Romola

GEORGE ELIOT'S COMPLETE WORKS

𝔥𝔞𝔫𝔡𝔶 𝔙𝔬𝔩𝔲𝔪𝔢 𝔈𝔡𝔦𝔱𝔦𝔬𝔫,

PRINTED FROM NEW ELECTROTYPE PLATES.

———◆———

This copy is one of an edition of one thousand immediately following the six hundred impressions of the ÉDITION DE LUXE.

THE VISIBLE MADONNA.

HANDY VOLUME EDITION

ROMOLA

VOL. II.

SILAS MARNER

BY GEORGE ELIOT

BOSTON
ESTES AND LAURIAT
1887

CONTENTS.

———•———

Book III. — *Continued.*

CONTENTS.

ILLUSTRATIONS.

Engraved by George T. Andrew.

ROMOLA.

1

ROMOLA.

CHAPTER XLIV.

THE VISIBLE MADONNA.

THE crowd had no sooner passed onward than Romola descended to the street, and hastened to the steps of San Stefano. Cecco had been attracted with the rest towards the piazza, and she found Baldassarre standing alone against the church door, with the horn-cup in his hand, waiting for her. There was a striking change in him: the blank, dreamy glance of a half-returned consciousness had given place to a fierceness which, as she advanced and spoke to him, flashed upon her as if she had been its object. It was the glance of caged fury that sees its prey passing safe beyond the bars.

Romola started as the glance was turned on her, but her immediate thought was that he had seen Tito. And as she felt the look of hatred grating on her, something like a hope arose that this man might be the criminal, and that her husband might not have been guilty towards him. If she could learn that now, by bringing Tito face to face with him, and have her mind set at rest!

"If you will come with me," she said, "I can give you shelter and food until you are quite rested and strong. Will you come?"

"Yes," said Baldassarre, "I shall be glad to get my strength. I want to get my strength," he repeated, as if he were muttering to himself, rather than speaking to her.

"Come!" she said, inviting him to walk by her side, and taking the way by the Arno towards the Ponte Rubaconte as the more private road.

the weapon, food to nourish the body which was the temple of vengeance. When he had had enough bread, he should be able to think and act — to think first how he could hide himself, lest Tito should have him dragged away again.

With that idea of hiding in his mind, Baldassarre turned up the narrowest streets, bought himself some meat and bread, and sat down under the first loggia to eat. The bells that swung out louder and louder peals of joy, laying hold of him and making him vibrate along with all the air, seemed to him simply part of that strong world which was against him.

Romola had watched Baldassarre until he had disappeared round the turning into the Piazza de' Mozzi, half feeling that his departure was a relief, half reproaching herself for not seeking with more decision to know the truth about him, for not assuring herself whether there were any guiltless misery in his lot which she was not helpless to relieve. Yet what could she have done if the truth had proved to be the burden of some painful secret about her husband, in addition to the anxieties that already weighed upon her? Surely a wife was permitted to desire ignorance of a husband's wrong-doing, since she alone must not protest and warn men against him. But that thought stirred too many intricate fibres of feeling to be pursued now in her weariness. It was a time to rejoice, since help had come to Florence; and she turned into the court to tell the good news to her patients on their straw beds.

She closed the door after her, lest the bells should drown her voice, and then throwing the black drapery from her head, that the women might see her better, she stood in the midst and told them that corn was coming, and that the bells were ringing for gladness at the news. They all sat up to listen, while the children trotted or crawled towards her, and pulled her black skirts, as if they were impatient at being all that long way off her face. She yielded to them, weary as she was, and sat down on the straw, while the little pale things peeped into her basket and pulled her hair down, and the feeble voices around her said, "The Holy Virgin be praised!" "It was the procession!" "The Mother of God has had pity on us!"

At last Romola rose from the heap of straw, too tired to try and smile any longer, saying as she turned up the stone steps —

" I will come by-and-by, to bring you your dinner."

" Bless you, Madonna! bless you!" said the faint chorus, in much the same tone as that in which they had a few minutes before praised and thanked the unseen Madonna.

Romola cared a great deal for that music. She had no innate taste for tending the sick and clothing the ragged, like some women to whom the details of such work are welcome in themselves, simply as an occupation. Her early training had kept her aloof from such womanly labors ; and if she had not brought to them the inspiration of her deepest feelings, they would have been irksome to her. But they had come to be the one unshaken resting-place of her mind, the one narrow pathway on which the light fell clear. If the gulf between herself and Tito which only gathered a more perceptible wideness from her attempts to bridge it by submission, brought a doubt whether, after all, the bond to which she had labored to be true might not itself be false — if she came away from her confessor, Fra Salvestro, or from some contact with the disciples of Savonarola among whom she worshipped, with a sickening sense that these people were miserably narrow, and with an almost impetuous reaction towards her old contempt for their superstition — she found herself recovering a firm footing in her works of womanly sympathy. Whatever else made her doubt, the help she gave to her fellow-citizens made her sure that Fra Girolamo had been right to call her back. According to his unforgotten words, her place had not been empty: it had been filled with her love and her labor. Florence had had need of her, and the more her own sorrow pressed upon her, the more gladness she felt in the memories, stretching through the two long years, of hours and moments in which she had lightened the burden of life to others. All that ardor of her nature which could no longer spend itself in the woman's tenderness for father and husband, had transformed itself into an enthusiasm of sympathy with the general life. She had ceased to think that her own lot could be happy

— had ceased to think of happiness at all : the one end of her
life seemed to her to be the diminishing of sorrow.

Her enthusiasm was continually stirred to fresh vigor by
the influence of Savonarola. In spite of the wearisome visions
and allegories from which she recoiled in disgust when they
came as stale repetitions from other lips than his, her strong
affinity for his passionate sympathy and the splendor of his
aims had lost none of its power. His burning indignation
against the abuses and oppression that made the daily story
of the Church and of States had kindled the ready fire in her
too. His special care for liberty and purity of government in
Florence, with his constant reference of this immediate object
to the wider end of a universal regeneration, had created in
her a new consciousness of the great drama of human existence in which her life was a part; and through her daily help-
ful contact with the less fortunate of her fellow-citizens this
new consciousness became something stronger than a vague
sentiment; it grew into a more and more definite motive of
self-denying practice. She thought little about dogmas, and
shrank from reflecting closely on the Frate's prophecies of the
immediate scourge and closely following regeneration. She
had submitted her mind to his and had entered into communion
with the Church, because in this way she had found an immediate satisfaction for moral needs which all the previous
culture and experience of her life had left hungering. Fra
Girolamo's voice had waked in her mind a reason for living,
apart from personal enjoyment and personal affection ; but it
was a reason that seemed to need feeding with greater forces
than she possessed within herself, and her submissive use of all
offices of the Church was simply a watching and waiting if by
any means fresh strength might come. The pressing problem
for Romola just then was not to settle questions of controversy, but to keep alive that flame of unselfish emotion by
which a life of sadness might still be a life of active love.

Her trust in Savonarola's nature as greater than her own
made a large part of the strength she had found. And the
trust was not to be lightly shaken. It is not force of intellect
which causes ready repulsion from the aberration and eccentri-

cities of greatness, any more than it is force of vision that
causes the eye to explore the warts on a face bright with
human expression; it is simply the negation of high sensibilities. Romola was so deeply moved by the grand energies of
Savonarola's nature, that she found herself listening patiently
to all dogmas and prophecies, when they came in the vehicle
of his ardent faith and believing utterance.[1]

No soul is desolate as long as there is a human being for
whom it can feel trust and reverence. Romola's trust in Savonarola was something like a rope suspended securely by her
path, making her step elastic while she grasped it; if it were
suddenly removed, no firmness of the ground she trod could
save her from staggering, or perhaps from falling.

CHAPTER XLV.

AT THE BARBER'S SHOP.

AFTER that welcome appearance as the messenger with the
olive-branch, which was an unpromised favor of fortune, Tito
had other commissions to fulfil of a more premeditated character. He paused at the Palazzo Vecchio, and awaited there the
return of the Ten, who managed external and war affairs, that
he might duly deliver to them the results of his private mission to Pisa, intended as a preliminary to an avowed embassy
of which Bernardo Rucellai was to be the head, with the object of coming, if possible, to a pacific understanding with the
Emperor Maximilian and the League.

---

[1] He himself had had occasion enough to note the efficacy of that vehicle.
"If," he says in the *Compendium Revelationum*, "you speak of such as have
not heard these things from me, I admit that they who disbelieve are more
than they who believe, because it is one thing to hear him who inwardly feels
these things, and another to hear him who feels them not; . . . and, therefore, it is well said by St. Jerome, ' Habet nescio quid latentis energiæ vivæ
vocis actus, et in aures discipuli de auctoris ore transfusa fortis sonat.'"

Tito's talents for diplomatic work had been well ascertained, and as he gave with fulness and precision the results of his inquiries and interviews, Bernardo del Nero, who was at that time one of the Ten, could not withhold his admiration. He would have withheld it if he could; for his original dislike of Tito had returned, and become stronger, since the sale of the library. Romola had never uttered a word to her godfather on the circumstances of the sale, and Bernardo had understood her silence as a prohibition to him to enter on the subject, but he felt sure that the breach of her father's wish had been a blighting grief to her, and the old man's observant eyes discerned other indications that her married life was not happy.

"Ah," he said, inwardly, "that doubtless is the reason she has taken to listening to Fra Girolamo, and going among the Piagnoni, which I never expected from her. These women, if they are not happy, and have no children, must either take to folly or to some overstrained religion that makes them think they've got all heaven's work on their shoulders. And as for my poor child Romola, it is as I always said — the cramming with Latin and Greek has left her as much a woman as if she had done nothing all day but prick her fingers with the needle. And this husband of hers, who gets employed everywhere, because he's a tool with a smooth handle, I wish Tornabuoni and the rest may not find their fingers cut. Well, well, *solco torto, sacco dritto* — many a full sack comes from a crooked furrow; and he who will be captain of none but honest men will have small hire to pay."

With this long-established conviction that there could be no moral sifting of political agents, the old Florentine abstained from all interference in Tito's disfavor. Apart from what must be kept sacred and private for Romola's sake, Bernardo had nothing direct to allege against the useful Greek, except that he was a Greek, and that he, Bernardo, did not like him; for the doubleness of feigning attachment to the popular government, while at heart a Medicean, was common to Tito with more than half the Medicean party. He only feigned with more skill than the rest: that was all. So Bernardo was simply cold to Tito, who returned the coldness with a scrupulous, distant respect. And it was still the notion in Florence that the old tie between Bernardo and Bardo made any service done to Romola's husband an acceptable homage to her godfather.

After delivering himself of his charge at the Old Palace, Tito felt that the avowed official work of the day was done. He was tired and adust with long riding; but he did not go home. There were certain things in his scarsella and on his mind, from which he wished to free himself as soon as possible, but the opportunities must be found so skilfully that they must not seem to be sought. He walked from the Palazzo in a sauntering fashion towards the Piazza del Duomo. The procession was at an end now, but the bells were still ringing, and the people were moving about the streets restlessly, longing for some more definite vent to their joy. If the Frate could have stood up in the great piazza and preached to them, they might have been satisfied, but now, in spite of the new discipline which declared Christ to be the special King of the Florentines and required all pleasures to be of a Christian sort, there was a secret longing in many of the youngsters who shouted "Viva Gesù!" for a little vigorous stone-throwing in sign of thankfulness.

Tito, as he passed along, could not escape being recognized by some as the welcome bearer of the olive-branch, and could only rid himself of an inconvenient ovation, chiefly in the form of eager questions, by telling those who pressed on him that Meo di Sasso, the true messenger from Leghorn, must now be entering, and might certainly be met towards the Porta San Frediano. He could tell much more than Tito knew.

Freeing himself from importunities in this adroit manner, he made his way to the Piazza del Duomo, casting his long eyes round the space with an air of the utmost carelessness, but really seeking to detect some presence which might furnish him with one of his desired opportunities. The fact of the procession having terminated at the Duomo made it probable that there would be more than the usual concentration of loungers and talkers in the piazza and round Nello's shop. It was as he expected. There was a group leaning against the

rails near the north gates of the baptistery, so exactly what
he sought, that he looked more indifferent than ever, and
seemed to recognize the tallest member of the group entirely
by chance as he had half passed him, just turning his head to
give him a slight greeting, while he tossed the end of his *becchetto* over his left shoulder.

Yet the tall, broad-shouldered personage greeted in that
slight way looked like one who had considerable claims. He
wore a richly embroidered tunic, with a great show of linen,
after the newest French mode, and at his belt there hung a
sword and poniard of fine workmanship. His hat, with a red
plume in it, seemed a scornful protest against the gravity of
Florentine costume, which had been exaggerated to the utmost under the influence of the Piagnoni. Certain undefinable indications of youth made the breadth of his face and the
large diameter of his waist appear the more emphatically a
stamp of coarseness, and his eyes had that rude desecrating
stare at all men and things which to a refined mind is as
intolerable as a bad odor or a flaring light.

He and his companions, also young men dressed expensively
and wearing arms, were exchanging jokes with that sort of
ostentatious laughter which implies a desire to prove that the
laughter is not mortified though some people might suspect it.
There were good reasons for such a suspicion ; for this broad-
shouldered man with the red feather was Dolfo Spini, leader
of the Compagnacci, or Evil Companions — that is to say, of
all the dissolute young men belonging to the old aristocratic
party, enemies of the Mediceans, enemies of the popular government, but still more bitter enemies of Savonarola. Dolfo
Spini, heir of the great house with the loggia, over the bridge
of the Santa Trinità, had organized these young men into an
armed band, as sworn champions of extravagant suppers and
all the pleasant sins of the flesh, against reforming pietists
who threatened to make the world chaste and temperate to so
intolerable a degree that there would soon be no reason for
living, except the extreme unpleasantness of the alternative.
Up to this very morning he had been loudly declaring that
Florence was given up to famine and ruin entirely through its

blind adherence to the advice of the Frate, and that there could be no salvation for Florence but in joining the League and driving the Frate out of the city — sending him to Rome, in fact, whither he ought to have gone long ago in obedience to the summons of the Pope. It was suspected, therefore, that Messer Dolfo Spini's heart was not aglow with pure joy at the unexpected succors which had come in apparent fulfilment of the Frate's prediction, and the laughter, which was ringing out afresh as Tito joined the group at Nello's door, did not serve to dissipate the suspicion. For leaning against the door-post in the centre of the group was a close-shaven, keen-eyed personage, named Niccolò Macchiavelli, who, young as he was, had penetrated all the small secrets of egoism.

"Messer Dolfo's head," he was saying, "is more of a pumpkin than I thought. I measure men's dulness by the devices they trust in for deceiving others. Your dullest animal of all is he who grins and says he does n't mind just after he has had his shins kicked. If I were a trifle duller, now," he went on, smiling as the circle opened to admit Tito, "I should pretend to be fond of this Melema, who has got a secretaryship that would exactly suit me — as if Latin ill-paid could love better Latin that 's better paid! Melema, you are a pestiferously clever fellow, very much in my way, and I 'm sorry to hear you 've had another piece of good-luck to-day."

"Questionable luck, Niccolò," said Tito, touching him on the shoulder in a friendly way; "I have got nothing by it yet but being laid hold of and breathed upon by wool-beaters, when I am as soiled and battered with riding as a *tabellario* (letter-carrier) from Bologna."

"Ah! you want a touch of my art, Messer Oratore," said Nello, who had come forward at the sound of Tito's voice; "your chin, I perceive, has yesterday's crop upon it. Come, come — consign yourself to the priest of all the Muses. Sandro, quick with the lather!"

"In truth, Nello, that is just what I most desire at this moment," said Tito, seating himself; "and that was why I turned my steps towards thy shop, instead of going home at once, when I had done my business at the Palazzo."

" Yes, indeed, it is not fitting that you should present yourself to Madonna Romola with a rusty chin and a tangled
zazzera. Nothing that is not dainty ought to approach the
Florentine lily; though I see her constantly going about like
a sunbeam among the rags that line our corners — if indeed
she is not more like a moonbeam now, for I thought yesterday, when I met her, that she looked as pale and worn as that
fainting Madonna of Fra Giovanni's. You must see to it, my
bel erudito: she keeps too many fasts and vigils in your
absence."

Tito gave a melancholy shrug. "It is too true, Nello. She
has been depriving herself of half her proper food every day
during this famine. But what can I do? Her mind has been
set all aflame. A husband's influence is powerless against the
Frate's."

" As every other influence is likely to be, that of the Holy
Father included," said Domenico Cennini, one of the group
at the door, who had turned in with Tito. "I don't know
whether you have gathered anything at Pisa about the way
the wind sits at Rome, Melema?"

"Secrets of the council chamber, Messer Domenico!" said
Tito, smiling and opening his palms in a deprecatory manner.
"An envoy must be as dumb as a father confessor."

" Certainly, certainly," said Cennini. "I ask for no breach
of that rule. Well, my belief is, that if his Holiness were to
drive Fra Girolamo to extremity, the Frate would move heaven
and earth to get a General Council of the Church — ay, and
would get it too; and I, for one, should not be sorry, though
I'm no Piagnone."

" With leave of your greater experience, Messer Domenico,"
said Macchiavelli, "I must differ from you — not in your wish
to see a General Council which might reform the Church, but
in your belief that the Frate will checkmate his Holiness.
The Frate's game is an impossible one. If he had contented
himself with preaching against the vices of Rome, and with
prophesying that in some way, not mentioned, Italy would be
scourged, depend upon it Pope Alexander would have allowed
him to spend his breath in that way as long as he could find

hearers. Such spiritual blasts as those knock no walls down. But the Frate wants to be something more than a spiritual trumpet: he wants to be a lever, and what is more, he *is* a lever. He wants to spread the doctrine of Christ by maintaining a popular government in Florence, and the Pope, as I know, on the best authority, has private views to the contrary."

"Then Florence will stand by the Frate," Cennini broke in, with some fervor. "I myself should prefer that he would let his prophesying alone, but if our freedom to choose our own government is to be attacked — I am an obedient son of the Church, but I would vote for resisting Pope Alexander the Sixth, as our forefathers resisted Pope Gregory the Eleventh."

"But pardon me, Messer Domenico," said Macchiavelli, sticking his thumbs into his belt, and speaking with that cool enjoyment of exposition which surmounts every other force in discussion. "Have you correctly seized the Frate's position? How is it that he has become a lever, and made himself worth attacking by an acute man like his Holiness? Because he has got the ear of the people: because he gives them threats and promises, which they believe come straight from God, not only about hell, purgatory, and paradise, but about Pisa and our Great Council. But let events go against him, so as to shake the people's faith, and the cause of his power will be the cause of his fall. He is accumulating three sorts of hatred on his head — the hatred of average mankind against every one who wants to lay on them a strict yoke of virtue; the hatred of the stronger powers in Italy who want to farm Florence for their own purposes; and the hatred of the people, to whom he has ventured to promise good in this world, instead of confining his promises to the next. If a prophet is to keep his power, he must be a prophet like Mahomet, with an army at his back, that when the people's faith is fainting it may be frightened into life again."

"Rather sum up the three sorts of hatred in one," said Francesco Cei, impetuously, "and say he has won the hatred of all men who have sense and honesty, by inventing hypocriti-

cal lies. His proper place is among the false prophets in the
Inferno, who walk with their heads turned hindforemost."

"You are too angry, my Francesco," said Macchiavelli, smiling; "you poets are apt to cut the clouds in your wrath. I
am no votary of the Frate's, and would not lay down my little
finger for his veracity. But veracity is a plant of paradise,
and the seeds have never flourished beyond the walls. You,
yourself, my Francesco, tell poetical lies only; partly compelled by the poet's fervor, partly to please your audience;
but you object to lies in prose. Well, the Frate differs from
you as to the boundary of poetry, that's all. When he gets
into the pulpit of the Duomo, he has the fervor within him,
and without him he has the audience to please. Ecco!"

"You are somewhat lax there, Niccolò," said Cennini, gravely.
"I myself believe in the Frate's integrity, though I don't believe in his prophecies, and as long as his integrity is not disproved, we have a popular party strong enough to protect him
and resist foreign interference."

"A party that seems strong enough," said Macchiavelli,
with a shrug, and an almost imperceptible glance towards
Tito, who was abandoning himself with much enjoyment to
Nello's combing and scenting. "But how many Mediceans
are there among you? How many who will not be turned
round by a private grudge?"

"As to the Mediceans," said Cennini, "I believe there is
very little genuine feeling left on behalf of the Medici. Who
would risk much for Piero de' Medici? A few old stanch
friends, perhaps, like Bernardo del Nero; but even some of
those most connected with the family are hearty friends of
the popular government, and would exert themselves for the
Frate. I was talking to Giannozzo Pucci only a little while
ago, and I am convinced there's nothing he would set his face
against more than against any attempt to alter the new order
of things."

"You are right there, Messer Domenico," said Tito, with a
laughing meaning in his eyes, as he rose from the shaving-
chair; "and I fancy the tender passion came in aid of hard
theory there. I am persuaded there was some jealousy at

the bottom of Giannozzo's alienation from Piero de' Medici; else so amiable a creature as he would never feel the bitterness he sometimes allows to escape him in that quarter. He was in the procession with you, I suppose ? "

"No," said Cennini; " he is at his villa — went there three days ago."

Tito was settling his cap and glancing down at his splashed hose as if he hardly heeded the answer. In reality he had obtained a much-desired piece of information. He had at that moment in his scarsella a crushed gold ring which he had engaged to deliver to Giannozzo Pucci. He had received it from an envoy of Piero de' Medici, whom he had ridden out of his way to meet at Certaldo on the Siena road. Since Pucci was not in the town, he would send the ring by Fra Michele, a Carthusian lay Brother in the service of the Mediceans, and the receipt of that sign would bring Pucci back to hear the verbal part of Tito's mission.

"Behold him ! " said Nello, flourishing his comb and pointing it at Tito, " the handsomest scholar in the world or in the wolds,[1] now he has passed through my hands ! A trifle thinner in the face, though, than when he came in his first bloom to Florence — eh ? and, I vow, there are some lines just faintly hinting themselves about your mouth, Messer Oratore ! Ah, mind is an enemy to beauty ! I myself was thought beautiful by the women at one time — when I was in my swaddling-bands. But now — oimè ! I carry my unwritten poems in cipher on my face ! "

Tito, laughing with the rest as Nello looked at himself tragically in the hand-mirror, made a sign of farewell to the company generally, and took his departure.

"I 'm of our old Piero di Cosimo's mind," said Francesco Cei. " I don't half like Melema. That trick of smiling gets stronger than ever — no wonder he has lines about the mouth."

" He 's too successful," said Macchiavelli, playfully. " I 'm sure there 's something wrong about him, else he would n't have that secretaryship."

[1] " Del mondo o di maremma."

"He's an able man," said Cennini, in a tone of judicial fairness. "I and my brother have always found him useful with our Greek sheets, and he gives great satisfaction to the Ten. I like to see a young man work his way upward by merit. And the secretary Scala, who befriended him from the first, thinks highly of him still, I know."

"Doubtless," said a notary in the background. "He writes Scala's official letters for him, or corrects them, and gets well paid for it too."

"I wish Messer Bartolommeo would pay *me* to doctor his gouty Latin," said Macchiavelli, with a shrug. "Did *he* tell you about the pay, Ser Ceccone, or was it Melema himself?" he added, looking at the notary with a face ironically innocent.

"Melema? no, indeed," answered Ser Ceccone. "He is as close as a nut. He never brags. That's why he's employed everywhere. They say he's getting rich with doing all sorts of underhand work."

"It *is* a little too bad," said Macchiavelli, "and so many able notaries out of employment!"

"Well, I must say I thought that was a nasty story a year or two ago about the man who said he had stolen jewels," said Cei. "It got hushed up somehow; but I remember Piero di Cosimo said, at the time, he believed there was something in it, for he saw Melema's face when the man laid hold of him, and he never saw a visage so 'painted with fear,' as our sour old Dante says."

"Come, spit no more of that venom, Francesco," said Nello, getting indignant, "else I shall consider it a public duty to cut your hair awry the next time I get you under my scissors. That story of the stolen jewels was a lie. Bernardo Rucellai and the Magnificent Eight knew all about it. The man was a dangerous madman, and he was very properly kept out of mischief in prison. As for our Piero di Cosimo, his wits are running after the wind of Mongibello: he has such an extravagant fancy that he would take a lizard for a crocodile. No: that story has been dead and buried too long — our noses object to it."

"It is true," said Macchiavelli. "You forget the danger of the precedent, Francesco. The next mad beggarman may accuse you of stealing his verses, or me, God help me! of stealing his coppers. Ah!" he went on, turning towards the door, "Dolfo Spini has carried his red feather out of the piazza. That captain of swaggerers would like the Republic to lose Pisa just for the chance of seeing the people tear the frock off the Frate's back. With your pardon, Francesco — I know he is a friend of yours — there are few things I should like better than to see him play the part of Capo d'Oca, who went out to the tournament blowing his trumpets and returned with them in a bag."

CHAPTER XLVI.

BY A STREET LAMP.

THAT evening, when it was dark and threatening rain, Romola, returning with Maso and the lantern by her side, from the hospital of San Matteo, which she had visited after vespers, encountered her husband just issuing from the monastery of San Marco. Tito, who had gone out again shortly after his arrival in the Via de' Bardi, and had seen little of Romola during the day, immediately proposed to accompany her home, dismissing Maso, whose short steps annoyed him. It was only usual for him to pay her such an official attention when it was obviously demanded from him. Tito and Romola never jarred, never remonstrated with each other. They were too hopelessly alienated in their inner life ever to have that contest which is an effort towards agreement. They talked of all affairs, public and private, with careful adherence to an adopted course. If Tito wanted a supper prepared in the old library, now pleasantly furnished as a banqueting-room, Romola assented, and saw that everything needful was done: and Tito, on his side, left her entirely uncontrolled in her daily habits, accepting the help she offered him in transcribing or making digests, and in return meeting her conjectured want of supplies for her charities. Yet he constantly, as on this very morning, avoided exchanging glances with her; affected to believe that she was out of the house, in order to avoid seeking her in her own room; and playfully attributed to her a perpetual preference of solitude to his society.

In the first ardor of her self-conquest, after she had renounced her resolution of flight, Romola had made many timid efforts towards the return of a frank relation between them. But to her such a relation could only come by open speech about their differences, and the attempt to arrive at a moral understanding; while Tito could only be saved from alienation from her by such a recovery of her effusive tenderness as would have presupposed oblivion of their differences. He cared for no explanation between them; he felt any thorough explanation impossible: he would have cared to have Romola fond again, and to her, fondness was impossible. She could be submissive and gentle, she could repress any sign of repulsion; but tenderness was not to be feigned. She was helplessly conscious of the result: her husband was alienated from her.

It was an additional reason why she should be carefully kept outside of secrets which he would in no case have chosen to communicate to her. With regard to his political action he sought to convince her that he considered the cause of the Medici hopeless; and that on that practical ground, as well as in theory, he heartily served the popular government, in which she had now a warm interest. But impressions subtle as odors made her uneasy about his relations with San Marco. She was painfully divided between the dread of seeing any evidence to arouse her suspicions, and the impulse to watch lest any harm should come that she might have arrested.

As they walked together this evening, Tito said — "The business of the day is not yet quite ended for me. I shall conduct you to our door, my Romola, and then I must fulfil another commission, which will take me an hour, perhaps, before I can return and rest, as I very much need to do."

And then he talked amusingly of what he had seen at Pisa, until they were close upon a loggia, near which there hung a lamp before a picture of the Virgin. The street was a quiet one, and hitherto they had passed few people; but now there was a sound of many approaching footsteps and confused voices.

"We shall not get home without a wetting, unless we take shelter under this convenient loggia," Tito said, hastily, hurrying Romola, with a slightly startled movement, up the step of the loggia.

"Surely it is useless to wait for this small drizzling rain," said Romola, in surprise.

"No: I felt it becoming heavier. Let us wait a little." With that wakefulness to the faintest indication which belongs to a mind habitually in a state of caution, Tito had detected by the glimmer of the lamp that the leader of the advancing group wore a red feather and a glittering sword-hilt — in fact, was almost the last person in the world he would have chosen to meet at this hour with Romola by his side. He had already during the day had one momentous interview with Dolfo Spini, and the business he had spoken of to Romola as yet to be done was a second interview with that personage, a sequence of the visit he had paid at San Marco. Tito, by a long-preconcerted plan, had been the bearer of letters to Savonarola — carefully forged letters; one of them, by a stratagem, bearing the very signature and seal of the Cardinal of Naples, who of all the Sacred College had most exerted his influence at Rome in favor of the Frate. The purport of the letters was to state that the Cardinal was on his progress from Pisa, and, unwilling for strong reasons to enter Florence, yet desirous of taking counsel with Savonarola at this difficult juncture, intended to pause this very day at San Casciano, about ten miles from the city, whence he would ride out the next morning in the plain garb of a priest, and meet Savonarola, as if casually, five miles on the Florence road, two hours after sunrise. The plot, of which these forged letters were the initial step, was that Dolfo Spini with a band of his Compagnacci was to be posted in ambush on the road, at a lonely spot about five miles from the gates; that he was to seize Savonarola with the Dominican brother who would accompany him according to rule, and deliver him over to a small detachment of Milanese horse in readiness near San Casciano, by whom he was to be carried into the Roman territory.

There was a strong chance that the penetrating Frate would suspect a trap, and decline to incur the risk, which he had for some time avoided, of going beyond the city walls. Even when he preached, his friends held it necessary that he should be attended by an armed guard; and here he was called on to commit himself to a solitary road, with no other attendant than a fellow-monk. On this ground the minimum of time had been given him for decision, and the chance in favor of his acting on the letters was, that the eagerness with which his mind was set on the combining of interests within and without the Church towards the procuring of a General Council, and also the expectation of immediate service from the Cardinal in the actual juncture of his contest with the Pope, would triumph over his shrewdness and caution in the brief space allowed for deliberation.

Tito had had an audience of Savonarola, having declined to put the letters into any hands but his, and with consummate art had admitted that incidentally, and by inference, he was able so far to conjecture their purport as to believe they referred to a rendezvous outside the gates, in which case he urged that the Frate should seek an armed guard from the Signoria, and offered his services in carrying the request with the utmost privacy. Savonarola had replied briefly that this was impossible: an armed guard was incompatible with privacy. He spoke with a flashing eye, and Tito felt convinced that he meant to incur the risk.

Tito himself did not much care for the result. He managed his affairs so cleverly, that all results, he considered, must turn to his advantage. Whichever party came uppermost, he was secure of favor and money. That is an indecorously naked statement; the fact, clothed as Tito habitually clothed it, was that his acute mind, discerning the equal hollowness of all parties, took the only rational course in making them subservient to his own interest.

If Savonarola fell into the snare, there were diamonds in question and papal patronage; if not, Tito's adroit agency had strengthened his position with Savonarola and with Spini, while any confidences he obtained from them made him the more valuable as an agent of the Mediceans.

But Spini was an inconvenient colleague. He had cunning enough to delight in plots, but not the ability or self-command necessary to so complex an effect as secrecy. He frequently got excited with drinking, for even sober Florence had its "Beoni," or topers, both lay and clerical, who became loud at taverns and private banquets; and in spite of the agreement between him and Tito, that their public recognition of each other should invariably be of the coolest sort, there was always the possibility that on an evening encounter he would be suddenly blurting and affectionate. The delicate sign of casting the becchetto over the left shoulder was understood in the morning, but the strongest hint short of a threat might not suffice to keep off a fraternal grasp of the shoulder in the evening.

Tito's chief hope now was that Dolfo Spini had not caught sight of him, and the hope would have been well founded if Spini had had no clearer view of him than he had caught of Spini. But, himself in shadow, he had seen Tito illuminated for an instant by the direct rays of the lamp, and Tito in his way was as strongly marked a personage as the captain of the Compagnacci. Romola's black-shrouded figure had escaped notice, and she now stood behind her husband's shoulder in the corner of the loggia. Tito was not left to hope long.

"Ha! my carrier-pigeon!" grated Spini's harsh voice, in what he meant to be an undertone, while his hand grasped Tito's shoulder; "what did you run into hiding for? You didn't know it was comrades who were coming. It's well I caught sight of you; it saves time. What of the chase to-morrow morning? Will the bald-headed game rise? Are the falcons to be got ready?"

If it had been in Tito's nature to feel an access of rage, he would have felt it against this bull-faced accomplice, unfit either for a leader or a tool. His lips turned white, but his excitement came from the pressing difficulty of choosing a safe device. If he attempted to hush Spini, that would only deepen Romola's suspicion, and he knew her well enough to know that if some strong alarm were roused in her, she was neither to be silenced nor hoodwinked : on the other hand, if he repelled Spini angrily the wine-breathing Compagnaccio might become savage, being more ready at resentment than at the divination of motives. He adopted a third course, which proved that Romola retained one sort of power over him — the power of dread.

He pressed her hand, as if intending a hint to her, and said in a good-humored tone of comradeship —

" Yes, my Dolfo, you may prepare in all security. But take no trumpets with you."

" Don't be afraid," said Spini, a little piqued. "No need to play Ser Saccente with me. I know where the devil keeps his tail as well as you do. What ! he swallowed the bait whole ? The prophetic nose did n't scent the hook at all ?" he went on, lowering his tone a little, with a blundering sense of secrecy.

" The brute will not be satisfied till he has emptied the bag," thought Tito : but aloud he said, — " Swallowed all as easily as you swallow a cup of Trebbiano. Ha ! I see torches : there must be a dead body coming. The pestilence has been spreading, I hear."

"Santiddio ! I hate the sight of those biers. Good-night," said Spini, hastily moving off.

The torches were really coming, but they preceded a church dignitary who was returning homeward ; the suggestion of the dead body and the pestilence was Tito's device for getting rid of Spini without telling him to go. The moment he had moved away, Tito turned to Romola, and said, quietly —

" Do not be alarmed by anything that *bestia* has said, my Romola. We will go on now : I think the rain has not increased."

She was quivering with indignant resolution ; it was of no use for Tito to speak in that unconcerned way. She distrusted every word he could utter.

" I will not go on," she said. " I will not move nearer

home until I have some security against this treachery being perpetrated."

"Wait, at least, until these torches have passed," said Tito, with perfect self-command, but with a new rising of dislike to a wife who this time, he foresaw, might have the power of thwarting him in spite of the husband's predominance.

The torches passed, with the Vicario dell' Arcivescovo, and due reverence was done by Tito, but Romola saw nothing outward. If for the defeat of this treachery, in which she believed with all the force of long presentiment, it had been necessary at that moment for her to spring on her husband and hurl herself with him down a precipice, she felt as if she could have done it. Union with this man! At that moment the self-quelling discipline of two years seemed to be nullified : she felt nothing but that they were divided.

They were nearly in darkness again, and could only see each other's faces dimly.

"Tell me the truth, Tito — this time tell me the truth," said Romola, in a low quivering voice. "It will be safer for you."

"Why should I desire to tell you anything else, my angry saint?" said Tito, with a slight touch of contempt, which was the vent of his annoyance; "since the truth is precisely that over which you have most reason to rejoice — namely, that my knowing a plot of Spini's enables me to secure the Frate from falling a victim to it."

"What is the plot?"

"That I decline to tell," said Tito. "It is enough that the Frate's safety will be secured."

"It is a plot for drawing him outside the gates that Spini may murder him."

"There has been no intention of murder. It is simply a plot for compelling him to obey the Pope's summons to Rome. But as I serve the popular government, and think the Frate's presence here is a necessary means of maintaining it at present, I choose to prevent his departure. You may go to sleep with entire ease of mind to-night."

For a moment Romola was silent. Then she said, in a voice of anguish, "Tito, it is of no use: I have no belief in you."

She could just discern his action as he shrugged his shoulders, and spread out his palms in silence. That cold dislike which is the anger of unimpassioned beings was hardening within him.

"If the Frate leaves the city — if any harm happens to him," said Romola, after a slight pause, in a new tone of indignant resolution, — "I will declare what I have heard to the Signoria, and you will be disgraced. What if I am your wife?" she went on, impetuously; "I will be disgraced with you. If we are united, I am that part of you that will save you from crime. Others shall not be betrayed."

"I am quite aware of what you would be likely to do, *anima mia,*" said Tito, in the coolest of his liquid tones; "therefore if you have a small amount of reasoning at your disposal just now, consider that if you believe me in nothing else, you may believe me when I say I will take care of myself, and not put it in your power to ruin me."

"Then you assure me that the Frate is warned — he will not go beyond the gates?"

"He shall not go beyond the gates."

There was a moment's pause, but distrust was not to be expelled.

"I will go back to San Marco now and find out," Romola said, making a movement forward.

"You shall not!" said Tito, in a bitter whisper, seizing her wrists with all his masculine force. "I am master of you. You shall not set yourself in opposition to me."

There were passers-by approaching. Tito had heard them, and that was why he spoke in a whisper. Romola was too conscious of being mastered to have struggled, even if she had remained unconscious that witnesses were at hand. But she was aware now of footsteps and voices, and her habitual sense of personal dignity made her at once yield to Tito's movement towards leading her from the loggia.

They walked on in silence for some time, under the small drizzling rain. The first rush of indignation and alarm in Romola had begun to give way to more complicated feelings, which rendered speech and action difficult. In that simpler state of vehemence, open opposition to the husband from whom she felt her soul revolting had had the aspect of temptation for her; it seemed the easiest of all courses. But now, habits of self-questioning, memories of impulse subdued, and that proud reserve which all discipline had left unmodified, began to emerge from the flood of passion. The grasp of her wrists, which asserted her husband's physical predominance, instead of arousing a new fierceness in her, as it might have done if her impetuosity had been of a more vulgar kind, had given her a momentary shuddering horror at this form of contest with him. It was the first time they had been in declared hostility to each other since her flight and return, and the check given to her ardent resolution then, retained the power to arrest her now. In this altered condition her mind began to dwell on the probabilities that would save her from any desperate course: Tito would not risk betrayal by her; whatever had been his original intention, he must be determined now by the fact that she knew of the plot. She was not bound now to do anything else than to hang over him that certainty, that if he deceived her, her lips would not be closed. And then, it was possible — yes, she must cling to that possibility till it was disproved — that Tito had never meant to aid in the betrayal of the Frate.

Tito, on his side, was busy with thoughts, and did not speak again till they were near home. Then he said —

"Well, Romola, have you now had time to recover calmness? If so, you can supply your want of belief in me by a little rational inference: you can see, I presume, that if I had had any intention of furthering Spini's plot, I should now be aware that the possession of a fair Piagnone for my wife, who knows the secret of the plot, would be a serious obstacle in my way."

Tito assumed the tone which was just then the easiest to him, conjecturing that in Romola's present mood persuasive deprecation would be lost upon her.

"Yes, Tito," she said, in a low voice, "I think you believe that I would guard the Republic from further treachery. You are right to believe it: if the Frate is betrayed, I will de-

nounce you." She paused a moment, and then said, with an
effort, "But it was not so. I have perhaps spoken too hastily
— you never meant it. Only, why will you seem to be that
man's comrade ? "

"Such relations are inevitable to practical men, my Romola,"
said Tito, gratified by discerning the struggle within her.
"You fair creatures live in the clouds. Pray go to rest with
an easy heart," he added, opening the door for her.

CHAPTER XLVII.

CHECK.

Tito's clever arrangements had been unpleasantly frustrated
by trivial incidents which could not enter into a clever man's
calculations. It was very seldom that he walked with Romola
in the evening, yet he had happened to be walking with her
precisely on this evening when her presence was supremely
inconvenient. Life was so complicated a game that the devices of skill were liable to be defeated at every turn by air-
blown chances, incalculable as the descent of thistle-down.

It was not that he minded about the failure of Spini's plot,
but he felt an awkward difficulty in so adjusting his warning
to Savonarola on the one hand, and to Spini on the other, as
not to incur suspicion. Suspicion roused in the popular party
might be fatal to his reputation and ostensible position in
Florence : suspicion roused in Dolfo Spini might be as disagreeable in its effects as the hatred of a fierce dog not to be
chained.

If Tito went forthwith to the monastery to warn Savonarola
before the monks went to rest, his warning would follow so
closely on his delivery of the forged letters that he could not
escape unfavorable surmises. He could not warn Spini at
once without telling him the true reason, since he could not
immediately allege the discovery that Savonarola had changed

his purpose; and he knew Spini well enough to know that his understanding would discern nothing but that Tito had "turned round" and frustrated the plot. On the other hand, by deferring his warning to Savonarola until the morning, he would be almost sure to lose the opportunity of warning Spini that the Frate had changed his mind; and the band of Compagnacci would come back in all the rage of disappointment. This last, however, was the risk he chose, trusting to his power of soothing Spini by assuring him that the failure was due only to the Frate's caution.

Tito was annoyed. If he had had to smile it would have been an unusual effort to him. He was determined not to encounter Romola again, and he did not go home that night.

She watched through the night, and never took off her clothes. She heard the rain become heavier and heavier. She liked to hear the rain: the stormy heavens seemed a safeguard against men's devices, compelling them to inaction. And Romola's mind was again assailed, not only by the utmost doubt of her husband, but by doubt as to her own conduct. What lie might he not have told her? What project might he not have, of which she was still ignorant? Every one who trusted Tito was in danger; it was useless to try and persuade herself of the contrary. And was not she selfishly listening to the promptings of her own pride, when she shrank from warning men against him? "If her husband was a malefactor, her place was in the prison by his side" — that might be; she was contented to fulfil that claim. But was she, a wife, to allow a husband to inflict the injuries that would make him a malefactor, when it might be in her power to prevent them? Prayer seemed impossible to her. The activity of her thought excluded a mental state of which the essence is expectant passivity.

The excitement became stronger and stronger. Her imagination, in a state of morbid activity, conjured up possible schemes by which, after all, Tito would have eluded her threat; and towards daybreak the rain became less violent, till at last it ceased, the breeze rose again and dispersed the clouds, and the morning fell clear on all the objects around her. It made her uneasiness all the less endurable. She wrapped her mantle round her, and ran up to the loggia, as if there could be anything in the wide landscape that might determine her action; as if there could be anything but roofs hiding the line of street along which Savonarola might be walking towards betrayal.

If she went to her godfather, might she not induce him, without any specific revelation, to take measures for preventing Fra Girolamo from passing the gates? But that might be too late. Romola thought, with new distress, that she had failed to learn any guiding details from Tito, and it was already long past seven. She must go to San Marco: there was nothing else to be done.

She hurried down the stairs, she went out into the street without looking at her sick people, and walked at a swift pace along the Via de' Bardi towards the Ponte Vecchio. She would go through the heart of the city; it was the most direct road, and, besides, in the great piazza there was a chance of encountering her husband, who, by some possibility to which she still clung, might satisfy her of the Frate's safety, and leave no need for her to go to San Marco. When she arrived in front of the Palazzo Vecchio, she looked eagerly into the pillared court; then her eyes swept the piazza; but the well-known figure, once painted in her heart by young love, and now branded there by eating pain, was nowhere to be seen. She hurried straight on to the Piazza del Duomo. It was already full of movement: there were worshippers passing up and down the marble steps, there were men pausing for chat, and there were market-people carrying their burdens. Between those moving figures Romola caught a glimpse of her husband. On his way from San Marco he had turned into Nello's shop, and was now leaning against the door-post. As Romola approached she could see that he was standing and talking, with the easiest air in the world, holding his cap in his hand, and shaking back his freshly combed hair. The contrast of this ease with the bitter anxieties he had created convulsed her with indignation: the new vision of his hardness heightened her dread. She recognized Cronaca and two other frequenters of San Marco standing near her husband. It flashed through her mind — "I will compel him to speak before those men." And her light step brought her close upon him before he had time to move, while Cronaca was saying, "Here comes Madonna Romola."

A slight shock passed through Tito's frame as he felt himself face to face with his wife. She was haggard with her anxious watching, but there was a flash of something else than anxiety in her eyes as she said —

"Is the Frate gone beyond the gates?"

"No," said Tito, feeling completely helpless before this woman, and needing all the self-command he possessed to preserve a countenance in which there should seem to be nothing stronger than surprise.

"And you are certain that he is not going?" she insisted.

"I am certain that he is not going."

"That is enough," said Romola, and she turned up the steps, to take refuge in the Duomo, till she could recover from her agitation.

Tito never had a feeling so near hatred as that with which his eyes followed Romola retreating up the steps.

There were present not only genuine followers of the Frate, but Ser Ceccone, the notary, who at that time, like Tito himself, was secretly an agent of the Mediceans.

Ser Francesco di Ser Barone, more briefly known to infamy as Ser Ceccone, was not learned, not handsome, not successful, and the reverse of generous. He was a traitor without charm. It followed that he was not fond of Tito Melema.

CHAPTER XLVIII.

COUNTER-CHECK.

It was late in the afternoon when Tito returned home. Romola, seated opposite the cabinet in her narrow room, copying documents, was about to desist from her work because the light was getting dim, when her husband entered. He had come straight to this room to seek her, with a thoroughly defined intention, and there was something new to Romola in his manner and expression as he looked at her silently on entering, and, without taking off his cap and mantle, leaned one elbow on the cabinet, and stood directly in front of her.

Romola, fully assured during the day of the Frate's safety, was feeling the reaction of some penitence for the access of distrust and indignation which had impelled her to address her husband publicly on a matter that she knew he wished to be private. She told herself that she had probably been wrong. The scheming duplicity which she had heard even her godfather allude to as inseparable from party tactics might be sufficient to account for the connection with Spini, without the supposition that Tito had ever meant to further the plot. She wanted to atone for her impetuosity by confessing that she had been too hasty, and for some hours her mind had been dwelling on the possibility that this confession of hers might lead to other frank words breaking the two years' silence of their hearts. The silence had been so complete, that Tito was ignorant of her having fled from him and come back again; they had never approached an avowal of that past which, both in its young love and in the shock that shattered the love, lay locked away from them like a banquet-room where death had once broken the feast.

She looked up at him with that submission in her glance which belonged to her state of self-reproof; but the subtle change in his face and manner arrested her speech. For a few moments they remained silent, looking at each other.

Tito himself felt that a crisis was come in his married life. The husband's determination to mastery, which lay deep below all blandness and beseechingness, had risen permanently to the surface now, and seemed to alter his face, as a face is altered by a hidden muscular tension with which a man is secretly throttling or stamping out the life from something feeble, yet dangerous.

"Romola," he began, in the cool liquid tone that made her

shiver, "it is time that we should understand each other."
He paused.

"That is what I most desire, Tito," she said, faintly. Her
sweet pale face, with all its anger gone and nothing but the
timidity of self-doubt in it, seemed to give a marked predominance to her husband's dark strength.

"You took a step this morning," Tito went on, "which you
must now yourself perceive to have been useless — which ex-
posed you to remark and may involve me in serious practical
difficulties."

"I acknowledge that I was too hasty; I am sorry for any
injustice I may have done you." Romola spoke these words
in a fuller and firmer tone; Tito, she hoped, would look less
hard when she had expressed her regret, and then she could
say other things.

"I wish you once for all to understand," he said, without
any change of voice, "that such collisions are incompatible
with our position as husband and wife. I wish you to reflect
on the mode in which you were led to that step, that the
process may not be repeated."

"That depends chiefly on you, Tito," said Romola, taking
fire slightly. It was not at all what she had thought of saying, but we see a very little way before us in mutual speech.

"You would say, I suppose," answered Tito, "that nothing
is to occur in future which can excite your unreasonable suspicions. You were frank enough to say last night that you
have no belief in me. I am not surprised at any exaggerated
conclusion you may draw from slight premises, but I wish to
point out to you what is likely to be the fruit of your making
such exaggerated conclusions a ground for interfering in affairs of which you are ignorant. Your attention is thoroughly
awake to what I am saying?"

He paused for a reply.

"Yes," said Romola, flushing in irrepressible resentment at
this cold tone of superiority.

"Well, then, it may possibly not be very long before some
other chance words or incidents set your imagination at work
devising crimes for me, and you may perhaps rush to the

Palazzo Vecchio to alarm the Signoria and set the city in an uproar. Shall I tell you what may be the result ? Not simply the disgrace of your husband, to which you look forward with so much courage, but the arrest and ruin of many among the chief men in Florence, including Messer Bernardo del Nero."

Tito had meditated a decisive move, and he had made it. The flush died out of Romola's face, and her very lips were pale — an unusual effect with her, for she was little subject to fear. Tito perceived his success.

"You would perhaps flatter yourself," he went on, "that you were performing a heroic deed of deliverance; you might as well try to turn locks with fine words as apply such notions to the politics of Florence. The question now is, not whether you can have any belief in me, but whether, now you have been warned, you will dare to rush, like a blind man with a torch in his hand, among intricate affairs of which you know nothing."

Romola felt as if her mind were held in a vice by Tito's : the possibilities he had indicated were rising before her with terrible clearness.

"I am too rash," she said. "I will try not to be rash."

"Remember," said Tito, with unsparing insistence, "that your act of distrust towards me this morning might, for aught you knew, have had more fatal effects than that sacrifice of your husband which you have learned to contemplate without flinching."

"Tito, it is not so," Romola burst forth in a pleading tone, rising and going nearer to him, with a desperate resolution to speak out. "It is false that I would willingly sacrifice you. It has been the greatest effort of my life to cling to you. I went away in my anger two years ago, and I came back again because I was more bound to you than to anything else on earth. But it is useless. You shut me out from your mind. You affect to think of me as a being too unreasonable to share in the knowledge of your affairs. You will be open with me about nothing."

She looked like his good angel pleading with him, as she bent her face towards him with dilated eyes, and laid her hand upon his arm. But Romola's touch and glance no longer stirred any fibre of tenderness in her husband. The good-humored, tolerant Tito, incapable of hatred, incapable almost of impatience, disposed always to be gentle towards the rest of the world, felt himself becoming strangely hard towards this wife whose presence had once been the strongest influence he had known. With all his softness of disposition, he had a masculine effectiveness of intellect and purpose which, like sharpness of edge, is itself an energy, working its way without any strong momentum. Romola had an energy of her own which thwarted his, and no man, who is not exceptionally feeble, will endure being thwarted by his wife. Marriage must be a relation either of sympathy or of conquest.

No emotion darted across his face as he heard Romola for the first time speak of having gone away from him. His lips only looked a little harder as he smiled slightly and said —

"My Romola, when certain conditions are ascertained, we must make up our minds to them. No amount of wishing will fill the Arno, as your people say, or turn a plum into an orange. I have not observed even that prayers have much efficacy that way. You are so constituted as to have certain strong impressions inaccessible to reason : I cannot share those impressions, and you have withdrawn all trust from me in consequence. You have changed towards me ; it has followed that I have changed towards you. It is useless to take any retrospect. We have simply to adapt ourselves to altered conditions."

"Tito, it would not be useless for us to speak openly," said Romola, with the sort of exasperation that comes from using living muscle against some lifeless insurmountable resistance. "It was the sense of deception in you that changed me, and that has kept us apart. And it is not true that I changed first. You changed towards me the night you first wore that chain-armor. You had some secret from me — it was about that old man — and I saw him again yesterday. Tito," she went on, in a tone of agonized entreaty, "if you would once tell me everything, let it be what it may — I would not mind pain — that there might be no wall between us ! Is it not possible that we could begin a new life ? "

This time there was a flash of emotion across Tito's face.
He stood perfectly still; but the flash seemed to have whitened
him. He took no notice of Romola's appeal, but after a moment's pause, said quietly —

"Your impetuosity about trifles, Romola, has a freezing influence that would cool the baths of Nero." At these cutting
words, Romola shrank and drew herself up into her usual self-
sustained attitude. Tito went on. "If by 'that old man'
you mean the mad Jacopo di Nola who attempted my life and
made a strange accusation against me, of which I told you
nothing because it would have alarmed you to no purpose, he,
poor wretch, has died in prison. .I saw his name in the list of
dead."

"I know nothing about his accusation," said Romola. "But
I know he is the man whom I saw with the rope round his
neck in the Duomo — the man whose portrait Piero di Cosimo
painted, grasping your arm as he saw him grasp it the day the
French entered, the day you first wore the armor."

"And where is he now, pray?" said Tito, still pale, but
governing himself.

"He was lying lifeless in the street from starvation," said
Romola. "I revived him with bread and wine. I brought
him to our door, but he refused to come in. Then I gave him
some money, and he went away without telling me anything.
But he had found out that I was your wife. *Who* is he?"

"A man, half mad, half imbecile, who was once my father's
servant in Greece, and who has a rancorous hatred towards me
because I got him dismissed for theft. Now you have the
whole mystery, and the further satisfaction of knowing that I
am again in danger of assassination. The fact of my wearing
the armor, about which you seem to have thought so much,
must have led you to infer that I was in danger from this
man. Was that the reason you chose to cultivate his acquaintance and invite him into the house?"

Romola was mute. To speak was only like rushing with
bare breast against a shield.

Tito moved from his leaning posture, slowly took off his cap
and mantle, and pushed back his hair. He was collecting him-

self for some final words. And Romola stood upright looking
at him as she might have looked at some on-coming deadly
force, to be met only by silent endurance.

"We need not refer to these matters again, Romola," he
said, precisely in the same tone as that in which he had
spoken at first. "It is enough if you will remember that the
next time your generous ardor leads you to interfere in political affairs, you are likely, not to save any one from danger,
but to be raising scaffolds and setting houses on fire. You are
not yet a sufficiently ardent Piagnone to believe that Messer
Bernardo del Nero is the prince of darkness, and Messer Francesco Valori the archangel Michael. I think I need demand
no promise from you ? "

"I have understood you too well, Tito."

"It is enough," he said, leaving the room.

Romola turned round with despair in her face and sank into
her seat. "O God, I have tried — I cannot help it. We shall
always be divided." Those words passed silently through her
mind. "Unless," she said aloud, as if some sudden vision had
startled her into speech — "unless misery should come and
join us ! "

Tito, too, had a new thought in his mind after he had closed
the door behind him. With the project of leaving Florence as
soon as his life there had become a high enough stepping-stone
to a life elsewhere, perhaps at Rome or Milan, there was now
for the first time associated a desire to be free from Romola,
and to leave her behind him. She had ceased to belong to the
desirable furniture of his life : there was no possibility of an
easy relation between them without genuineness on his part.
Genuineness implied confession of the past, and confession
involved a change of purpose. But Tito had as little bent
that way as a leopard has to lap milk when its teeth are
grown. From all relations that were not easy and agreeable,
we know that Tito shrank : why should he cling to them ?

And Romola had made his relations difficult with others
besides herself. He had had a troublesome interview with
Dolfo Spini, who had come back in a rage after an ineffectual
soaking with rain and long waiting in ambush, and that scene

between Romola and himself at Nello's door, once reported in
Spini's ear, might be a seed of something more unmanageable
than suspicion. But now, at least, he believed that he had
mastered Romola by a terror which appealed to the strongest
forces of her nature. He had alarmed her affection and her
conscience by the shadowy image of consequences; he had
arrested her intellect by hanging before it the idea of a hopeless complexity in affairs which defied any moral judgment.

Yet Tito was not at ease. The world was not yet quite
cushioned with velvet, and, if it had been, he could not have
abandoned himself to that softness with thorough enjoyment;
for before he went out again this evening he put on his coat
of chain-armor.

CHAPTER XLIX.

THE PYRAMID OF VANITIES.

THE wintry days passed for Romola as the white ships pass
one who is standing lonely on the shore — passing in silence
and sameness, yet each bearing a hidden burden of coming
change. Tito's hint had mingled so much dread with her
interest in the progress of public affairs that she had begun
to court ignorance rather than knowledge. The threatening
German Emperor was gone again; and, in other ways besides,
the position of Florence was alleviated; but so much distress remained that Romola's active duties were hardly diminished, and in these, as usual, her mind found a refuge from its
doubt.

She dared not rejoice that the relief which had come in
extremity and had appeared to justify the policy of the Frate's
party was making that party so triumphant, that Francesco
Valori, hot-tempered chieftain of the Piagnoni, had been elected
Gonfaloniere at the beginning of the year, and was making
haste to have as much of his own liberal way as possible during his two months of power. That seemed for the moment

like a strengthening of the party most attached to freedom, and a reinforcement of protection to Savonarola; but Romola was now alive to every suggestion likely to deepen her foreboding, that whatever the present might be, it was only an unconscious brooding over the mixed germs of Change which might any day become tragic. And already by Carnival time, a little after mid-February, her presentiment was confirmed by the signs of a very decided change : the Mediceans had ceased to be passive, and were openly exerting themselves to procure the election of Bernardo del Nero as the new Gonfaloniere.

On the last day of the Carnival, between ten and eleven in the morning, Romola walked out, according to promise, towards the Corso degli Albizzi, to fetch her cousin Brigida, that they might both be ready to start from the Via de' Bardi early in the afternoon, and take their places at a window which Tito had had reserved for them in the Piazza della Signoria, where there was to be a scene of so new and striking a sort, that all Florentine eyes must desire to see it. For the Piagnoni were having their own way thoroughly about the mode of keeping the Carnival. In vain Dolfo Spini and his companions had struggled to get up the dear old masks and practical jokes, well spiced with indecency. Such things were not to be in a city where Christ had been declared king.

Romola set out in that languid state of mind with which every one enters on a long day of sight-seeing purely for the sake of gratifying a child, or some dear childish friend. The day was certainly an epoch in carnival-keeping; but this phase of reform had not touched her enthusiasm : and she did not know that it was an epoch in her own life when *another* lot would begin to be no longer secretly but visibly entwined with her own.

She chose to go through the great piazza that she might take a first survey of the unparalleled sight there while she was still alone. Entering it from the south, she saw something monstrous and many-colored in the shape of a pyramid, or, rather, like a huge fir-tree, sixty feet high, with shelves on the branches, widening and widening towards the base till they reached a circumference of eighty yards. The piazza was full of life: slight young figures, in white garments, with olive wreaths on their heads, were moving to and fro about the base of the pyramidal tree, carrying baskets full of bright-colored things; and maturer forms, some in the monastic frock, some in the loose tunics and dark-red caps of artists, were helping and examining, or else retreating to various points in the distance to survey the wondrous whole: while a consider-able group, among whom Romola recognized Piero di Cosimo, standing on the marble steps of Orgagna's Loggia, seemed to be keeping aloof in discontent and scorn.

Approaching nearer, she paused to look at the multifarious objects ranged in gradation from the base to the summit of the pyramid. There were tapestries and brocades of immod-est design, pictures and sculptures held too likely to incite to vice; there were boards and tables for all sorts of games, · playing-cards along with the blocks for printing them, dice, and other apparatus for gambling; there were worldly music-books, and musical instruments in all the pretty varieties of lute, drum, cymbal, and trumpet; there were masks and mas-querading-dresses used in the old Carnival shows; there were handsome copies of Ovid, Boccaccio, Petrarca, Pulci, and other books of a vain or impure sort; there were all the implements of feminine vanity — rouge-pots, false hair, mirrors, perfumes, powders, and transparent veils intended to provoke inquisitive glances: lastly, at the very summit, there was the unflattering effigy of a probably mythical Venetian merchant, who was understood to have offered a heavy sum for this collection of marketable abominations, and, soaring above him in sur-passing ugliness, the symbolic figure of the old debauched Carnival.

This was the preparation for a new sort of bonfire — the Burning of Vanities. Hidden in the interior of the pyramid was a plentiful store of dry fuel and gunpowder; and on this last day of the festival, at evening, the pile of vanities was to be set ablaze to the sound of trumpets, and the ugly old Car-nival was to tumble into the flames amid the songs of reform-ing triumph.

This crowning act of the new festivities could hardly have

been prepared but for a peculiar organization which had been started by Savonarola two years before. The mass of the Florentine boyhood and youth was no longer left to its own genial promptings towards street mischief and crude dissoluteness. Under the training of Fra Domenico, a sort of lieutenant to Savonarola, lads and striplings, the hope of Florence, were to have none but pure words on their lips, were to have a zeal for Unseen Good that should put to shame the lukewarmness of their elders, and were to know no pleasures save of an angelic sort — singing divine praises and walking in white robes. It was for them that the ranges of seats had been raised high against the walls of the Duomo; and they had been used to hear Savonarola appeal to them as the future glory of a city specially appointed to do the work of God.

These fresh-cheeked troops were the chief agents in the regenerated merriment of the new Carnival, which was a sort of sacred parody of the old. Had there been bonfires in the old time? There was to be a bonfire now, consuming impurity from off the earth. Had there been symbolic processions? There were to be processions now, but the symbols were to be white robes and red crosses and olive wreaths — emblems of peace and innocent gladness — and the banners and images held aloft were to tell the triumphs of goodness. Had there been dancing in a ring under the open sky of the piazza, to the sound of choral voices chanting loose songs? There was to be dancing in a ring now, but dancing of monks and laity in fraternal love and divine joy, and the music was to be the music of hymns. As for the collections from street passengers, they were to be greater than ever — not for gross and superfluous suppers, but — for the benefit of the hungry and needy; and, besides, there was the collecting of the *Anathema*, or the Vanities to be laid on the great pyramidal bonfire.

Troops of young inquisitors went from house to house on this exciting business of asking that the Anathema should be given up to them. Perhaps, after the more avowed vanities had been surrendered, Madonna, at the head of the household, had still certain little reddened balls brought from the Levant, intended to produce on a sallow cheek a sudden bloom of the

most ingenuous falsity ? If so, let her bring them down and
cast them into the basket of doom. Or, perhaps, she had
ringlets and coils of "dead hair" ? — if so, let her bring them
to the street-door, not on her head, but in her hands, and publicly renounce the Anathema which hid the respectable signs
of age under a ghastly mockery of youth. And, in reward,
she would hear fresh young voices pronounce a blessing on her
and her house.

The beardless inquisitors, organized into little regiments,
doubtless took to their work very willingly. To coerce people
by shame, or other spiritual pelting, into the giving up of
things it will probably vex them to part with, is a form of
piety to which the boyish mind is most readily converted; and
if some obstinately wicked men got enraged and threatened
the whip or the cudgel, this also was exciting. Savonarola
himself evidently felt about the training of these boys the
difficulty weighing on all minds with noble yearnings towards
great ends, yet with that imperfect perception of means which
forces a resort to some supernatural constraining influence as
the only sure hope. The Florentine youth had had very evil
habits and foul tongues: it seemed at first an unmixed blessing when they were got to shout " *Viva Gesù!* " But Savonarola was forced at last to say from the pulpit, "There is a
little too much shouting of ' *Viva Gesù!* ' This constant
utterance of sacred words brings them into contempt. Let
me have no more of that shouting till the next Festa."

Nevertheless, as the long stream of white-robed youthful-
ness, with its little red crosses and olive wreaths, had gone to
the Duomo at dawn this morning to receive the communion
from the hands of Savonarola, it was a sight of beauty; and,
doubtless, many of those young souls were laying up memories of hope and awe that might save them from ever resting
in a merely vulgar view of their work as men and citizens.
There is no kind of conscious obedience that is not an advance
on lawlessness, and these boys became the generation of men
who fought greatly and endured greatly in the last struggle of
their Republic. Now, in the intermediate hours between the
early communion and dinner-time, they were making their

last perambulations to collect alms and vanities, and this was why Romola saw the slim white figures moving to and fro about the base of the great pyramid.

"What think you of this folly, Madonna Romola?" said a brusque voice close to her ear. "Your Piagnoni will make *l'inferno* a pleasant prospect to us, if they are to carry things their own way on earth. It's enough to fetch a cudgel over the mountains to see painters, like Lorenzo di Credi and young Baccio there, helping to burn color out of life in this fashion."

"My good Piero," said Romola, looking up and smiling at the grim man, "even you must be glad to see some of these things burnt. Look at those gewgaws and wigs and rouge-pots: I have heard you talk as indignantly against those things as Fra Girolamo himself."

"What then?" said Piero, turning round on her sharply. "I never said a woman should make a black patch of herself against the background. Va! Madonna Antigone, it's a shame for a woman with your hair and shoulders to run into such nonsense — leave it to women who are not worth painting. What! the most holy Virgin herself has always been dressed well; that's the doctrine of the Church: — talk of heresy, indeed! And I should like to know what the excellent Messer Bardo would have said to the burning of the divine poets by these Frati, who are no better an imitation of men than if they were onions with the bulbs uppermost. Look at that Petrarca sticking up beside a rouge-pot: do the idiots pretend that the heavenly Laura was a painted harridan? And Boccaccio, now: do you mean to say, Madonna Romola — you who are fit to be a model for a wise Saint Catherine of Egypt — do you mean to say you have never read the stories of the immortal Messer Giovanni?"

"It is true I have read them, Piero," said Romola. "Some of them a great many times over, when I was a little girl. I used to get the book down when my father was asleep, so that I could read to myself."

"*Ebbene?*" said Piero, in a fiercely challenging tone.

"There are some things in them I do not want ever to forget," said Romola; "but you must confess, Piero, that a great many of those stories are only about low deceit for the lowest ends. Men do not want books to make them think lightly of vice, as if life were a vulgar joke. And I cannot blame Fra Girolamo for teaching that we owe our time to something better."

"Yes, yes, it's very well to say so now you've read them," said Piero, bitterly, turning on his heel and walking away from her.

Romola, too, walked on, smiling at Piero's innuendo, with a sort of tenderness towards the old painter's anger, because she knew that her father would have felt something like it. For herself, she was conscious of no inward collision with the strict and sombre view of pleasure which tended to repress poetry in the attempt to repress vice. Sorrow and joy have each their peculiar narrowness; and a religious enthusiasm like Savonarola's which ultimately blesses mankind by giving the soul a strong propulsion towards sympathy with pain, indignation against wrong, and the subjugation of sensual desire, must always incur the reproach of a great negation. Romola's life had given her an affinity for sadness which inevitably made her unjust towards merriment. That subtle result of culture which we call Taste was subdued by the need for deeper motive; just as the nicer demands of the palate are annihilated by urgent hunger. Moving habitually among scenes of suffering, and carrying woman's heaviest disappointment in her heart, the severity which allied itself with self-renouncing beneficent strength had no dissonance for her.

CHAPTER L.

ANOTHER figure easily recognized by us — a figure not clad in black, but in the old red, green, and white — was approaching the piazza that morning to see the Carnival. She came from an opposite point, for Tessa no longer lived on the hill of San Giorgio. After what had happened there with Baldassarre, Tito had thought it best for that and other reasons to find her a new home, but still in a quiet airy quarter, in a house bordering on the wide garden grounds north of the Porta Santa Croce.

Tessa was not come out sight-seeing without special leave. Tito had been with her the evening before, and she had kept back the entreaty which she felt to be swelling her heart and throat until she saw him in a state of radiant ease, with one arm round the sturdy Lillo, and the other resting gently on her own shoulder as she tried to make the tiny Ninna steady on her legs. She was sure then that the weariness with which he had come in and flung himself into his chair had quite melted away from his brow and lips. Tessa had not been slow at learning a few small stratagems by which she might avoid vexing Naldo and yet have a little of her own way. She could read nothing else, but she had learned to read a good deal in her husband's face.

And certainly the charm of that bright, gentle-humored Tito who woke up under the Loggia de' Cerchi on a Lenten morning five years before, not having yet given any hostages to deceit, never returned so nearly as in the person of Naldo, seated in that straight-backed, carved arm-chair which he had provided for his comfort when he came to see Tessa and the children. Tito himself was surprised at the growing sense of relief which he felt in these moments. No guile was needed towards Tessa: she was too ignorant and too innocent to suspect him of anything. And the little voices calling him "Babbo" were very sweet in his ears for the short while that he heard them. When he thought of leaving Florence, he never thought of leaving Tessa and the little ones behind. He was very fond of these round-cheeked, wide-eyed human things that clung about him and knew no evil of him. And wherever affection can spring, it is like the green leaf and the blossom — pure, and breathing purity, whatever soil it may grow in. Poor Romola, with all her self-sacrificing effort, was really helping to harden Tito's nature by chilling it with a positive dislike

which had beforehand seemed impossible in him; but Tessa
kept open the fountains of kindness.

"Ninna is very good without me now," began Tessa, feeling
her request rising very high in her throat, and letting Ninna
seat herself on the floor. "I can leave her with Monna Lisa
any time, and if she is in the cradle and cries, Lillo is as
sensible as can be — he goes and thumps Monna Lisa."

Lillo, whose great dark eyes looked all the darker because
his curls were of a light brown like his mother's, jumped off
Babbo's knee, and went forthwith to attest his intelligence by
thumping Monna Lisa, who was shaking her head slowly over
her spinning at the other end of the room.

"A wonderful boy!" said Tito, laughing.

"Is n't he?" said Tessa, eagerly, getting a little closer to
him; "and I might go and see the Carnival to-morrow, just
for an hour or two, might n't I?"

"Oh, you wicked pigeon!" said Tito, pinching her cheek;
"those are your longings, are they? What have you to do
with carnivals now you are an old woman with two children?"

"But old women like to see things," said Tessa, her lower
lip hanging a little. "Monna Lisa said she should like to go,
only she's so deaf she can't hear what is behind her, and she
thinks we could n't take care of both the children."

"No, indeed, Tessa," said Tito, looking rather grave, "you
must not think of taking the children into the crowded streets,
else I shall be angry."

"But I have never been into the piazza without leave," said
Tessa, in a frightened, pleading tone, "since the Holy Saturday, and I think Nofri is dead, for you know the poor *madre*
died; and I shall never forget the Carnival I saw once; it was
so pretty — all roses and a king and queen under them — and
singing. I liked it better than the San Giovanni."

"But there's nothing like that now, my Tessa. They are
going to make a bonfire in the piazza — that's all. But I
cannot let you go out by yourself in the evening."

"Oh no, no! I don't want to go in the evening. I only
want to go and see the procession by daylight. There *will* be
a procession — is it not true?"

"Yes, after a sort," said Tito, "as lively as a flight of cranes. You must not expect roses and glittering kings and queens, my Tessa. However, I suppose any string of people to be called a procession will please your blue eyes. And there's a thing they have raised in the Piazza de' Signori for the bonfire. You may like to see that. But come home early, and look like a grave little old woman; and if you see any men with feathers and swords, keep out of their way: they are very fierce, and like to cut old women's heads off."

"Santa Madonna! where do they come from? Ah! you are laughing; it is not so bad. But I will keep away from them. Only," Tessa went on in a whisper, putting her lips near Naldo's ear, "if I might take Lillo with me! He is very sensible."

"But who will thump Monna Lisa then, if she does n't hear?" said Tito, finding it difficult not to laugh, but thinking it necessary to look serious. "No, Tessa, you could not take care of Lillo if you got into a crowd, and he's too heavy for you to carry him."

"It is true," said Tessa, rather sadly, "and he likes to run away. I forgot that. Then I will go alone. But now look at Ninna — you have not looked at her enough."

Ninna was a blue-eyed thing, at the tottering, tumbling age — a fair solid, which, like a loaded die, found its base with a constancy that warranted prediction. Tessa went to snatch her up, and when Babbo was paying due attention to the recent teeth and other marvels, she said, in a whisper, "And shall I buy some confetti for the children?"

Tito drew some small coins from his scarsella, and poured them into her palm.

"That will buy no end," said Tessa, delighted at this abundance. "I shall not mind going without Lillo so much, if I bring him something."

So Tessa set out in the morning towards the great piazza where the bonfire was to be. She did not think the February breeze cold enough to demand further covering than her green woollen dress. A mantle would have been oppressive, for it would have hidden a new necklace and a new clasp, mounted

with silver, the only ornamental presents Tito had ever made
her. Tessa did not think at all of showing her figure, for no
one had ever told her it was pretty; but she was quite sure
that her necklace and clasp were of the prettiest sort ever
worn by the richest contadina, and she arranged her white
hood over her head so that the front of her necklace might be
well displayed. These ornaments, she considered, must inspire
respect for her as the wife of some one who could afford to
buy them.

She tripped along very cheerily in the February sunshine,
thinking much of the purchases for the little ones, with which
she was to fill her small basket, and not thinking at all of any
one who might be observing her. Yet her descent from her
upper story into the street had been watched, and she was
being kept in sight as she walked by a person who had often
waited in vain to see if it were not Tessa who lived in that
house to which he had more than once dogged Tito. Baldassarre was carrying a package of yarn: he was constantly employed in that way, as a means of earning his scanty bread,
and keeping the sacred fire of vengeance alive; and he had
come out of his way this morning, as he had often done before,
that he might pass by the house to which he had followed
Tito in the evening. His long imprisonment had so intensi-
fied his timid suspicion and his belief in some diabolic fortune
favoring Tito, that he had not dared to pursue him, except
under cover of a crowd or of the darkness; he felt, with instinctive horror, that if Tito's eyes fell upon him, he should
again be held up to obloquy, again be dragged away; his
weapon would be taken from him, and he should be cast helpless into a prison-cell. His fierce purpose had become as
stealthy as a serpent's, which depends for its prey on one dart
of the fang. Justice was weak and unfriended; and he could
not hear again the voice that pealed the promise of vengeance
in the Duomo; he had been there again and again, but that
voice, too, had apparently been stifled by cunning strong-armed
wickedness. For a long while, Baldassarre's ruling thought
was to ascertain whether Tito still wore the armor, for now
at last his fainting hope would have been contented with a

successful stab on this side the grave ; but he would never risk
his precious knife again. It was a weary time he had had to
wait for the chance of answering this question by touching
Tito's back in the press of the street. Since then, the knowledge that the sharp steel was useless, and that he had no
hope but in some new device, had fallen with leaden weight
on his enfeebled mind. A dim vision of winning one of
those two wives to aid him came before him continually,
and continually slid away. The wife who had lived on the
hill was no longer there. If he could find her again, he might
grasp some thread of a project, and work his way to more
clearness.

And this morning he had succeeded. He was quite certain
now where this wife lived, and as he walked, bent a little
under his burden of yarn, yet keeping the green and white
figure in sight, his mind was dwelling upon her and her circumstances as feeble eyes dwell on lines and colors, trying
to interpret them into consistent significance.

Tessa had to pass through various long streets without seeing any other sign of the Carnival than unusual groups of the
country people in their best garments, and that disposition in
everybody to chat and loiter which marks the early hours of
a holiday, before the spectacle has begun. Presently, in her
disappointed search for remarkable objects, her eyes fell on a
man with a pedler's basket before him, who seemed to be selling nothing but little red crosses to all the passengers. A
little red cross would be pretty to hang up over ·her bed ; it
would also help to keep off harm, and would perhaps make
Ninna stronger. Tessa went to the other side of the street
that she might ask the pedler the price of the crosses, fearing
that they would cost a little too much for her to spare from
her purchase of sweets. The pedler's back had been turned
towards her hitherto, but when she came near him she recognized an old acquaintance of the Mercato, Bratti Ferravecchi,
and, accustomed to feel that she was to avoid old acquaintances, she turned away again and passed to the other side of
the street. But Bratti's eye was too well practised in looking
out at the corner after possible customers, for her movement

to have escaped him, and she was presently arrested by a tap
on the arm from one of the red crosses.

"Young woman," said Bratti, as she unwillingly turned her
head, "you come from some castello a good way off, it seems
to me, else you'd never think of walking about, this blessed
Carnival, without a red cross in your hand. Santa Madonna!
Four white quattrini is a small price to pay for your soul —
prices rise in purgatory, let me tell you."

"Oh, I should like one," said Tessa, hastily, "but I couldn't
spare four white quattrini."

Bratti had at first regarded Tessa too abstractedly as a mere
customer to look at her with any scrutiny, but when she began
to speak he exclaimed, "By the head of San Giovanni, it must
be the little Tessa, and looking as fresh as a ripe apple!
What! you've done none the worse, then, for running away
from father Nofri? You were in the right of it, for he goes
on crutches now, and a crabbed fellow with crutches is dangerous; he can reach across the house and beat a woman as
he sits."

"I'm married," said Tessa, rather demurely, remembering
Naldo's command that she should behave with gravity; "and
my husband takes great care of me."

"Ah, then, you've fallen on your feet! Nofri said you
were good-for-nothing vermin; but what then? An ass may
bray a good while before he shakes the stars down. I always
said you did well to run away, and it isn't often Bratti's in
the wrong. Well, and so you've got a husband and plenty of
money? Then you'll never think much of giving four white
quattrini for a red cross. I get no profit; but what with the
famine and the new religion, all other merchandise is gone
down. You live in the country where the chestnuts are
plenty, eh? You've never wanted for polenta, I can see."

"No, I've never wanted anything," said Tessa, still on her
guard.

"Then you can afford to buy a cross. I got a Padre to
bless them, and you get blessing and all for four quattrini.
It isn't for the profit; I hardly get a danaro by the whole
lot. But then they're holy wares, and it's getting harder and

harder work to see your way to Paradise: the very Carnival
is like Holy Week, and the least you can do to keep the Devil
from getting the upper hand is to buy a cross. God guard
you! think what the Devil's tooth is! You've seen him
biting the man in San Giovanni. I should hope?"

Tessa felt much teased and frightened. "Oh, Bratti," she
said, with a discomposed face, "I want to buy a great many
confetti: I've got little Lillo and Ninna at home. And nice
colored sweet things cost a great deal. And they will not
like the cross so well, though I know it would be good to
have it."

"Come, then," said Bratti, fond of laying up a store of
merits by imagining possible extortions and then heroically
renouncing them, "since you're an old acquaintance, you
shall have it for two quattrini. It's making you a present of
the cross, to say nothing of the blessing."

Tessa was reaching out her two quattrini with trembling
hesitation, when Bratti said abruptly, "Stop a bit! Where
do you live?"

"Oh, a long way off," she answered, almost automatically,
being preoccupied with her quattrini; "beyond San Ambrogio,
in the Via Piccola, at the top of the house where the wood is
stacked below."

"Very good," said Bratti, in a patronizing tone; "then I'll
let you have the cross on trust, and call for the money. So
you live inside the gates? Well, well, I shall be passing."

"No, no!" said Tessa, frightened lest Naldo should be
angry at this revival of an old acquaintance. "I can spare
the money. Take it now."

"No," said Bratti, resolutely; "I'm not a hard-hearted
pedler. I'll call and see if you've got any rags, and you shall
make a bargain. See, here's the cross: and there's Pippo's
shop not far behind you; you can go and fill your basket, and
I must go and get mine empty. *Addio, piccina.*"

Bratti went on his way, and Tessa, stimulated to change her
money into confetti before further accident, went into Pippo's
shop, a little fluttered by the thought that she had let Bratti
know more about her than her husband would approve. There

were certainly more dangers in coming to see the Carnival
than in staying at home; and she would have felt this more
strongly if she had known that the wicked old man, who had
wanted to kill her husband on the hill, was still keeping her
in sight. But she had not noticed the man with the burden
on his back.

The consciousness of having a small basketful of things to
make the children glad, dispersed her anxiety, and as she
entered the Via de' Libraj her face had its usual expression
of childlike content. And now she thought there was really
a procession coming, for she saw white robes and a banner,
and her heart began to palpitate with expectation. She stood
a little aside, but in that narrow street there was the pleasure
of being obliged to look very close. The banner was pretty :
it was the Holy Mother with the Babe, whose love for her
Tessa had believed in more and more since she had had her
babies; and the figures in white had not only green wreaths
on their heads, but little red crosses by their side, which
caused her some satisfaction that she also had her red cross.
Certainly, they looked as beautiful as the angels on the clouds,
and to Tessa's mind they too had a background of cloud, like
everything else that came to her in life. How and whence
did they come? She did not mind much about knowing.
But one thing surprised her as newer than wreaths and
crosses; it was that some of the white figures carried baskets
between them. What could the baskets be for ?

But now they were very near, and, to her astonishment, they
wheeled aside and came straight up to her. She trembled as
she would have done if St. Michael in the picture had shaken
his head at her, and was conscious of nothing but terrified
wonder till she saw close to her a round boyish face, lower
than her own, and heard a treble voice saying, " Sister, you
carry the Anathema about you. Yield it up to the blessed
Gesù, and He will adorn you with the gems of His grace."

Tessa was only more frightened, understanding nothing.
Her first conjecture settled on her basket of sweets. They
wanted that, these alarming angels. Oh dear, dear ! She
looked down at it.

"No, sister," said a taller youth, pointing to her necklace and the clasp of her belt, "it is those vanities that are the Anathema. Take off that necklace and unclasp that belt, that they may be burned in the holy Bonfire of Vanities, and save *you* from burning."

"It is the truth, my sister," said a still taller youth, evidently the archangel of this band. "Listen to these voices speaking the divine message. You already carry a red cross : let that be your only adornment. Yield up your necklace and belt, and you shall obtain grace."

This was too much. Tessa, overcome with awe, dared not say "no," but she was equally unable to render up her beloved necklace and clasp. Her pouting lips were quivering, the tears rushed to her eyes, and a great drop fell. For a moment she ceased to see anything; she felt nothing but confused terror and misery. Suddenly a gentle hand was laid on her arm, and a soft, wonderful voice, as if the Holy Madonna were speaking, said, "Do not be afraid; no one shall harm you."

Tessa looked up and saw a lady in black, with a young heavenly face and loving hazel eyes. She had never seen any one like this lady before, and under other circumstances might have had awe-struck thoughts about her; but now everything else was overcome by the sense that loving protection was near her. The tears only fell the faster, relieving her swelling heart, as she looked up at the heavenly face, and, putting her hand to her necklace, said sobbingly —

"I can't give them to be burnt. My husband — he bought them for me — and they are so pretty — and Ninna — oh, I wish I'd never come!"

"Do not ask her for them," said Romola, speaking to the white-robed boys in a tone of mild authority. "It answers no good end for people to give up such things against their will. That is not what Fra Girolamo approves : he would have such things given up freely."

Madonna Romola's word was not to be resisted, and the white train moved on. They even moved with haste, as if some new object had caught their eyes; and Tessa felt with bliss that they were gone, and that her necklace and clasp were still with her.

"Oh, I will go back to the house," she said, still agitated; "I will go nowhere else. But if I should meet them again, and you not be there?" she added, expecting everything from this heavenly lady.

"Stay a little," said Romola. "Come with me under this doorway, and we will hide the necklace and clasp, and then you will be in no danger."

She led Tessa under the archway, and said, "Now, can we find room for your necklace and belt in your basket? Ah! your basket is full of crisp things that will break: let us be careful, and lay the heavy necklace under them."

It was like a change in a dream to Tessa—the escape from nightmare into floating safety and joy—to find herself taken care of by this lady, so lovely, and powerful, and gentle. She let Romola unfasten her necklace and clasp, while she herself did nothing but look up at the face that bent over her.

"They are sweets for Lillo and Ninna," she said, as Romola carefully lifted up the light parcels in the basket, and placed the ornaments below them.

"Those are your children?" said Romola, smiling. "And you would rather go home to them than see any more of the Carnival? Else you have not far to go to the Piazza de' Signori, and there you would see the pile for the great bonfire."

"No, oh no!" said Tessa, eagerly; "I shall never like bonfires again. I will go back."

"You live at some castello, doubtless," said Romola, not waiting for an answer. "Towards which gate do you go?"

"Towards Por' Santa Croce."

"Come, then," said Romola, taking her by the hand and leading her to the corner of a street nearly opposite. "If you go down there," she said, pausing, "you will soon be in a straight road. And I must leave you now, because some one else expects me. You will not be frightened. Your pretty things are quite safe now. Addio."

"Addio, Madonna," said Tessa, almost in a whisper, not

knowing what else it would be right to say; and in an instant
the heavenly lady was gone. Tessa turned to catch a last
glimpse, but she only saw the tall gliding figure vanish round
the projecting stonework. So she went on her way in wonder,
longing to be once more safely housed with Monna Lisa, un-
desirous of carnivals forevermore.

Baldassarre had kept Tessa in sight till the moment of her
parting with Romola: then he went away with his bundle of
yarn. It seemed to him that he had discerned a clew which
might guide him if he could only grasp the necessary details
firmly enough. He had seen the two wives together, and the
sight had brought to his conceptions that vividness which had
been wanting before. His power of imagining facts needed
to be reinforced continually by the senses. The tall wife was
the noble and rightful wife; she had the blood in her that
would be readily kindled to resentment; she would know
what scholarship was, and how it might lie locked in by the
obstructions of the stricken body, like a treasure buried by
earthquake. She could believe him: she would be *inclined* to
believe him, if he proved to her that her husband was unfaith-
ful. Women cared about that: they would take vengeance
for that. If this wife of Tito's loved him, she would have a
sense of injury which Baldassarre's mind dwelt on with keen
longing, as if it would be the strength of another Will added
to his own, the strength of another mind to form devices.

Both these wives had been kind to Baldassarre, and their
acts towards him, being bound up with the very image of
them, had not vanished from his memory; yet the thought
of their pain could not present itself to him as a check. To
him it seemed that pain was the order of the world for all
except the hard and base. If any were innocent, if any were
noble, where could the utmost gladness lie for them? Where
it lay for him — in unconquerable hatred and triumphant vengeance. But he must be cautious: he must watch this wife
in the Via de' Bardi, and learn more of her; for even here
frustration was possible. There was no power for him now
but in patience.

CHAPTER LI.

WHEN Romola said that some one else expected her, she meant her cousin Brigida, but she was far from suspecting how much that good kinswoman was in need of her. Returning together towards the piazza, they had descried the company of youths coming to a stand before Tessa, and when Romola, having approached near enough to see the simple little contadina's distress, said, "Wait for me a moment, cousin," Monna Brigida said hastily, "Ah, I will not go on : come for me to Boni's shop, — I shall go back there."

The truth was, Monna Brigida had a consciousness on the one hand of certain "vanities" carried on her person, and on the other of a growing alarm lest the Piagnoni should be right in holding that rouge, and false hair, and pearl embroidery, endamaged the soul. Their serious view of things filled the air like an odor ; nothing seemed to have exactly the same flavor as it used to have ; and there was the dear child Romola, in her youth and beauty, leading a life that was uncomfortably suggestive of rigorous demands on woman. A widow at fifty-five whose satisfaction has been largely drawn from what she thinks of her own person, and what she believes others think of it, requires a great fund of imagination to keep her spirits buoyant. And Monna Brigida had begun to have frequent struggles at her toilet. If her soul would prosper better without them, was it really worth while to put on the rouge and the braids ? But when she lifted up the hand-mirror and saw a sallow face with baggy cheeks, and crows'-feet that were not to be dissimulated by any simpering of the lips — when she parted her gray hair, and let it lie in simple Piagnone fashion round her face, her courage failed. Monna Berta would certainly burst out laughing at her, and call her an old hag, and as Monna Berta was really only fifty-two, she had a superiority which would make the observation cutting. Every woman who was not a Piagnone would give a shrug at the sight of her, and the men would accost her as if she were their grandmother. Whereas, at fifty-five a woman was not so very old — she only required making up a little. So the rouge and the braids and the embroidered berretta went on again, and Monna Brigida was satisfied with the accustomed effect; as for her neck, if she covered it up, people might suppose it was too old to show, and, on the contrary, with the necklaces round it, it looked better than Monna Berta's. This very day, when she was preparing for the Piagnone Carnival, such a struggle had occurred, and the conflicting fears and longings which caused the struggle, caused her to turn back and seek refuge in the druggist's shop rather than encounter the collectors of the Anathema when Romola was not by her side. But Monna Brigida was not quite rapid enough in her retreat. She had been descried, even before she turned away, by the white-robed boys in the rear of those who wheeled round towards Tessa, and the willingness with which Tessa was given up was, perhaps, slightly due to the fact that part of the troop had already accosted a personage carrying more markedly upon her the dangerous weight of the Anathema. It happened that several of this troop were at the youngest age taken into peculiar training; and a small fellow of ten, his olive wreath resting above cherubic cheeks and wide brown eyes, his imagination really possessed with a hovering awe at existence as something in which great consequences impended on being good or bad, his longings nevertheless running in the direction of mastery and mischief, was the first to reach Monna Brigida and place himself across her path. She felt angry, and looked for an open door, but there was not one at hand, and by attempting to escape now, she would only make things worse. But it was not the cherubic-faced young one who first addressed her; it was a youth of fifteen, who held one handle of a wide basket.

"Venerable mother!" he began, "the blessed Jesus commands you to give up the Anathema which you carry upon you. That cap embroidered with pearls, those jewels that fasten up your false hair — let them be given up and sold for the poor; and cast the hair itself away from you, as a lie that is only fit for burning. Doubtless, too, you have other jewels under your silk mantle."

"Yes, lady," said the youth at the other handle, who had many of Fra Girolamo's phrases by heart, "they are too heavy for you: they are heavier than a millstone, and are weighting you for perdition. Will you adorn yourself with the hunger of the poor, and be proud to carry God's curse upon your head?"

"In truth you are old, buona madre," said the cherubic boy, in a sweet soprano. "You look very ugly with the red on your cheeks and that black glistening hair, and those fine things. It is only Satan who can like to see you. Your Angel is sorry. He wants you to rub away the red."

The little fellow snatched a soft silk scarf from the basket, and held it towards Monna Brigida, that she might use it as her guardian angel desired. Her anger and mortification were fast giving way to spiritual alarm. Monna Berta and that cloud of witnesses, highly dressed society in general, were not looking at her, and she was surrounded by young monitors, whose white robes, and wreaths, and red crosses, and dreadful candor, had something awful in their unusualness. Her Franciscan confessor, Fra Cristoforo, of Santa Croce, was not at hand to reinforce her distrust of Dominican teaching, and she was helplessly possessed and shaken by a vague sense that a supreme warning was come to her. Unvisited by the least suggestion of any other course that was open to her, she took the scarf that was held out, and rubbed her cheeks, with trembling submissiveness.

"It is well, madonna," said the second youth. "It is a holy beginning. And when you have taken those vanities from your head, the dew of heavenly grace will descend on it." The infusion of mischief was getting stronger, and putting his hand to one of the jewelled pins that fastened her braids to the berretta, he drew it out. The heavy black plait fell down over Monna Brigida's face, and dragged the rest of the head-gear forward. It was a new reason for not hesitating: she put up her hands hastily, undid the other fastenings, and flung down into the basket of doom her beloved crimson-velvet berretta, with all its unsurpassed embroidery of seed-pearls, and stood an' unrouged woman, with gray hair pushed backward from a face where certain deep lines of age had triumphed over *embonpoint*.

But the berretta was not allowed to lie in the basket. With impish zeal the youngsters lifted it, and held it up pitilessly, with the false hair dangling.

"See, venerable mother," said the taller youth, "what ugly lies you have delivered yourself from! And now you look like the blessed Saint Anna, the mother of the Holy Virgin."

Thoughts of going into a convent forthwith, and never showing herself in the world again, were rushing through Monna Brigida's mind. There was nothing possible for her but to take care of her soul. Of course, there were spectators laughing: she had no need to look round to assure herself of that. Well! it would, perhaps, be better to be forced to think more of Paradise. But at the thought that the dear accustomed world was no longer in her choice, there gathered some of those hard tears which just moisten elderly eyes, and she could see but dimly a large rough hand holding a red cross, which was suddenly thrust before her over the shoulders of the boys, while a strong guttural voice said —

"Only four quattrini, madonna, blessing and all! Buy it. You'll find a comfort in it now your wig's gone. Deh! what are we sinners doing all our lives? Making soup in a basket, and getting nothing but the scum for our stomachs. Better buy a blessing, madonna! Only four quattrini; the profit is not so much as the smell of a danaro, and it goes to the poor."

Monna Brigida, in dim-eyed confusion, was proceeding to the further submission of reaching money from her embroidered scarsella, at present hidden by her silk mantle, when the group round her, which she had not yet entertained the idea of escaping, opened before a figure as welcome as an angel loosing prison-bolts.

"Romola, look at me!" said Monna Brigida, in a piteous tone, putting out both her hands.

The white troop was already moving away, with a slight consciousness that its zeal about the head-gear had been super-abundant enough to afford a dispensation from any further demand for penitential offerings.

"Dear cousin, don't be distressed," said Romola, smitten with pity, yet hardly able to help smiling at the sudden apparition of her kinswoman in a genuine, natural guise, strangely contrasted with all memories of her. She took the black drapery from her own head, and threw it over Monna Brigida's. "There," she went on soothingly, "no one will remark you now. We will turn down the Via del Palagio and go straight to our house."

They hastened away, Monna Brigida grasping Romola's hand tightly, as if to get a stronger assurance of her being actually there.

"Ah, my Romola, my dear child!" said the short fat woman, hurrying with frequent steps to keep pace with the majestic young figure beside her; "what an old scarecrow I am! I must be good — I mean to be good!"

"Yes, yes; buy a cross!" said the guttural voice, while the rough hand was thrust once more before Monna Brigida: for Bratti was not to be abashed by Romola's presence into re-nouncing a probable customer, and had quietly followed up their retreat. "Only four quattrini, blessing and all — and if there was any profit, it would all go to the poor."

Monna Brigida would have been compelled to pause, even if she had been in a less submissive mood. She put up one hand deprecatingly to arrest Romola's remonstrance, and with the other reached out a grosso, worth many white quattrini, saying, in an entreating tone —

"Take it, good man, and begone."

"You're in the right, madonna," said Bratti, taking the coin quickly, and thrusting the cross into her hand; "I'll not offer you change, for I might as well rob you of a mass. What! we must all be scorched a little, but you'll come off the easier; better fall from the window than the roof. A good Easter and a good year to you!"

"Well, Romola," cried Monna Brigida, pathetically, as Bratti left them, " if I'm to be a Piagnone it's no matter how I look ! "

" Dear cousin," said Romola, smiling at her affectionately, " you don't know how much better you look than you ever did before. I see now how good-natured your face is, like yourself. That red and finery seemed to thrust themselves forward and hide expression. Ask our Piero or any other painter if he would not rather paint your portrait now than before. I think all lines of the human face have something either touching or grand, unless they seem to come from low passions. How fine old men are, like my godfather! Why should not old women look grand and simple ? "

" Yes, when one gets to be sixty, my Romola," said Brigida, relapsing a little ; " but I'm only fifty-five, and Monna Berta, and everybody — but it's no use : I will be good, like you. Your mother, if she'd been alive, would have been as old as I am ; we were cousins together. One *must* either die or get old. But it doesn't matter about being old, if one's a Piagnone."

CHAPTER LII.

A PROPHETESS.

THE incidents of that Carnival day seemed to Romola to carry no other personal consequences to her than the new care of supporting poor cousin Brigida in her fluctuating resignation to age and gray hairs ; but they introduced a Lenten time in which she was kept at a high pitch of mental excitement and active effort.

Bernardo del Nero had been elected Gonfaloniere. By great exertions the Medicean party had so far triumphed, and that triumph had deepened Romola's presentiment of some secretly prepared scheme likely to ripen either into success or betrayal during these two months of her godfather's authority. Every morning the dim daybreak as it peered into her room seemed

to be that haunting fear coming back to her. Every morning
the fear went with her as she passed through the streets on
her way to the early sermon in the Duomo : but there she
gradually lost the sense of its chill presence, as men lose the
dread of death in the clash of battle.

In the Duomo she felt herself sharing in a passionate conflict
which had wider relations than any enclosed within the walls
of Florence. For Savonarola was preaching — preaching the
last course of Lenten sermons he was ever allowed to finish in
the Duomo : he knew that excommunication was imminent,
and he had reached the point of defying it. He held up the
condition of the Church in the terrible mirror of his unflinching speech, which called things by their right names and dealt
in no polite periphrases ; he proclaimed with heightening confidence the advent of renovation — of a moment when there
would be a general revolt against corruption. As to his own
destiny, he seemed to have a double and alternating prevision :
sometimes he saw himself taking a glorious part in that revolt, sending forth a voice that would be heard through all
Christendom, and making the dead body of the Church tremble into new life, as the body of Lazarus trembled when the
Divine voice pierced the sepulchre ; sometimes he saw no
prospect for himself but persecution and martyrdom : — this
life for him was only a vigil, and only after death would come
the dawn.

The position was one which must have had its impressive-
ness for all minds that were not of the dullest order, even
if they were inclined, as Macchiavelli was, to interpret the
Frate's character by a key that presupposed no loftiness. To
Romola, whose kindred ardor gave her a firm belief in Savonarola's genuine greatness of purpose, the crisis was as stirring
as if it had been part of her personal lot. It blent itself as an
exalting memory with all her daily labors ; and those labors
were calling not only for difficult perseverance, but for new
courage. Famine had never yet taken its flight from Florence,
and all distress, by its long continuance, was getting harder
to bear ; disease was spreading in the crowded city, and the
Plague was expected. As Romola walked, often in weariness,

among the sick, the hungry, and the murmuring, she felt it
good to be inspired by something more than her pity — by the
belief in a heroism struggling for sublime ends, towards which
the daily action of her pity could only tend feebly, as the
dews that freshen the weedy ground to-day tend to prepare an
unseen harvest in the years to come.

But that mighty music which stirred her in the Duomo was
not without its jarring notes. Since those first days of glowing hope when the Frate, seeing the near triumph of good in
the reform of the Republic and the coming of the French deliverer, had preached peace, charity, and oblivion of political
differences, there had been a marked change of conditions:
political intrigue had been too obstinate to allow of the desired
oblivion; the belief in the French deliverer, who had turned
his back on his high mission, seemed to have wrought harm;
and hostility, both on a petty and on a grand scale, was attacking the Prophet with new weapons and new determination.

It followed that the spirit of contention and self-vindication
pierced more and more conspicuously in his sermons; that he
was urged to meet the popular demands not only by increased
insistence and detail concerning visions and private revelations,
but by a tone of defiant confidence against objectors; and from
having denounced the desire for the miraculous, and declared
that miracles had no relation to true faith, he had come to assert that at the right moment the Divine power would attest
the truth of his prophetic preaching by a miracle. And continually, in the rapid transitions of excited feeling, as the
vision of triumphant good receded behind the actual predominance of evil, the threats of coming vengeance against vicious
tyrants and corrupt priests gathered some impetus from personal exasperation, as well as from indignant zeal.

In the career of a great public orator who yields himself to
the inspiration of the moment, that conflict of selfish and unselfish emotion which in most men is hidden in the chamber
of the soul, is brought into terrible evidence: the language of
the inner voices is written out in letters of fire.

But if the tones of exasperation jarred on Romola, there was
often another member of Fra Girolamo's audience to whom

they were the only thrilling tones, like the vibration of deep bass notes to the deaf. Baldassarre had found out that the wonderful Frate was preaching again, and as often as he could, he went to hear the Lenten sermon, that he might drink in the threats of a voice which seemed like a power on the side of justice. He went the more because he had seen that Romola went too; for he was waiting and watching for a time when not only outward circumstances, but his own varying mental state, would mark the right moment for seeking an interview with her. Twice Romola had caught sight of his face in the Duomo — once when its dark glance was fixed on hers. She wished not to see it again, and yet she looked for it, as men look for the reappearance of a portent. But any revelation that might be yet to come about this old man was a subordinate fear now : it referred, she thought, only to the past, and her anxiety was almost absorbed by the present.

Yet the stirring Lent passed by ; April, the second and final month of her godfather's supreme authority, was near its close ; and nothing had occurred to fulfil her presentiment. In the public mind, too, there had been fears, and rumors had spread from Rome of a menacing activity on the part of Piero de' Medici ; but in a few days the suspected Bernardo would go out of power.

Romola was trying to gather some courage from the review of her futile fears, when on the 27th, as she was walking out on her usual errands of mercy in the afternoon, she was met by a messenger from Camilla Rucellai, chief among the feminine seers of Florence, desiring her presence forthwith on matters of the highest moment. Romola, who shrank with unconquerable repulsion from the shrill volubility of those illuminated women, and had just now a special repugnance towards Camilla because of a report that she had announced revelations hostile to Bernardo del Nero, was at first inclined to send back a flat refusal. Camilla's message might refer to public affairs, and Romola's immediate prompting was to close her ears against knowledge that might only make her mental burden heavier. But it had become so thoroughly her habit to reject her impulsive choice, and to obey passively the guidance of outward claims, that, reproving herself for allowing her presentiments to make her cowardly and selfish, she ended by compliance, and went straight to Camilla.

She found the nervous gray-haired woman in a chamber arranged as much as possible like a convent cell. The thin fingers clutching Romola as she sat, and the eager voice addressing her at first in a loud whisper, caused her a physical shrinking that made it difficult for her to keep her seat.

Camilla had a vision to communicate — a vision in which it had been revealed to her by Romola's Angel, that Romola knew certain secrets concerning her godfather, Bernardo del Nero, which, if disclosed, might save the Republic from peril. Camilla's voice rose louder and higher as she narrated her vision, and ended by exhorting Romola to obey the command of her Angel, and separate herself from the enemy of God.

Romola's impetuosity was that of a massive nature, and, except in moments when she was deeply stirred, her manner was calm and self-controlled. She had a constitutional disgust for the shallow excitability of women like Camilla, whose faculties seemed all wrought up into fantasies, leaving nothing for emotion and thought. The exhortation was not yet ended when she started up and attempted to wrench her arm from Camilla's tightening grasp. It was of no use. The prophetess kept her hold like a crab, and, only incited to more eager exhortation by Romola's resistance, was carried beyond her own intention into a shrill statement of other visions which were to corroborate this. Christ himself had appeared to her and ordered her to send his commands to certain citizens in office that they should throw Bernardo del Nero from the window of the Palazzo Vecchio. Fra Girolamo himself knew of it, and had not dared this time to say that the vision was not of Divine authority.

"And since then," said Camilla, in her excited treble, straining upward with wild eyes towards Romola's face, "the Blessed Infant has come to me and laid a wafer of sweetness on my tongue in token of his pleasure that I had done his will."

"Let me go!" said Romola, in a deep voice of anger. "God grant you are mad! else you are detestably wicked!"

The violence of her effort to be free was too strong for Camilla now. She wrenched away her arm and rushed out of the room, not pausing till she had hurriedly gone far along the street, and found herself close to the church of the Badia. She had but to pass behind the curtain under the old stone arch, and she would find a sanctuary shut in from the noise and hurry of the street, where all objects and all uses suggested the thought of an eternal peace subsisting in the midst of turmoil.

She turned in, and sinking down on the step of the altar in front of Filippino Lippi's serene Virgin appearing to St. Bernard, she waited in hope that the inward tumult which agitated her would by-and-by subside.

The thought which pressed on her the most acutely was that Camilla could allege Savonarola's countenance of her wicked folly. Romola did not for a moment believe that he had sanctioned the throwing of Bernardo del Nero from the window as a Divine suggestion; she felt certain that there was falsehood or mistake in that allegation. Savonarola had become more and more severe in his views of resistance to malcontents; but the ideas of strict law and order were fundamental to all his political teaching. Still, since he knew the possibly fatal effects of visions like Camilla's, since he had a marked distrust of such spirit-seeing women, and kept aloof from them as much as possible, why, with his readiness to denounce wrong from the pulpit, did he not publicly denounce these pretended revelations which brought new darkness instead of light across the conception of a Supreme Will? Why? The answer came with painful clearness: he was fettered inwardly by the consciousness that such revelations were not, in their basis, distinctly separable from his own visions; he was fettered outwardly by the foreseen consequence of raising a cry against himself even among members of his own party, as one who would suppress all Divine inspiration of which he himself was not the vehicle — he or his confidential and supplementary seer of visions, Fra Salvestro.

Romola, kneeling with buried face on the altar-step, was enduring one of those sickening moments, when the enthu-

siasm which had come to her as the only energy strong enough
to make life worthy, seemed to be inevitably bound up with
vain dreams and wilful eye-shutting. Her mind rushed back
with a new attraction towards the strong worldly sense, the
dignified prudence, the untheoretic virtues of her godfather,
who was to be treated as a sort of Agag because he held that
a more restricted form of government was better than the
Great Council, and because he would not pretend to forget old
ties to the banished family.

But with this last thought rose the presentiment of some
plot to restore the Medici; and then again she felt that the
popular party was half justified in its fierce suspicion. Again
she felt that to keep the Government of Florence pure, and
to keep out a vicious rule, was a sacred cause; the Frate was
right there, and had carried her understanding irrevocably
with him. But at this moment the assent of her understanding went alone; it was given unwillingly. Her heart was
recoiling from a right allied to so much narrowness; a right
apparently entailing that hard systematic judgment of men
which measures them by assents and denials quite superficial
to the manhood within them. Her affection and respect were
clinging with new tenacity to her godfather, and with him to
those memories of her father which were in the same opposition to the division of men into sheep and goats by the easy
mark of some political or religious symbol.

After all has been said that can be said about the widening
influence of ideas, it remains true that they would hardly be
such strong agents unless they were taken in a solvent of
feeling. The great world-struggle of developing thought is
continually foreshadowed in the struggle of the affections,
seeking a justification for love and hope.

If Romola's intellect had been less capable of discerning
the complexities in human things, all the early loving associations of her life would have forbidden her to accept im-
plicitly the denunciatory exclusiveness of Savonarola. She
had simply felt that his mind had suggested deeper and more
efficacious truth to her than any other, and the large breathing-
room she found in his grand view of human duties had made

her patient towards that part of his teaching which she could not absorb, so long as its practical effect came into collision with no strong force in her. But now a sudden insurrection of feeling had brought about that collision. Her indignation, once roused by Camilla's visions, could not pause there, but ran like an illuminating fire over all the kindred facts in Savonarola's teaching, and for the moment she felt what was true in the scornful sarcasms she heard continually flung against him, more keenly than she felt what was false.

But it was an illumination that made all life look ghastly to her. Where were the beings to whom she could cling, with whom she could work and endure, with the belief that she was working for the right? On the side from which moral energy came lay a fanaticism from which she was shrinking with newly startled repulsion; on the side to which she was drawn by affection and memory, there was the presentiment of some secret plotting, which her judgment told her would not be unfairly called crime. And still surmounting every other thought was the dread inspired by Tito's hints, lest that presentiment should be converted into knowledge, in such a way that she would be torn by irreconcilable claims.

Calmness would not come even on the altar-steps; it would not come from looking at the serene picture where the saint, writing in the rocky solitude, was being visited by faces with celestial peace in them. Romola was in the hard press of human difficulties, and that rocky solitude was too far off. She rose from her knees that she might hasten to her sick people in the courtyard, and by some immediate beneficent action, revive that sense of worth in life which at this moment was unfed by any wider faith. But when she turned round, she found herself face to face with a man who was standing only two yards off her. The man was Baldassarre.

CHAPTER LIII.

ON SAN MINIATO.

"I WOULD speak with you," said Baldassarre, as Romola looked at him in silent expectation. It was plain that he had followed her, and had been waiting for her. She was going at last to know the secret about him.

" Yes," she said, with the same sort of submission that she might have shown under an imposed penance. " But you wish to go where no one can hear us ? "

" Where *he* will not come upon us," said Baldassarre, turn-ing and glancing behind him timidly. " Out — in the air — away from the streets."

" I sometimes go to San Miniato at this hour," said Romola. "If you like, I will go now, and you can follow me. It is far, but we can be solitary there."

He nodded assent, and Romola set out. To some women it might have seemed an alarming risk to go to a comparatively solitary spot with a man who had some of the outward signs of that madness which Tito attributed to him. But Romola was not given to personal fears, and she was glad of the dis-tance that interposed some delay before another blow fell on her. The afternoon was far advanced, and the sun was al-ready low in the west, when she paused on some rough ground in the shadow of the cypress-trunks, and looked round for Baldassarre. He was not far off, but when he reached her, he was glad to sink down on an edge of stony earth. His thick-set frame had no longer the sturdy vigor which belonged to it when he first appeared with the rope round him in the Duomo; and under the transient tremor caused by the exertion of walking up the hill, his eyes seemed to have a more helpless vagueness.

" The hill is steep," said Romola, with compassionate gentle-ness, seating herself by him. " And I fear you have been weakened by want ? "

He turned his head and fixed his eyes on her in silence,
unable, now the moment of speech was come, to seize the
words that would convey the thought he wanted to utter : and
she remained as motionless as she could, lest he should suppose her impatient. He looked like nothing higher than a
common-bred, neglected old man ; but she was used now to be
very near to such people, and to think a great deal about their
troubles. Gradually his glance gathered a more definite expression, and at last he said with abrupt emphasis —

"Ah ! you would have been my daughter !"

The swift flush came in Romola's face and went back again
as swiftly, leaving her with white lips a little apart, like a
marble image of horror. For her mind, the revelation was
made. She divined the facts that lay behind that single word,
and in the first moment there could be no check to the impulsive belief which sprang from her keen experience of Tito's
nature. The sensitive response of her face was a stimulus to
Baldassarre ; for the first time his words had wrought their
right effect. He went on with gathering eagerness and firmness, laying his hand on her arm.

"You are a woman of proud blood — is it not true ? You
go to hear the preacher ; you hate baseness — baseness that
smiles and triumphs. You hate your husband ? "

"Oh, God ! were you really his father ? " said Romola, in a
low voice, too entirely possessed by the images of the past to
take any note of Baldassarre's question. "Or was it as he
said ? Did you take him when he was little ? "

"Ah, you believe me — you know what he is ! " said Baldassarre, exultingly, tightening the pressure on her arm, as if
the contact gave him power. "You will help me ? "

"Yes," said Romola, not interpreting the words as he
meant them. She laid her palm gently on the rough hand
that grasped her arm, and the tears came to her eyes as she
looked at him. "Oh, it is piteous ! Tell me — you were a
great scholar ; you taught him. *How* is it ? "

She broke off. Tito's allegation of this man's madness had
come across her ; and where were the signs even of past refinement ? But she had the self-command not to move her

hand. She sat perfectly still, waiting to listen with new caution.

"It is gone! — it is all gone!" said Baldassarre; "and they would not believe me, because he lied, and said I was mad; and they had me dragged to prison. And I am old — my mind will not come back. And the world is against me."

He paused a moment, and his eyes sank as if he were under a wave of despondency. Then he looked up at her again, and said with renewed eagerness —

"But *you* are not against me. He made you love him, and he has been false to you; and you hate him. Yes, he made *me* love him: he was beautiful and gentle, and I was a lonely man. I took him when they were beating him. He slept in my bosom when he was little, and I watched him as he grew, and gave him all my knowledge, and everything that was mine I meant to be his. I had many things; money, and books, and gems. He had my gems — he sold them; and he left me in slavery. He never came to seek me, and when I came back poor and in misery, he denied me. He said I was a madman."

"He told us his father was dead — was drowned," said Romola, faintly. "Surely he must have believed it then. Oh! he could not have been so base *then!*"

A vision had risen of what Tito was to her in those first days when she thought no more of wrong in him than a child thinks of poison in flowers. The yearning regret that lay in that memory brought some relief from the tension of horror. With one great sob the tears rushed forth.

"Ah, you are young, and the tears come easily," said Baldassarre, with some impatience. "But tears are no good; they only put out the fire within, and it is the fire that works. Tears will hinder us. Listen to me."

Romola turned towards him with a slight start. Again the possibility of his madness had darted through her mind, and checked the rush of belief. If, after all, this man were only a mad assassin? But her deep belief in this story still lay behind, and it was more in sympathy than in fear that she avoided the risk of paining him by any show of doubt.

"Tell me," she said, as gently as she could, "how did you lose your memory — your scholarship."

"I was ill. I can't tell how long — it was a blank. I remember nothing, only at last I was sitting in the sun among the stones, and everything else was darkness. And slowly, and by degrees, I felt something besides that: a longing for something — I did not know what — that never came. And when I was in the ship on the waters I began to know what I longed for; it was for the Boy to come back — it was to find all my thoughts again, for I was locked away outside them all. And I am outside now. I feel nothing but a wall and darkness."

Baldassarre had become dreamy again, and sank into silence, resting his head between his hands : and again Romola's belief in him had submerged all cautioning doubts. The pity with which she dwelt on his words seemed like the revival of an old pang. Had she not daily seen how her father missed Dino and the future he had dreamed of in that son?

"It all came back once," Baldassarre went on presently. "I was master of everything. I saw all the world again, and my gems, and my books; and I thought I had him in my power, and I went to expose him where — where the lights were and the trees; and he lied again, and said I was mad, and they dragged me away to prison. . . . Wickedness is strong; and he wears armor."

The fierceness had flamed up again. He spoke with his former intensity, and again he grasped Romola's arm.

"But you will help me? He has been false to you too. He has another wife, and she has children. He makes her believe he is her husband, and she is a foolish, helpless thing. I will show you where she lives."

The first shock that passed through Romola was visibly one of anger. The woman's sense of indignity was inevitably foremost. Baldassarre instinctively felt her in sympathy with him.

"You hate him," he went on. "Is it not true? There is no love between you; I know that. I know women can hate; and you have proud blood. You hate falseness, and you can love revenge."

Romola sat paralyzed by the shock of conflicting feelings. She was not conscious of the grasp that was bruising her tender arm.

"You shall contrive it," said Baldassarre, presently, in an eager whisper. "I have learned by heart that you are his rightful wife. You are a noble woman. You go to hear the preacher of vengeance; you will help justice. But you will think for me. My mind goes — everything goes sometimes — all but the fire. The fire is God: it is justice: it will not die. You believe that — is it not true? If they will not hang him for robbing me, you will take away his armor — you will make him go without it, and I will stab him. I have a knife, and my arm is still strong enough."

He put his hand under his tunic, and reached out the hidden knife, feeling the edge abstractedly, as if he needed the sensation to keep alive his ideas.

It seemed to Romola as if every fresh hour of her life were to become more difficult than the last. Her judgment was too vigorous and rapid for her to fall into the mistake of using futile deprecatory words to a man in Baldassarre's state of mind. She chose not to answer his last speech. She would win time for his excitement to allay itself by asking something else that she cared to know. She spoke rather tremulously —

"You say she is foolish and helpless — that other wife — and believes him to be her real husband. Perhaps he is: perhaps he married her before he married me."

"I cannot tell," said Baldassarre, pausing in that action of feeling the knife, and looking bewildered. "I can remember no more. I only know where she lives. You shall see her. I will take you; but not now," he added hurriedly, "*he* may be there. The night is coming on."

"It is true," said Romola, starting up with a sudden consciousness that the sun had set and the hills were darkening; "but you will come and take me — when?"

"In the morning," said Baldassarre, dreaming that she, too, wanted to hurry to her vengeance.

"Come to me, then, where you came to me to-day, in the

church. I will be there at ten; and if you are not there, I will go again towards mid-day. Can you remember?"

"Mid-day," said Baldassarre — "only mid-day. The same place, and mid-day. And, after that," he added, rising and grasping her arm again with his left hand, while he held the knife in his right; "we will have our revenge. He shall feel the sharp edge of justice. The world is against me, but you will help me."

"I would help you in other ways," said Romola, making a first, timid effort to dispel his illusion about her. "I fear you are in want; you have to labor, and get little. I should like to bring you comforts, and make you feel again that there is some one who cares for you."

"Talk no more about that," said Baldassarre, fiercely. "I will have nothing else. Help me to wring one drop of vengeance on this side of the grave. I have nothing but my knife. It is sharp; but there is a moment after the thrust when men see the face of death, — and it shall be *my* face that he will see."

He loosed his hold, and sank down again in a sitting posture. Romola felt helpless: she must defer all intentions till the morrow.

"Mid-day, then," she said, in a distinct voice.

"Yes," he answered, with an air of exhaustion. "Go; I will rest here."

She hastened away. Turning at the last spot whence he was likely to be in sight, she saw him seated still.

----•----

CHAPTER LIV.

THE EVENING AND THE MORNING.

ROMOLA had a purpose in her mind as she was hastening away; a purpose which had been growing through the afternoon hours like a side-stream, rising higher and higher along with the main current. It was less a resolve than a necessity of her feeling. Heedless of the darkening streets, and not caring to call for Maso's slow escort, she hurried across the bridge where the river showed itself black before the distant dying red, and took the most direct way to the Old Palace. She might encounter her husband there. No matter. She could not weigh probabilities; she must discharge her heart. She did not know what she passed in the pillared court or up the wide stairs; she only knew that she asked an usher for the Gonfaloniere, giving her name, and begging to be shown into a private room.

She was not left long alone with the frescoed figures and the newly lit tapers. Soon the door opened, and Bernardo del Nero entered, still carrying his white head erect above his silk lucco.

"Romola, my child, what is this?" he said, in a tone of anxious surprise as he closed the door.

She had uncovered her head and went towards him without speaking. He laid his hand on her shoulder, and held her a little way from him that he might see her better. Her face was haggard from fatigue and long agitation, her hair had rolled down in disorder; but there was an excitement in her eyes that seemed to have triumphed over the bodily consciousness.

"What has he done?" said Bernardo, abruptly. "Tell me everything, child; throw away pride. I am your father."

"It is not about myself — nothing about myself," said Romola, hastily. "Dearest godfather, it is about you. I have heard things — some I cannot tell you. But you are in danger in the palace; you are in danger everywhere. There are fanatical men who would harm you, and — and there are traitors. Trust nobody. If you trust, you will be betrayed."

Bernardo smiled.

"Have you worked yourself up into this agitation, my poor child," he said, raising his hand to her head and patting it gently, "to tell such old truth as that to an old man like me?"

"Oh, no, no! they are not old truths that I mean," said Romola, pressing her clasped hands painfully together, as if that action would help her to suppress what must not be told. "They are fresh things that I know, but cannot tell. Dearest godfather, you know I am not foolish. I would not come to you without reason. Is it too late to warn you against any one, *every* one who seems to be working on your side ? Is it too late to say, 'Go to your villa and keep away in the country when these three more days of office are over ? ' Oh, God! perhaps it is too late ! and if any harm comes to you, it will be as if I had done it !"

The last words had burst from Romola involuntarily : a long-stifled feeling had found spasmodic utterance. But she herself was startled and arrested.

"I mean," she added, hesitatingly, "I know nothing positive. I only know what fills me with fears."

"Poor child !" said Bernardo, looking at her with quiet penetration for a moment or two. Then he said : "Go, Romola — go home and rest. These fears may be only big ugly shadows of something very little and harmless. Even traitors must see their interest in betraying ; the rats will run where they smell the cheese, and there is no knowing yet which way the scent will come."

He paused, and turned away his eyes from her with an air of abstraction, till, with a slow shrug, he added —

"As for warnings, they are of no use to me, child. I enter into no plots, but I never forsake my colors. If I march abreast with obstinate men, who will rush on guns and pikes, I must share the consequences. Let us say no more about that. I have not many years left at the bottom of my sack for them to rob me of. Go, child ; go home and rest."

He put his hand on her head again caressingly, and she could not help clinging to his arm, and pressing her brow against his shoulder. Her godfather's caress seemed the last thing that was left to her out of that young filial life, which now looked so happy to her even in its troubles, for they were troubles untainted by anything hateful.

"Is silence best, my Romola ? " said the old man.

"Yes, now; but I cannot tell whether it always will be," she answered, hesitatingly, raising her head with an appealing look.

"Well, you have a father's ear while I am above ground" —he lifted the black drapery and folded it round her head, adding — "and a father's home; remember that." Then opening the door, he said: "There, hasten away. You are like a black ghost; you will be safe enough."

When Romola fell asleep that night, she slept deep. Agitation had reached its limits; she must gather strength before she could suffer more; and, in spite of rigid habit, she slept on far beyond sunrise.

When she awoke, it was to the sound of guns. Piero de' Medici, with thirteen hundred men at his back, was before the gate that looks towards Rome.

So much Romola learned from Maso, with many circumstantial additions of dubious quality. A countryman had come in and alarmed the Signoria before it was light, else the city would have been taken by surprise. His master was not in the house, having been summoned to the Palazzo long ago. She sent out the old man again, that he might gather news, while she went up to the loggia from time to time to try and discern any signs of the dreaded entrance having been made, or of its having been effectively repelled. Maso brought her word that the great piazza was full of armed men, and that many of the chief citizens suspected as friends of the Medici had been summoned to the palace and detained there. Some of the people seemed not to mind whether Piero got in or not, and some said the Signoria itself had invited him; but however that might be, they were giving him an ugly welcome; and the soldiers from Pisa were coming against him.

In her memory of those morning hours, there were not many things that Romola could distinguish as actual external experiences standing markedly out above the tumultuous waves of retrospect and anticipation. She knew that she had really walked to the Badia by the appointed time in spite of street alarms; she knew that she had waited there in vain. And the scene she had witnessed when she came out of the church, and stood watching on the steps while the doors were being closed behind her for the afternoon interval, always came back to her like a remembered waking.

There was a change in the faces and tones of the people, armed and unarmed, who were pausing or hurrying along the streets. The guns were firing again, but the sound only provoked laughter. She soon knew the cause of the change. Piero de' Medici and his horsemen had turned their backs on Florence, and were galloping as fast as they could along the Siena road. She learned this from a substantial shopkeeping Piagnone, who had not yet laid down his pike.

"It is true," he ended, with a certain bitterness in his emphasis. "Piero is gone, but there are those left behind who were in the secret of his coming — we all know that; and if the new Signoria does its duty we shall soon know *who* they are."

The words darted through Romola like a sharp spasm; but the evil they foreshadowed was not yet close upon her, and as she entered her home again, her most pressing anxiety was the possibility that she had lost sight for a long while of Baldassarre.

CHAPTER LV.

WAITING.

THE lengthening sunny days went on without bringing either what Romola most desired or what she most dreaded. They brought no sign from Baldassarre, and, in spite of special watch on the part of the Government, no revelation of the suspected conspiracy. But they brought other things which touched her closely, and bridged the phantom-crowded space of anxiety with active sympathy in immediate trial. They brought the spreading Plague and the Excommunication of Savonarola.

Both these events tended to arrest her incipient alienation

from the Frate, and to rivet again her attachment to the man
who had opened to her the new life of duty, and who seemed
now to be worsted in the fight for principle against profligacy.
For Romola could not carry from day to day into the abodes
of pestilence and misery the sublime excitement of a gladness
that, since such anguish existed, she too existed to make some
of the anguish less bitter, without remembering that she owed
this transcendent moral life to Fra Girolamo. She could not
witness the silencing and excommunication of a man whose
distinction from the great mass of the clergy lay, not in any
heretical belief, not in his superstitions, but in the energy with
which he sought to make the Christian life a reality, without
feeling herself drawn strongly to his side.

Far on in the hot days of June the Excommunication, for
some weeks arrived from Rome, was solemnly published in
the Duomo. Romola went to witness the scene, that the
resistance it inspired might invigorate that sympathy with
Savonarola which was one source of her strength. It was in
memorable contrast with the scene she had been accustomed
to witness there.

Instead of upturned citizen-faces filling the vast area under
the morning light, the youngest rising amphitheatre-wise
towards the walls, and making a garland of hope around the
memories of age — instead of the mighty voice thrilling all
hearts with the sense of great things, visible and invisible, to
be struggled for — there were the bare walls at evening made
more sombre by the glimmer of tapers ; there was the black
and gray flock of monks and secular clergy with bent, unex-
pectant faces ; there was the occasional tinkling of little bells
in the pauses of a monotonous voice reading a sentence which
had already been long hanging up in the churches ; and at last
there was the extinction of the tapers, and the slow, shuffling
tread of monkish feet departing in the dim silence.

Romola's ardor on the side of the Frate was doubly strengthened by the gleeful triumph she saw in hard and coarse faces,
and by the fear-stricken confusion in the faces and speech of
many among his strongly attached friends. The question
where the duty of obedience ends, and the duty of resistance

begins, could in no case be an easy one; but it was made over-
whelmingly difficult by the belief that the Church was — not
a compromise of parties to secure a more or less approximate
justice in the appropriation of funds, but — a living organism,
instinct with Divine power to bless and to curse. To most of
the pious Florentines, who had hitherto felt no doubt in their
adherence to the Frate, that belief in the Divine potency of
the Church was not an embraced opinion, it was an inalienable
impression, like the concavity of the blue firmament; and the
boldness of Savonarola's written arguments that the Excommunication was unjust, and that, being unjust, it was not valid,
only made them tremble the more, as a defiance cast at a mystic image, against whose subtle immeasurable power there was
neither weapon nor defence.

But Romola, whose mind had not been allowed to draw its
early nourishment from the traditional associations of the
Christian community in which her father had lived a life
apart, felt her relation to the Church only through Savonarola; his moral force had been the only authority to which
she had bowed; and in his excommunication she only saw the
menace of hostile vice: on one side she saw a man whose life
was devoted to the ends of public virtue and spiritual purity,
and on the other the assault of alarmed selfishness, headed by
a lustful, greedy, lying, and murderous old man, once called
Rodrigo Borgia, and now lifted to the pinnacle of infamy as
Pope Alexander the Sixth. The finer shades of fact which
soften the edge of such antitheses are not apt to be seen
except by neutrals, who are not distressed to discern some
folly in martyrs and some judiciousness in the men who burnt
them.

But Romola required a strength that neutrality could not
give; and this Excommunication, which simplified and en-
nobled the resistant position of Savonarola by bringing into
prominence its wider relations, seemed to come to her like a
rescue from the threatening isolation of criticism and doubt.
The Frate was now withdrawn from that smaller antagonism
against Florentine enemies into which he continually fell in
the unchecked excitement of the pulpit, and presented him-

self simply as appealing to the Christian world against a vicious exercise of ecclesiastical power. He was a standard-bearer leaping into the breach. Life never seems so clear and easy as when the heart is beating faster at the sight of some generous self-risking deed. We feel no doubt then what is the highest prize the soul can win; we almost believe in our own power to attain it. By a new current of such enthusiasm Romola was helped through these difficult summer days. She had ventured on no words to Tito that would apprise him of her late interview with Baldassarre, and the revelation he had made to her. What would such agitating, difficult words win from him? No admission of the truth; nothing, probably, but a cool sarcasm about her sympathy with his assassin. Baldassarre was evidently helpless: the thing to be feared was, not that he should injure Tito, but that Tito, coming upon his traces, should carry out some new scheme for ridding himself of the injured man who was a haunting dread to him. Romola felt that she could do nothing decisive until she had seen Baldassarre again, and learned the full truth about that "other wife" — learned whether she were the wife to whom Tito was first bound.

The possibilities about that other wife, which involved the worst wound to her hereditary pride, mingled themselves as a newly embittering suspicion with the earliest memories of her illusory love, eating away the lingering associations of tenderness with the past image of her husband; and her irresistible belief in the rest of Baldassarre's revelation made her shrink from Tito with a horror which would perhaps have urged some passionate speech in spite of herself if he had not been more than usually absent from home. Like many of the wealthier citizens in that time of pestilence, he spent the intervals of business chiefly in the country: the agreeable Melema was welcome at many villas, and since Romola had refused to leave the city, he had no need to provide a country residence of his own.

But at last, in the later days of July, the alleviation of those public troubles which had absorbed her activity and much of her thought, left Romola to a less counteracted sense

of her personal lot. The Plague had almost disappeared, and
the position of Savonarola was made more hopeful by a
favorable magistracy, who were writing urgent vindicatory
letters to Rome on his behalf, entreating the withdrawal of
the Excommunication.

Romola's healthy and vigorous frame was undergoing the
reaction of languor inevitable after continuous excitement and
over-exertion; but her mental restlessness would not allow
her to remain at home without peremptory occupation, except
during the sultry hours. In the cool of the morning and
evening she walked out constantly, varying her direction as
much as possible, with the vague hope that if Baldassarre
were still alive she might encounter him. Perhaps some illness had brought a new paralysis of memory, and he had
forgotten where she lived — forgotten even her existence.
That was her most sanguine explanation of his non-appearance.
The explanation she felt to be most probable was, that he had
died of the Plague.

CHAPTER LVI.

THE OTHER WIFE.

THE morning warmth was already beginning to be rather
oppressive to Romola, when, after a walk along by the walls
on her way from San Marco, she turned towards the intersect-
ing streets again at the gate of Santa Croce.

The Borgo La Croce was so still, that she listened to her
own footsteps on the pavement in the sunny silence, until, on
approaching a bend in the street, she saw, a few yards before
her, a little child not more than three years old, with no other
clothing than his white shirt, pause from a waddling run and
look around him. In the first moment of coming nearer she
could only see his back — a boy's back, square and sturdy,
with a cloud of reddish-brown curls above it; but in the next
he turned towards her, and she could see his dark eyes wide

with tears, and his lower lip pushed up and trembling, while his fat brown fists clutched his shirt helplessly. The glimpse of a tall black figure sending a shadow over him brought his bewildered fear to a climax, and a loud crying sob sent the big tears rolling.

Romola, with the ready maternal instinct which was one hidden source of her passionate tenderness, instantly uncovered her head, and, stooping down on the pavement, put her arms round him, and her cheeks against his, while she spoke to him in caressing tones. At first his sobs were only the louder, but he made no effort to get away, and presently the outburst ceased with that strange abruptness which belongs to childish joys and griefs: his face lost its distortion, and was fixed in an open-mouthed gaze at Romola.

"You have lost yourself, little one," she said, kissing him. "Never mind! we will find the house again. Perhaps mamma will meet us."

She divined that he had made his escape at a moment when the mother's eyes were turned away from him, and thought it likely that he would soon be followed.

"Oh, what a heavy, heavy boy!" she said, trying to lift him. "I cannot carry you. Come, then, you must toddle back by my side."

The parted lips remained motionless in awed silence, and one brown fist still clutched the shirt with as much tenacity as ever; but the other yielded itself quite willingly to the wonderful white hand, strong but soft.

"You *have* a mamma?" said Romola, as they set out, looking down at the boy with a certain yearning. But he was mute. A girl under those circumstances might perhaps have chirped abundantly; not so this square-shouldered little man with the big cloud of curls.

He was awake to the first sign of his whereabout, however. At the turning by the front of San Ambrogio he dragged Romola towards it, looking up at her.

"Ah, that is the way home, is it?" she said, smiling at him. He only thrust his head forward and pulled, as an admonition that they should go faster.

There was still another turning that he had a decided opinion about, and then Romola found herself in a short street leading to open garden ground. It was in front of a house at the end of this street that the little fellow paused, pulling her towards some stone stairs. He had evidently no wish for her to loose his hand, and she would not have been willing to leave him without being sure that she was delivering him to his friends. They mounted the stairs, seeing but dimly in that sudden withdrawal from the sunlight, till, at the final landing-place, an extra stream of light came from an open doorway. Passing through a small lobby, they came to another open door, and there Romola paused. Her approach had not been heard.

On a low chair at the farther end of the room, opposite the light, sat Tessa, with one hand on the edge of the cradle, and her head hanging a little on one side, fast asleep. Near one of the windows, with her back turned towards the door, sat Monna Lisa at her work of preparing salad, in deaf unconsciousness. There was only an instant for Romola's eyes to take in that still scene; for Lillo snatched his hand away from her and ran up to his mother's side, not making any direct effort to wake her, but only leaning his head back against her arm, and surveying Romola seriously from that distance.

As Lillo pushed against her, Tessa opened her eyes, and looked up in bewilderment; but her glance had no sooner rested on the figure at the opposite doorway than she started up, blushed deeply, and began to tremble a little, neither speaking nor moving forward.

"Ah! we have seen each other before," said Romola, smiling, and coming forward. "I am glad it was *your* little boy. He was crying in the street; I suppose he had run away. So we walked together a little way, and then he knew where he was, and brought me here. But you had not missed him? That is well, else you would have been frightened."

The shock of finding that Lillo had run away overcame every other feeling in Tessa for the moment. Her color went again, and, seizing Lillo's arm, she ran with him to Monna Lisa, saying, with a half sob, loud in the old woman's ear —

"Oh, Lisa, you are wicked! Why will you stand with your back to the door? Lillo ran away ever so far into the street."

"Holy Mother!" said Monna Lisa, in her meek, thick tone, letting the spoon fall from her hands. "Where were *you*, then? I thought you were there, and had your eye on him."

"But you *know* I go to sleep when 1 am rocking," said Tessa, in pettish remonstrance.

"Well, well, we must keep the outer door shut, or else tie him up," said Monna Lisa, "for he 'll be as cunning as Satan before long, and that 's the holy truth. But how came he back, then?"

This question recalled Tessa to the consciousness of Romola's presence. Without answering, she turned towards her, blushing and timid again, and Monna Lisa's eyes followed her movement. The old woman made a low reverence, and said —

"Doubtless the most noble lady brought him back." Then, advancing a little nearer to Romola, she added, "It 's my shame for him to have been found with only his shirt on; but he kicked, and would n't have his other clothes on this morning, and the mother, poor thing, will never hear of his being beaten. But what 's an old woman to do without a stick when the lad's legs get so strong? Let your nobleness look at his legs."

Lillo, conscious that his legs were in question, pulled his shirt up a little higher, and looked down at their olive roundness with a dispassionate and curious air. Romola laughed, and stooped to give him a caressing shake and a kiss, and this action helped the reassurance that Tessa had already gathered from Monna Lisa's address to Romola. For when Naldo had been told about the adventure at the Carnival, and Tessa had asked him who the heavenly lady that had come just when she was wanted, and had vanished so soon, was likely to be — whether she could be the Holy Madonna herself? — he had answered, "Not exactly, my Tessa; only one of the saints," and had not chosen to say more. So that in the dream-like combination of small experience which made up Tessa's thought, Romola had remained confusedly associated with the pictures in the churches, and when she reappeared, the grateful remembrance of her protection was slightly tinctured with religious awe — not deeply, for Tessa's dread was chiefly of ugly and evil beings. It seemed unlikely that good beings would be angry and punish her, as it was the nature of Nofri and the devil to do. And now that Monna Lisa had spoken freely about Lillo's legs and Romola had laughed, Tessa was more at her ease.

"Ninna's in the cradle," she said. "*She's* pretty too."

Romola went to look at the sleeping Ninna, and Monna Lisa, one of the exceptionally meek deaf, who never expect to be spoken to, returned to her salad.

"Ah! she is waking : she has opened her blue eyes," said Romola. "You must take her up, and I will sit down in this chair — may I ? — and nurse Lillo. Come, Lillo!"

She sat down in Tito's chair, and put out her arms towards the lad, whose eyes had followed her. He hesitated : and, pointing his small fingers at her with a half-puzzled, half-angry feeling, said, "That's Babbo's chair," not seeing his way out of the difficulty if Babbo came and found Romola in his place.

"But Babbo is not here, and I shall go soon. Come, let me nurse you as he does," said Romola, wondering to herself for the first time what sort of Babbo he was whose wife was dressed in contadina fashion, but had a certain daintiness about her person that indicated idleness and plenty. Lillo consented to be lifted up, and, finding the lap exceedingly comfortable, began to explore her dress and hands, to see if there were any ornaments beside the rosary.

Tessa, who had hitherto been occupied in coaxing Ninna out of her waking peevishness, now sat down in her low chair, near Romola's knee, arranging Ninna's tiny person to advantage, jealous that the strange lady too seemed to notice the boy most, as Naldo did.

"Lillo was going to be angry with me, because I sat in Babbo's chair," said Romola, as she bent forward to kiss Ninna's little foot. "Will he come soon and want it ?"

"Ah, no!" said Tessa, "you can sit in it a long while. I

shall be sorry when you go. When you first came to take
care of me at the Carnival, I thought it was wonderful; you
came and went away again so fast. And Naldo said, perhaps
you were a saint, and that made me tremble a little, though
the saints are very good, I know; and you were good to me,
and now you have taken care of Lillo. Perhaps you will always come and take care of me. That was how Naldo did a
long while ago; he came and took care of me when I was
frightened, one San Giovanni. I could n't think where he
came from — he was so beautiful and good. And so are you,"
ended Tessa, looking up at Romola with devout admiration.

"Naldo is your husband. His eyes are like Lillo's," said
Romola, looking at the boy's darkly pencilled eyebrows, unusual at his age. She did not speak interrogatively, but with
a quiet certainty of inference which was necessarily mysterious to Tessa.

"Ah! you know him!" she said, pausing a little in wonder.
"Perhaps you know Nofri and Peretola, and our house on the
hill, and everything. Yes, like Lillo's; but not his hair. His
hair is dark and long — " she went on, getting rather excited.
"Ah! if you know it, ecco!"

She had put her hand to a thin red silk cord that hung
round her neck, and drew from her bosom the tiny old parch-
ment *breve*, the horn of red coral, and a long dark curl
carefully tied at one end and suspended with those mystic
treasures. She held them towards Romola, away from Ninna's
snatching hand.

"It is a fresh one. I cut it lately. See how bright it is!"
she said, laying it against the white background of Romola's
fingers. "They get dim, and then he lets me cut another
when his hair is grown; and I put it with the *breve*, because
sometimes he is away a long while, and then I think it helps
to take care of me."

A slight shiver passed through Romola as the curl was laid
across her fingers. At Tessa's first mention of her husband as
having come mysteriously she knew not whence, a possibility
had risen before Romola that made her heart beat faster; for
to one who is anxiously in search of a certain object the faint-

est suggestions have a peculiar significance. And when the
curl was held towards her, it seemed for an instant like a
mocking phantasm of the lock she herself had cut to wind
with one of her own five years ago. But she preserved her
outward calmness, bent not only on knowing the truth, but
also on coming to that knowledge in a way that would not
pain this poor, trusting, ignorant thing, with the child's mind
in the woman's body. "Foolish and helpless:" yes; so far
she corresponded to Baldassarre's account.

"It is a beautiful curl," she said, resisting the impulse to
withdraw her hand. "Lillo's curls will be like it, perhaps,
for *his* cheek, too, is dark. And you never know where your
husband goes to when he leaves you?"

"No," said Tessa, putting back her treasures out of the
children's way. "But I know Messer San Michele takes care
of him, for he gave him a beautiful coat, all made of little
chains; and if he puts that on, nobody can kill him. And
perhaps, if —" Tessa hesitated a little, under a recurrence of
that original dreamy wonder about Romola which had been
expelled by chatting contact — "if you *were* a saint, you would
take care of him, too, because you have taken care of me and
Lillo."

An agitated flush came over Romola's face in the first moment of certainty, but she had bent her cheek against Lillo's
head. The feeling that leaped out in that flush was something like exultation at the thought that the wife's burden
might be about to slip from her overladen shoulders; that this
little ignorant creature might prove to be Tito's lawful wife.
A strange exultation for a proud and high-born woman to have
been brought to! But it seemed to Romola as if that were
the only issue that would make duty anything else for her
than an insoluble problem. Yet she was not deaf to Tessa's
last appealing words; she raised her head, and said, in her
clearest tones —

"I will always take care of you if I see you need me. But
that beautiful coat? your husband did not wear it when you
were first married? Perhaps he used not to be so long away
from you then?"

"Ah, yes! he was. Much — much longer. So long, I thought he would never come back. I used to cry. Oh me! I was beaten then; a long, long while ago at Peretola, where we had the goats and mules."

"And how long had you been married before your husband had that chain coat ? " said Romola, her heart beating faster and faster.

Tessa looked meditative, and began to count on her fingers, and Romola watched the fingers as if they would tell the secret of her destiny.

"The chestnuts were ripe when we were married," said Tessa, marking off her thumb and fingers again as she spoke; "and then again they were ripe at Peretola before he came back, and then again, after that, on the hill. And soon the soldiers came, and we heard the trumpets, and then Naldo had the coat."

"You had been married more than two years. In which church were you married ? " said Romola, too entirely absorbed by one thought to put any question that was less direct. Perhaps before the next morning she might go to her godfather and say that she was not Tito Melema's lawful wife — that the vows which had bound her to strive after an impossible union had been made void beforehand.

Tessa gave a slight start at Romola's new tone of inquiry, and looked up at her with a hesitating expression. Hitherto she had prattled on without consciousness that she was making revelations, any more than when she said old things over and over again to Monna Lisa.

"Naldo said I was never to tell about that," she said, doubtfully. "Do you think he would not be angry if I told you ?"

"It is right that you should tell me. Tell me everything," said Romola, looking at her with mild authority.

If the impression from Naldo's command had been much more recent than it was, the constraining effect of Romola's mysterious authority would have overcome it. But the sense that she was telling what she had never told before made her begin with a lowered voice.

"It was not in a church — it was at the Natività, when there

was a fair, and all the people went overnight to see the Madonna in the Nunziata, and my mother was ill and couldn't
go, and I took the bunch of cocoons for her; and then he came
to me in the church and I heard him say, 'Tessa!' I knew
him because he had taken care of me at the San Giovanni,
and then we went into the piazza where the fair was, and I
had some *berlingozzi*, for I was hungry and he was very good
to me; and at the end of the piazza there was a holy father,
and an altar like what they have at the processions outside
the churches. So he married us, and then Naldo took me back
into the church and left me; and I went home, and my mother
died, and Nofri began to beat me more, and Naldo never came
back. And I used to cry, and once at the Carnival I saw him
and followed him, and he was angry, and said he would come
some time, I must wait. So I went and waited; but, oh! it
was a long while before he came; but he would have come if
he could, for he was good; and then he took me away, because
I cried and said I could not bear to stay with Nofri. And,
oh! I was so glad, and since then I have been always happy,
for I don't mind about the goats and mules, because I have
Lillo and Ninna now; and Naldo is never angry, only I think
he doesn't love Ninna so well as Lillo, and she *is* pretty."

Quite forgetting that she had thought her speech rather momentous at the beginning, Tessa fell to devouring Ninna with
kisses, while Romola sat in silence with absent eyes. It was
inevitable that in this moment she should think of the three
beings before her chiefly in their relation to her own lot, and
she was feeling the chill of disappointment that her difficulties
were not to be solved by external law. She had relaxed her
hold of Lillo, and was leaning her cheek against her hand, seeing nothing of the scene around her. Lillo was quick in per-
ceiving a change that was not agreeable to him; he had not
yet made any return to her caresses, but he objected to their
withdrawal, and putting up both his brown arms to pull her
head towards him, he said, "Play with me again!"

Romola, roused from her self-absorption, clasped the lad
anew, and looked from him to Tessa, who had now paused
from her shower of kisses, and seemed to have returned to the

more placid delight of contemplating the heavenly lady's face. That face was undergoing a subtle change, like the gradual oncoming of a warmer, softer light. Presently Romola took her scissors from her scarsella, and cut off one of her long wavy locks, while the three pair of wide eyes followed her movements with kitten-like observation.

"I must go away from you now," she said, "but I will leave this lock of hair that it may remind you of me, because if you are ever in trouble you can think that perhaps God will send me to take care of you again. I cannot tell you where to find me, but if I ever know that you want me, I will come to you. Addio!"

She had set down Lillo hurriedly, and held out her hand to Tessa, who kissed it with a mixture of awe and sorrow at this parting. Romola's mind was oppressed with thoughts; she needed to be alone as soon as possible, but with her habitual care for the least fortunate, she turned aside to put her hand in a friendly way on Monna Lisa's shoulder and make her a farewell sign. Before the old woman had finished her deep reverence, Romola had disappeared.

Monna Lisa and Tessa moved towards each other by simultaneous impulses, while the two children stood clinging to their mother's skirts as if they, too, felt the atmosphere of awe.

"Do you think she *was* a saint?" said Tessa, in Lisa's ear, showing her the lock.

Lisa rejected that notion very decidedly by a backward movement of her fingers, and then stroking the rippled gold, said —

"She's a great and noble lady. I saw such in my youth."

Romola went home and sat alone through the sultry hours of that day with the heavy certainty that her lot was unchanged. She was thrown back again on the conflict between the demands of an outward law, which she recognized as a widely ramifying obligation, and the demands of inner moral facts which were becoming more and more peremptory. She had drunk in deeply the spirit of that teaching by which Savonarola had urged her to return to her place. She felt that the sanctity attached to all close relations, and, therefore, pre-eminently to the closest, was but the expression in outward law of that result towards which all human goodness and nobleness must spontaneously tend; that the light abandonment of ties, whether inherited or voluntary, because they had ceased to be pleasant, was the uprooting of social and personal virtue. What else had Tito's crime towards Baldassarre been but that abandonment working itself out to the most hideous extreme of falsity and ingratitude?

And the inspiring consciousness breathed into her by Savonarola's influence that her lot was vitally united with the general lot had exalted even the minor details of obligation into religion. She was marching with a great army; she was feeling the stress of a common life. If victims were needed, and it was uncertain on whom the lot might fall, she would stand ready to answer to her name. She had stood long; she had striven hard to fulfil the bond, but she had seen all the conditions which made the fulfilment possible gradually forsaking her. The one effect of her marriage-tie seemed to be the stifling predominance over her of a nature that she despised. All her efforts at union had only made its impossibility more palpable, and the relation had become for her simply a degrading servitude. The law was sacred. Yes, but rebellion might be sacred too. It flashed upon her mind that the problem before her was essentially the same as that which had lain before Savonarola — the problem where the sacredness of obedience ended, and where the sacredness of rebellion began. To her, as to him, there had come one of those moments in life when the soul must dare to act on its own warrant, not only without external law to appeal to, but in the face of a law which is not unarmed with Divine lightnings — lightnings that may yet fall if the warrant has been false.

Before the sun had gone down she had adopted a resolve. She would ask no counsel of her godfather or of Savonarola until she had made one determined effort to speak freely with Tito and obtain his consent that she should live apart from him. She desired not to leave him clandestinely again, or to forsake Florence. She would tell him that if he ever felt a

real need of her, she would come back to him. Was not that
the utmost faithfulness to her bond that could be required of
her ? A shuddering anticipation came over her that he would
clothe a refusal in a sneering suggestion that she should enter
a convent as the only mode of quitting him that would not be
scandalous. He knew well that her mind revolted from that
means of escape, not only because of her own repugnance to a
narrow rule, but because all the cherished memories of her
father forbade that she should adopt a mode of life which was
associated with his deepest griefs and his bitterest dislike.

Tito had announced his intention of coming home this evening. She would wait for him, and say what she had to say at
once, for it was difficult to get his ear during the day. If he
had the slightest suspicion that personal words were coming,
he slipped away with an appearance of unpremeditated ease.
When she sent for Maso to tell him that she would wait for
his master, she observed that the old man looked at her and
lingered with a mixture of hesitation and wondering anxiety ;
but finding that she asked him no question, he slowly turned
away. Why should she ask questions ? Perhaps Maso only
knew or guessed something of what she knew already.

It was late before Tito came. Romola had been pacing up
and down the long room which had once been the library, with
the windows open, and a loose white linen robe on instead of
her usual black garment. She was glad of that change after
the long hours of heat and motionless meditation ; but the
coolness and exercise made her more intensely wakeful, and
as she went with the lamp in her hand to open the door for
Tito, he might well have been startled by the vividness of her
eyes and the expression of painful resolution, which was in
contrast with her usual self-restrained quiescence before him.
But it seemed that this excitement was just what he expected.

"Ah! it is you, Romola. Maso is gone to bed," he said,
in a grave, quiet tone, interposing to close the door for her.
Then, turning round, he said, looking at her more fully than
he was wont, "You have heard it all, I see."

Romola quivered. *He* then was inclined to take the ini-
tiative. He had been to Tessa. She led the way through

the nearest door, set down her lamp, and turned towards him
again.

"You must not think despairingly of the consequences,"
said Tito, in a tone of soothing encouragement, at which
Romola stood wondering, until he added, "The accused have
too many family ties with all parties not to escape; and
Messer Bernardo del Nero has other things in his favor
besides his age."

Romola started, and gave a cry as if she had been suddenly
stricken by a sharp weapon.

"What! you did not know it?" said Tito, putting his hand
under her arm that he might lead her to a seat; but she seemed
to be unaware of his touch.

"Tell me," she said, hastily — "tell me what it is."

"A man, whose name you may forget — Lamberto dell'
Antella — who was banished, has been seized within the territory: a letter has been found on him of very dangerous import
to the chief Mediceans, and the scoundrel, who was once a
favorite hound of Piero de' Medici, is ready now to swear
what any one pleases against him or his friends. Some have
made their escape, but five are now in prison."

"My godfather?" said Romola, scarcely above a whisper,
as Tito made a slight pause.

"Yes: I grieve to say it. But along with him there are
three, at least, whose names have a commanding interest even
among the popular party — Niccolò Ridolfi, Lorenzo Tornabuoni,
and Giannozzo Pucci."

The tide of Romola's feelings had been violently turned
into a new channel. In the tumult of that moment there
could be no check to the words which came as the impulsive
utterance of her long-accumulating horror. When Tito had
named the men of whom she felt certain he was the con-
federate, she said, with a recoiling gesture and low-toned
bitterness —

"And *you* — you are safe?"

"You are certainly an amiable wife, my Romola," said Tito,
with the coldest irony. "Yes; I am safe."

They turned away from each other in silence.

CHAPTER LVII.

WHY TITO WAS SAFE.

TITO had good reasons for saying that he was safe. In the last three months, during which he had foreseen the discovery of the Medicean conspirators as a probable event, he had had plenty of time to provide himself with resources. He had been strengthening his influence at Rome and at Milan, by being the medium of secret information and indirect measures against the Frate and the popular party; he had cultivated more assiduously than ever the regard of this party, by showing subtle evidence that his political convictions were entirely on their side; and all the while, instead of withdrawing his agency from the Mediceans, he had sought to be more actively employed and exclusively trusted by them. It was easy to him to keep up this triple game. The principle of duplicity admitted by the Mediceans on their own behalf deprived them of any standard by which they could measure the trustworthiness of a colleague who had not, like themselves, hereditary interests, alliances, and prejudices, which were intensely Medicean. In their minds, to deceive the opposite party was fair stratagem; to deceive their own party was a baseness to which they felt no temptation; and, in using Tito's facile ability, they were not keenly awake to the fact that the absence of traditional attachments which made him a convenient agent was also the absence of what among themselves was the chief guarantee of mutual honor. Again, the Roman and Milanese friends of the aristocratic party, or Arrabbiati, who were the bitterest enemies of Savonarola, carried on a system of underhand correspondence and espionage, in which the deepest hypocrisy was the best service, and demanded the heaviest pay; so that to suspect an agent because he played a part strongly would have been an absurd want of logic. On the other hand, the Piagnoni of the popular party, who had the directness

that belongs to energetic conviction, were the more inclined to
credit Tito with sincerity in his political adhesion to them,
because he affected no religious sympathies.

By virtue of these conditions, the last three months had
been a time of flattering success to Tito. The result he most
cared for was the securing of a future position for himself at
Rome or at Milan ; for he had a growing determination, when
the favorable moment should come, to quit Florence for one of
those great capitals where life was easier, and the rewards of
talent and learning were more splendid. At present, the scale
dipped in favor of Milan ; and if within the year he could
render certain services to Duke Ludovico Sforza, he had the
prospect of a place at the Milanese court which outweighed
the advantages of Rome.

The revelation of the Medicean conspiracy, then, had been
a subject of forethought to Tito ; but he had not been able to
foresee the mode in which it would be brought about. The
arrest of Lamberto dell' Antella with a tell-tale letter on his
person, and a bitter rancor against the Medici in his heart,
was an incalculable event. It was not possible, in spite of the
careful pretexts with which his agency had been guarded, that
Tito should escape implication : he had never expected this
in case of any wide discovery concerning the Medicean plots.
But his quick mind had soon traced out the course that would
secure his own safety with the fewest unpleasant concomitants.
It is agreeable to keep a whole skin ; but the skin still remains
an organ sensitive to the atmosphere.

His reckoning had not deceived him. That night, before he
returned home, he had secured the three results for which he
most cared : he was to be freed from all proceedings against
him on account of complicity with the Mediceans ; he was to
retain his secretaryship for another year, unless he previously
resigned it ; and, lastly, the price by which he had obtained
these guarantees was to be kept as a State secret. The price
would have been thought heavy by most men ; and Tito himself would rather not have paid it.

He had applied himself first to win the mind of Francesco
Valori, who was not only one of the Ten under whom he im-

mediately held his secretaryship, but one of the special council appointed to investigate the evidence of the plot. Francesco Valori, as we have seen, was the head of the Piagnoni, a man with certain fine qualities that were not incompatible with violent partisanship, with an arrogant temper that alienated his friends, nor with bitter personal animosities — one of the bitterest being directed against Bernardo del Nero. To him, in a brief private interview, after obtaining a pledge of secrecy, Tito avowed his own agency for the Mediceans — an agency induced by motives about which he was very frank, declaring at the same time that he had always believed their efforts futile, and that he sincerely preferred the maintenance of the popular government; affected to confide to Valori, as a secret, his own personal dislike for Bernardo del Nero; and, after this preparation, came to the important statement that there was another Medicean plot, of which, if he obtained certain conditions from the government, he could, by a journey to Siena and into Romagna, where Piero de' Medici was again trying to gather forces, obtain documentary evidence to lay before the council. To this end it was essential that his character as a Medicean agent should be unshaken for all Mediceans, and hence the fact that he had been a source of information to the authorities must be wrapped in profound secrecy. Still, some odor of the facts might escape in spite of precaution, and before Tito could incur the unpleasant consequences of acting against his friends, he must be assured of immunity from any prosecution as a Medicean, and from deprivation of office for a year to come.

These propositions did not sound in the ear of Francesco Valori precisely as they sound to us. Valori's mind was not intensely bent on the estimation of Tito's conduct; and it *was* intensely bent on procuring an extreme sentence against the five prisoners. There were sure to be immense efforts to save them; and it was to be wished (on public grounds) that the evidence against them should be of the strongest, so as to alarm all well-affected men at the dangers of clemency. The character of legal proceedings at that time implied that evidence was one of those desirable things which could only be

come at by foul means. To catch a few people and torture
them into confessing everybody's guilt was one step towards
justice; and it was not always easy to see the next, unless a
traitor turned up. Lamberto dell' Antella had been tortured
in aid of his previous willingness to tell more than he knew;
nevertheless, additional and stronger facts were desirable, especially against Bernardo del Nero, who, so far as appeared
hitherto, had simply refrained from betraying the late plot
after having tried in vain to discourage it; for the welfare of
Florence demanded that the guilt of Bernardo del Nero should
be put in the strongest light. So Francesco Valori zealously
believed; and perhaps he was not himself aware that the
strength of his zeal was determined by his hatred. He decided that Tito's proposition ought to be accepted, laid it
before his colleagues without disclosing Tito's name, and won
them over to his opinion. Late in the day, Tito was admitted
to an audience of the Special Council, and produced a deep
sensation among them by revealing another plot for insuring
the mastery of Florence to Piero de' Medici, which was to
have been carried into execution in the middle of this very
month of August. Documentary evidence on this subject
would do more than anything else to make the right course
clear. He received a commission to start for Siena by break
of day; and, besides this, he carried away with him from the
council chamber a written guarantee of his immunity and of
his retention of office.

Among the twenty Florentines who bent their grave eyes
on Tito, as he stood gracefully before them, speaking of startling things with easy periphrasis, and with that apparently
unaffected admission of being actuated by motives short of the
highest, which is often the intensest affectation, there were
several whose minds were not too entirely preoccupied to pass
a new judgment on him in these new circumstances; they
silently concluded that this ingenious and serviceable Greek
was in future rather to be used for public needs than for private intimacy. Unprincipled men were useful, enabling those
who had more scruples to keep their hands tolerably clean
in a world where there was much dirty work to be done.

Indeed, it was not clear to respectable Florentine brains, unless
they held the Frate's extravagant belief in a possible purity
and loftiness to be striven for on this earth, how life was to
be carried on in any department without human instruments
whom it would not be unbecoming to kick or to spit upon in
the act of handing them their wages. Some of these very
men who passed a tacit judgment on Tito were shortly to be
engaged in a memorable transaction that could by no means
have been carried through without the use of an unscrupulous-
ness as decided as his; but, as their own bright poet Pulci
had said for them, it is one thing to love the fruits of treachery, and another thing to love traitors —

> "Il tradimento a molti piace assai,
>   Ma il traditore a gnun non piacque mai."

The same society has had a gibbet for the murderer and a
gibbet for the martyr, an execrating hiss for a dastardly act,
and as loud a hiss for many a word of generous truthfulness
or just insight: a mixed condition of things which is the sign,
not of hopeless confusion, but of struggling order.

For Tito himself, he was not unaware that he had sunk a
little in the estimate of the men who had accepted his services.
He had that degree of self-contemplation which necessarily
accompanies the habit of acting on well-considered reasons, of
whatever quality; and if he could have chosen, he would have
declined to see himself disapproved by men of the world. He
had never meant to be disapproved; he had meant always to
conduct himself so ably that if he acted in opposition to the
standard of other men they should not be aware of it; and the
barrier between himself and Romola had been raised by the
impossibility of such concealment with her. He shrank from
condemnatory judgments as from a climate to which he could
not adapt himself. But things were not so plastic in the hands
of cleverness as could be wished, and events had turned out
inconveniently. He had really no rancor against Messer Bernardo del Nero; he had a personal liking for Lorenzo Tornabuoni and Giannozzo Pucci. He had served them very ably,
and in such a way that if their party had been winners he

would have merited high reward; but was he to relinquish all the agreeable fruits of life because their party had failed? His proffer of a little additional proof against them would probably have no influence on their fate; in fact, he felt convinced they would escape any extreme consequences; but if he had not given it, his own fortunes, which made a promising fabric, would have been utterly ruined. And what motive could any man really have, except his own interest? Florentines whose passions were engaged in their petty and precarious political schemes might have no self-interest separable from family pride and tenacity in old hatreds and attachments; a modern simpleton who swallowed whole one of the old systems of philosophy, and took the indigestion it occasioned for the signs of a divine afflux or the voice of an inward monitor, might see his interest in a form of self-conceit which he called self-rewarding virtue; fanatics who believed in the coming Scourge and Renovation might see their own interest in a future palm-branch and white robe: but no man of clear intellect allowed his course to be determined by such puerile impulses or questionable inward fumes. Did not Pontanus, poet and philosopher of unrivalled Latinity, make the finest possible oration at Naples to welcome the French king, who had come to dethrone the learned orator's royal friend and patron? and still Pontanus held up his head and prospered. Men did not really care about these things, except when their personal spleen was touched. It was weakness only that was despised; power of any sort carried its immunity; and no man, unless by very rare good fortune, could mount high in the world without incurring a few unpleasant necessities which laid him open to enmity, and perhaps to a little hissing, when enmity wanted a pretext.

It was a faint prognostic of that hissing, gathered by Tito from certain indications when he was before the council, which gave his present conduct the character of an epoch to him, and made him dwell on it with argumentative vindication. It was not that he was taking a deeper step in wrong-doing, for it was not possible that he should feel any tie to the Mediceans to be stronger than the tie to his father; but his conduct to his father had been hidden by successful lying: his present act did not admit of total concealment — in its very nature it was a revelation. And Tito winced under his new liability to disesteem.

Well! a little patience, and in another year, or perhaps in half a year, he might turn his back on these hard, eager Florentines, with their futile quarrels and sinking fortunes. His brilliant success at Florence had had some ugly flaws in it: he had fallen in love with the wrong woman, and Baldassarre had come back under incalculable circumstances. But as Tito galloped with a loose rein towards Siena, he saw a future before him in which he would no longer be haunted by those mistakes. He had much money safe out of Florence already; he was in the fresh ripeness of eight-and-twenty; he was conscious of well-tried skill. Could he not strip himself of the past, as of rehearsal clothing, and throw away the old bundle, to robe himself for the real scene?

It did not enter into Tito's meditations on the future, that, on issuing from the council chamber and descending the stairs, he had brushed against a man whose face he had not stayed to recognize in the lamp-light. The man was Ser Ceccone — also willing to serve the State by giving information against unsuccessful employers.

CHAPTER LVIII.

A FINAL UNDERSTANDING.

TITO soon returned from Siena, but almost immediately set out on another journey, from which he did not return till the 17th of August. Nearly a fortnight had passed since the arrest of the accused, and still they were in prison, still their fate was uncertain. Romola had felt during this interval as if all cares were suspended for her, other than watching the fluctuating probabilities concerning that fate. Sometimes they seemed strongly in favor of the prisoners; for the chances

of effective interest on their behalf were heightened by delay,
and an indefinite prospect of delay was opened by the reluc-
tance of all persons in authority to incur the odium attendant
on any decision. On the one side there was a loud cry that
the Republic was in danger, and that lenity to the prisoners
would be the signal of attack for all its enemies; on the
other, there was a certainty that a sentence of death and
confiscation of property passed on five citizens of distinguished name, would entail the rancorous hatred of their
relatives on all who were conspicuously instrumental to such a
sentence.

The final judgment properly lay with the Eight, who pre-
sided over the administration of criminal justice; and the
sentence depended on a majority of six votes. But the Eight
shrank from their onerous responsibility, and asked in this
exceptional case to have it shared by the Signoria (or the
Gonfaloniere and the eight Priors). The Signoria in its turn
shrugged its shoulders, and proposed the appeal to the Great
Council. For, according to a law passed by the earnest persuasion of Savonarola nearly three years before, whenever a
citizen was condemned to death by the fatal six votes (called
the *sei fave* or *six beans*, beans being in more senses than one
the political pulse of Florence), he had the right of appealing
from that sentence to the Great Council.

But in this stage of the business, the friends of the accused
resisted the appeal, determined chiefly by the wish to gain
delay; and, in fact, strict legality required that sentence
should have been passed prior to the appeal. Their resistance
prevailed, and a middle course was taken; the sentence was
referred to a large assembly convened on the 17th, consisting of all the higher magistracies, the smaller council or
Senate of Eighty, and a select number of citizens.

On this day Romola, with anxiety heightened by the possibility that before its close her godfather's fate might be
decided, had obtained leave to see him for the second time,
but only in the presence of witnesses. She had returned to
the Via de' Bardi in company with her cousin Brigida, still
ignorant whether the council had come to any decisive issue;

and Monna Brigida had gone out again to await the momentous news at the house of a friend belonging to one of the magistracies, that she might bring back authentic tidings as soon as they were to be had.

Romola had sunk on the first seat in the bright saloon, too much agitated, too sick at heart, to care about her place, or be conscious of discordance in the objects that surrounded her. She sat with her back to the door, resting her head on her hands. It seemed a long while since Monna Brigida had gone, and Romola was expecting her return. But when the door opened she knew it was not Monna Brigida who entered.

Since she had parted from Tito on that memorable night, she had had no external proof to warrant her belief that he had won his safety by treachery; on the contrary, she had had evidence that he was still trusted by the Mediceans, and was believed by them to be accomplishing certain errands of theirs in Romagna, under cover of fulfilling a commission of the government. For the obscurity in which the evidence concerning the conspirators was shrouded allowed it to be understood that Tito had escaped any implication.

But Romola's suspicion was not to be dissipated: her horror of his conduct towards Baldassarre projected itself over every conception of his acts; it was as if she had seen him committing a murder, and had had a diseased impression ever after that his hands were covered with fresh blood.

As she heard his step on the stone floor, a chill shudder passed through her; she could not turn round, she could not rise to give any greeting. He did not speak, but after an instant's pause took a seat on the other side of the table just opposite to her. Then she raised her eyes and looked at him; but she was mute. He did not show any irritation, but said, coolly —

"This meeting corresponds with our parting, Romola. But I understand that it is a moment of terrible suspense. I am come, however, if you will listen to me, to bring you the relief of hope."

She started, and altered her position, but looked at him dubiously.

"It will not be unwelcome to you to hear — even though it is I who tell it — that the council is prorogued till the 21st. The Eight have been frightened at last into passing a sentence of condemnation, but the demand has now been made on behalf of the condemned for the Appeal to the Great Council."

Romola's face lost its dubious expression; she asked eagerly —

"And when is it to be made ? "

"It has not yet been granted ; but it *may* be granted. The Special Council is to meet again on the 21st to deliberate whether the Appeal shall be allowed or not. In the mean time there is an interval of three days, in which chances may occur in favor of the prisoners — in which interest may be used on their behalf."

Romola started from her seat. The color had risen to her face like a visible thought, and her hands trembled. In that moment her feeling towards Tito was forgotten.

"Possibly," said Tito, also rising, "your own intention may have anticipated what I was going to say. You are thinking of the Frate."

"I am," said Romola, looking at him with surprise. "Has he done anything ? Is there anything to tell me ? "

"Only this. It was Messer Francesco Valori's bitterness and violence which chiefly determined the course of things in the council to-day. Half the men who gave in their opinion against the prisoners were frightened into it, and there are numerous friends of Fra Girolamo both in this Special Council and out of it who are strongly opposed to the sentence of death — Piero Guicciardini, for example, who is one member of the Signoria that made the stoutest resistance ; and there is Giovan Battista Ridolfi, who, Piagnone as he is, will not lightly forgive the death of his brother Niccolò."

"But how can the Appeal be denied," said Romola, indignantly, "when it is the law — when it was one of the chief glories of the popular government to have passed the law ? "

"They call this an exceptional case. Of course there are ingenious arguments, but there is much more of loud bluster about the danger of the Republic. But, you see, no opposition could prevent the assembly from being prorogued, and a certain powerful influence rightly applied during the next three days might determine the wavering courage of those who desire that the Appeal should be granted, and might even give a check to the headlong enmity of Francesco Valori. It happens to have come to my knowledge that the Frate has so far interfered as to send a message to him in favor of Lorenzo Tornabuoni. I know you can sometimes have access to the Frate: it might at all events be worth while to use your privilege now."

"It is true," said Romola, with an air of abstraction. "I cannot believe that the Frate would approve denying the Appeal."

"I heard it said by more than one person in the court of the Palazzo, before I came away, that it would be to the everlasting discredit of Fra Girolamo if he allowed a government which is almost entirely made up of his party, to deny the Appeal, without entering his protest, when he has been boasting in his books and sermons that it was he who got the law passed.[1] But between ourselves, with all respect for your Frate's ability, my Romola, he has got into the practice of preaching that form of human sacrifices called killing tyrants and wicked malcontents, which some of his followers are likely to think inconsistent with lenity in the present case."

"I know, I know," said Romola, with a look and tone of pain. "But he is driven into those excesses of speech. It used to be different. I *will* ask for an interview. I cannot rest without it. I trust in the greatness of his heart."

She was not looking at Tito; her eyes were bent with a

---

[1] The most recent, and in some respects the best, biographer of Savonarola, Signor Villari, endeavors to show that the Law of Appeal ultimately enacted, being wider than the law originally contemplated by Savonarola, was a source of bitter annoyance to him, as a contrivance of the aristocratic party for attaching to the measures of the popular government the injurious results of license. But in taking this view the estimable biographer lost sight of the fact that, not only in his sermons, but in a deliberately prepared book (the *Compendium Revelationum*) written long after the Appeal had become law, Savonarola enumerates among the benefits secured to Florence, "*the Appeal from the Six Votes, advocated by me, for the greater security of the citizens.*"

vague gaze towards the ground, and she had no distinct consciousness that the words she heard came from her husband.

"Better lose no time, then," said Tito, with unmixed suavity,
moving his cap round in his hands as if he were about to put
it on and depart. "And now, Romola, you will perhaps be
able to see, in spite of prejudice, that my wishes go with yours
in this matter. You will not regard the misfortune of my
safety as an offence."

Something like an electric shock passed through Romola: it
was the full consciousness of her husband's presence returning
to her. She looked at him without speaking.

"At least," he added, in a slightly harder tone, "you will
endeavor to base our intercourse on some other reasonings
than that because an evil deed is possible, *I* have done it. Am
I alone to be beyond the pale of your extensive charity?"

The feeling which had been driven back from Romola's lips
a fortnight before rose again with the gathered force of a
tidal wave. She spoke with a decision which told him that
she was careless of consequences.

"It is too late, Tito. There is no killing the suspicion that
deceit has once begotten. And now I know everything. I
know who that old man was: he was your father, to whom
you owe everything — to whom you owe more than if you had
been his own child. By the side of that, it is a small thing
that you broke my trust and my father's. As long as you
deny the truth about that old man, there is a horror rising
between us: the law that should make us one can never be
obeyed. I too am a human being. I have a soul of my own
that abhors your actions. Our union is a pretence — as if a
perpetual lie could be a sacred marriage."

Tito did not answer immediately. When he did speak it
was with a calculated caution, that was stimulated by alarm.

"And you mean to carry out that independence by quitting
me, I presume?"

"I desire to quit you," said Romola, impetuously.

"And supposing I do not submit to part with what the law
gives me some security for retaining? You will then, of
course, proclaim your reasons in the ear of all Florence. You

will bring forward your mad assassin, who is doubtless ready
to obey your call, and you will tell the world that you believe
his testimony because he is so rational as to desire to assassi-
nate me.   You will first inform the Signoria that I am a Medicean conspirator, and then you will inform the Mediceans that
I have betrayed them, and in both cases you will offer the
excellent proof that you believe me capable in general of
everything bad.   It will certainly be a striking position for
a wife to adopt.   And if, on such evidence, you succeed in
holding me up to infamy, you will have surpassed all the
heroines of the Greek drama."

He paused a moment, but she stood mute.   He went on
with the sense of mastery.

"I believe you have no other grievance against me — except
that I have failed in fulfilling some lofty indefinite conditions
on which you gave me your wifely affection, so that, by withdrawing it, you have gradually reduced me to the careful supply of your wants as a fair Piagnone of high condition and
liberal charities.   I think your success in gibbeting me is not
certain.   But doubtless you would begin by winning the ear
of Messer Bernardo del Nero ? "

"Why do I speak of anything ? " cried Romola, in anguish,
sinking on her chair again.   "It is hateful in me to be thinking of myself."

She did not notice when Tito left the room, or know how
long it was before the door opened to admit Monna Brigida.
But in that instant she started up and said —

"Cousin, we must go to San Marco directly.   I must see
my confessor, Fra Salvestro."

CHAPTER LIX.

PLEADING.

THE morning was in its early brightness when Romola was again on her way to San Marco, having obtained through Fra Salvestro, the evening before, the promise of an interview with Fra Girolamo in the chapter-house of the convent. The rigidity with which Savonarola guarded his life from all the pretexts of calumny made such interviews very rare, and whenever they were granted, they were kept free from any appearance of mystery. For this reason the hour chosen was one at which there were likely to be other visitors in the outer cloisters of San Marco.

She chose to pass through the heart of the city that she might notice the signs of public feeling. Every loggia, every convenient corner of the piazza, every shop that made a rendezvous for gossips, was astir with the excitement of gratuitous debate; a languishing trade tending to make political discussion all the more vigorous. It was clear that the parties for and against the death of the conspirators were bent on making the fullest use of the three days' interval in order to determine the popular mood. Already handbills were in circulation; some presenting, in large print, the alternative of justice on the conspirators or ruin to the Republic; others in equally large print urging the observance of the law and the granting of the Appeal. Round these jutting islets of black capitals there were lakes of smaller characters setting forth arguments less necessary to be read: for it was an opinion entertained at that time (in the first flush of triumph at the discovery of printing), that there was no argument more widely convincing than question-begging phrases in large type.

Romola, however, cared especially to become acquainted with the arguments in smaller type, and, though obliged to

hasten forward, she looked round anxiously as she went that
she might miss no opportunity of securing copies. For a long
way she saw none but such as were in the hands of eager
readers, or else fixed on the walls, from which in some places
the sbirri were tearing them down. But at last, passing
behind San Giovanni with a quickened pace that she might
avoid the many acquaintances who frequented the piazza, she
saw Bratti with a stock of handbills which he appeared to be
exchanging for small coin with the passers-by. She was too
familiar with the humble life of Florence for Bratti to be any
stranger to her, and turning towards him she said, "Have you
two sorts of handbills, Bratti? Let me have them quickly."

"Two sorts," said Bratti, separating the wet sheets with a
slowness that tried Romola's patience. "There's 'Law,' and
there's 'Justice.'"

"Which sort do you sell most of?"

"'Justice' — 'Justice' goes the quickest, — so I raised the
price, and made it two danari. But then I bethought me
the 'Law' was good ware too, and had as good a right to be
charged for as 'Justice;' for people set no store by cheap
things, and if I sold the 'Law' at one danaro, I should be
doing it a wrong. And I'm a fair trader. 'Law,' or 'Justice,'
it's all one to me; they're good wares. I got 'em both for
nothing, and I sell 'em at a fair profit. But you'll want more
than one of a sort?"

"No, no: here's a white quattrino for the two," said Romola,
folding up the bills and hurrying away.

She was soon in the outer cloisters of San Marco, where Fra
Salvestro was awaiting her under the cloister, but did not
notice the approach of her light step. He was chatting, according to his habit, with lay visitors; for under the auspices
of a government friendly to the Frate, the timidity about fre-
quenting San Marco, which had followed on the first shock of
the Excommunication, had been gradually giving way. In
one of these lay visitors she recognized a well-known satellite
of Francesco Valori, named Andrea Cambini, who was narrating or expounding with emphatic gesticulation, while Fra
Salvestro was listening with that air of trivial curiosity which

tells that the listener cares very much about news and very
little about its quality. This characteristic of her confessor,
which was always repulsive to Romola, was made exasperating to her at this moment by the certainty she gathered, from
the disjointed words which reached her ear, that Cambini was
narrating something relative to the fate of the conspirators.
She chose not to approach the group, but as soon as she saw
that she had arrested Fra Salvestro's attention, she turned
towards the door of the chapter-house, while he, making a
sign of approval, disappeared within the inner cloister. A lay
Brother stood ready to open the door of the chapter-house for
her, and closed it behind her as she entered.

Once more looked at by those sad frescoed figures which
had seemed to be mourning with her at the death of her
brother Dino, it was inevitable that something of that scene
should come back to her; but the intense occupation of her
mind with the present made the remembrance less a retrospect
than an indistinct recurrence of impressions which blended
themselves with her agitating fears, as if her actual anxiety
were a revival of the strong yearning she had once before
brought to this spot — to be repelled by marble rigidity. She
gave no space for the remembrance to become more definite,
for she at once opened the handbills, thinking she should
perhaps be able to read them in the interval before Fra
Girolamo appeared. But by the time she had read to the
end of the one that recommended the observance of the law,
the door was opening, and doubling up the papers she stood
expectant.

When the Frate had entered she knelt, according to the
usual practice of those who saw him in private; but as soon
as he had uttered a benedictory greeting she rose and stood
opposite to him at a few yards' distance. Owing to his seclusion since he had been excommunicated, it had been an unusually long while since she had seen him, and the late months
had visibly deepened in his face the marks of overtaxed
mental activity and bodily severities; and yet Romola was
not so conscious of this change as of another, which was less
definable. Was it that the expression of serene elevation and

pure human fellowship which had once moved her was no longer present in the same force, or was it that the sense of his being divided from her in her feeling about her godfather roused the slumbering sources of alienation, and marred her own vision? Perhaps both causes were at work. Our relations with our fellow-men are most often determined by co-incident currents of that sort; the inexcusable word or deed seldom comes until after affection or reverence has been already enfeebled by the strain of repeated excuses.

It was true that Savonarola's glance at Romola had some of that hardness which is caused by an egotistic prepossession. He divined that the interview she had sought was to turn on the fate of the conspirators, a subject on which he had already had to quell inner voices that might become loud again when encouraged from without. Seated in his cell, correcting the sheets of his "Triumph of the Cross," it was easier to repose on a resolution of neutrality.

"It is a question of moment, doubtless, on which you wished to see me, my daughter," he began, in a tone which was gentle rather from self-control than from immediate inclination. "I know you are not wont to lay stress on small matters."

"Father, you know what it is before I tell you," said Romola, forgetting everything else as soon as she began to pour forth her plea. "You know what I am caring for — it is for the life of the old man I love best in the world. The thought of him has gone together with the thought of my father as long as I remember the daylight. That is my warrant for coming to you, even if my coming should have been needless. Perhaps it is: perhaps you have already determined that your power over the hearts of men shall be used to prevent them from denying to Florentines a right which you yourself helped to earn for them."

"I meddle not with the functions of the State, my daughter," said Fra Girolamo, strongly disinclined to reopen externally a debate which he had already gone through inwardly. "I have preached and labored that Florence should have a good government, for a good government is needful to the perfecting of the Christian life; but I keep away my hands from

particular affairs which it is the office of experienced citizens
to administer."

"Surely, father — " Romola broke off. She had uttered
this first word almost impetuously, but she was checked by the
counter-agitation of feeling herself in an attitude of remonstrance towards the man who had been the source of guidance
and strength to her. In the act of rebelling she was bruising
her own reverence.

Savonarola was too keen not to divine something of the conflict that was arresting her — too noble, deliberately to assume
in calm speech that self-justifying evasiveness into which he
was often hurried in public by the crowding impulses of the
orator.

"Say what is in your heart; speak on, my daughter," he
said, standing with his arms laid one upon the other, and looking at her with quiet expectation.

"I was going to say, father, that this matter is surely of
higher moment than many about which I have heard you
preach and exhort fervidly. If it belonged to you to urge
that men condemned for offences against the State should have
the right to appeal to the Great Council — if — " Romola was
getting eager again — "if you count it a glory to have won
that right for them, can it less belong to you to declare yourself against the right being denied to almost the first men who
need it? Surely that touches the Christian life more closely
than whether you knew beforehand that the Dauphin would
die, or whether Pisa will be conquered."

There was a subtle movement, like a subdued sign of pain,
in Savonarola's strong lips, before he began to speak.

"My daughter, I speak as it is given me to speak — I am
not master of the times when I may become the vehicle of
knowledge beyond the common lights of men. In this case I
have no illumination beyond what wisdom may give to those
who are charged with the safety of the State. As to the law
of Appeal against the Six Votes, I labored to have it passed
in order that no Florentine should be subject to loss of life
and goods through the private hatred of a few who might
happen to be in power; but these five men, who have desired

to overthrow a free government and restore a corrupt tyrant, have been condemned with the assent of a large assembly of their fellow-citizens. They refused at first to have their cause brought before the Great Council. They have lost the right to the appeal."

"How can they have lost it?" said Romola. "It is the right to appeal against condemnation, and they have never been condemned till now; and, forgive me, father, it *is* private hatred that would deny them the appeal; it *is* the violence of the few that frightens others; else why was the assembly divided again directly after it had seemed to agree? And if anything weighs against the observance of the law, let this weigh *for* it — this, that you used to preach more earnestly than all else, that there should be no place given to hatred and bloodshed because of these party strifes, so that private ill-will should not find its opportunities in public acts. Father, you *know* that there is private hatred concerned here: will it not dishonor you not to have interposed on the side of mercy, when there are many who hold that it is also the side of law and justice?"

"My daughter," said Fra Girolamo, with more visible emotion than before, "there is a mercy which is weakness, and even treason against the common good. The safety of Florence, which means even more than the welfare of Florentines, now demands severity, as it once demanded mercy. It is not only for a past plot that these men are condemned, but also for a plot which has not yet been executed; and the devices that were leading to its execution are not put an end to: the tyrant is still gathering his forces in Romagna, and the enemies of Florence, who sit in the highest places of Italy, are ready to hurl any stone that will crush her."

"What plot?" said Romola, reddening, and trembling with alarmed surprise.

"You carry papers in your hand, I see," said Fra Girolamo, pointing to the handbills. "One of them will, perhaps, tell you that the government has had new information."

Romola hastily opened the handbill she had not yet read, and saw that the government had now positive evidence of a second plot, which was to have been carried out in this August time. To her mind it was like reading a confirmation that Tito had won his safety by foul means; his pretence of wishing that the Frate should exert himself on behalf of the condemned only helped the wretched conviction. She crushed up the paper in her hand, and, turning to Savonarola, she said, with new passion, "Father, what safety can there be for Florence when the worst man can always escape? And," she went on, a sudden flash of remembrance coming from the thought about her husband, "have not you yourself encouraged this deception which corrupts the life of Florence, by wanting more favor to be shown to Lorenzo Tornabuoni, who has worn two faces, and flattered you with a show of affection, when my godfather has always been honest? Ask all Florence who of those five men has the truest heart, and there will not be many who will name any other name than Bernardo del Nero. You did interpose with Francesco Valori for the sake of one prisoner: you have *not* then been neutral; and you know that your word will be powerful."

"I do not desire the death of Bernardo," said Savonarola, coloring deeply. "It would be enough if he were sent out of the city."

"Then why do you not speak to save an old man of seventy-five from dying a death of ignominy — to give him at least the fair chances of the law?" burst out Romola, the impetuosity of her nature so roused that she forgot everything but her indignation. "It is not that you feel bound to be neutral; else why did you speak for Lorenzo Tornabuoni? You spoke for him because he is more friendly to San Marco; my godfather feigns no friendship. It is not, then, as a Medicean that my godfather is to die; it is as a man you have no love for!"

When Romola paused, with cheeks glowing, and with quivering lips, there was dead silence. As she saw Fra Girolamo standing motionless before her, she seemed to herself to be hearing her own words over again; words that in this echo of consciousness were in strange, painful dissonance with the memories that made part of his presence to her. The moments of silence were expanded by gathering compunction and self-doubt. She had committed sacrilege in her passion. And even the sense that she could retract nothing of her plea, that her mind could not submit itself to Savonarola's negative, made it the more needful to her to satisfy those reverential memories. With a sudden movement towards him she said —

"Forgive me, father; it is pain to me to have spoken those words — yet I cannot help speaking. I am little and feeble compared with you; you brought me light and strength. But I submitted because I felt the proffered strength — because I saw the light. *Now* I cannot see it. Father, you yourself declare that there comes a moment when the soul must have no guide but the voice within it, to tell whether the consecrated thing has sacred virtue. And therefore I must speak."

Savonarola had that readily roused resentment towards opposition, hardly separable from a power-loving and powerful nature, accustomed to seek great ends that cast a reflected grandeur on the means by which they are sought. His sermons have much of that red flame in them. And if he had been a meaner man his susceptibility might have shown itself in irritation at Romola's accusatory freedom, which was in strong contrast with the deference he habitually received from his disciples. But at this moment such feelings were nullified by that hard struggle which made half the tragedy of his life — the struggle of a mind possessed by a never-silent hunger after purity and simplicity, yet caught in a tangle of egoistic demands, false ideas, and difficult outward conditions, that made simplicity impossible. Keenly alive to all the suggestions of Romola's remonstrating words, he was rapidly surveying, as he had done before, the courses of action that were open to him, and their probable results. But it was a question on which arguments could seem decisive only in proportion as they were charged with feeling, and he had received no impulse that could alter his bias. He looked at Romola, and said —

"You have full pardon for your frankness, my daughter. You speak, I know, out of the fulness of your family affections. But these affections must give way to the needs of the

Republic. If those men who have a close acquaintance with the affairs of the State believe, as I understand they do, that the public safety requires the extreme punishment of the law to fall on the five conspirators, I cannot control their opinion, seeing that I stand aloof from such affairs."

"Then you desire that they should die ? You desire that the Appeal should be denied them ? " said Romola, feeling anew repelled by a vindication which seemed to her to have the nature of a subterfuge.

"I have said that I do not desire their death."

"Then," said Romola, her indignation rising again, "you can be indifferent that Florentines should inflict death which you do not desire, when you might have protested against it — when you might have helped to hinder it, by urging the observance of a law which you held it good to get passed. Father, you used not to stand aloof : you used not to shrink from protesting. Do not say you cannot protest where the lives of men are concerned; say rather, you desire their death. Say rather, you hold it good for Florence that there shall be more blood and more hatred. Will the death of five Mediceans put an end to parties in Florence ? Will the death of a noble old man like Bernardo del Nero save a city that holds such men as Dolfo Spini ? "

"My daughter, it is enough. The cause of freedom, which is the cause of God's kingdom upon earth, is often most injured by the enemies who carry within them the power of certain human virtues. The wickedest man is often not the most insurmountable obstacle to the triumph of good."

"Then why do you say again, that you do not desire my godfather's death ? " said Romola, in mingled anger and despair. "Rather, you hold it the more needful he should die because he is the better man. I cannot unravel your thoughts, father; I cannot hear the real voice of your judgment and conscience."

There was a moment's pause. Then Savonarola said, with keener emotion than he had yet shown —

"Be thankful, my daughter, if your own soul has been spared perplexity; and judge not those to whom a harder lot

has been given. *You* see one ground of action in this matter.
I see many. I have to choose that which will further the
work intrusted to me. The end I seek is one to which minor
respects must be sacrificed. The death of five men — were
they less guilty than these — is a light matter weighed against
the withstanding of the vicious tyrannies which stifle the life
of Italy, and foster the corruption of the Church; a light
matter weighed against the furthering of God's kingdom
upon earth, the end for which I live and am willing myself
to die."

Under any other circumstances, Romola would have been
sensitive to the appeal at the beginning of Savonarola's speech;
but at this moment she was so utterly in antagonism with
him, that what he called perplexity seemed to her sophistry
and doubleness; and as he went on, his words only fed that
flame of indignation, which now again, more fully than ever
before, lit up the memory of all his mistakes, and made her
trust in him seem to have been a purblind delusion. She
spoke almost with bitterness.

"Do you, then, know so well what will further the coming
of God's kingdom, father, that you will dare to despise the
plea of mercy — of justice — of faithfulness to your own
teaching? Has the French king, then, brought renovation to
Italy? Take care, father, lest your enemies have some reason
when they say, that in your visions of what will further God's
kingdom you see only what will strengthen your own party."

"And that is true!" said Savonarola, with flashing eyes.
Romola's voice had seemed to him in that moment the voice
of his enemies. "The cause of my party *is* the cause of God's
kingdom."

"I do not believe it!" said Romola, her whole frame
shaken with passionate repugnance. "God's kingdom is something wider — else, let me stand outside it with the beings
that I love."

The two faces were lit up, each with an opposite emotion,
each with an opposite certitude. Further words were impossible. Romola hastily covered her head and went out in
silence.

CHAPTER LX.

THREE days later the moon that was just surmounting the buildings of the piazza in front of the Old Palace within the hour of midnight, did not make the usual broad lights and shadows on the pavement. Not a hand's-breadth of pavement was to be seen, but only the heads of an eager struggling multitude. And instead of that background of silence in which the pattering footsteps and buzzing voices, the lute-thrumming or rapid scampering of the many night wanderers of Florence stood out in obtrusive distinctness, there was the background of a roar from mingled shouts and imprecations, tramplings and pushings, and accidental clashing of weapons, across which nothing was distinguishable but a darting shriek, or the heavy dropping toll of a bell.

Almost all who could call themselves the public of Florence were awake at that hour, and either enclosed within the limits of that piazza, or struggling to enter it. Within the palace were still assembled in the council chamber all the chief magistracies, the eighty members of the senate, and the other select citizens who had been in hot debate through long hours of daylight and torchlight whether the Appeal should be granted or whether the sentence of death should be executed on the prisoners forthwith, to forestall the dangerous chances of delay. And the debate had been so much like fierce quarrel that the noise from the council chamber had reached the crowd outside. Only within the last hour had the question been decided: the Signoria had remained divided, four of them standing out resolutely for the Appeal in spite of the strong argument that if they did not give way their houses should be sacked, until Francesco Valori, in brief and furious speech, made the determination of his party more ominously distinct by declaring that if the Signoria would not defend

NICCOLÒ MACCHIAVELLI.

the liberties of the Florentine people by executing those five perfidious citizens, there would not be wanting others who would take that cause in hand to the peril of all who opposed it. The Florentine Cato triumphed. When the votes were counted again, the four obstinate white beans no longer appeared; the whole nine were of the fatal affirmative black, deciding the death of the five prisoners without delay — deciding also, only tacitly and with much more delay, the death of Francesco Valori.

And now, while the judicial Eight were gone to the Bargello to prepare for the execution, the five condemned men were being led barefoot and in irons through the midst of the council. It was their friends who had contrived this: would not Florentines be moved by the visible association of such cruel ignominy with two venerable men like Bernardo del Nero and Niccolò Ridolfi, who had taken their bias long before the new order of things had come to make Mediceanism retrograde — with two brilliant popular young men like Tornabuoni and Pucci, whose absence would be felt as a haunting vacancy wherever there was a meeting of chief Florentines? It was useless: such pity as could be awakened now was of that hopeless sort which leads not to rescue, but to the tardier action of revenge.

While this scene was passing up-stairs Romola stood below against one of the massive pillars in the court of the palace, expecting the moment when her godfather would appear, on his way to execution. By the use of strong interest she had gained permission to visit him in the evening of this day, and remain with him until the result of the council should be determined. And now she was waiting with his confessor to follow the guard that would lead him to the Bargello. Her heart was bent on clinging to the presence of the childless old man to the last moment, as her father would have done; and she had overpowered all remonstrances. Giovan Battista Ridolfi, a disciple of Savonarola, who was going in bitterness to behold the death of his elder brother Niccolò, had promised that she should be guarded, and now stood by her side.

Tito, too, was in the palace; but Romola had not seen him.

Since the evening of the 17th they had avoided each other,
and Tito only knew by inference from the report of the Frate's
neutrality that her pleading had failed. He was now surrounded with official and other personages, both Florentine
and foreign, who had been awaiting the issue of the long-
protracted council, maintaining, except when he was directly
addressed, the subdued air and grave silence of a man whom
actual events are placing in a painful state of strife between
public. and private feeling. When an allusion was made to
his wife in relation to those events, he implied that, owing to
the violent excitement of her mind, the mere fact of his continuing to hold office under a government concerned in her
godfather's condemnation, roused in her a diseased hostility
towards him; so that for her sake he felt it best not to approach her.

"Ah, the old Bardi blood!" said Cennini, with a shrug.
"I shall not be surprised if this business shakes *her* loose from
the Frate, as well as some others I could name."

"It is excusable in a woman, who is doubtless beautiful,
since she is the wife of Messer Tito," said a young French
envoy, smiling and bowing to Tito, "to think that her affections must overrule the good of the State, and that nobody
is to be beheaded who is anybody's cousin; but such a view is
not to be encouraged in the male population. It seems to me
your Florentine polity is much weakened by it."

"That is true," said Niccolò Macchiavelli; "but where personal ties are strong, the hostilities they raise must be taken
due account of. Many of these half-way severities are mere
hot-headed blundering. The only safe blows to be inflicted
on men and parties are the blows that are too heavy to be
avenged."

"Niccolò," said Cennini, "there is a clever wickedness in
thy talk sometimes that makes me mistrust thy pleasant young
face as if it were a mask of Satan."

"Not at all, my good Domenico," said Macchiavelli, smiling,
and laying his hand on the elder's shoulder. "Satan was a
blunderer, an introducer of *novità*, who made a stupendous
failure. If he had succeeded, we should all have been

worshipping him, and his portrait would have been more flattered."

"Well, well," said Cennini, "I say not thy doctrine is not too clever for Satan: I only say it is wicked enough for him."

"I tell you," said Macchiavelli, "my doctrine is the doctrine of all men who seek an end a little farther off than their own noses. Ask our Frate, our prophet, how his universal renovation is to be brought about: he will tell you, first, by getting a free and pure government; and since it appears that this cannot be done by making all Florentines love each other, it must be done by cutting off every head that happens to be obstinately in the way. Only if a man incurs odium by sanctioning a severity that is not thorough enough to be final, he commits a blunder. And something like that blunder, I suspect, the Frate has committed. It was an occasion on which he might have won some lustre by exerting himself to maintain the Appeal; instead of that, he has lost lustre, and has gained no strength."

Before any one else could speak, there came the expected announcement that the prisoners were about to leave the council chamber; and the majority of those who were present hurried towards the door, intent on securing the freest passage to the Bargello in the rear of the prisoners' guard; for the scene of the execution was one that drew alike those who were moved by the deepest passions and those who were moved by the coldest curiosity.

Tito was one of those who remained behind. He had a native repugnance to sights of death and pain, and five days ago whenever he had thought of this execution as a possibility he had hoped that it would not take place, and that the utmost sentence would be exile: his own safety demanded no more. But now he felt that it would be a welcome guarantee of his security when he had learned that Bernardo del Nero's head was off the shoulders. The new knowledge and new attitude towards him disclosed by Romola on the day of his return, had given him a new dread of the power she possessed to make his position insecure. If any act of hers only succeeded in making him an object of suspicion and odium, he foresaw not only frustration, but frustration under unpleasant circumstances. Her belief in Baldassarre had clearly determined her wavering feelings against further submission, and if her godfather lived she would win him to share her belief without much trouble. Romola seemed more than ever an unmanageable fact in his destiny. But if Bernardo del Nero were dead, the difficulties that would beset her in placing herself in opposition to her husband would probably be insurmountable to her shrinking pride. Therefore Tito had felt easier when he knew that the Eight had gone to the Bargello to order the instant erection of the scaffold. Four other men — his intimates and confederates — were to die, besides Bernardo del Nero. But a man's own safety is a god that sometimes makes very grim demands. Tito felt them to be grim : even in the pursuit of what was agreeable, this paradoxical life forced upon him the desire for what was disagreeable. But he had had other experience of this sort, and as he heard through the open doorway the shuffle of many feet and the clanking of metal on the stairs, he was able to answer the questions of the young French envoy without showing signs of any other feeling than that of sad resignation to State necessities.

Those sounds fell on Romola as if her power of hearing had been exalted along with every other sensibility of her nature. She needed no arm to support her ; she shed no tears. She felt that intensity of life which seems to transcend both grief and joy — in which the mind seems to itself akin to elder forces that wrought out existence before the birth of pleasure and pain. Since her godfather's fate had been decided, the previous struggle of feeling in her had given way to an identification of herself with him in these supreme moments : she was inwardly asserting for him that, if he suffered the punishment of treason, he did not deserve the name of traitor ; he was the victim to a collision between two kinds of faithfulness. It was not given him to die for the noblest cause, and yet he died because of his nobleness. He might have been a meaner man and found it easier not to incur this guilt. Romola was feeling the full force of that sympathy with the individual lot that is continually opposing itself to the formulæ by which actions and parties are judged. She was treading the way with her second father to the scaffold, and nerving herself to defy ignominy by the consciousness that it was not deserved.

The way was fenced in by three hundred armed men, who had been placed as a guard by the orders of Francesco Valori, for among the apparent contradictions that belonged to this event, not the least striking was the alleged alarm on the one hand at the popular rage against the conspirators, and the alleged alarm on the other lest there should be an attempt to rescue them in the midst of a hostile crowd. When they had arrived within the court of the Bargello, Romola was allowed to approach Bernardo with his confessor for a moment of farewell. Many eyes were bent on them even in that struggle of an agitated throng, as the aged man, forgetting that his hands were bound with irons, lifted them towards the golden head that was bent towards him, and then, checking that movement, leaned to kiss her. She seized the fettered hands that were hung down again, and kissed them as if they had been sacred things.

"My poor Romola," said Bernardo, in a low voice, "I have only to die, but thou hast to live — and I shall not be there to help thee."

"Yes," said Romola, hurriedly, "you *will* help me — always — because I shall remember you."

She was taken away and conducted up the flight of steps that led to the loggia surrounding the grand old court. She took her place there, determined to look till the moment when her godfather laid his head on the block. Now while the prisoners were allowed a brief interval with their confessor, the spectators were pressing into court until the crowd became dense around the black scaffold, and the torches fixed in iron rings against the pillars threw a varying startling light at one moment on passionless stone carvings, at another on some pale face agitated with suppressed rage or suppressed grief — the face of one among the many near relatives of the condemned, who were presently to receive their dead and carry them home.

Romola's face looked like a marble image against the dark

arch as she stood watching for the moment when her god-father would appear at the foot of the scaffold. He was to suffer first, and Battista Ridolfi, who was by her side, had promised to take her away through a door behind them when she would have seen the last look of the man who alone in all the world had shared her pitying love for her father. And still, in the background of her thought, there was the possibility striving to be a hope, that some rescue might yet come, something that would keep that scaffold unstained by blood.

For a long while there was constant movement, lights flickering, heads swaying to and fro, confused voices within the court, rushing waves of sound through the entrance from without. It seemed to Romola as if she were in the midst of a storm-troubled sea, caring nothing about the storm, caring only to hold out a signal till the eyes that looked for it could seek it no more.

Suddenly there was stillness, and the very tapers seemed to tremble into quiet. The executioner was ready on the scaffold, and Bernardo del Nero was seen ascending it with a slow firm step. Romola made no visible movement, uttered not even a suppressed sound: she stood more firmly, caring for *his* firmness. She saw him pause, saw the white head kept erect, while he said in a voice distinctly audible —

"It is but a short space of life that my fellow-citizens have taken from me."

She perceived that he was gazing slowly round him as he spoke. She felt that his eyes were resting on her, and that she was stretching out her arms towards him. Then she saw no more till — a long while after, as it seemed — a voice said, "My daughter, all is peace now. I can conduct you to your house."

She uncovered her head and saw her godfather's confessor standing by her, in a room where there were other grave men talking in subdued tones.

"I am ready," she said, starting up. "Let us lose no time."

She thought all clinging was at an end for her: all her strength now should be given to escape from a grasp under which she shuddered.

CHAPTER LXI.

DRIFTING AWAY.

On the eighth day from that memorable night Romola was standing on the brink of the Mediterranean, watching the gentle summer pulse of the sea just above what was then the little fishing village of Viareggio.

Again she had fled from Florence, and this time no arresting voice had called her back. Again she wore the gray religious dress ; and this time, in her heart-sickness, she did not care that it was a disguise. A new rebellion had risen within her, a new despair. Why should she care about wearing one badge more than another, or about being called by her own name ? She despaired of finding any consistent duty belonging to that name. What force was there to create for her that supremely hallowed motive which men call duty, but which can have no inward constraining existence save through some form of believing love ?

The bonds of all strong affection were snapped. In her marriage, the highest bond of all, she had ceased to see the mystic union which is its own guarantee of indissolubleness, had ceased even to see the obligation of a voluntary pledge : had she not proved that the things to which she had pledged herself were impossible ? The impulse to set herself free had risen again with overmastering force ; yet the freedom could only be an exchange of calamity. There is no compensation for the woman who feels that the chief relation of her life has been no more than a mistake. She has lost her crown. The deepest secret of human blessedness has half whispered itself to her, and then forever passed her by.

And now Romola's best support under that supreme woman's sorrow had slipped away from her. The vision of any great purpose, any end of existence which could ennoble endurance and exalt the common deeds of a dusty life with divine ardors,

was utterly eclipsed for her now by the sense of a confusion
in human things which made all effort a mere dragging at
tangled threads; all fellowship, either for resistance or advo-
cacy, mere unfairness and exclusiveness.   What, after all, was
the man who had represented for her the highest heroism: the
heroism not of hard, self-contained endurance, but of willing,
self-offering love ?   What was the cause he was struggling
for ?   Romola had lost her trust in Savonarola, had lost that
fervor of admiration which had made her unmindful of his
aberrations, and attentive only to the grand curve of his orbit.
And now that her keen feeling for her godfather had thrown
her into antagonism with the Frate, she saw all the repulsive
and inconsistent details in his teaching with a painful lucidity
which exaggerated their proportions.   In the bitterness of her
disappointment she said that his striving after the renovation
of the Church and the world was a striving after a mere name
which told no more than the title of a book : a name that had
come to mean practically the measures that would strengthen
his own position in Florence ; nay, often questionable deeds
and words, for the sake of saving his influence from suffering
by his own errors.   And that political reform which had once
made a new interest in her life seemed now to reduce itself to
narrow devices for the safety of Florence, in contemptible
contradiction with the alternating professions of blind trust in
the Divine care.

It was inevitable that she should judge the Frate unfairly
on a question of individual suffering, at which *she* looked with
the eyes of personal tenderness, and *he* with the eyes of theoretic
conviction.   In that declaration of his, that the cause of his
party was the cause of God's kingdom, she heard only the
ring of egoism.   Perhaps such words have rarely been uttered
without that meaner ring in them ; yet they are the implicit
formula of all energetic belief.   And if such energetic belief,
pursuing a grand and remote end, is often in danger of becoming a demon-worship, in which the votary lets his son and
daughter pass through the fire with a readiness that hardly
looks like sacrifice; tender fellow-feeling for the nearest has
its danger too, and is apt to be timid and sceptical towards the

larger aims without which life cannot rise into religion. In this way poor Romola was being blinded by her tears.

No one who has ever known what it is thus to lose faith in a fellow-man whom he has profoundly loved and reverenced, will lightly say that the shock can leave the faith in the Invisible Goodness unshaken. With the sinking of high human trust, the dignity of life sinks too; we cease to believe in our own better self, since that also is part of the common nature which is degraded in our thought; and all the finer impulses of the soul are dulled. Romola felt even the springs of her once active pity drying up, and leaving her to barren egoistic complaining. Had not *she* had her sorrows too ? And few had cared for her, while she had cared for many. She had done enough; she had striven after the impossible, and was weary of this stifling crowded life. She longed for that repose in mere sensation which she had sometimes dreamed of in the sultry afternoons of her early girlhood, when she had fancied herself floating naïad-like in the waters.

The clear waves seemed to invite her : she wished she could lie down to sleep on them and pass from sleep into death. But Romola could not directly seek death ; the fulness of young life in her forbade that. She could only wish that death would come.

At the spot where she had paused there was a deep bend in the shore, and a small boat with a sail was moored there. In her longing to glide over the waters that were getting golden with the level sun-rays, she thought of a story which had been one of the things she had loved to dwell on in Boccaccio, when her father fell asleep and she glided from her stool to sit on the floor and read the "Decamerone." It was the story of that fair Gostanza who in her love-lornness desired to live no longer, but not having the courage to attack her young life, had put herself into a boat and pushed off to sea ; then, lying down in the boat, had wrapped her mantle round her head, hoping to be wrecked, so that her fear would be helpless to flee from death. The memory had remained a mere thought in Romola's mind, without budding into any distinct wish ; but now, as she paused again in her walking to and fro, she

saw gliding black against the red gold another boat with one
man in it, making towards the bend where the first and smaller
boat was moored. Walking on again, she at length saw the
man land, pull his boat ashore and begin to unlade something
from it. He was perhaps the owner of the smaller boat also:
he would be going away soon, and her opportunity would be
gone with him — her opportunity of buying that smaller boat.
She had not yet admitted to herself that she meant to use it,
but she felt a sudden eagerness to secure the possibility of
using it, which disclosed the half-unconscious growth of a
thought into a desire.

"Is that little boat yours also?" she said to the fisherman,
who had looked up, a little startled by the tall gray figure, and
had made a reverence to this holy Sister wandering thus mysteriously in the evening solitude.

It *was* his boat; an old one, hardly seaworthy, yet worth
repairing to any man who would buy it. By the blessing of
San Antonio, whose chapel was in the village yonder, his fishing had prospered, and he had now a better boat, which had
once been Gianni's who died. But he had not yet sold the old
one. Romola asked him how much it was worth, and then,
while he was busy, thrust the price into a little satchel lying
on the ground and containing the remnant of his dinner. After
that, she watched him furling his sail and asked him how he
should set it if he wanted to go out to sea, and then pacing up
and down again, waited to see him depart.

The imagination of herself gliding away in that boat on the
darkening waters was growing more and more into a longing,
as the thought of a cool brook in sultriness becomes a painful
thirst. To be freed from the burden of choice when all motive
was bruised, to commit herself, sleeping, to destiny which
would either bring death or else new necessities that might
rouse a new life in her! — it was a thought that beckoned her
the more because the soft evening air made her long to rest in
the still solitude, instead of going back to the noise and heat
of the village.

At last the slow fisherman had gathered up all his movables
and was walking away. Soon the gold was shrinking and get-

ting duskier in sea and sky, and there was no living thing in sight, no sound but the lulling monotony of the lapping waves. In this sea there was no tide that would help to carry her away if she waited for its ebb; but Romola thought the breeze from the land was rising a little. She got into the boat, unfurled the sail, and fastened it as she had learned in that first brief lesson. She saw that it caught the light breeze, and this was all she cared for. Then she loosed the boat from its moorings, and tried to urge it with an oar, till she was far out from the land, till the sea was dark even to the west, and the stars were disclosing themselves like a palpitating life over the wide heavens. Resting at last, she threw back her cowl, and, taking off the kerchief underneath, which confined her hair, she doubled them both under her head for a pillow on one of the boat's ribs. The fair head was still very young and could bear a hard pillow.

And so she lay, with the soft night air breathing on her while she glided on the water and watched the deepening quiet of the sky. She was alone now: she had freed herself from all claims, she had freed herself even from that burden of choice which presses with heavier and heavier weight when claims have loosed their guiding hold.

Had she found anything like the dream of her girlhood? No. Memories hung upon her like the weight of broken wings that could never be lifted — memories of human sympathy which even in its pains leaves a thirst that the Great Mother has no milk to still. Romola felt orphaned in those wide spaces of sea and sky. She read no message of love for her in that far-off symbolic writing of the heavens, and with a great sob she wished that she might be gliding into death.

She drew the cowl over her head again and covered her face, choosing darkness rather than the light of the stars, which seemed to her like the hard light of eyes that looked at her without seeing her. Presently she felt that she was in the grave, but not resting there: she was touching the hands of the beloved dead beside her, and trying to wake them.

CHAPTER LXII.

THE BENEDICTION.

About ten o'clock on the morning of the 27th of February the currents of passengers along the Florentine streets set decidedly towards San Marco. It was the last morning of the Carnival, and every one knew there was a second Bonfire of Vanities being prepared in front of the Old Palace; but at this hour it was evident that the centre of popular interest lay elsewhere.

The Piazza di San Marco was filled by a multitude who showed no other movement than that which proceeded from the pressure of new-comers trying to force their way forward from all the openings: but the front ranks were already closeserried and resisted the pressure. Those ranks were ranged around a semicircular barrier in front of the church, and within this barrier were already assembling the Dominican Brethren of San Marco.

But the temporary wooden pulpit erected over the churchdoor was still empty. It was presently to be entered by the man whom the Pope's command had banished from the pulpit of the Duomo, whom the other ecclesiastics of Florence had been forbidden to consort with, whom the citizens had been forbidden to hear on pain of excommunication. This man had said, "A wicked, unbelieving Pope who has gained the pontifical chair by bribery is not Christ's Vicar. His curses are broken swords: he grasps a hilt without a blade. His commands are contrary to the Christian life: it is lawful to disobey them — nay, *it is not lawful to obey them.*" And the people still flocked to hear him as he preached in his own church of San Marco, though the Pope was hanging terrible threats over Florence if it did not renounce the pestilential schismatic and send him to Rome to be "converted" — still, as on this very morning, accepted the Communion from his

excommunicated hands. For how if this Frate had really
more command over the Divine lightnings than that official
successor of Saint Peter? It was a momentous question,
which for the mass of citizens could never be decided by the
Frate's ultimate test, namely, what was and what was not
accordant with the highest spiritual law. No: in such a case
as this, if God had chosen the Frate as his prophet to rebuke
the High Priest who carried the mystic raiment unworthily,
he would attest his choice by some unmistakable sign. As
long as the belief in the Prophet carried no threat of outward
calamity, but rather the confident hope of exceptional safety,
no sign was needed: his preaching was a music to which the
people felt themselves marching along the way they wished
to go; but now that belief meant an immediate blow to their
commerce, the shaking of their position among the Italian
States, and an interdict on their city, there inevitably came
the question, "What miracle showest thou?" Slowly at
first, then faster and faster, that fatal demand had been swelling in Savonarola's ear, provoking a response, outwardly in
the declaration that at the fitting time the miracle would
come; inwardly in the faith — not unwavering, for what faith
is so? — that if the need for miracle became urgent, the work
he had before him was too great for the Divine power to leave
it halting. His faith wavered, but not his speech: it is the
lot of every man who has to speak for the satisfaction of the
crowd, that he must often speak in virtue of yesterday's faith,
hoping it will come back to-morrow.

It was in preparation for a scene which was really a
response to the popular impatience for some supernatural
guarantee of the Prophet's mission, that the wooden pulpit
had been erected above the church-door. But while the ordinary Frati in black mantles were entering and arranging themselves, the faces of the multitude were not yet eagerly directed
towards the pulpit: it was felt that Savonarola would not
appear just yet, and there was some interest in singling out
the various monks, some of them belonging to high Florentine
families, many of them having fathers, brothers, or cousins
among the artisans and shopkeepers who made the majority

of the crowd.   It was not till the tale of monks was complete, not till they had fluttered their books and had begun to chant, that people said to each other, " Fra Girolamo must be coming now."

That expectation rather than any spell from the accustomed wail of psalmody was what made silence and expectation seem to spread like a paling solemn light over the multitude of up-turned faces, all now directed towards the empty pulpit.

The next instant the pulpit was no longer empty.   A figure covered from head to foot in black cowl and mantle had en-tered it, and was kneeling with bent head and with face turned away.   It seemed a weary time to the eager people while the black figure knelt and the monks chanted.   But the stillness was not broken, for the Frate's audiences with Heaven were yet charged with electric awe for that mixed multitude, so that those who had already the will to stone him felt their arms unnerved.

At last there was a vibration among the multitude, each seeming to give his neighbor a momentary aspen-like touch, as when men who have been watching for something in the heavens see the expected presence silently disclosing itself. The Frate had risen, turned towards the people, and partly pushed back his cowl.   The monotonous wail of psalmody had ceased, and to those who stood near the pulpit, it was as if the sounds which had just been filling their ears had suddenly merged themselves in the force of Savonarola's flashing glance, as he looked round him in the silence.   Then he stretched out his hands, which, in their exquisite delicacy, seemed trans-figured from an animal organ for grasping into vehicles of sen-sibility too acute to need any gross contact: hands that came like an appealing speech from that part of his soul which was masked by his strong passionate face, written on now with deeper lines about the mouth and brow than are made by forty-four years of ordinary life.

At the first stretching out of the hands some of the crowd in the front ranks fell on their knees, and here and there a de-vout disciple farther off; but the great majority stood firm, some resisting the impulse to kneel before this excommunicated man (might not a great judgment fall upon him even in this act of blessing?) — others jarred with scorn and hatred of the ambitious deceiver who was getting up this new comedy, before which, nevertheless, they felt themselves impotent, as before the triumph of a fashion.

But then came the voice, clear and low at first, uttering the words of absolution — "*Misereatur vestri*" — and more fell on their knees : and as it rose higher and yet clearer, the erect heads became fewer and fewer, till, at the words "*Benedicat vos omnipotens Deus,*" it rose to a masculine cry, as if protesting its power to bless under the clutch of a demon that wanted to stifle it : it rang like a trumpet to the extremities of the piazza, and under it every head was bowed.

After the utterance of that blessing, Savonarola himself fell on his knees and hid his face in temporary exhaustion. Those great jets of emotion were a necessary part of his life; he himself had said to the people long ago, "Without preaching I cannot live." But it was a life that shattered him.

In a few minutes more, some had risen to their feet, but a larger number remained kneeling, and all faces were intently watching him. He had taken into his hands a crystal vessel, containing the consecrated Host, and was about to address the people.

"You remember, my children, three days ago I besought you, when I should hold this Sacrament in my hand in the face of you all, to pray fervently to the Most High that if this work of mine does not come from Him, He will send a fire and consume me, that I may vanish into the eternal darkness away from His light which I have hidden with my falsity. Again I beseech you to make that prayer, and to make it *now.*"

It was a breathless moment : perhaps no man really prayed, if some in a spirit of devout obedience made the effort to pray. Every consciousness was chiefly possessed by the sense that Savonarola was praying, in a voice not loud, but distinctly audible in the wide stillness.

"Lord, if I have not wrought in sincerity of soul, if my word cometh not from Thee, strike me in this moment with Thy thunder, and let the fires of Thy wrath enclose me."

He ceased to speak, and stood motionless, with the consecrated Mystery in his hand, with eyes uplifted and a quivering
excitement in his whole aspect. Every one else was motionless and silent too, while the sunlight, which for the last
quarter of an hour had here and there been piercing the grayness, made fitful streaks across the convent wall, causing some
awe-stricken spectators to start timidly. But soon there was
a wider parting, and with a gentle quickness, like a smile,
a stream of brightness poured itself on the crystal vase,
and then spread itself over Savonarola's face with mild
glorification.

An instantaneous shout rang through the piazza, " Behold
the answer ! "

The warm radiance thrilled through Savonarola's frame,
and so did the shout. It was his last moment of untroubled
triumph, and in its rapturous confidence he felt carried to a
grander scene yet to come, before an audience that would represent all Christendom, in whose presence he should again be
sealed as the messenger of the supreme righteousness, and
feel himself full charged with Divine strength. It was but a
moment that expanded itself in that prevision. While the
shout was still ringing in his ears he turned away within the
church, feeling the strain too great for him to bear it longer.

But when the Frate had disappeared, and the sunlight
seemed no longer to have anything special in its illumination,
but was spreading itself impartially over all things clean and
unclean, there began, along with the general movement of the
crowd, a confusion of voices in which certain strong discords
and varying scales of laughter made it evident that, in the
previous silence and universal kneeling, hostility and scorn
had only submitted unwillingly to a momentary spell.

"It seems to me the plaudits are giving way to criticism,"
said Tito, who had been watching the scene attentively from
an upper loggia in one of the houses opposite the church.
" Nevertheless it was a striking moment, eh, Messer Pietro ?
Fra Girolamo is a man to make one understand that there was
a time when the monk's frock was a symbol of power over
men's minds rather than over the keys of women's cupboards."

"Assuredly," said Pietro Cennini. "And until I have seen proof that Fra Girolamo has much less faith in God's judgments than the common run of men, instead of having considerably more, I shall not believe that he would brave Heaven in this way if his soul were laden with a conscious lie."

CHAPTER LXIII.

RIPENING SCHEMES.

A MONTH after that Carnival, one morning near the end of March, Tito descended the marble steps of the Old Palace, bound on a pregnant errand to San Marco. For some reason, he did not choose to take the direct road, which was but a slightly bent line from the Old Palace; he chose rather to make a circuit by the Piazza di Santa Croce, where the people would be pouring out of the church after the early sermon.

It was in the grand church of Santa Croce that the daily Lenten sermon had of late had the largest audience. For Savonarola's voice had ceased to be heard even in his own church of San Marco, a hostile Signoria having imposed silence on him in obedience to a new letter from the Pope, threatening the city with an immediate interdict if this "wretched worm" and "monstrous idol" were not forbidden to preach, and sent to demand pardon at Rome. And next to hearing Fra Girolamo himself, the most exciting Lenten occupation was to hear him argued against and vilified. This excitement was to be had in Santa Croce, where the Franciscan appointed to preach the Quaresimal sermons had offered to clench his arguments by walking through the fire with Fra Girolamo. Had not that schismatical Dominican said, that his prophetic doctrine would be proved by a miracle at the fitting time? Here, then, was the fitting time. Let Savonarola walk through the fire, and if he came out unhurt, the Divine origin of his doctrine would be demonstrated; but if the fire consumed him, his falsity would

be manifest; and that he might have no excuse for evading
the test, the Franciscan declared himself willing to be a victim
to this high logic, and to be burned for the sake of securing
the necessary minor premiss.

Savonarola, according to his habit, had taken no notice
of these pulpit attacks. But it happened that the zealous
preacher of Santa Croce was no other than the Fra Francesco
di Puglia, who at Prato the year before had been engaged in a
like challenge with Savonarola's fervent follower Fra Domenico, but had been called home by his superiors while the heat
was simply oratorical. Honest Fra Domenico, then, who was
preaching Lenten sermons to the women in the Via del Coco-
mero, no sooner heard of this new challenge, than he took up
the gauntlet for his master, and declared himself ready to walk
through the fire with Fra Francesco. Already the people were
beginning to take a strong interest in what seemed to them a
short and easy method of argument (for those who were to be
convinced), when Savonarola, keenly alive to the dangers that
lay in the mere discussion of the case, commanded Fra Domenico to withdraw his acceptance of the challenge and secede
from the affair. The Franciscan declared himself content:
he had not directed his challenge to any subaltern, but to Fra
Girolamo himself.

After that, the popular interest in the Lenten sermons had
flagged a little. But this morning, when Tito entered the
Piazza di Santa Croce, he found, as he expected, that the
people were pouring from the church in large numbers. Instead of dispersing, many of them concentrated themselves
towards a particular spot near the entrance of the Franciscan
monastery, and Tito took the same direction, threading the
crowd with a careless and leisurely air, but keeping careful
watch on that monastic entrance, as if he expected some object
of interest to issue from it.

It was no such expectation that occupied the crowd. The
object they were caring about was already visible to them in
the shape of a large placard, affixed by order of the Signoria,
and covered with very legible official handwriting. But curiosity was somewhat balked by the fact that the manuscript

was chiefly in Latin, and though nearly every man knew
beforehand approximately what the placard contained, he had
an appetite for more exact knowledge, which gave him an irritating sense of his neighbor's ignorance in not being able to
interpret the learned tongue. For that aural acquaintance
with Latin phrases which the unlearned might pick up from
pulpit quotations constantly interpreted by the preacher could
help them little when they saw written Latin; the spelling
even of the modern language being in an unorganized and
scrambling condition for the mass of people who could read
and write,[1] while the majority of those assembled nearest to
the placard were not in the dangerous predicament of posses-
sing that little knowledge.

"It's the Frate's doctrines that he's to prove by being
burned," said that large public character Goro, who happened
to be among the foremost gazers. "The Signoria has taken it
in hand, and the writing is to let us know. It's what the
Padre has been telling us about in his sermon."

"Nay, Goro," said a sleek shopkeeper, compassionately,
"thou hast got thy legs into twisted hose there. The Frate
has to prove his doctrines by *not* being burned : he is to walk
through the fire, and come out on the other side sound and
whole."

"Yes, yes," said a young sculptor, who wore his white-
streaked cap and tunic with a jaunty air. "But Fra Girolamo
objects to walking through the fire. Being sound and whole
already, he sees no reason why he should walk through the
fire to come out in just the same condition. He leaves such
odds and ends of work to Fra Domenico."

"Then I say he flinches like a coward," said Goro, in a
wheezy treble. "Suffocation! that was what he did at the
Carnival. He had us all in the piazza to see the lightning
strike him, and nothing came of it."

"Stop that bleating," said a tall shoemaker, who had stepped
in to hear part of the sermon, with bunches of slippers hang-

---

[1] The old diarists throw in their consonants with a regard rather to quan-
tity than position, well typified by the *Ragnolo Braghiello* (Agnolo Gabriello)
of Boccaccio's Ferondo.

ing over his shoulders. "It seems to me, friend, that you are
about as wise as a calf with water on its brain. The Frate
will flinch from nothing: he'll say nothing beforehand, perhaps, but when the moment comes he'll walk through the
fire without asking any gray-frock to keep him company. But
I would give a shoestring to know what this Latin all is."

"There's so much of it," said the shopkeeper, "else I'm
pretty good at guessing. Is there no scholar to be seen?"
he added, with a slight expression of disgust.

There was a general turning of heads, which caused the
talkers to descry Tito approaching in their rear.

"Here is one," said the young sculptor, smiling and raising
his cap.

"It is the secretary of the Ten: he is going to the convent,
doubtless; make way for him," said the shopkeeper, also doff-
ing, though that mark of respect was rarely shown by Florentines except to the highest officials. The exceptional reverence
was really exacted by the splendor and grace of Tito's appearance, which made his black mantle, with its gold fibula, look
like a regal robe, and his ordinary black velvet cap like an
entirely exceptional head-dress. The hardening of his cheeks
and mouth, which was the chief change in his face since he
came to Florence, seemed to a superficial glance only to give
his beauty a more masculine character. He raised his own
cap immediately and said —

"Thanks, my friend, I merely wished, as you did, to see
what is at the foot of this placard — ah, it is as I expected.
I had been informed that the government permits any one
who will, to subscribe his name as a candidate to enter the
fire — which is an act of liberality worthy of the magnificent
Signoria — reserving of course the right to make a selection.
And doubtless many believers will be eager to subscribe their
names. For what is it to enter the fire, to one whose faith is
firm? A man is afraid of the fire, because he believes it will
burn him; but if he believes the contrary?" — here Tito lifted
his shoulders and made an oratorical pause — "for which reason I have never been one to disbelieve the Frate, when he
has said that he would enter the fire to prove his doctrine.

For in his place, if you believed the fire would not burn you, which of you, my friends, would not enter it as readily as you would walk along the dry bed of the Mugnone ? "

As Tito looked round him during this appeal, there was a change in some of his audience very much like the change in an eager dog when he is invited to smell something pungent. Since the question of burning was becoming practical, it was not every one who would rashly commit himself to any general view of the relation between faith and fire. The scene might have been too much for a gravity less under command than Tito's.

"Then, Messer Segretario," said the young sculptor, "it seems to me Fra Francesco is the greater hero, for he offers to enter the fire for the truth, though he is sure the fire will burn him."

"I do not deny it," said Tito, blandly. "But if it turns out that Fra Francesco is mistaken, he will have been burned for the wrong side, and the Church has never reckoned such victims to be martyrs. We must suspend our judgment until the trial has really taken place."

"It is true, Messer Segretario," said the shopkeeper, with subdued impatience. "But will you favor us by interpreting the Latin ? "

"Assuredly," said Tito. "It does but express the conclusions or doctrines which the Frate specially teaches, and which the trial by fire is to prove true or false. They are doubtless familiar to you. First, that Florence —-"

"Let us have the Latin bit by bit, and then tell us what it means," said the shoemaker, who had been a frequent hearer of Fra Girolamo.

"Willingly," said Tito, smiling. "You will then judge if I give you the right meaning."

"Yes, yes ; that's fair," said Goro.

"*Ecclesia Dei indiget renovatione;* that is, the Church of God needs purifying or regenerating."

"It is true," said several voices at once.

"That means, the priests ought to lead better lives; there needs no miracle to prove that. That's what the Frate has always been saying," said the shoemaker.

"*Flagellabitur*," Tito went on. "That is, it will be scourged. *Renovabitur:* it will be purified. *Florentia quoque post flagellam renovabitur et prosperabitur:* Florence also, after the scourging, shall be purified and shall prosper."

"That means we are to get Pisa again," said the shop-keeper.

"And get the wool from England as we used to do, I should hope," said an elderly man, in an old-fashioned berretta, who had been silent till now. "There's been scourging enough with the sinking of the trade."

At this moment, a tall personage, surmounted by a red feather, issued from the door of the convent, and exchanged an indifferent glance with Tito; who, tossing his becchetto carelessly over his left shoulder, turned to his reading again, while the bystanders, with more timidity than respect, shrank to make a passage for Messer Dolfo Spini.

"*Infideles convertentur ad Christum,*" Tito went on. "That is, the infidels shall be converted to Christ."

"Those are the Turks and the Moors. Well, I've nothing to say against that," said the shopkeeper, dispassionately.

"*Hæc autem omnia erunt temporibus nostris:* and all these things shall happen in our times."

"Why, what use would they be else?" said Goro.

"*Excommunicatio nuper luta contra Reverendum Patrem nostrum Fratrem Hieronymum nulla est:* the excommunication lately pronounced against our reverend father, Fra Girolamo, is null. *Non observantes eum non peccant:* those who disregard it are not committing a sin."

"I shall know better what to say to that when we have had the Trial by Fire," said the shopkeeper.

"Which doubtless will clear up everything," said Tito. "That is all the Latin — all the conclusions that are to be proved true or false by the trial. The rest you can perceive is simply a proclamation of the Signoria in good Tuscan, calling on such as are eager to walk through the fire, to come to the Palazzo and subscribe their names. Can I serve you further? If not —"

Tito, as he turned away, raised his cap and bent slightly,

with so easy an air that the movement seemed a natural prompting of deference.

He quickened his pace as he left the piazza, and after two or three turnings he paused in a quiet street before a door at which he gave a light and peculiar knock. It was opened by a young woman whom he chucked under the chin as he asked her if the Padrone was within, and he then passed, without further ceremony, through another door which stood ajar on his right hand. It admitted him into a handsome but untidy room, where Dolfo Spini sat playing with a fine stag-hound which alternately snuffed at a basket of pups and licked his hands with that affectionate disregard of her master's morals sometimes held to be one of the most agreeable attributes of her sex. He just looked up as Tito entered, but continued his play, simply from that disposition to persistence in some irrelevant action, by which slow-witted sensual people seem to be continually counteracting their own purposes. Tito was patient.

"A handsome *bracca* that," he said, quietly, standing with his thumbs in his belt. Presently he added, in that cool liquid tone which seemed mild, but compelled attention, "When you have finished such caresses as cannot possibly be deferred, my Dolfo, we will talk of business, if you please. My time, which I could wish to be eternity at your service, is not entirely my own this morning."

"Down, Mischief, down!" said Spini, with sudden roughness. "Malediction!" he added, still more gruffly, pushing the dog aside; then, starting from his seat, he stood close to Tito, and put a hand on his shoulder as he spoke.

"I hope your sharp wits see all the ins and outs of this business, my fine necromancer, for it seems to me no clearer than the bottom of a sack."

"What is your difficulty, my cavalier?"

"These accursed Frati Minori at Santa Croce. They are drawing back now. Fra Francesco himself seems afraid of sticking to his challenge; talks of the Prophet being likely to use magic to get up a false miracle — thinks he himself might be dragged into the fire and burned, and the Prophet might come out whole by magic, and the Church be none the better. And then, after all our talking, there's not so much as a blessed lay brother who will offer himself to pair with that pious sheep Fra Domenico."

"It is the peculiar stupidity of the tonsured skull that prevents them from seeing of how little consequence it is whether they are burned or not," said Tito. "Have you sworn well to them that they shall be in no danger of entering the fire?"

"No," said Spini, looking puzzled; "because one of them will be obliged to go in with Fra Domenico, who thinks it a thousand years till the fagots are ready."

"Not at all. Fra Domenico himself is not likely to go in. I have told you before, my Dolfo, only your powerful mind is not to be impressed without more repetition than suffices for the vulgar — I have told you that now you have got the Signoria to take up this affair and prevent it from being hushed up by Fra Girolamo, nothing is necessary but that on a given day the fuel should be prepared in the piazza, and the people got together with the expectation of seeing something prodigious. If, after that, the Prophet quits the piazza without any appearance of a miracle on his side, he is ruined with the people : they will be ready to pelt him out of the city, the Signoria will find it easy to banish him from the territory, and his Holiness may do as he likes with him. Therefore, my Alcibiades, swear to the Franciscans that their gray frocks shall not come within singeing distance of the fire."

Spini rubbed the back of his head with one hand, and tapped his sword against his leg with the other, to stimulate his power of seeing these intangible combinations.

"But," he said presently, looking up again, "unless we fall on him in the piazza, when the people are in a rage, and make an end of him and his lies then and there, Valori and the Salviati and the Albizzi will take up arms and raise a fight for him. I know that was talked of when there was the hubbub on Ascension Sunday. And the people may turn round again : there may be a story raised of the French king coming again, or some other cursed chance in the hypocrite's favor. The city will never be safe till he's out of it."

"He *will* be out of it before long, without your giving yourself any further trouble than this little comedy of the Trial by Fire. The wine and the sun will make vinegar without any shouting to help them, as your Florentine sages would say. You will have the satisfaction of delivering your city from an incubus by an able stratagem, instead of risking blunders with sword-thrusts."

"But suppose he *did* get magic and the devil to help him, and walk through the fire after all?" said Spini, with a grimace intended to hide a certain shyness in trenching on this speculative ground. "How do you know there's nothing in those things? Plenty of scholars believe in them, and this Frate is bad enough for anything."

"Oh, of course there are such things," said Tito, with a shrug: "but I have particular reasons for knowing that the Frate is not on such terms with the devil as can give him any confidence in this affair. The only magic he relies on is his own ability."

"Ability!" said Spini. "Do you call it ability to be setting Florence at loggerheads with the Pope and all the powers of Italy — all to keep beckoning at the French king who never comes? You may call him able, but I call him a hypocrite, who wants to be master of everybody, and get himself made Pope."

"You judge with your usual penetration, my captain, but our opinions do not clash. The Frate, wanting to be master, and to carry out his projects against the Pope, requires the lever of a foreign power, and requires Florence as a fulcrum. I used to think him a narrow-minded bigot, but now, I think him a shrewd ambitious man who knows what he is aiming at, and directs his aim as skilfully as you direct a ball when you are playing at *maglio*."

"Yes, yes," said Spini, cordially, "I can aim a ball."

"It is true," said Tito, with bland gravity; "and I should not have troubled you with my trivial remark on the Frate's ability, but that you may see how this will heighten the credit of your success against him at Rome and at Milan, which is sure to serve you in good stead when the city comes to change its policy."

"Well, thou art a good little demon, and shalt have good pay," said Spini, patronizingly; whereupon he thought it only natural that the useful Greek adventurer should smile with gratification as he said —

"Of course, any advantage to me depends entirely on your — "

"We shall have our supper at my palace to-night," interrupted Spini, with a significant nod and an affectionate pat on Tito's shoulder, "and I shall expound the new scheme to them all."

"Pardon, my magnificent patron," said Tito; "the scheme has been the same from the first — it has never varied except in your memory. Are you sure you have fast hold of it now ? "

Spini rehearsed.

"One thing more," he said, as Tito was hastening away. "There is that sharp-nosed notary, Ser Ceccone ; he has been handy of late. Tell me, you who can see a man wink when you 're behind him, do you think I may go on making use of him ? "

Tito dared not say "No." He knew his companion too well to trust him with advice when all Spini's vanity and self-interest were not engaged in concealing the adviser.

"Doubtless," he answered, promptly. "I have nothing to say against Ceccone."

That suggestion of the notary's intimate access to Spini caused Tito a passing twinge, interrupting his amused satisfaction in the success with which he made a tool of the man who fancied himself a patron. For he had been rather afraid of Ser Ceccone. Tito's nature made him peculiarly alive to circumstances that might be turned to his disadvantage ; his memory was much haunted by such possibilities, stimulating him to contrivances by which he might ward them off. And it was not likely that he should forget that October morning more than a year ago, when Romola had appeared suddenly before him at the door of Nello's shop, and had compelled him to declare his certainty that Fra Girolamo was not going outside the gates. The fact that Ser Ceccone had been a witness of that scene, together with Tito's perception that for some reason or other he was an object of dislike to the notary, had received a new importance from the recent turn of events. For after having been implicated in the Medicean plots, and having found it advisable in consequence to retire into the country for some time, Ser Ceccone had of late, since his reappearance in the city, attached himself to the Arrabbiati, and cultivated the patronage of Dolfo Spini. Now that captain of the Compagnacci was much given, when in the company of intimates, to confidential narrative about his own doings, and if Ser Ceccone's powers of combination were sharpened by enmity, he might gather some knowledge which he could use against Tito with very unpleasant results.

It would be pitiable to be balked in well-conducted schemes by an insignificant notary; to be lamed by the sting of an insect whom he had offended unawares. "But," Tito said to himself, "the man's dislike to me can be nothing deeper than the ill-humor of a dinnerless dog; I shall conquer it if I can make him prosperous." And he had been very glad of an opportunity which had presented itself of providing the notary with a temporary post as an extra *cancelliere* or registering secretary under the Ten, believing that with this sop and the expectation of more, the waspish cur must be quite cured of the disposition to bite him.

But perfect scheming demands omniscience, and the notary's envy had been stimulated into hatred by causes of which Tito knew nothing. That evening when Tito, returning from his critical audience with the Special Council, had brushed by Ser Ceccone on the stairs, the notary, who had only just returned from Pistoja, and learned the arrest of the conspirators, was bound on an errand which bore a humble resemblance to Tito's. He also, without giving up a show of popular zeal, had been putting in the Medicean lottery. He also had been privy to the unexecuted plot, and was willing to tell what he knew, but knew much less to tell. He also would have been willing to go on treacherous errands, but a more eligible agent had forestalled him. His propositions were received coldly; the council, he was told, was already in possession of the needed information, and since he had been thus busy in sedition, it would be well for him to retire out of the way of mischief, otherwise the government might be obliged to take note of him. Ser Ceccone wanted no evidence to make him attribute his failure to Tito, and his spite was the more bitter because the nature of the case compelled him to hold his peace about it. Nor was this the whole of his grudge against the flourishing Melema. On issuing from his hiding-place, and attaching himself to the Arrabbiati, he had earned some pay as one of the spies who reported information on Florentine affairs to the Milanese court; but his pay had been small, notwithstanding his pains to write full letters, and he had lately been apprised that his news was seldom more than a late and imperfect edition of what was known already. Now Ser Ceccone had no positive knowledge that Tito had an underhand connection with the Arrabbiati and the Court of Milan, but he had a suspicion of which he chewed the cud with as strong a sense of flavor as if it had been a certainty.

This fine-grown vigorous hatred could swallow the feeble opiate of Tito's favors, and be as lively as ever after it. Why should Ser Ceccone like Melema any the better for doing him favors? Doubtless the suave secretary had his own ends to serve; and what right had he to the superior position which made it possible for him to show favor? But since he had tuned his voice to flattery, Ser Ceccone would pitch his in the same key, and it remained to be seen who would win at the game of outwitting.

To have a mind well oiled with that sort of argument which prevents any claim from grasping it, seems eminently convenient sometimes : only the oil becomes objectionable when we find it anointing other minds on which we want to establish a hold.

Tito, however, not being quite omniscient, felt now no more than a passing twinge of uneasiness at the suggestion of Ser Ceccone's power to hurt him. It was only for a little while that he cared greatly about keeping clear of suspicions and hostility. He was now playing his final game in Florence, and the skill he was conscious of applying gave him a pleasure

in it even apart from the expected winnings. The errand on
which he was bent to San Marco was a stroke in which he felt
so much confidence that he had already given notice to the
Ten of his desire to resign his office at an indefinite period
within the next month or two, and had obtained permission to
make that resignation suddenly, if his affairs needed it, with
the understanding that Niccolò Macchiavelli was to be his pro-
visional substitute, if not his successor. He was acting on
hypothetic grounds, but this was the sort of action that had
the keenest interest for his diplomatic mind. From a combination of general knowledge concerning Savonarola's purposes
with diligently observed details he had framed a conjecture
which he was about to verify by this visit to San Marco. If
he proved to be right, his game would be won, and he might
soon turn his back on Florence. He looked eagerly towards
that consummation, for many circumstances besides his own
weariness of the place told him that it was time for him to be
gone.

CHAPTER LXIV.

THE PROPHET IN HIS CELL.

TITO's visit to San Marco had been announced beforehand,
and he was at once conducted by Fra Niccolò, Savonarola's
secretary, up the spiral staircase into the long corridors lined
with cells — corridors where Fra Angelico's frescos, delicate
as the rainbow on the melting cloud, startled the unaccustomed
eye here and there, as if they had been sudden reflections cast
from an ethereal world, where the Madonna sat crowned in
her radiant glory, and the Divine infant looked forth with
perpetual promise.

It was an hour of relaxation in the monastery, and most of
the cells were empty. The light through the narrow windows
looked in on nothing but bare walls, and the hard pallet and
the crucifix. And even behind that door at the end of a long
corridor, in the inner cell opening from an antechamber where

the Prior usually sat at his desk or received private visitors,
the high jet of light fell on only one more object that looked
quite as common a monastic sight as the bare walls and hard
pallet. It was but the back of a figure in the long white Dominican tunic and scapulary, kneeling with bowed head before
a crucifix. It might have been any ordinary Fra Girolamo,
who had nothing worse to confess than thinking of wrong
things when he was singing *in coro,* or feeling a spiteful joy
when Fra Benedetto dropped the ink over his own miniatures
in the breviary he was illuminating — who had no higher
thought than that of climbing safely into Paradise up the
narrow ladder of prayer, fasting, and obedience. But under
this particular white tunic there was a heart beating with a
consciousness inconceivable to the average monk, and perhaps
hard to be conceived by any man who has not arrived at self-
knowledge through a tumultuous inner life : a consciousness
in which irrevocable errors and lapses from veracity were so
entwined with noble purposes and sincere beliefs, in which
self-justifying expediency was so inwoven with the tissue of a
great work which the whole being seemed as unable to abandon as the body was unable to abandon glowing and trembling
before the objects of hope and fear, that it was perhaps impossible, whatever course might be adopted, for the conscience
to find perfect repose.

Savonarola was not only in the attitude of prayer, there
were Latin words of prayer on his lips ; and yet he was not
praying. He had entered his cell, had fallen on his knees,
and burst into words of supplication, seeking in this way for
an influx of calmness which would be a warrant to him that
the resolutions urged on him by crowding thoughts and passions were not wresting him away from the Divine support ;
but the previsions and impulses which had been at work within
him for the last hour were too imperious ; and while he
pressed his hands against his face, and while his lips were
uttering audibly, " *Cor mundum crea in me,*" his mind was
still filled with the images of the snare his enemies had prepared for him, was still busy with the arguments by which he
could justify himself against their taunts and accusations.

And it was not only against his opponents that Savonarola
had to defend himself. This morning he had had new proof
that his friends and followers were as much inclined to urge
on the Trial by Fire as his enemies: desiring and tacitly expecting that he himself would at last accept the challenge and
evoke the long-expected miracle which was to dissipate doubt
and triumph over malignity. Had he not said that God would
declare himself at the fitting time? And to the understanding of plain Florentines, eager to get party questions settled,
it seemed that no time could be more fitting than this. Certainly, if Fra Domenico walked through the fire unhurt, *that*
would be a miracle, and the faith and ardor of that good
brother were felt to be a cheering augury; but Savonarola was
acutely conscious that the secret longing of his followers to
see him accept the challenge had not been dissipated by any
reasons he had given for his refusal.

Yet it was impossible to him to satisfy them; and with bitter distress he saw now that it was impossible for· him any
longer to resist the prosecution of the trial in Fra Domenico's
case. Not that Savonarola had uttered and written a falsity
when he declared his belief in a future supernatural attesta-
tion of his work; but his mind was so constituted that while
it was easy for him to believe in a miracle which, being distant
and undefined, was screened behind the strong reasons he saw
for its occurrence, and yet easier for him to have a belief in
inward miracles such as his own prophetic inspiration and
divinely wrought intuitions; it was at the same time insur-
mountably difficult to him to believe in the probability of a
miracle which, like this of being carried unhurt through the
fire, pressed in all its details on his imagination and involved
a demand not only for belief but for exceptional action.

Savonarola's nature was one of those in which opposing
tendencies co-exist in almost equal strength: the passionate
sensibility which, impatient of definite thought, floods every
idea with emotion and tends towards contemplative ecstasy,
alternated in him with a keen perception of outward facts
and a vigorous practical judgment of men and things. And
in this case of the Trial by Fire, the latter characteristics were

stimulated into unusual activity by an acute physical sensitiveness which gives overpowering force to the conception of pain and destruction as a necessary sequence of facts which have already been causes of pain in our experience. The promptitude with which men will consent to touch red-hot iron with a wet finger is not to be measured by their theoretic acceptance of the impossibility that the iron will burn them : practical belief depends on what is most strongly represented in the mind at a given moment. And with the Frate's constitution, when the Trial by Fire was urged on his imagination as an immediate demand, it was impossible for him to believe that he or any other man could walk through the flames unhurt — impossible for him to believe that even if he resolved to offer himself, he would not shrink at the last moment.

But the Florentines were not likely to make these fine distinctions. To the common run of mankind it has always seemed a proof of mental vigor to find moral questions easy, and judge conduct according to concise alternatives. And nothing was likely to seem plainer than that a man who at one time declared that God would not leave him without the guarantee of a miracle, and yet drew back when it was proposed to test his declaration, had said what he did not believe. Were not Fra Domenico and Fra Mariano, and scores of Piagnoni besides, ready to enter the fire ? What was the cause of their superior courage, if it was not their superior faith ? Savonarola could not have explained his conduct satisfactorily to his friends, even if he had been able to explain it thoroughly to himself. And he was not. Our naked feelings make haste to clothe themselves in propositions which lie at hand among our store of opinions, and to give a true account of what passes within us something else is necessary besides sincerity, even when sincerity is unmixed. In these very moments, when Savonarola was kneeling in audible prayer, he had ceased to hear the words on his lips. They were drowned by argumentative voices within him that shaped their reasons more and more for an outward audience.

"To appeal to heaven for a miracle by a rash acceptance of

a challenge, which is a mere snare prepared for me by ignoble foes, would be a tempting of God, and the appeal would not be responded to. Let the Pope's legate come, let the ambassadors of all the great Powers come and promise that the calling of a General Council and the reform of the Church shall hang on the miracle, and I will enter the flames, trusting that God will not withhold His seal from that great work. Until then I reserve myself for higher duties which are directly laid upon me: it is not permitted to me to leap from the chariot for the sake of wrestling with every loud vaunter. But Fra Domenico's invincible zeal to enter into the trial may be the sign of a Divine vocation, may be a pledge that the miracle — "

But no! when Savonarola brought his mind close to the threatened scene in the piazza, and imagined a human body entering the fire, his belief recoiled again. It was not an event that his imagination could simply see: he felt it with shuddering vibrations to the extremities of his sensitive fingers. The miracle could not be. Nay, the trial itself was not to happen: he was warranted in doing all in his power to hinder it. The fuel might be got ready in the piazza, the people might be assembled, the preparatory formalities might be gone through: all this was perhaps inevitable now, and he could no longer resist it without bringing dishonor on — himself? Yes, and therefore on the cause of God. But it was not really intended that the Franciscan should enter the fire, and while *he* hung back there would be the means of preventing Fra Domenico's entrance. At the very worst, if Fra Domenico were compelled to enter, he should carry the consecrated Host with him, and with that Mystery in his hand, there might be a warrant for expecting that the ordinary effects of fire would be stayed; or, more probably, this demand would be resisted, and might thus be a final obstacle to the trial.

But these intentions could not be avowed: he must appear frankly to await the trial, and to trust in its issue. That dissidence between inward reality and outward seeming was not the Christian simplicity after which he had striven through

years of his youth and prime, and which he had preached as a
chief fruit of the Divine life. In the stress and heat of the
day, with cheeks burning, with shouts ringing in the ears,
who is so blest as to remember the yearnings he had in
the cool and silent morning and know that he has not belied
them?

"O God, it is for the sake of the people — because they are
blind — because their faith depends on me. If I put on sack-
cloth and cast myself among the ashes, who will take up the
standard and head the battle? Have I not been led by a way
which I knew not to the work that lies before me?"

The conflict was one that could not end, and in the effort at
prayerful pleading the uneasy mind laved its smart continually in thoughts of the greatness of that task which there was
no man else to fulfil if he forsook it. It was not a thing of
every day that a man should be inspired with the vision and
the daring that made a sacred rebel.

Even the words of prayer had died away. He continued to
kneel, but his mind was filled with the images of results to
be felt through all Europe; and the sense of immediate difficulties was being lost in the glow of that vision, when the
knocking at the door announced the expected visit.

Savonarola drew on his mantle before he left his cell, as
was his custom when he received visitors; and with that
immediate response to any appeal from without which belongs
to a power-loving nature accustomed to make its power felt by
speech, he met Tito with a glance as self-possessed and strong
as if he had risen from resolution instead of conflict.

Tito did not kneel, but simply made a greeting of profound
deference, which Savonarola received quietly without any
sacerdotal words, and then desiring him to be seated, said at
once —

"Your business is something of weight, my son, that could
not be conveyed through others?"

"Assuredly, father, else I should not have presumed to ask
it. I will not trespass on your time by any proem. I
gathered from a remark of Messer Domenico Mazzinghi that
you might be glad to make use of the next special courier who

is sent to France with despatches from the Ten. I must entreat you to pardon me if I have been too officious; but inasmuch as Messer Domenico is at this moment away at his villa, I wished to apprise you that a courier carrying important letters is about to depart for Lyons at daybreak to-morrow."

The muscles of Fra Girolamo's face were eminently under command, as must be the case with all men whose personality is powerful, and in deliberate speech he was habitually cautious, confiding his intentions to none without necessity. But under any strong mental stimulus, his eyes were liable to a dilatation and added brilliancy that no strength of will could control. He looked steadily at Tito, and did not answer immediately, as if he had to consider whether the information he had just heard met any purpose of his.

Tito, whose glance never seemed observant, but rarely let anything escape it, had expected precisely that dilatation and flash of Savonarola's eyes which he had noted on other occasions. He saw it, and then immediately busied himself in adjusting his gold fibula, which had got wrong; seeming to imply that he awaited an answer patiently.

The fact was that Savonarola had expected to receive this intimation from Domenico Mazzinghi, one of the Ten, an ardent disciple of his whom he had already employed to write a private letter to the Florentine ambassador in France, to prepare the way for a letter to the French king himself in Savonarola's handwriting, which now lay ready in the desk at his side. It was a letter calling on the king to assist in summoning a General Council, that might reform the abuses of the Church, and begin by deposing Pope Alexander, who was not rightfully Pope, being a vicious unbeliever, elected by corruption and governing by simony.

This fact was not what Tito knew, but what his constructive talent, guided by subtle indications, had led him to guess and hope.

"It is true, my son," said Savonarola. quietly, — "it is true I have letters which I would gladly send by safe conveyance under cover to our ambassador. Our community of San Marco, as you know, has affairs in France, being, among other things, responsible for a debt to that singularly wise and experienced Frenchman, Signor Philippe de Comines, on the library of the Medici, which we purchased; but I apprehend that Domenico Mazzinghi himself may return to the city before evening, and I should gain more time for preparation of the letters if I waited to deposit them in his hands."

"Assuredly, reverend father, that might be better on all grounds, except one, namely, that if anything occurred to hinder Messer Domenico's return, the despatch of the letters would require either that I should come to San Marco again at a late hour, or that you should send them to me by your secretary; and I am aware that you wish to guard against the false inferences which might be drawn from a too frequent communication between yourself and any officer of the government." In throwing out this difficulty Tito felt that the more unwillingness the Frate showed to trust him, the more certain he would be of his conjecture.

Savonarola was silent; but while he kept his mouth firm, a slight glow rose in his face with the suppressed excitement that was growing within him. It would be a critical moment — that in which he delivered the letter out of his own hands.

"It is most probable that Messer Domenico will return in time," said Tito, affecting to consider the Frate's determination settled, and rising from his chair as he spoke. "With your permission, I will take my leave, father, not to trespass on your time when my errand is done; but as I may not be favored with another interview, I venture to confide to you — what is not yet known to others, except to the magnificent Ten — that I contemplate resigning my secretaryship, and leaving Florence shortly. Am I presuming too much on your interest in stating what relates chiefly to myself?"

"Speak on, my son," said the Frate; "I desire to know your prospects."

"I find, then, that I have mistaken my real vocation in forsaking the career of pure letters, for which I was brought up. The politics of Florence, father, are worthy to occupy the greatest mind — to occupy yours — when a man is in a position to execute his own ideas; but when, like me, he can only hope to be the mere instrument of changing schemes, he requires to be animated by the minor attachments of a born Florentine : also, my wife's unhappy alienation from a Florentine residence since the painful events of August naturally influences me. I wish to join her."

Savonarola inclined his head approvingly.

"I intend, then, soon to leave Florence, to visit the chief courts of Europe, and to widen my acquaintance with the men of letters in the various universities. I shall go first to the court of Hungary, where scholars are eminently welcome; and I shall probably start in a week or ten days. I have not concealed from you, father, that I am no religious enthusiast; I have not my wife's ardor; but religious enthusiasm, as I conceive, is not necessary in order to appreciate the grandeur and justice of your views concerning the government of nations and the Church. And if you condescend to intrust me with any commission that will further the relations you wish to establish, I shall feel honored. May I now take my leave ? "

"Stay, my son. When you depart from Florence I will send a letter to your wife, of whose spiritual welfare I would fain be assured, for she left me in anger. As for the letters to France, such as I have ready — "

Savonarola rose and turned to his desk as he spoke. He took from it a letter on which Tito could see, but not read, an address in the Frate's own minute and exquisite handwriting, still to be seen covering the margins of his Bibles. He took a large sheet of paper, enclosed the letter, and sealed it.

"Pardon me, father," said Tito, before Savonarola had time to speak, "unless it were your decided wish, I would rather not incur the responsibility of carrying away the letter. Messer Domenico Mazzinghi will doubtless return, or, if not, Fra Niccolò can convey it to me at the second hour of the evening, when I shall place the other despatches in the courier's hands."

"At present, my son," said the Frate, waiving that point, "I wish you to address this packet to our ambassador in your own handwriting, which is preferable to my secretary's."

Tito sat down to write the address while the Frate stood by
him with folded arms, the glow mounting in his cheek, and
his lip at last quivering. Tito rose and was about to move
away, when Savonarola said abruptly — "Take it, my son.
There is no use in waiting. It does not please me that Fra
Niccolò should have needless errands to the Palazzo."

As Tito took the letter, Savonarola stood in suppressed
excitement that forbade further speech. There seems to be a
subtle emanation from passionate natures like his, making
their mental states tell immediately on others; when they
are absent-minded and inwardly excited there is silence in
the air.

Tito made a deep reverence and went out with the letter
under his mantle.

The letter was duly delivered to the courier and carried out
of Florence. But before that happened another messenger,
privately employed by Tito, had conveyed information in
cipher, which was carried by a series of relays to armed agents
of Ludovico Sforza, Duke of Milan, on the watch for the
very purpose of intercepting despatches on the borders of the
Milanese territory.

———◆———

CHAPTER LXV.

THE TRIAL BY FIRE.

LITTLE more than a week after, on the 7th of April, the
great Piazza della Signoria presented a stranger spectacle even
than the famous Bonfire of Vanities. And a greater multitude had assembled to see it than had ever before tried to find
place for themselves in the wide piazza, even on the day of
San Giovanni.

It was near mid-day, and since the early morning there had
been a gradual swarming of the people at every coign of van-
tage or disadvantage offered by the façades and roofs of the
houses, and such spaces of the pavement as were free to the

public. Men were seated on iron rods that made a sharp
angle with the rising wall, were clutching slim pillars with
arms and legs, were astride on the necks of the rough statuary
that here and there surmounted the entrances of the grander
houses, were finding a palm's-breadth of seat on a bit of archi-
trave, and a footing on the rough projections of the rustic
stonework, while they clutched the strong iron rings or staples
driven into the walls beside them.

For they were come to see a Miracle : cramped limbs and
abraded flesh seemed slight inconveniences with that prospect
close at hand. It is the ordinary lot of mankind to hear of
miracles, and more or less to believe in them ; but now the
Florentines were going to see one. At the very least they
would see half a miracle ; for if the monk did not come whole
out of the fire, they would see him enter it, and infer that he
was burned in the middle.

There could be no reasonable doubt, it seemed, that the fire
would be kindled, and that the monks would enter it. For
there, before their eyes, was the long platform, eight feet
broad, and twenty yards long, with a grove of fuel heaped up
terribly, great branches of dry oak as a foundation, crackling
thorns above, and well-anointed tow and rags, known to make
fine flames in Florentine illuminations. The platform began
at the corner of the marble terrace in front of the Old Palace,
close to Marzocco, the stone lion, whose aged visage looked
frowningly along the grove of fuel that stretched obliquely
across the piazza.

Besides that, there were three large bodies of armed men :
five hundred hired soldiers of the Signoria stationed before
the palace ; five hundred Compagnacci under Dolfo Spini, far
off on the opposite side of the piazza ; and three hundred
armed citizens of another sort, under Marco Salviati, Savonarola's friend, in front of Orgagna's Loggia, where the
Franciscans and Dominicans were to be placed with their
champions.

Here had been much expense of money and labor, and high
dignities were concerned. There could be no reasonable doubt
that something great was about to happen ; and it would cer-

tainly be a great thing if the two monks were simply burned,
for in that case too God would have spoken, and said very
plainly that Fra Girolamo was not His prophet.

And there was not much longer to wait, for it was now near
mid-day. Half the monks were already at their post, and
that half of the Loggia that lies towards the Palace was already filled with gray mantles ; but the other half, divided off
by boards, was still empty of everything except a small altar.
The Franciscans had entered and taken their places in silence.
But now, at the other side of the piazza was heard loud chanting from two hundred voices, and there was general satisfaction, if not in the chanting, at least in the evidence that the
Dominicans were come. That loud chanting repetition of the
prayer, "Let God arise, and let His enemies be scattered,"
was unpleasantly suggestive to some impartial ears of a desire
to vaunt confidence and excite dismay : and so was the flame-
colored velvet cope in which Fra Domenico was arrayed as he
headed the procession, cross in hand, his simple mind really
exalted with faith, and with the genuine intention to enter the
flames for the glory of God and Fra Girolamo. Behind him
came Savonarola in the white vestment of a priest, carrying in
his hands a vessel containing the consecrated Host. He, too,
was chanting loudly ; he, too, looked firm and confident, and
as all eyes were turned eagerly on him, either in anxiety, curiosity, or malignity, from the moment when he entered the
piazza till he mounted the steps of the Loggia and deposited
the Sacrament on the altar, there was an intensifying flash
and energy in his countenance responding to that scrutiny.

We are so made, almost all of us, that the false seeming
which we have thought of with painful shrinking when beforehand in our solitude it has urged itself on us as a necessity,
will possess our muscles and move our lips as if nothing but
that were easy when once we have come under the stimulus of
expectant eyes and ears. And the strength of that stimulus
to Savonarola can hardly be measured by the experience of ordinary lives. Perhaps no man has ever had a mighty influence
over his fellows without having the innate need to dominate,
and this need usually becomes the more imperious in propor-

tion as the complications of life make Self inseparable from a purpose which is not selfish. In this way it came to pass that on the day of the Trial by Fire, the doubleness which is the pressing temptation in every public career, whether of priest, orator, or statesman, was more strongly defined in Savonarola's consciousness as the acting of a part, than at any other period in his life. He was struggling not against impending martyrdom, but against impending ruin.

Therefore he looked and acted as if he were thoroughly confident, when all the while foreboding was pressing with leaden weight on his heart, not only because of the probable issues of this trial, but because of another event already past — an event which was spreading a sunny satisfaction through the mind of a man who was looking down at the passion-worn prophet from a window of the Old Palace. It was a common turning-point towards which those widely sundered lives had been converging, that two evenings ago the news had come that the Florentine courier of the Ten had been arrested and robbed of all his despatches, so that Savonarola's letter was already in the hands of the Duke of Milan, and would soon be in the hands of the Pope, not only heightening rage, but giving a new justification to extreme measures. There was no malignity in Tito Melema's satisfaction : it was the mild self-gratulation of a man who has won a game that has employed hypothetic skill, not a game that has stirred the muscles and heated the blood. Of course that bundle of desires and contrivances called human nature, when moulded into the form of a plain-featured Frate Predicatore, more or less of an impostor, could not be a pathetic object to a brilliant-minded scholar who understood everything. Yet this tonsured Girolamo with the high nose and large under lip was an immensely clever Frate, mixing with his absurd superstitions or fabrications very remarkable notions about government : no babbler, but a man who could keep his secrets. Tito had no more spite against him than against Saint Dominic. On the contrary, Fra Girolamo's existence had been highly convenient to Tito Melema, furnishing him with that round of the ladder from which he was about to leap on to a new and smooth foot-

ing very much to his heart's content. And everything now
was in forward preparation for that leap: let one more sun
rise and set, and Tito hoped to quit Florence. He had been
so industrious that he felt at full leisure to amuse himself
with to-day's comedy, which the thick-headed Dolfo Spini
could never have brought about but for him.

Not yet did the loud chanting cease, but rather swelled to a
deafening roar, being taken up in all parts of the piazza by
the Piagnoni, who carried their little red crosses as a badge,
and, most of them, chanted the prayer for the confusion of
God's enemies with the expectation of an answer to be given
through the medium of a more signal personage than Fra Domenico. This good Frate in his flame-colored cope was now
kneeling before the little altar on which the Sacrament was
deposited, awaiting his summons.

On the Franciscan side of the Loggia there was no chanting
and no flame-color: only silence and grayness. But there was
this counterbalancing difference, that the Franciscans had two
champions: a certain Fra Giuliano was to pair with Fra Domenico, while the original champion, Fra Francesco, confined
his challenge to Savonarola.

"Surely," thought the men perched uneasily on the rods
and pillars, "all must be ready now. This chanting might
stop, and we should see better when the Frati are moving
towards the platform."

But the Frati were not to be seen moving yet. Pale Franciscan faces were looking uneasily over the boarding at that
flame-colored cope. It had an evil look and might be enchanted, so that a false miracle would be wrought by magic.
Your monk may come whole out of the fire, and yet it may be
the work of the devil.

And now there was passing to and fro between the Loggia
and the marble terrace of the Palazzo, and the roar of chanting became a little quieter, for every one at a distance was
beginning to watch more eagerly. But it soon appeared that
the new movement was not a beginning, but an obstacle to
beginning. The dignified Florentines appointed to preside
over this affair as moderators on each side, went in and out

of the Palace, and there was much debate with the Franciscans. But at last it was clear that Fra Domenico, conspicuous in his flame-color, was being fetched towards the Palace.
Probably the fire had already been kindled — it was difficult to
see at a distance — and the miracle was going to begin.

Not at all. The flame-colored cope disappeared within the
Palace; then another Dominican was fetched away; and for
a long while everything went on as before — the tiresome
chanting, which was not miraculous, and Fra Girolamo in his
white vestment standing just in the same place. But at last
something happened: Fra Domenico was seen coming out
of the Palace again, and returning to his brethren. He had
changed all his clothes with a brother monk, but he was
guarded on each flank by a Franciscan, lest coming into the
vicinity of Savonarola he should be enchanted again.

"Ah, then," thought the distant spectators, a little less conscious of cramped limbs and hunger, "Fra Domenico is not
going to enter the fire. It is Fra Girolamo who offers himself
after all. We shall see him move presently, and if he comes
out of the flames we shall have a fine view of him!"

But Fra Girolamo did not move, except with the ordinary
action accompanying speech. The speech was bold and firm,
perhaps somewhat ironically remonstrant, like that of Elijah
to the priests of Baal, demanding the cessation of these trivial
delays. But speech is the most irritating kind of argument
for those who are out of hearing, cramped in the limbs, and
empty in the stomach. And what need was there for speech?
If the miracle did not begin, it could be no one's fault but Fra
Girolamo's, who might put an end to all difficulties by offering himself now the fire was ready, as he had been forward
enough to do when there was no fuel in sight.

More movement to and fro, more discussion; and the afternoon seemed to be slipping away all the faster because the
clouds had gathered, and changed the light on everything,
and sent a chill through the spectators, hungry in mind and
body.

Now it was the crucifix which Fra Domenico wanted to
carry into the fire and must not be allowed to profane in that

manner. After some little resistance Savonarola gave way
to this objection, and thus had the advantage of making one
more concession; but he immediately placed in Fra Domenico's
hands the vessel containing the consecrated Host. The idea
that the presence of the sacred Mystery might in the worst
extremity avert the ordinary effects of fire hovered in his
mind as a possibility; but the issue on which he counted
was of a more positive kind. In taking up the Host he said
quietly, as if he were only doing what had been presupposed
from the first —

"Since they are not willing that you should enter with the
crucifix, my brother, enter simply with the Sacrament."

New horror in the Franciscans; new firmness in Savonarola.
" It was impious presumption to carry the Sacrament into the
fire: if it were burned the scandal would be great in the minds
of the weak and ignorant." "Not at all: even if it were
burned, the Accidents only would be consumed, the Substance
would remain." Here was a question that might be argued
till set of sun and remain as elastic as ever; and no one could
propose settling it by proceeding to the trial, since it was essentially a preliminary question. It was only necessary that
both sides should remain firm — that the Franciscans should
persist in not permitting the Host to be carried into the fire,
and that Fra Domenico should persist in refusing to enter
without it.

Meanwhile the clouds were getting darker, the air chiller.
Even the chanting was missed now it had given way to in-
audible argument; and the confused sounds of talk from all
points of the piazza, showing that expectation was everywhere relaxing, contributed to the irritating presentiment
that nothing decisive would be done. Here and there a dropping shout was heard; then, more frequent shouts in a rising
scale of scorn.

"Light the fire and drive them in !" "Let us have a smell
of roast — we want our dinner!" "Come, Prophet, let us
know whether anything is to happen before the twenty-four
hours are over!" "Yes, yes, what's your last vision?" "Oh,
he's got a dozen in his inside; they're the small change for

a miracle!" "Olà, Frate, where are you? Never mind wasting the fuel!"

Still the same movement to and fro between the Loggia and the Palace; still the same debate, slow and unintelligible to the multitude as the colloquies of insects that touch antennæ to no other apparent effect than that of going and coming. But an interpretation was not long wanting to unheard debates in which Fra Girolamo was constantly a speaker: it was he who was hindering the trial; everybody was appealing to him now, and he was hanging back.

Soon the shouts ceased to be distinguishable, and were lost in an uproar not simply of voices, but of clashing metal and trampling feet. The suggestions of the irritated people had stimulated old impulses in Dolfo Spini and his band of Compagnacci; it seemed an opportunity not to be lost for putting an end to Florentine difficulties by getting possession of the arch-hypocrite's person; and there was a vigorous rush of the armed men towards the Loggia, thrusting the people aside, or driving them on to the file of soldiery stationed in front of the Palace. At this movement, everything was suspended both with monks and embarrassed magistrates except the palpitating watch to see what would come of the struggle.

But the Loggia was well guarded by the band under the brave Salviati; the soldiers of the Signoria assisted in the repulse; and the trampling and rushing were all backward again towards the Tetto de' Pisani, when the blackness of the heavens seemed to intensify in this moment of utter confusion; and the rain, which had already been felt in scattered drops, began to fall with rapidly growing violence, wetting the fuel, and running in streams off the platform, wetting the weary hungry people to the skin, and driving every man's disgust and rage inwards to ferment there in the damp darkness.

Everybody knew now that the Trial by Fire was not to happen. The Signoria was doubtless glad of the rain, as an obvious reason, better than any pretext, for declaring that both parties might go home. It was the issue which Savonarola had expected and desired; yet it would be an ill description

of what he felt to say that he was glad. As that rain fell,
and plashed on the edge of the Loggia, and sent spray over
the altar and all garments and faces, the Frate knew that the
demand for him to enter the fire was at an end. But he knew
too, with a certainty as irresistible as the damp chill that had
taken possession of his frame, that the design of his enemies
was fulfilled, and that his honor was not saved. He knew
that he should have to make his way to San Marco again
through the enraged crowd, and that the hearts of many friends
who would once have defended him with their lives would
now be turned against him.

When the rain had ceased he asked for a guard from the
Signoria, and it was given him. Had he said that he was
willing to die for the work of his life ? Yes, and he had not
spoken falsely. But to die in dishonor — held up to scorn as
a hypocrite and a false prophet ? "O God ! *that* is not martyrdom ! It is the blotting out of a life that has been a protest against wrong. Let me die because of the worth that is
in me, not because of my weakness."

The rain had ceased, and the light from the breaking clouds
fell on Savonarola as he left the Loggia in the midst of his
guard, walking as he had come, with the Sacrament in his
hand. But there seemed no glory in the light that fell on him
now, no smile of heaven : it was only that light which shines
on, patiently and impartially, justifying or condemning by
simply showing all things in the slow history of their ripen-
ing. He heard no blessing, no tones of pity, but only taunts
and threats. He knew this was a foretaste of coming bitterness ; yet his courage mounted under all moral attack, and he
showed no sign of dismay.

"Well parried, Frate !" said Tito, as Savonarola descended
the steps of the Loggia. "But I fear your career at Florence
is ended. What say you, my Niccolò ? "

"It is a pity his falsehoods were not all of a wise sort," said
Macchiavelli, with a melancholy shrug. "With the times so
much on his side as they are about Church affairs, he might
have done something great."

CHAPTER LXVI.

A MASQUE OF THE FURIES.

The next day was Palm Sunday, or Olive Sunday, as it was chiefly called in the olive-growing Valdarno ; and the morning sun shone with a more delicious clearness for the yesterday's rain. Once more Savonarola mounted the pulpit in San Marco, and saw a flock around him whose faith in him was still unshaken ; and this morning in calm and sad sincerity he declared himself ready to die : in front of all visions he saw his own doom. Once more he uttered the benediction, and saw the faces of men and women lifted towards him in venerating love. Then he descended the steps of the pulpit and turned away from that sight forever.

For before the sun had set Florence was in an uproar. The passions which had been roused the day before had been smouldering through that quiet morning, and had now burst out again with a fury not unassisted by design, and not without official connivance. The uproar had begun at the Duomo in an attempt of some Compagnacci to hinder the evening sermon, which the Piagnoni had assembled to hear. But no sooner had men's blood mounted and the disturbances had become an affray than the cry arose, "To San Marco ! the fire to San Marco ! "

And long before the daylight had died, both the church and convent were being besieged by an enraged and continually increasing multitude. Not without resistance. For the monks, long conscious of growing hostility without, had arms within their walls, and some of them fought as vigorously in their long white tunics as if they had been Knights Templars. Even the command of Savonarola could not prevail against the impulse to self-defence in arms that were still muscular under the Dominican serge. There were laymen too who had not chosen to depart, and some of them fought fiercely : there

was firing from the high altar close by the great crucifix, there
was pouring of stones and hot embers from the convent roof,
there was close fighting with swords in the cloisters. Notwithstanding the force of the assailants, the attack lasted till
deep night.

The demonstrations of the Government had all been against
the convent; early in the attack guards had been sent for, not
to disperse the assailants, but to command all within the convent to lay down their arms, all laymen to depart from it, and
Savonarola himself to quit the Florentine territory within
twelve hours. Had Savonarola quitted the convent then, he
could hardly have escaped being torn to pieces; he was willing to go, but his friends hindered him. It was felt to be a
great risk even for some laymen of high name to depart by
the garden wall, but among those who had chosen to do so was
Francesco Valori, who hoped to raise rescue from without.

And now when it was deep night — when the struggle could
hardly have lasted much longer, and the Compagnacci might
soon have carried their swords into the library, where Savonarola was praying with the Brethren who had either not taken
up arms or had laid them down at his command — there came
a second body of guards, commissioned by the Signoria to
demand the persons of Fra Girolamo and his two coadjutors,
Fra Domenico and Fra Salvestro.

Loud was the roar of triumphant hate when the light of
lanterns showed the. Frate issuing from the door of the convent with a guard who promised him no other safety than that
of the prison. The struggle now was, who should get first
in the stream that rushed up the narrow street to see the
Prophet carried back in ignominy to the piazza where he had
braved it yesterday — who should be in the best place for
reaching his ear with insult, nay, if possible, for smiting him
and kicking him. This was not difficult for some of the armed
Compagnacci who were not prevented from mixing themselves
with the guards.

When Savonarola felt himself dragged and pushed along in
the midst of that hooting multitude; when lanterns were
lifted to show him deriding faces; when he felt himself spit

upon, smitten and kicked with grossest words of insult, it seemed to him that the worst bitterness of life was past. If men judged him guilty, and were bent on having his blood, it was only death that awaited him. But the worst drop of bitterness can never be wrung on to our lips from without: the lowest depth of resignation is not to be found in martyrdom; it is only to be found when we have covered our heads in silence and felt, "I am not worthy to be a martyr; the Truth shall prosper, but not by me."

But that brief imperfect triumph of insulting the Frate, who had soon disappeared under the doorway of the Old Palace, was only like the taste of blood to the tiger. Were there not the houses of the hypocrite's friends to be sacked? Already one-half of the armed multitude, too much in the rear to share greatly in the siege of the convent, had been employed in the more profitable work of attacking rich houses, not with planless desire for plunder, but with that discriminating selection of such as belonged to chief Piagnoni, which showed that the riot was under guidance, and that the rabble with clubs and staves was well officered by sword-girt Compagnacci. Was there not — next criminal after the Frate — the ambitious Francesco Valori, suspected of wanting with the Frate's help to make himself a Doge or Gonfaloniere for life? And the gray-haired man who, eight months ago, had lifted his arm and his voice in such ferocious demand for justice on five of his fellow-citizens, only escaped from San Marco to experience what *others* called justice — to see his house surrounded by an angry, greedy multitude, to see his wife shot dead with an arrow, and to be himself murdered, as he was on his way to answer a summons to the Palazzo, by the swords of men named Ridolfi and Tornabuoni.

In this way that Masque of the Furies, called Riot, was played on in Florence through the hours of night and early morning.

But the chief director was not visible: he had his reasons for issuing his orders from a private retreat, being of rather too high a name to let his red feather be seen waving among all the work that was to be done before the dawn. The retreat was the same house and the same room in a quiet street between Santa Croce and San Marco, where we have seen Tito paying a secret visit to Dolfo Spini. Here the Captain of the Compagnacci sat through this memorable night, receiving visitors who came and went, and went and came, some of them in the guise of armed Compagnacci, others dressed obscurely and without visible arms. There was abundant wine on the table, with drinking-cups for chance comers; and though Spini was on his guard against excessive drinking, he took enough from time to time to heighten the excitement produced by the news that was being brought to him continually.

Among the obscurely dressed visitors Ser Ceccone was one of the most frequent, and as the hours advanced towards the morning twilight he had remained as Spini's constant companion, together with Francesco Cei, who was then in rather careless hiding in Florence, expecting to have his banishment revoked when the Frate's fall had been accomplished.

The tapers had burnt themselves into low shapeless masses, and holes in the shutters were just marked by a sombre outward light, when Spini, who had started from his seat and walked up and down with an angry flush on his face at some talk that had been going forward with those two unmilitary companions, burst out —

"The devil spit him! he shall pay for it, though. Ha, ha! the claws shall be down on him when he little thinks of them. So *he* was to be the great man after all! He's been pretending to chuck everything towards my cap, as if I were a blind beggarman, and all the while he's been winking and filling his own scarsella. I should like to hang skins about him and set my hounds on him! And he's got that fine ruby of mine, I was fool enough to give him yesterday. Malediction! And he was laughing at me in his sleeve two years ago, and spoiling the best plan that ever was laid. I was a fool for trusting myself with a rascal who had long-twisted contrivances that nobody could see to the end of but himself."

"A Greek, too, who dropped into Florence with gems packed about him," said Francesco Cei, who had a slight smile of amusement on his face at Spini's fuming. "You did *not* choose your confidant very wisely, my Dolfo."

"He's a cursed deal cleverer than you, Francesco, and handsomer too," said Spini, turning on his associate with a general desire to worry anything that presented itself.

"I humbly conceive," said Ser Ceccone, "that Messer Francesco's poetic genius will outweigh — "

"Yes, yes, rub your hands! I hate that notary's trick of yours," interrupted Spini, whose patronage consisted largely in this sort of frankness. "But there comes Taddeo, or somebody: now's the time! What news, eh?" he went on, as two Compagnacci entered with heated looks.

"Bad!" said one. "The people have made up their minds they were going to have the sacking of Soderini's house, and now they have been balked we shall have them turning on us, if we don't take care. I suspect there are some Mediceans buzzing about among them, and we may see them attacking your palace over the bridge before long, unless we can find a bait for them another way."

"I have it!" said Spini, and seizing Taddeo by the belt he drew him aside to give him directions, while the other went on telling Cei how the Signoria had interfered about Soderini's house.

"Ecco!" exclaimed Spini, presently, giving Taddeo a slight push towards the door. "Go, and make quick work."

CHAPTER LXVII.

WAITING BY THE RIVER.

ABOUT the time when the two Compagnacci went on their errand, there was another man who, on the opposite side of the Arno, was also going out into the chill gray twilight. His errand, apparently, could have no relation to theirs; he was making his way to the brink of the river at a spot which, though within the city walls, was overlooked by no dwellings, and which only seemed the more shrouded and lonely for the warehouses and granaries which at some little distance backward turned their shoulders to the river. There was a sloping width of long grass and rushes made all the more dank by broad gutters which here and there emptied themselves into the Arno.

The gutters and the loneliness were the attraction that drew this man to come and sit down among the grass, and bend over the waters that ran swiftly in the channelled slope at his side. For he had once had a large piece of bread brought to him by one of those friendly runlets, and more than once a raw carrot and apple-parings. It was worth while to wait for such chances in a place where there was no one to see, and often in his restless wakefulness he came to watch here before daybreak; it might save him for one day the need of that silent begging which consisted in sitting on a church-step by the wayside out beyond the Porta San Frediano.

For Baldassarre hated begging so much that he would perhaps have chosen to die rather than make even that silent appeal, but for one reason that made him desire to live. It was no longer a hope; it was only that possibility which clings to every idea that has taken complete possession of the mind: the sort of possibility that makes a woman watch on a headland for the ship which held something dear, though all her neighbors are certain that the ship was a wreck long years ago. After he had come out of the convent hospital, where the monks of San Miniato had taken care of him as long as he was helpless; after he had watched in vain for the Wife who was to help him, and had begun to think that she was dead of the pestilence that seemed to fill all the space since the night he parted from her, he had been unable to conceive any way in which sacred vengeance could satisfy itself through his arm. His knife was gone, and he was too feeble in body to win another by work, too feeble in mind, even if he had had the knife, to contrive that it should serve its one purpose. He was a shattered, bewildered, lonely old man ; yet he desired to live : he waited for something of which he had no distinct vision — something dim, formless — that startled him, and made strong pulsations within him, like that unknown thing which we look for when we start from sleep, though no voice or touch has waked us. Baldassarre desired to live ; and therefore he crept out in the gray light, and seated himself in the long grass, and watched the waters that had a faint promise in them.

Meanwhile the Compagnacci were busy at their work. The formidable bands of armed men, left to do their will with very little interference from an embarrassed if not conniving Signoria, had parted into two masses, but both were soon making their way by different roads towards the Arno. The smaller mass was making for the Ponte Rubaconte, the larger for the Ponte Vecchio ; but in both the same words had passed from mouth to mouth as a signal, and almost every man of the multitude knew that he was going to the Via de' Bardi to sack a house there. If he knew no other reason, could he demand a better ?

The armed Compagnacci knew something more, for a brief word of command flies quickly, and the leaders of the two streams of rabble had a perfect understanding that they would meet before a certain house a little towards the eastern end of the Via de' Bardi, where the master would probably be in bed, and be surprised in his morning sleep.

But the master of that house was neither sleeping nor in bed ; he had not been in bed that night. For Tito's anxiety to quit Florence had been stimulated by the events of the previous day : investigations would follow in which appeals might be made to him delaying his departure : and in all delay he had an uneasy sense that there was danger. Falsehood had prospered and waxed strong ; but it had nourished the twin life, Fear. He no longer wore his armor, he was no longer afraid of Baldassarre ; but from the corpse of that dead fear a spirit had risen — the undying *habit* of fear. He felt he should not be safe till he was out of this fierce, turbid Florence ; and now he was ready to go. Maso was to deliver up his house to the new tenant ; his horses and mules were awaiting him in San Gallo; Tessa and the children had been lodged for the night in the Borgo outside the gate, and would be dressed in readiness to mount the mules and join him. He descended the stone steps into the courtyard, he passed through the great doorway, not the same Tito, but nearly as brilliant as on the day when he had first entered that house and made the mistake of falling in love with Romola. The mistake was remedied now: the old life was cast off, and was soon to be far behind him.

He turned with rapid steps towards the Piazza dei Mozzi, intending to pass over the Ponte Rubaconte; but as he went along certain sounds came upon his ears that made him turn round and walk yet more quickly in the opposite direction. Was the mob coming into Oltrarno? It was a vexation, for he would have preferred the more private road. He must now go by the Ponte Vecchio; and unpleasant sensations made him draw his mantle close round him, and walk at his utmost speed. There was no one to see him in that gray twilight. But before he reached the end of the Via de' Bardi, like sounds fell on his ear again, and this time they were much louder and nearer. Could he have been deceived before? The mob must be coming over the Ponte Vecchio. Again he turned, from an impulse of fear that was stronger than reflection; but it was only to be assured that the mob was actually entering the street from the opposite end. He chose not to go back to his house: after all they would not attack *him*. Still, he had some valuables about him; and all things except reason and order are possible with a mob. But necessity does the work of courage. He went on towards the Ponte Vecchio, the rush and the trampling and the confused voices getting so loud before him that he had ceased to hear them behind.

For he had reached the end of the street, and the crowd pouring from the bridge met him at the turning and hemmed in his way. He had not time to wonder at a sudden shout before he felt himself surrounded, not, in the first instance, by an unarmed rabble, but by armed Compagnacci; the next sensation was that his cap fell off, and that he was thrust

violently forward among the rabble, along the narrow passage
of the bridge. Then he distinguished the shouts, " Piagnone!
Medicean! Piagnone! Throw him over the bridge!"

His mantle was being torn off him with strong pulls that
would have throttled him if the fibula had not given way.
Then his scarsella was snatched at; but all the while he was
being hustled and dragged; and the snatch failed — his scarsella still hung at his side. Shouting, yelling, half motive-
less execration rang stunningly in his ears, spreading even
among those who had not yet seen him, and only knew there
was a man to be reviled. Tito's horrible dread was that he
should be struck down or trampled on before he reached
the open arches that surmount the centre of the bridge.
There was one hope for him, that they might throw him over
before they had wounded him or beaten the strength out of
him; and his whole soul was absorbed in that one hope and
its obverse terror.

Yes — they *were* at the arches. In that moment Tito, with
bloodless face and eyes dilated, had one of the self-preserving
inspirations that come in extremity. With a sudden desperate
effort he mastered the clasp of his belt, and flung belt and
scarsella forward towards a yard of clear space against the
parapet, crying in a ringing voice —

"There are diamonds! there is gold!"

In the instant the hold on him was relaxed, and there was a
rush towards the scarsella. He threw himself on the parapet
with a desperate leap, and the next moment plunged —
plunged with a great plash into the dark river far below.

It was his chance of salvation; and it was a good chance.
His life had been saved once before by his fine swimming, and
as he rose to the surface again after his long dive he had a
sense of deliverance. He struck out with all the energy of
his strong prime, and the current helped him. If he could
only swim beyond the Ponte alla Carrara he might land in a
remote part of the city, and even yet reach San Gallo. Life
was still before him. And the idiot mob, shouting and bellow-
ing on the bridge there, would think he was drowned.

They did think so. Peering over the parapet along the

dark stream, they could not see afar off the moving blackness of the floating hair, and the velvet tunic-sleeves.

It was only from the other way that a pale olive face could be seen looking white above the dark water: a face not easy even for the indifferent to forget, with its square forehead, the long low arch of the eyebrows, and the long lustrous agate-like eyes. Onward the face went on the dark current, with inflated quivering nostrils, with the blue veins distended on the temples. One bridge was passed — the bridge of Santa Trinità. Should he risk landing now rather than trust to his strength? No. He heard, or fancied he heard, yells and cries pursuing him. Terror pressed him most from the side of his fellow-men: he was less afraid of indefinite chances, and he swam on, panting and straining. He was not so fresh as he would have been if he had passed the night in sleep.

Yet the next bridge — the last bridge — was passed. He was conscious of it; but in the tumult of his blood, he could only feel vaguely that he was safe and might land. But where? The current was having its way with him: he hardly knew where he was: exhaustion was bringing on the dreamy state that precedes unconsciousness.

But now there were eyes that discerned him — aged eyes, strong for the distance. Baldassarre, looking up blankly from the search in the runlet that brought him nothing, had seen a white object coming along the broader stream. Could that be any fortunate chance for *him?* He looked and looked till the object gathered form: then he leaned forward with a start as he sat among the rank green stems, and his eyes seemed to be filled with a new light. Yet he only watched — motionless. Something was being brought to him.

The next instant a man's body was cast violently on the grass two yards from him, and he started forward like a panther, clutching the velvet tunic as he fell forward on the body and flashed a look in the man's face.

Dead — was he dead? The eyes were rigid. But no, it could not be — Justice had brought him. Men looked dead sometimes, and yet the life came back into them. Baldassarre did not feel feeble in that moment. He knew just what he could do. He got his large fingers within the neck of the tunic and held them there, kneeling on one knee beside the body and watching the face. There was a fierce hope in his heart, but it was mixed with trembling. In his eyes there was only fierceness : all the slow-burning remnant of life within him seemed to have leaped into flame.

Rigid — rigid still. Those eyes with the half-fallen lids were locked against vengeance. *Could* it be that he was dead ? There was nothing to measure the time : it seemed long enough for hope to freeze into despair.

Surely at last the eyelids were quivering : the eyes were no longer rigid. There was a vibrating light in them : they opened wide.

" Ah, yes ! You see me — you know me ! "

Tito knew him ; but he did not know whether it was life or death that had brought him into the presence of his injured father. It might be death — and death might mean this chill gloom with the face of the hideous past hanging over him forever.

But now Baldassarre's only dread was, lest the young limbs should escape him. He pressed his knuckles against the round throat, and knelt upon the chest with all the force of his aged frame. Let death come now !

Again he kept his watch on the face. And when the eyes were rigid again, he dared not trust them. He would never lose his hold till some one came and found them. Justice would send some witness, and then he, Baldassarre, would declare that he had killed this traitor, to whom he had once been a father. They would perhaps believe him now, and then he would be content with the struggle of justice on earth — then he would desire to die with his hold on this body, and follow the traitor to hell that he might clutch him there.

And so he knelt, and so he pressed his knuckles against the round throat, without trusting to the seeming death, till the light got strong and he could kneel no longer. Then he sat on the body, still clutching the neck of the tunic. But the hours went on, and no witness came. No eyes descried afar off the two human bodies among the tall grass by the riverside. Florence was busy with greater affairs, and the preparation of a deeper tragedy.

Not long after those two bodies were lying in the grass, Savonarola was being tortured, and crying out in his agony, "I will confess!"

It was not until the sun was westward that a wagon drawn by a mild gray ox came to the edge of the grassy margin, and as the man who led it was leaning to gather up the round stones that lay heaped in readiness to be carried away, he detected some startling object in the grass. The aged man had fallen forward, and his dead clutch was on the garment of the other. It was not possible to separate them: nay, it was better to put them into the wagon and carry them as they were into the great piazza, that notice might be given to the Eight.

As the wagon entered the frequented streets there was a growing crowd escorting it with its strange burden. No one knew the bodies for a long while, for the aged face had fallen forward, half hiding the younger. But before they had been moved out of sight, they had been recognized.

"I know that old man," Piero di Cosimo had testified. "I painted his likeness once. He is the prisoner who clutched Melema on the steps of the Duomo."

"He is perhaps the same old man who appeared at supper in my gardens," said Bernardo Rucellai, one of the Eight. "I had forgotten him. I thought he had died in prison. But there is no knowing the truth now."

Who shall put his finger on the work of justice, and say, "It is there"? Justice is like the Kingdom of God — it is not without us as a fact, it is within us as a great yearning.

CHAPTER LXVIII.

ROMOLA'S WAKING.

ROMOLA in her boat passed from dreaming into long deep sleep, and then again from deep sleep into busy dreaming, till at last she felt herself stretching out her arms in the court of the Bargello, where the flickering flames of the tapers seemed to get stronger and stronger till the dark scene was blotted out with light. Her eyes opened and she saw it was the light of morning. Her boat was lying still in a little creek; on her right hand lay the speckless sapphire-blue of the Mediterranean; on her left one of those scenes which were and still are repeated again and again like a sweet rhythm, on the shores of that loveliest sea.

In a deep curve of the mountains lay a breadth of green land, curtained by gentle tree-shadowed slopes leaning towards the rocky heights. Up these slopes might be seen here and there, gleaming between the tree-tops, a pathway leading to a little irregular mass of building that seemed to have clambered in a hasty way up the mountain-side, and taken a difficult stand there for the sake of showing the tall belfry as a sight of beauty to the scattered and clustered houses of the village below. The rays of the newly risen sun fell obliquely on the westward horn of this crescent-shaped nook: all else lay in dewy shadow. No sound came across the stillness; the very waters seemed to have curved themselves there for rest.

The delicious sun-rays fell on Romola and thrilled her gently like a caress. She lay motionless, hardly watching the scene; rather, feeling simply the presence of peace and beauty. While we are still in our youth there can always come, in our early waking, moments when mere passive existence is itself a Lethe, when the exquisiteness of subtle indefinite sensation creates a bliss which is without memory and without desire. As the soft warmth penetrated Romola's young limbs, as her eyes rested on this sequestered luxuriance, it seemed that the agitating past had glided away like that dark scene in the Bargello, and that the afternoon dreams of her girlhood had really come back to her. For a minute or two the oblivion was untroubled; she did not even think that she could rest here forever, she only felt that she rested. Then she became distinctly conscious that she was lying in the boat which had been bearing her over the waters all through the night. Instead of bringing her to death, it had been the gently lulling cradle of a new life. And in spite of her evening despair she was glad that the morning had come to her again: glad to think that she was resting in the familiar sunlight rather than in the unknown regions of death. *Could* she not rest here? No sound from Florence would reach her. Already oblivion was troubled; from behind the golden haze were piercing domes and towers and walls, parted by a river and enclosed by the green hills.

She rose from her reclining posture and sat up in the boat, willing, if she could, to resist the rush of thoughts that urged themselves along with the conjecture how far the boat had carried her. Why need she mind? This was a sheltered nook where there were simple villagers who would not harm her. For a little while, at least, she might rest and resolve on nothing. Presently she would go and get some bread and milk, and then she would nestle in the green quiet, and feel that there was a pause in her life. She turned to watch the crescent-shaped valley, that she might get back the soothing sense of peace and beauty which she had felt in her first waking.

She had not been in this attitude of contemplation more than a few minutes when across the stillness there came a piercing cry; not a brief cry, but continuous and more and more intense. Romola felt sure it was the cry of a little child in distress that no one came to help. She started up and put one foot on the side of the boat ready to leap on to the beach; but she paused there and listened: the mother of the child must be near, the cry must soon cease. But it went on, and drew Romola so irresistibly, seeming the more piteous to her for the sense of peace which had preceded it, that she jumped on to the beach and walked many paces before she knew what direction she would take. The cry, she thought, came from some rough garden growth many yards on her right hand, where she saw a half-ruined hovel. She climbed over a low broken stone fence, and made her way across patches of weedy green crops and ripe but neglected corn. The cry grew plainer, and convinced that she was right she hastened towards the hovel; but even in that hurried walk she felt an oppressive change in the air as she left the sea behind. Was there some taint lurking among the green luxuriance that had seemed such an inviting shelter from the heat of the coming day? She could see the opening into the hovel now, and the cry was darting through her like a pain. The next moment her foot was within the doorway, but the sight she beheld in the sombre light arrested her with a shock of awe and horror. On the straw, with which the floor was scattered, lay three dead bodies, one of a tall man, one of a girl about eight years old, and one of a young woman whose long black hair was being clutched and pulled by a living child — the child that was sending forth the piercing cry. Romola's experience in the haunts of death and disease made thought and action prompt: she lifted the little living child, and in trying to soothe it on her bosom, still bent to look at the bodies and see if they were really dead. The strongly marked type of race in their features, and their peculiar garb, made her conjecture that they were Spanish or Portuguese Jews, who had perhaps been put ashore and abandoned there by rapacious sailors, to whom their property remained as a prey. Such things were happening continually to Jews compelled to abandon their homes by the Inquisition: the cruelty of greed thrust them from the sea, and the cruelty of superstition thrust them back to it.

"But, surely," thought Romola, "I shall find some woman in the village whose mother's heart will not let her refuse to tend this helpless child — if the real mother is indeed dead."

This doubt remained, because while the man and girl looked emaciated and also showed signs of having been long dead,

the woman seemed to have been hardier, and had not quite
lost the robustness of her form. Romola, kneeling, was about
to lay her hand on the heart; but as she lifted the piece of
yellow woollen drapery that lay across the bosom, she saw the
purple spots which marked the familiar pestilence. Then it
struck her that if the villagers knew of this, she might have
more difficulty than she had expected in getting help from
them; they would perhaps shrink from her with that child in
her arms. But she had money to offer them, and they would
not refuse to give her some goat's milk in exchange for it.

She set out at once towards the village, her mind filled now
with the effort to soothe the little dark creature, and with
wondering how she should win some woman to be good to it.
She could not help hoping a little in a certain awe she had
observed herself to inspire, when she appeared, unknown and
unexpected, in her religious dress. As she passed across a
breadth of cultivated ground, she noticed, with wonder, that
little patches of corn mingled with the other crops had been
left to over-ripeness untouched by the sickle, and that golden
apples and dark figs lay rotting on the weedy earth. There
were grassy spaces within sight, but no cow, or sheep, or goat.
The stillness began to have something fearful in it to Romola;
she hurried along towards the thickest cluster of houses, where
there would be the most life to appeal to on behalf of the helpless life she carried in her arms. But she had picked up two
figs, and bit little pieces from the sweet pulp to still the child
with.

She entered between two lines of dwellings. It was time
that villagers should have been stirring long ago, but not a
soul was in sight. The air was becoming more and more
oppressive, laden, it seemed, with some horrible impurity.
There was a door open; she looked in, and saw grim empti-
ness. Another open door; and through that she saw a man
lying dead with all his garments on, his head lying athwart a
spade handle, and an earthenware cruse in his hand, as if he
had fallen suddenly.

Romola felt horror taking possession of her. Was she in a
village of the unburied dead? She wanted to listen if there

were any faint sound, but the child cried out afresh when she ceased to feed it, and the cry filled her ears. At last she saw a figure crawling slowly out of a house, and soon sinking back in a sitting posture against the wall. She hastened towards the figure; it was a young woman in fevered anguish, and she, too, held a pitcher in her hand. As Romola approached her she did not start; the one need was too absorbing for any other idea to impress itself on her.

"Water! get me water!" she said, with a moaning utterance.

Romola stooped to take the pitcher, and said gently in her ear, "You shall have water; can you point towards the well?"

The hand was lifted towards the more distant end of the little street, and Romola set off at once with as much speed as she could use under the difficulty of carrying the pitcher as well as feeding the child. But the little one was getting more content as the morsels of sweet pulp were repeated, and ceased to distress her with its cry, so that she could give a less distracted attention to the objects around her.

The well lay twenty yards or more beyond the end of the street, and as Romola was approaching it her eyes were directed to the opposite green slope immediately below the church. High up, on a patch of grass between the trees, she had descried a cow and a couple of goats, and she tried to trace a line of path that would lead her close to that cheering sight, when once she had done her errand to the well. Occupied in this way, she was not aware that she was very near the well, and that some one approaching it on the other side had fixed a pair of astonished eyes upon her.

Romola certainly presented a sight which, at that moment and in that place, could hardly have been seen without some pausing and palpitation. With her gaze fixed intently on the distant slope, the long lines of her thick gray garment giving a gliding character to her rapid walk, her hair rolling backward and illuminated on the left side by the sun-rays, the little olive baby on her right arm now looking out with jet-black eyes, she might well startle that youth of fifteen, accustomed to swing the censer in the presence of a Madonna less fair and marvellous than this.

"She carries a pitcher in her hand — to fetch water for the
sick. It is the Holy Mother, come to take care of the people
who have the pestilence."

It was a sight of awe : she would, perhaps, be angry with
those who fetched water for themselves only. The youth
flung down his vessel in terror, and Romola, aware now of
some one near her, saw the black and white figure fly as if for
dear life towards the slope she had just been contemplating.
But remembering the parched sufferer, she half-filled her
pitcher quickly and hastened back.

Entering the house to look for a small cup, she saw salt
meat and meal : there were no signs of want in the dwelling.
With nimble movement she seated baby on the ground, and
lifted a cup of water to the sufferer, who drank eagerly and
then closed her eyes and leaned her head backward, seeming
to give herself up to the sense of relief. Presently she opened
her eyes, and, looking at Romola, said languidly —

"Who are you ? "

"I came over the sea," said Romola. "I only came this
morning. Are all the people dead in these houses ? "

"I think they are all ill now — all that are not dead. My
father and my sister lie dead up-stairs, and there is no one to
bury them : and soon I shall die."

"Not so, I hope," said Romola. "I am come to take care
of you. I am used to the pestilence ; I am not afraid. But
there must be some left who are not ill. I saw a youth running towards the mountain when I went to the well."

"I cannot tell. When the pestilence came, a great many
people went away, and drove off the cows and goats. Give me
more water ! "

Romola, suspecting that if she followed the direction of the
youth's flight, she should find some men and women who were
still healthy and able, determined to seek them out at once,
that she might at least win them to take care of the child, and
leave her free to come back and see how many living needed
help, and how many dead needed burial. She trusted to her
powers of persuasion to conquer the aid of the timorous, when
once she knew what was to be done.

At the Well.

Promising the sick woman to come back to her, she lifted the dark bantling again, and set off towards the slope. She felt no burden of choice on her now, no longing for death. She was thinking how she would go to the other sufferers, as she had gone to that fevered woman.

But, with the child on her arm, it was not so easy to her as usual to walk up a slope, and it seemed a long while before the winding path took her near the cow and the goats. She was beginning herself to feel faint from heat, hunger, and thirst, and as she reached a double turning, she paused to consider whether she would not wait near the cow, which some one was likely to come and milk soon, rather than toil up to the church before she had taken any rest. Raising her eyes to measure the steep distance, she saw peeping between the boughs, not more than five yards off, a broad round face, watching her attentively, and lower down the black skirt of a priest's garment, and a hand grasping a bucket. She stood mutely observing, and the face, too, remained motionless. Romola had often witnessed the overpowering force of dread in cases of pestilence, and she was cautious.

Raising her voice in a tone of gentle pleading, she said, " I came over the sea. I am hungry, and so is the child. Will you not give us some milk ? "

Romola had divined part of the truth, but she had not divined that preoccupation of the priest's mind which charged her words with a strange significance. Only a little while ago, the young acolyte had brought word to the Padre that he had seen the Holy Mother with the Babe. fetching water for the sick : she was as tall as the cypresses, and had a light about her head, and she looked up at the church. The pievano[1] had not listened with entire belief : he had been more than fifty years in the world without having any vision of the Madonna, and he thought the boy might have misinterpreted the unexpected appearance of a villager. But he had been made uneasy, and before venturing to come down and milk his cow, he had repeated many Aves. The pievano's conscience tormented him a little : he trembled at the pestilence, but he

[1] Parish priest.

also trembled at the thought of the mild-faced Mother, conscious that that Invisible Mercy might demand something more of him than prayers and " Hails." In this state of mind — unable to banish the image the boy had raised of the Mother with the glory about her tending the sick — the pievano had come down to milk his cow, and had suddenly caught sight of Romola pausing at the parted way. Her pleading words, with their strange refinement of tone and accent, instead of being explanatory, had a preternatural sound for him. Yet he did not quite believe he saw the Holy Mother: he was in a state of alarmed hesitation. If anything miraculous were happening, he felt there was no strong presumption that the miracle would be in his favor. He dared not run away ; he dared not advance.

" Come down," said Romola, after a pause. " Do not fear. Fear rather to deny food to the hungry when they ask you."

A moment after, the boughs were parted, and the complete figure of a thick-set priest with a broad, harmless face, his black frock much worn and soiled, stood, bucket in hand, looking at her timidly, and still keeping aloof as he took the path towards the cow in silence.

Romola followed him and watched him without speaking again, as he seated himself against the tethered cow, and, when he had nervously drawn some milk, gave it to her in a brass cup he carried with him in the bucket. As Romola put the cup to the lips of the eager child, and afterwards drank some milk herself, the Padre observed her from his wooden stool with a timidity that changed its character a little. He recognized the Hebrew baby, he was certain that he had a substantial woman before him ; but there was still something strange and unaccountable in Romola's presence in this spot, and the Padre had a presentiment that things were going to change with him. Moreover, that Hebrew baby was terribly associated with the dread of pestilence.

Nevertheless, when Romola smiled at the little one sucking its own milky lips, and stretched out the brass cup again, saying, " Give us more, good father," he obeyed less nervously than before.

Romola on her side was not unobservant; and when the second supply of milk had been drunk, she looked down at the round-headed man, and said with mild decision —

"And now tell me, father, how this pestilence came, and why you let your people die without the sacraments, and lie unburied. For I am come over the sea to help those who are left alive — and you, too, will help them now."

He told her the story of the pestilence: and while he was telling it, the youth, who had fled before, had come peeping and advancing gradually, till at last he stood and watched the scene from behind a neighboring bush.

Three families of Jews, twenty souls in all, had been put ashore many weeks ago, some of them already ill of the pestilence. The villagers, said the priest, had of course refused to give shelter to the miscreants, otherwise than in a distant hovel, and under heaps of straw. But when the strangers had died of the plague, and some of the people had thrown the bodies into the sea, the sea had brought them back again in a great storm, and everybody was smitten with terror. A grave was dug, and the bodies were buried; but then the pestilence attacked the Christians, and the greater number of the villagers went away over the mountain, driving away their few cattle, and carrying provisions. The priest had not fled; he had stayed and prayed for the people, and he had prevailed on the youth Jacopo to stay with him; but he confessed that a mortal terror of the plague had taken hold of him, and he had not dared to go down into the valley.

"You will fear no longer, father," said Romola, in a tone of encouraging authority; "you will come down with me, and we will see who is living, and we will look for the dead to bury them. I have walked about for months where the pestilence was, and see, I am strong. Jacopo will come with us," she added, motioning to the peeping lad, who came slowly from behind his defensive bush, as if invisible threads were dragging him.

"Come, Jacopo," said Romola again, smiling at him, "you will carry the child for me. See! your arms are strong, and I am tired."

That was a dreadful proposal to Jacopo, and to the priest also ; but they were both under a peculiar influence forcing them to obey. The suspicion that Romola was a supernatural form was dissipated, but their minds were filled instead with the more effective sense that she was a human being whom God had sent over the sea to command them.

" Now we will carry down the milk," said Romola, " and see if any one wants it."

So they went all together down the slope, and that morning the sufferers saw help come to them in their despair. There were hardly more than a score alive in the whole valley ; but all of these were comforted, most were saved, and the dead were buried.

In this way days, weeks, and months passed with Romola till the men were digging and sowing again, till the women smiled at her as they carried their great vases on their heads to the well, and the Hebrew baby was a tottering tumbling Christian, Benedetto by name, having been baptized in the church on the mountain-side. But by that time she herself was suffering from the fatigue and languor that must come after a continuous strain on mind and body. She had taken for her dwelling one of the houses abandoned by their owners, standing a little aloof from the village street ; and here on a thick heap of clean straw — a delicious bed for those who do not dream of down — she felt glad to lie still through most of the daylight hours, taken care of along with the little Benedetto by a woman whom the pestilence had widowed.

Every day the Padre and Jacopo and the small flock of surviving villagers paid their visit to this cottage to see the blessed Lady, and to bring her of their best as an offering — honey, fresh cakes, eggs, and polenta. It was a sight they could none of them forget, a sight they all told of in their old age — how the sweet and sainted lady with her fair face, her golden hair, and her brown eyes that had a blessing in them, lay weary with her labors after she had been sent over the sea to help them in their extremity, and how the queer little black Benedetto used to crawl about the straw by her side and want everything that was brought to her, and she always gave him a bit of what she took, and told them if they loved her they must be good to Benedetto.

Many legends were afterwards told in that valley about the blessed Lady who came over the sea, but they were legends by which all who heard might know that in times gone by a woman had done beautiful loving deeds there, rescuing those who were ready to perish.

CHAPTER LXIX.

HOMEWARD.

In those silent wintry hours when Romola lay resting from her weariness, her mind, travelling back over the past, and gazing across the undefined distance of the future, saw all objects from a new position. Her experience since the moment of her waking in the boat had come to her with as strong an effect as that of the fresh seal on the dissolving wax. She had felt herself without bonds, without motive; sinking in mere egoistic complaining that life could bring her no content; feeling a right to say, "I am tired of life, I want to die." That thought had sobbed within her as she fell asleep, but from the moment after her waking when the cry had drawn her, she had not even reflected, as she used to do in Florence, that she was glad to live because she could lighten sorrow — she had simply lived, with so energetic an impulse to share the life around her, to answer the call of need and do the work which cried aloud to be done, that the reasons for living, enduring, laboring, never took the form of argument.

The experience was like a new baptism to Romola. In Florence the simpler relations of the human being to his fellow-men had been complicated for her with all the special ties of marriage, the State, and religious discipleship, and when these had disappointed her trust, the shock seemed to have shaken her aloof from life and stunned her sympathy. But now she said, "It was mere baseness in me to desire death. If everything else is doubtful, this suffering that I can help is certain; if the glory of the cross is an illusion, the sorrow is only the truer. While the strength is in my arm I will stretch it out to the fainting; while the light visits my eyes they shall seek the forsaken."

And then the past arose with a fresh appeal to her. Her work in this green valley was done, and the emotions that were disengaged from the people immediately around her rushed back into the old deep channels of use and affection. That rare possibility of self-contemplation which comes in any complete severance from our wonted life made her judge herself as she had never done before: the compunction which is inseparable from a sympathetic nature keenly alive to the possible experience of others, began to stir in her with growing force. She questioned the justness of her own conclusions, of her own deeds: she had been rash, arrogant, always dissatisfied that others were not good enough, while she herself had not been true to what her soul had once recognized as the best. She began to condemn her flight: after all, it had been cowardly self-care; the grounds on which Savonarola had once taken her back were truer, deeper than the grounds she had had for her second flight. How could she feel the needs of others and not feel, above all, the needs of the nearest?

But then came reaction against such self-reproach. The memory of her life with Tito, of the conditions which made their real union impossible, while their external union imposed a set of false duties on her which were essentially the concealment and sanctioning of what her mind revolted from, told her that flight had been her only resource. All minds, except such as are delivered from doubt by dulness of sensibility, must be subject to this recurring conflict where the many-twisted conditions of life have forbidden the fulfilment of a bond. For in strictness there is no replacing of relations: the presence of the new does not nullify the failure and breach of the old. Life has lost its perfection: it has been maimed; and until the wounds are quite scarred, conscience continually casts backward, doubting glances.

Romola shrank with dread from the renewal of her prox-
imity to Tito, and yet she was uneasy that she had put herself out of reach of knowing what was his fate — uneasy that
the moment might yet come when he would be in misery and
need her. There was still a thread of pain within her, testi-
fying to those words of Fra Girolamo, that she could not
cease to be a wife. Could anything utterly cease for her that
had once mingled itself with the current of her heart's
blood ?

Florence, and all her life there, had come back to her like
hunger; her feelings could not go wandering after the possible and the vague : their living fibre was fed with the memory
of familiar things. And the thought that she had divided
herself from them forever became more and more importunate
in these hours that were unfilled with action. What if Fra
Girolamo had been wrong ? What if the life of Florence was
a web of inconsistencies? Was she, then, something higher,
that she should shake the dust from off her feet, and say,
" This world is not good enough for me " ? If she had been
really higher, she would not so easily have lost all her trust.

Her indignant grief for her godfather had no longer complete possession of her, and her sense of debt to Savonarola
was recovering predominance. Nothing that had come, or
was to come, could do away with the fact that there had been
a great inspiration in him which had waked a new life in
her. Who, in all her experience, could demand the same
gratitude from her as he ? His errors — might they not bring
calamities ?

She could not rest. She hardly knew whether it was her
strength returning with the budding leaves that made her
active again, or whether it was her eager longing to get nearer
Florence. She did not imagine herself daring to enter Florence,
but the desire to be near enough to learn what was happening there urged itself with a strength that excluded all other
purposes.

And one March morning the people in the valley were gathered together to see the blessed Lady depart. Jacopo had
fetched a mule for her, and was going with her over the

mountains. The Padre, too, was going with her to the nearest town, that he might help her in learning the safest way by which she might get to Pistoja. Her store of trinkets and money, untouched in this valley, was abundant for her needs.

If Romola had been less drawn by the longing that was taking her away, it would have been a hard moment for her when she walked along the village street for the last time, while the Padre and Jacopo, with the mule, were awaiting her near the well. Her steps were hindered by the wailing people, who knelt and kissed her hands, then clung to her skirts and kissed the gray folds, crying, "Ah, why will you go, when the good season is beginning and the crops will be plentiful? Why will you go?"

"Do not be sorry," said Romola, "you are well now, and I shall remember you. I must go and see if my own people want me."

"Ah, yes, if they have the pestilence!"

"Look at us again, Madonna!"

"Yes, yes, we will be good to the little Benedetto!"

At last Romola mounted her mule, but a vigorous screaming from Benedetto as he saw her turn from him in this new position, was an excuse for all the people to follow her and insist that he must ride on the mule's neck to the foot of the slope.

The parting must come at last, but as Romola turned continually before she passed out of sight, she saw the little flock lingering to catch the last waving of her hand.

CHAPTER LXX.

MEETING AGAIN.

On the 14th of April Romola was once more within the walls of Florence. Unable to rest at Pistoja, where contradictory reports reached her about the Trial by Fire, she had

gone on to Prato; and was beginning to think that she should
be drawn on to Florence in spite of dread, when she encountered that monk of San Spirito who had been her godfather's
confessor. From him she learned the full story of Savonarola's
arrest, and of her husband's death. This Augustinian monk
had been in the stream of people who had followed the wagon
with its awful burthen into the piazza, and he could tell her
what was generally known in Florence — that Tito had escaped
from an assaulting mob by leaping into the Arno, but had been
murdered on the bank by an old man who had long had an
enmity against him. But Romola understood the catastrophe
as no one else did. Of Savonarola the monk told her, in that
tone of unfavorable prejudice which was usual in the Black
Brethren (Frati Neri) towards the brother who showed white
under his black, that he had confessed himself a deceiver of
the people.

Romola paused no longer. That evening she was in Florence, sitting in agitated silence under the exclamations of joy
and wailing, mingled with exuberant narrative, which were
poured into her ears by Monna Brigida, who had backslided
into false hair in Romola's absence, but now drew it off again
and declared she would not mind being gray, if her dear child
would stay with her.

Romola was too deeply moved by the main events which
she had known before coming to Florence, to be wrought upon
by the doubtful gossiping details added in Brigida's narrative.
The tragedy of her husband's death, of Fra Girolamo's confession of duplicity under the coercion of torture, left her hardly
any power of apprehending minor circumstances. All the
mental activity she could exert under that load of awe-stricken
grief, was absorbed by two purposes which must supersede
every other; to try and see Savonarola, and to learn what had
become of Tessa and the children.

"Tell me, cousin," she said abruptly, when Monna Brigida's tongue had run quite away from troubles into projects
of Romola's living with her, "has anything been seen or
said since Tito's death of a young woman with two little
children ?"

Brigida started, rounded her eyes, and lifted up her hands.

"Cristo! no. What! was he so bad as that, my poor child?
Ah, then, that was why you went away, and left me word only
that you went of your own free will. Well, well; if I'd
known that, I should n't have thought you so strange and
flighty. For I did say to myself, though I did n't tell anybody else, 'What was she to go away from her husband for,
leaving him to mischief, only because they cut poor Bernardo's
head off? She's got her father's temper,' I said, 'that's
what it is.' Well, well; never scold me, child: Bardo *was*
fierce, you can't deny it. But if you had only told me the
truth, that there was a young hussy and children, I should
have understood it all. Anything seen or said of her? No;
and the less the better. They say enough of ill about him
without that. But since that was the reason you went — "

"No, dear cousin," said Romola, interrupting her earnestly,
"pray do not talk so. I wish above all things to find that
young woman and her children, and to take care of them.
They are quite helpless. Say nothing against it; that is the
thing I shall do first of all."

"Well," said Monna Brigida, shrugging her shoulders and
lowering her voice with an air of puzzled discomfiture, "if
that's being a Piagnone, I've been taking peas for pater-
nosters. Why, Fra Girolamo said as good as that widows
ought not to marry again. Step in at the door and it's a sin
and a shame, it seems; but come down the chimney and you're
welcome. *Two* children — Santiddio!"

"Cousin, the poor thing has done no conscious wrong: she
is ignorant of everything. I will tell you — but not now."

Early the next morning Romola's steps were directed to
the house beyond San Ambrogio where she had once found
Tessa; but it was as she had feared: Tessa was gone. Romola conjectured that Tito had sent her away beforehand to
some spot where he had intended to join her, for she did not
believe that he would willingly part with those children. It
was a painful conjecture, because, if Tessa were out of Florence, there was hardly a chance of finding her, and Romola
pictured the childish creature waiting and waiting at some

wayside spot in wondering, helpless misery. Those who lived near could tell her nothing except that old deaf Lisa had gone away a week ago with her goods, but no one knew where Tessa had gone. Romola saw no further active search open to her; for she had no knowledge that could serve as a starting-point for inquiry, and not only her innate reserve but a more noble sensitiveness made her shrink from assuming an attitude of generosity in the eyes of others by publishing Tessa's relation to Tito, along with her own desire to find her. Many days passed in anxious inaction. Even under strong solicitation from other thoughts Romola found her heart palpitating if she caught sight of a pair of round brown legs, or of a short woman in the contadina dress.

She never for a moment told herself that it was heroism or exalted charity in her to seek these beings; she needed something that she was bound specially to care for; she yearned to clasp the children and to make them love her. This at least would be some sweet result, for others as well as herself, from all her past sorrow. It appeared there was much property of Tito's to which she had a claim; but she distrusted the cleanness of that money, and she had determined to make it all over to the State, except so much as was equal to the price of her father's library. This would be enough for the modest support of Tessa and the children. But Monna Brigida threw such planning into the background by clamorously insisting that Romola must live with her and never forsake her till she had seen her safe in Paradise — else why had she persuaded her to turn Piagnone? — and if Romola wanted to rear other people's children, she, Monna Brigida, must rear them too. Only they must be found first.

Romola felt the full force of that innuendo. But strong feeling unsatisfied is never without its superstition, either of hope or despair. Romola's was the superstition of hope: *somehow* she was to find that mother and the children. And at last another direction for active inquiry suggested itself. She learned that Tito had provided horses and mules to await him in San Gallo; he was therefore going to leave Florence by the gate of San Gallo, and she determined, though without

much confidence in the issue, to try and ascertain from the
gatekeepers if they had observed any one corresponding to the
description of Tessa, with her children, to have passed the gates
before the morning of the 9th of April. Walking along the
Via San Gallo, and looking watchfully about her through her
long widow's veil, lest she should miss any object that might
aid her, she descried Bratti chaffering with a customer. That
roaming man, she thought, might aid her : she would not mind
talking of Tessa to *him*. But as she put aside her veil and
crossed the street towards him, she saw something hanging
from the corner of his basket which made her heart leap with
a much stronger hope.

"Bratti, my friend," she said abruptly, "where did you get
that necklace ? "

"Your servant, Madonna," said Bratti, looking round at her
very deliberately, his mind not being subject to surprise.
"It's a necklace worth money, but I shall get little by it, for
my heart's too tender for a trader's ; I have promised to keep
it in pledge."

"Pray tell me where you got it ; — from a little woman
named Tessa, is it not true ? "

"Ah ! if you know her," said Bratti, "and would redeem it
of me at a small profit, and give it her again, you'd be doing
a charity, for she cried at parting with it — you'd have thought
she was running into a brook. It's a small profit I'll charge
you. You shall have it for a florin, for I don't like to be
hard-hearted."

"Where is she ? " said Romola, giving him the money, and
unclasping the necklace from the basket in joyful agitation.

"Outside the gate there, at the other end of the Borgo,
at old Sibilla Manetti's : anybody will tell you which is the
house."

Romola went along with winged feet, blessing that incident
of the Carnival which had made her learn by heart the appearance of this necklace. Soon she was at the house she sought.
The young woman and the children were in the inner room —
were to have been fetched away a fortnight ago and more —
had no money, only their clothes, to pay a poor widow with

for their food and lodging. But since Madonna knew them —
Romola waited to hear no more, but opened the door.

Tessa was seated on the low bed: her crying had passed into
tearless sobs, and she was looking with sad blank eyes at the
two children, who were playing in an opposite corner — Lillo
covering his head with his skirt and roaring at Ninna to
frighten her, then peeping out again to see how she bore it.
The door was a little behind Tessa, and she did not turn round
when it opened, thinking it was only the old woman: expectation was no longer alive. Romola had thrown aside her veil
and paused a moment, holding the necklace in sight. Then
she said, in that pure voice that used to cheer her father —

" Tessa ! "

Tessa started to her feet and looked round.

" See," said Romola, clasping the beads on Tessa's neck,
" God has sent me to you again."

The poor thing screamed and sobbed, and clung to the arms
that fastened the necklace. She could not speak. The two
children came from their corner, laid hold of their mother's
skirts, and looked up with wide eyes at Romola.

That day they all went home to Monna Brigida's, in the
Borgo degli Albizzi. Romola had made known to Tessa by
gentle degrees, that Naldo could never come to her again: not
because he was cruel, but because he was dead.

" But be comforted, my Tessa," said Romola. " I am come
to take care of you always. And we have got Lillo and
Ninna."

Monna Brigida's mouth twitched in the struggle between her
awe of Romola and the desire to speak unseasonably.

" Let be, for the present," she thought; " but it seems to me
a thousand years till I tell this little contadina, who seems not
to know how many fingers she's got on her hand, who Romola
is. And I *will* tell her some day, else she 'll never know her
place. It 's all very well for Romola; — nobody will call their
souls their own when she 's by; but if I 'm to have this puss-
faced minx living in my house she must be humble to me."

However, Monna Brigida wanted to give the children too
many sweets for their supper, and confessed to Romola, the

last thing before going to bed, that it would be a shame not to take care of such cherubs.

"But you must give up to me a little, Romola, about their eating, and those things. For you have never had a baby, and I had twins, only they died as soon as they were born."

———•———

CHAPTER LXXI.

THE CONFESSION.

When Romola brought home Tessa and the children, April was already near its close, and the other great anxiety on her mind had been wrought to its highest pitch by the publication in print of Fra Girolamo's Trial, or rather of the confessions drawn from him by the sixteen Florentine citizens commissioned to interrogate him. The appearance of this document, issued by order of the Signoria, had called forth such strong expressions of public suspicion and discontent, that severe measures were immediately taken for recalling it. Of course there were copies accidentally mislaid, and a second edition, *not* by order of the Signoria, was soon in the hands of eager readers.

Romola, who began to despair of ever speaking with Fra Girolamo, read this evidence again and again, desiring to judge it by some clearer light than the contradictory impressions that were taking the form of assertions in the mouths of both partisans and enemies.

In the more devout followers of Savonarola his want of constancy under torture, and his retractation of prophetic claims, had produced a consternation too profound to be at once displaced as it ultimately was by the suspicion, which soon grew into a positive datum, that any reported words of his which were in inexplicable contradiction to their faith in him, had not come from the lips of the prophet, but from the falsifying pen of Ser Ceccone, that notary of evil repute, who had made the digest of the examination. But there were obvious facts that at once threw discredit on the printed document. Was not the list of sixteen examiners half made up of the prophet's bitterest enemies? Was not the notorious Dolfo Spini one of the new Eight prematurely elected, in order to load the dice against a man whose ruin had been determined on by the party in power? It was but a murder with slow formalities that was being transacted in the Old Palace. The Signoria had resolved to drive a good bargain with the Pope and the Duke of Milan, by extinguishing the man who was as great a molestation to vicious citizens and greedy foreign tyrants as to a corrupt clergy. The Frate had been doomed beforehand, and the only question that was pretended to exist now was, whether the Republic, in return for a permission to lay a tax on ecclesiastical property, should deliver him alive into the hands of the Pope, or whether the Pope should further concede to the Republic what its dignity demanded — the privilege of hanging and burning its own prophet on its own piazza.

Who, under such circumstances, would give full credit to this so-called confession? If the Frate had denied his prophetic gift, the denial had only been wrenched from him by the agony of torture — agony that, in his sensitive frame, must quickly produce raving. What if these wicked examiners declared that he had only had the torture of the rope and pulley thrice, and only on one day, and that his confessions had been made when he was under no bodily coercion — was that to be believed? He had been tortured much more; he had been tortured in proportion to the distress his confessions had created in the hearts of those who loved him.

Other friends of Savonarola, who were less ardent partisans, did not doubt the substantial genuineness of the confession, however it might have been colored by the transpositions and additions of the notary; but they argued indignantly that there was nothing which could warrant a condemnation to death, or even to grave punishment. It must be clear to all impartial men that if this examination represented the only evidence against the Frate, he would die, not for any crime,

but because he had made himself inconvenient to the Pope, to
the rapacious Italian States that wanted to dismember their
Tuscan neighbor, and to those unworthy citizens who sought
to gratify their private ambition in opposition to the common
weal.

Not a shadow of political crime had been proved against him.
Not one stain had been detected on his private conduct: his
fellow-monks, including one who had formerly been his secretary for several years, and who, with more than the average
culture of his companions, had a disposition to criticise Fra
Girolamo's rule as Prior, bore testimony, even after the shock
of his retractation, to an unimpeachable purity and consistency
in his life, which had commanded their unsuspecting venera-
tion. The Pope himself had not been able to raise a charge of
heresy against the Frate, except on the ground of disobedience
to a mandate, and disregard of the sentence of excommunication. It was difficult to justify that breach of discipline by
argument, but there was a moral insurgence in the minds of
grave men against the Court of Rome, which tended to confound the theoretic distinction between the Church and
churchmen, and to lighten the scandal of disobedience.

Men of ordinary morality and public spirit felt that the
triumph of the Frate's enemies was really the triumph of
gross license. And keen Florentines like Soderini and Piero
Guicciardini may well have had an angry smile on their lips
at a severity which dispensed with all law in order to hang
and burn a man in whom the seductions of a public career
had warped the strictness of his veracity; may well have
remarked that if the Frate had mixed a much deeper fraud
with a zeal and ability less inconvenient to high personages,
the fraud would have been regarded as an excellent oil for
ecclesiastical and political wheels.

Nevertheless such shrewd men were forced to admit that,
however poor a figure the Florentine government made in its
clumsy pretence of a judicial warrant for what had in fact
been predetermined as an act of policy, the measures of the
Pope against Savonarola were necessary measures of self-
defence. Not to try and rid himself of a man who wanted to

stir up the Powers of Europe to summon a General Council and depose him, would have been adding ineptitude to iniquity. There was no denying that towards Alexander the Sixth Savonarola was a rebel, and, what was much more, a dangerous rebel. Florence had heard him say, and had well understood what he meant, that he would not *obey the devil*. It was inevitably a life-and-death struggle between the Frate and the Pope; but it was less inevitable that Florence should make itself the Pope's executioner.

Romola's ears were filled in this way with the suggestions of a faith still ardent under its wounds, and the suggestions of worldly discernment, judging things according to a very moderate standard of what is possible to human nature. She could be satisfied with neither. She brought to her long meditations over that printed document many painful observations, registered more or less consciously through the years of her discipleship, which whispered a presentiment that Savonarola's retractation of his prophetic claims was not merely a spasmodic effort to escape from torture. But, on the other hand, her soul cried out for some explanation of his lapses which would make it still possible for her to believe that the main striving of his life had been pure and grand. The recent memory of the selfish discontent which had come over her like a blighting wind along with the loss of her trust in the man who had been for her an incarnation of the highest motives, had produced a reaction which is known to many as a sort of faith that has sprung up to them out of the very depths of their despair. It was impossible, she said now, that the negative disbelieving thoughts which had made her soul arid of all good, could be founded in the truth of things: impossible that it had not been a living spirit, and no hollow pretence, which had once breathed in the Frate's words, and kindled a new life in her. Whatever falsehood there had been in him, had been a fall and not a purpose; a gradual entanglement in which he struggled, not a contrivance encouraged by success.

Looking at the printed confessions, she saw many sentences which bore the stamp of bungling fabrication: they had that emphasis and repetition in self-accusation which none but **very**

low hypocrites use to their fellow-men. But the fact that
these sentences were in striking opposition, not only to the
character of Savonarola, but also to the general tone of the confessions, strengthened the impression that the rest of the text
represented in the main what had really fallen from his lips
Hardly a word was dishonorable to him except what turned
on his prophetic annunciations. He was unvarying in his
statement of the ends he had pursued for Florence, the Church,
and the world; and, apart from the mixture of falsity in that
claim to special inspiration by which he sought to gain hold
of men's minds, there was no admission of having used unworthy means. Even in this confession, and without expur-
gation of the notary's malign phrases, Fra Girolamo shone
forth as a man who had sought his own glory indeed, but
sought it by laboring for the very highest end — the moral
welfare of men — not by vague exhortations, but by striving
to turn beliefs into energies that would work in all the details
of life.

"Everything that I have done," said one memorable passage,
which may perhaps have had its erasures and interpolations,
"I have done with the design of being forever famous in the
present and in future ages; and that I might win credit in
Florence; and that nothing of great import should be done
without my sanction. And when I had thus established my
position in Florence, I had it in my mind to do great things in
Italy and beyond Italy, by means of those chief personages
with whom I had contracted friendship and consulted on high
matters, such as this of the General Council. And in proportion as my first efforts succeeded, I should have adopted
further measures. Above all, when the General Council had
once been brought about, I intended to rouse the princes of
Christendom, and especially those beyond the borders of Italy,
to subdue the infidels. It was not much in my thoughts to
get myself made a Cardinal or Pope, for when I should have
achieved the work I had in view, I should, without being
Pope, have been the first man in the world in the authority I
should have possessed, and the reverence that would have
been paid me. If I had been made Pope, I would not have

refused the office : but it seemed to me that to be the head of that work was a greater thing than to be Pope, because a man without virtue may be Pope ; but *such a work as I contemplated demanded a man of excellent virtues."*

That blending of ambition with belief in the supremacy of goodness made no new tone to Romola, who had been used to hear it in the voice that rang through the Duomo. It was the habit of Savonarola's mind to conceive great things, and to feel that he was the man to do them. Iniquity should be brought low ; the cause of justice, purity, and love should triumph ; and it should triumph by his voice, by his work, by his blood. In moments of ecstatic contemplation, doubtless, the sense of self melted in the sense of the Unspeakable, and in that part of his experience lay the elements of genuine self-abasement ; but in the presence of his fellow-men for whom he was to act, pre-eminence seemed a necessary condition of his life.

And perhaps this confession, even when it described a doubleness that was conscious and deliberate, really implied no more than that wavering of belief concerning his own impressions and motives which most human beings who have not a stupid inflexibility of self-confidence must be liable to under a marked change of external conditions. In a life where the experience was so tumultuously mixed as it must have been in the Frate's, what a possibility was opened for a change of self-judgment, when, instead of eyes that venerated and knees that knelt, instead of a great work on its way to accomplishment, and in its prosperity stamping the agent as a chosen instrument, there came the hooting and the spitting and the curses of the crowd ; and then the hard faces of enemies made judges ; and then the horrible torture, and with the torture the irrepressible cry, " It is true, what you would have me say : let me go : do not torture me again : yes, yes, I am guilty. O God ! Thy stroke has reached me ! "

As Romola thought of the anguish that must have followed the confession — whether, in the subsequent solitude of the prison, conscience retracted or confirmed the self-taxing words — that anguish seemed to be pressing on her own heart and urging the slow bitter tears. Every vulgar self-ignorant person in Florence was glibly pronouncing on this man's demerits, while *he* was knowing a depth of sorrow which can only be known to the soul that has loved and sought the most perfect thing, and beholds itself fallen.

She had not then seen — what she saw afterwards — the evidence of the Frate's mental state after he had had thus to lay his mouth in the dust. As the days went by, the reports of new unpublished examinations, eliciting no change of confessions, ceased; Savonarola was left alone in his prison and allowed pen and ink for a while, that, if he liked, he might use his poor bruised and strained right arm to write with. He wrote; but what he wrote was no vindication of his innocence, no protest against the proceedings used towards him: it was a continued colloquy with that divine purity with which he sought complete reunion; it was the outpouring of self-abasement; it was one long cry for inward renovation. No lingering echoes of the old vehement self-assertion, " Look at my work, for it is good, and those who set their faces against it are the children of the devil! " The voice of Sadness tells him, "God placed thee in the midst of the people even as if thou hadst been one of the excellent. In this way thou hast taught others, and hast failed to learn thyself. Thou hast cured others: and thou thyself hast been still diseased. Thy heart was lifted up at the beauty of thy own deeds, and through this thou hast lost thy wisdom and art become, and shalt be to all eternity, nothing. . . . After so many benefits with which God has honored thee, thou art fallen into the depths of the sea; and after so many gifts bestowed on thee, thou, by thy pride and vainglory, hast scandalized all the world." And when Hope speaks and argues that the divine love has not forsaken him, it says nothing now of a great work to be done, but only says, " Thou art not forsaken, else why is thy heart bowed in penitence? That too is a gift."

There is no jot of worthy evidence that from the time of his imprisonment to the supreme moment, Savonarola thought or spoke of himself as a martyr. The idea of martyrdom had been to him a passion dividing the dream of the future with the triumph of beholding his work achieved. And now, in place of both, had come a resignation which he called by no glorifying name.

But therefore he may the more fitly be called a martyr by his fellow-men to all time. For power rose against him not because of his sins, but because of his greatness — not because he sought to deceive the world, but because he sought to make it noble. And through that greatness of his he endured a double agony : not only the reviling, and the torture, and the death-throe, but the agony of sinking from the vision of glorious achievement into that deep shadow where he could only say, "I count as nothing : darkness encompasses me : yet the light I saw was the true light."

CHAPTER LXXII.

THE LAST SILENCE.

ROMOLA had seemed to hear, as if they had been a cry, the words repeated to her by many lips — the words uttered by Savonarola when he took leave of those brethren of San Marco who had come to witness his signature of the confession : "Pray for me, for God has withdrawn from me the spirit of prophecy."

Those words had shaken her with new doubts as to the mode in which he looked back at the past in moments of complete self-possession. And the doubts were strengthened by more piteous things still, which soon reached her ears.

The 19th of May had come, and by that day's sunshine there had entered into Florence the two Papal Commissaries, charged with the completion of Savonarola's trial. They entered amid the acclamations of the people, calling for the death of the Frate. For now the popular cry was, "It is the Frate's deception that has brought on all our misfortunes ; let him be burned, and all things right will be done, and our evils will cease."

The next day it is well certified that there was fresh and
fresh torture of the shattered sensitive frame; and now, at
the first sight of the horrible implements, Savonarola, in convulsed agitation, fell on his knees, and in brief passionate
words *retracted his confession*, declared that he had spoken
falsely in denying his prophetic gift, and that if he suffered,
he would suffer for the truth — "The things that I have
spoken, I had them from God."

But not the less the torture was laid upon him, and when
he was under it he was asked why he had uttered those
retracting words. Men were not demons in those days, and
yet nothing but confessions of guilt were held a reason for
release from torture. The answer came: "I said it that I
might seem good: tear me no more, I will tell you the
truth."

There were Florentine assessors at this new trial, and those
words of twofold retractation had soon spread. They filled
Romola with dismayed uncertainty.

"But" — it flashed across her — "there will come a moment
when he may speak. When there is no dread hanging over
him but the dread of falsehood, when they have brought him
into the presence of death, when he is lifted above the people,
and looks on them for the last time, they cannot hinder him
from speaking a last decisive word. I will be there."

Three days after, on the 23d of May, 1498, there was again
a long narrow platform stretching across the great piazza,
from the Palazzo Vecchio towards the Tetta de' Pisani. But
there was no grove of fuel as before: instead of that, there
was one great heap of fuel placed on the circular area which
made the termination of the long narrow platform. And
above this heap of fuel rose a gibbet with three halters on it;
a gibbet which, having two arms, still looked so much like a
cross as to make some beholders uncomfortable, though one
arm had been truncated to avoid the resemblance.

On the marble terrace of the Palazzo were three tribunals;
one near the door for the Bishop, who was to perform the ceremony of degradation on Fra Girolamo and the two brethren
who were to suffer as his followers and accomplices; another

for the Papal Commissaries, who were to pronounce them heretics and schismatics, and deliver them over to the secular arm; and a third, close to Marzocco, at the corner of the terrace where the platform began, for the Gonfaloniere, and the Eight who were to pronounce the sentence of death.

Again the piazza was thronged with expectant faces: again there was to be a great fire kindled. In the majority of the crowd that pressed around the gibbet the expectation was that of ferocious hatred, or of mere hard curiosity to behold a barbarous sight. But there were still many spectators on the wide pavement, on the roofs, and at the windows, who, in the midst of their bitter grief and their own endurance of insult as hypocritical Piagnoni, were not without a lingering hope, even at this eleventh hour, that God would interpose, by some sign, to manifest their beloved prophet as His servant. And there were yet more who looked forward with trembling eagerness, as Romola did, to that final moment when Savonarola might say, "O people, I was innocent of deceit."

Romola was at a window on the north side of the piazza, far away from the marble terrace where the tribunals stood; and near her, also looking on in painful doubt concerning the man who had won his early reverence, was a young Florentine of two-and-twenty, named Jacopo Nardi, afterwards to deserve honor as one of the very few who, feeling Fra Girolamo's eminence, have written about him with the simple desire to be veracious. He had said to Romola, with respectful gentleness, when he saw the struggle in her between her shuddering horror of the scene and her yearning to witness what might happen in the last moment —

"Madonna, there is no need for you to look at these cruel things. I will tell you when he comes out of the Palazzo. Trust to me; I know what you would see."

Romola covered her face, but the hootings that seemed to make the hideous scene still visible could not be shut out. At last her arm was touched, and she heard the words, "He comes." She looked towards the Palace, and could see Savonarola led out in his Dominican garb; could see him standing before the Bishop, and being stripped of the black mantle, the white scapulary and long white tunic, till he stood in a close woollen under-tunic, that told of no sacred office, no rank. He had been degraded, and cut off from the Church Militant.

The baser part of the multitude delight in degradations, apart from any hatred; it is the satire they best understand. There was a fresh hoot of triumph as the three degraded brethren passed on to the tribunal of the Papal Commissaries, who were to pronounce them schismatics and heretics. Did not the prophet look like a schismatic and heretic now? It is easy to believe in the damnable state of a man who stands stripped and degraded.

Then the third tribunal was passed — that of the Florentine officials who were to pronounce sentence, and among whom, even at her distance, Romola could discern the odious figure of Dolfo Spini, indued in the grave black lucco, as one of the Eight.

Then the three figures, in their close white raiment, trod their way along the platform, amidst yells and grating tones of insult.

"Cover your eyes, Madonna," said Jacopo Nardi; "Fra Girolamo will be the last."

It was not long before she had to uncover them again. Savonarola was there. He was not far off her now. He had mounted the steps; she could see him look round on the multitude.

But in the same moment expectation died, and she only saw what he was seeing — torches waving to kindle the fuel beneath his dead body, faces glaring with a yet worse light; she only heard what *he* was hearing — gross jests, taunts, and curses.

The moment was past. Her face was covered again, and she only knew that Savonarola's voice had passed into eternal silence.

EPILOGUE.

On the evening of the 22d of May, 1509, five persons, of whose history we have known something, were seated in a handsome upper room opening on to a loggia which, at its right-hand corner, looked all along the Borgo Pinti, and over the city gate towards Fiesole, and the solemn heights beyond it.

At one end of the room was an archway opening into a narrow inner room, hardly more than a recess, where the light fell from above on a small altar covered with fair white linen. Over the altar was a picture, discernible at the distance where the little party sat only as the small full-length portrait of a Dominican Brother. For it was shaded from the light above by overhanging branches and wreaths of flowers, and the fresh tapers below it were unlit. But it seemed that the decoration of the altar and its recess was not complete. For part of the floor was strewn with a confusion of flowers and green boughs, and among them sat a delicate blue-eyed girl of thirteen, tossing her long light-brown hair out of her eyes, as she made selections for the wreaths she was weaving, or looked up at her mother's work in the same kind, and told her how to do it with a little air of instruction.

For that mother was not very clever at weaving flowers or at any other work. Tessa's fingers had not become more adroit with the years — only very much fatter. She got on slowly and turned her head about a good deal, and asked Ninna's opinion with much deference; for Tessa never ceased to be astonished at the wisdom of her children. She still wore her contadina gown: it was only broader than the old one; and there was the silver pin in her rough curly brown hair, and round her neck the memorable necklace, with a red cord under it, that ended mysteriously in her bosom. Her

rounded face wore even a more perfect look of childish content than in her younger days: everybody was so good in the
world, Tessa thought; even Monna Brigida never found fault
with her now, and did little else than sleep, which was an
amiable practice in everybody, and one that Tessa liked for
herself.

Monna Brigida was asleep at this moment, in a straight-
backed arm-chair, a couple of yards off. Her hair, parting
backward under her black hood, had that soft whiteness which
is not like snow or anything else, but is simply the lovely
whiteness of aged hair. Her chin had sunk on her bosom, and
her hands rested on the elbow of her chair. She had not been
weaving flowers or doing anything else: she had only been
looking on as usual, and as usual had fallen asleep.

The other two figures were seated farther off, at the wide
doorway that opened on to the loggia. Lillo sat on the ground
with his back against the angle of the door-post, and his long
legs stretched out, while he held a large book open on his
knee, and occasionally made a dash with his hand at an inquisitive fly, with an air of interest stronger than that excited
by the finely-printed copy of Petrarch which he kept open at
one place, as if he were learning something by heart.

Romola sat nearly opposite Lillo, but she was not observing
him. Her hands were crossed on her lap and her eyes were
fixed absently on the distant mountains: she was evidently
unconscious of anything around her. An eager life had left
its marks upon her: the finely-moulded cheek had sunk a
little, the golden crown was less massive; but there was a
placidity in Romola's face which had never belonged to it in
youth. It is but once that we can know our worst sorrows,
and Romola had known them while life was new.

Absorbed in this way, she was not at first aware that Lillo
had ceased to look at his book, and was watching her with a
slightly impatient air, which meant that he wanted to talk to
her, but was not quite sure whether she would like that entertainment just now. But persevering looks make themselves
felt at last. Romola did presently turn away her eyes from
the distance and met Lillo's impatient dark gaze with a brighter

and brighter smile. He shuffled along the floor, still keeping the book on his lap, till he got close to her and lodged his chin on her knee.

"What is it, Lillo?" said Romola, pulling his hair back from his brow. Lillo was a handsome lad, but his features were turning out to be more massive and less regular than his father's. The blood of the Tuscan peasant was in his veins.

"Mamma Romola, what am I to be?" he said, well contented that there was a prospect of talking till it would be too late to con "Spirto gentil" any longer.

"What should you like to be, Lillo? You might be a scholar. My father was a scholar, you know, and taught me a great deal. That is the reason why I can teach you."

"Yes," said Lillo, rather hesitatingly. "But he is old and blind in the picture. Did he get a great deal of glory?"

"Not much, Lillo. The world was not always very kind to him, and he saw meaner men than himself put into higher places, because they could flatter and say what was false. And then his dear son thought it right to leave him and become a monk; and after that, my father, being blind and lonely, felt unable to do the things that would have made his learning of greater use to men, so that he might still have lived in his works after he was in his grave."

"I should not like that sort of life," said Lillo. "I should like to be something that would make me a great man, and very happy besides — something that would not hinder me from having a good deal of pleasure."

"That is not easy, my Lillo. It is only a poor sort of happiness that could ever come by caring very much about our own narrow pleasures. We can only have the highest happiness, such as goes along with being a great man, by having wide thoughts, and much feeling for the rest of the world as well as ourselves; and this sort of happiness often brings so much pain with it, that we can only tell it from pain by its being what we would choose before everything else, because our souls see it is good. There are so many things wrong and difficult in the world, that no man can be great — he can hardly keep himself from wickedness — unless he gives up thinking much about pleasure or rewards, and gets strength to endure what is hard and painful. My father had the greatness that belongs to integrity; he chose poverty and obscurity rather than falsehood. And there was Fra Girolamo — you know why I keep to-morrow sacred: *he* had the greatness which belongs to a life spent in struggling against powerful wrong, and in trying to raise men to the highest deeds they are capable of. And so, my Lillo, if you mean to act nobly and seek to know the best things God has put within reach of men, you must learn to fix your mind on that end, and not on what will happen to you because of it. And remember, if you were to choose something lower, and make it the rule of your life to seek your own pleasure and escape from what is disagreeable, calamity might come just the same; and it would be calamity falling on a base mind, which is the one form of sorrow that has no balm in it, and that may well make a man say, — 'It would have been better for me if I had never been born.' I will tell you something, Lillo."

Romola paused for a moment. She had taken Lillo's cheeks between her hands, and his young eyes were meeting hers.

"There was a man to whom I was very near, so that I could see a great deal of his life, who made almost every one fond of him, for he was young, and clever, and beautiful, and his manners to all were gentle and kind. I believe, when I first knew him, he never thought of anything cruel or base. But because he tried to slip away from everything that was unpleasant, and cared for nothing else so much as his own safety, he came at last to commit some of the basest deeds — such as make men infamous. He denied his father, and left him to misery; he betrayed every trust that was reposed in him, that he might keep himself safe and get rich and prosperous. Yet calamity overtook him."

Again Romola paused. Her voice was unsteady, and Lillo was looking up at her with awed wonder.

"Another time, my Lillo — I will tell you another time. See, there are our old Piero di Cosimo and Nello coming up the Borgo Pinti, bringing us their flowers. Let us go and wave our hands to them, that they may know we see them."

"How queer old Piero is!" said Lillo, as they stood at the corner of the loggia, watching the advancing figures. "He abuses you for dressing the altar, and thinking so much of Fra Girolamo, and yet he brings you the flowers."

"Never mind," said Romola. "There are many good people who did not love Fra Girolamo. Perhaps I should never have learned to love him if he had not helped me when I was in great need."

SILAS MARNER AND EPPIE.

SILAS MARNER:

THE WEAVER OF RAVELOE.

A child, more than all other gifts
That earth can offer to declining man,
Brings hope with it, and forward-looking thoughts.
WORDSWORTH.

SILAS MARNER:

THE WEAVER OF RAVELOE.

———•———

PART I.

CHAPTER I.

In the days when the spinning-wheels hummed busily in the farmhouses — and even great ladies, clothed in silk and thread-lace, had their toy spinning-wheels of polished oak — there might be seen in districts far away among the lanes, or deep in the bosom of the hills, certain pallid undersized men, who, by the side of the brawny country-folk, looked like the remnants of a disinherited race. The shepherd's dog barked fiercely when one of these alien-looking men appeared on the upland, dark against the early winter sunset; for what dog likes a figure bent under a heavy bag? — and these pale men rarely stirred abroad without that mysterious burden. The shepherd himself, though he had good reason to believe that the bag held nothing but flaxen thread, or else the long rolls of strong linen spun from that thread, was not quite sure that this trade of weaving, indispensable though it was, could be carried on entirely without the help of the Evil One. In that far-off time superstition clung easily round every person or thing that was at all unwonted, or even intermittent and occasional merely, like the visits of the pedler or the knife-grinder. No one knew where wandering men had their homes or their origin; and how was a man to be explained unless you at least knew somebody who knew his father and mother? To the peasants of old times, the world outside their own

direct experience was a region of vagueness and mystery: to
their untravelled thought a state of wandering was a conception as dim as the winter life of the swallows that came back
with the spring; and even a settler, if he came from distant
parts, hardly ever ceased to be viewed with a remnant of distrust, which would have prevented any surprise if a long
course of inoffensive conduct on his part had ended in the
commission of a crime; especially if he had any reputation
for knowledge, or showed any skill in handicraft. All cleverness, whether in the rapid use of that difficult instrument the
tongue, or in some other art unfamiliar to villagers, was in
itself suspicious: honest folk, born and bred in a visible
manner, were mostly not over wise or clever — at least, not
beyond such a matter as knowing the signs of the weather;
and the process by which rapidity and dexterity of any kind
were acquired was so wholly hidden, that they partook of the
nature of conjuring. In this way it came to pass that those
scattered linen-weavers — emigrants from the town into the
country — were to the last regarded as aliens by their rustic
neighbors, and usually contracted the eccentric habits which
belong to a state of loneliness.

In the early years of this century, such a linen-weaver,
named Silas Marner, worked at his vocation in a stone cottage
that stood among the nutty hedgerows near the village of
Raveloe, and not far from the edge of a deserted stone-pit.
The questionable sound of Silas's loom, so unlike the natural
cheerful trotting of the winnowing-machine, or the simpler
rhythm of the flail, had a half-fearful fascination for the
Raveloe boys, who would often leave off their nutting or
birds'-nesting to peep in at the window of the stone cottage,
counterbalancing a certain awe at the mysterious action of the
loom, by a pleasant sense of scornful superiority, drawn from
the mockery of its alternating noises, along with the bent,
tread-mill attitude of the weaver. But sometimes it happened
that Marner, pausing to adjust an irregularity in his thread,
became aware of the small scoundrels, and, though chary of
his time, he liked their intrusion so ill that he would descend
from his loom, and, opening the door, would fix on them a

gaze that was always enough to make them take to their legs in terror. For how was it possible to believe that those large brown protuberant eyes in Silas Marner's pale face really saw nothing very distinctly that was not close to them, and not rather that their dreadful stare could dart cramp, or rickets, or a wry mouth at any boy who happened to be in the rear? They had, perhaps, heard their fathers and mothers hint that Silas Marner could cure folk's rheumatism if he had a mind, and add, still more darkly, that if you could only speak the devil fair enough, he might save you the cost of the doctor. Such strange lingering echoes of the old demon-worship might perhaps even now be caught by the diligent listener among the gray-haired peasantry; for the rude mind with difficulty associates the ideas of power and benignity. A shadowy conception of power that by much persuasion can be induced to refrain from inflicting harm, is the shape most easily taken by the sense of the Invisible in the minds of men who have always been pressed close by primitive wants, and to whom a life of hard toil has never been illuminated by any enthusiastic religious faith. To them pain and mishap present a far wider range of possibilities than gladness and enjoyment: their imagination is almost barren of the images that feed desire and hope, but is all overgrown by recollections that are a perpetual pasture to fear. "Is there anything you can fancy that you would like to eat?" I once said to an old laboring man, who was in his last illness, and who had refused all the food his wife had offered him. "No," he answered, "I've never been used to nothing but common victual, and I can't eat that." Experience had bred no fancies in him that could raise the phantasm of appetite.

And Raveloe was a village where many of the old echoes lingered, undrowned by new voices. Not that it was one of those barren parishes lying on the outskirts of civilization — inhabited by meagre sheep and thinly-scattered shepherds: on the contrary, it lay in the rich central plain of what we are pleased to call Merry England, and held farms which, speaking from a spiritual point of view, paid highly desirable tithes. But it was nestled in a snug well-wooded hollow, quite an hour's journey on horseback from any turnpike, where it was never reached by the vibrations of the coach-horn, or of public opinion. It was an important-looking village, with a fine old church and large churchyard in the heart of it, and two or three large brick-and-stone homesteads, with well-walled orchards and ornamental weathercocks, standing close upon the road, and lifting more imposing fronts than the rectory, which peeped from among the trees on the other side of the churchyard : — a village which showed at once the summits of its social life, and told the practised eye that there was no great park and manor-house in the vicinity, but that there were several chiefs in Raveloe who could farm badly quite at their ease, drawing enough money from their bad farming, in those war times, to live in a rollicking fashion, and keep a jolly Christmas, Whitsun, and Easter tide.

It was fifteen years since Silas Marner had first come to Raveloe; he was then simply a pallid young man, with prominent short-sighted brown eyes, whose appearance would have had nothing strange for people of average culture and experience, but for the villagers near whom he had come to settle it had mysterious peculiarities which corresponded with the exceptional nature of his occupation, and his advent from an unknown region called "North'ard." So had his way of life : — he invited no comer to step across his door-sill, and he never strolled into the village to drink a pint at the Rainbow, or to gossip at the wheelwright's : he sought no man or woman, save for the purposes of his calling, or in order to supply himself with necessaries; and it was soon clear to the Raveloe lasses that he would never urge one of them to accept him against her will — quite as if he had heard them declare that they would never marry a dead man come to life again. This view of Marner's personality was not without another ground than his pale face and unexampled eyes; for Jem Rodney, the mole-catcher, averred that one evening as he was returning homeward he saw Silas Marner leaning against a stile with a heavy bag on his back, instead of resting the bag on the stile as a man in his senses would have done; and that, on coming up to him, he saw that Marner's eyes were set like a dead man's, and he spoke to him, and shook him, and his limbs were stiff, and his hands clutched the bag as if they 'd been made of iron; but just as he had made up his mind that the weaver was dead, he came all right again, like, as you might say, in the winking of an eye, and said " Good-night," and walked off. All this Jem swore he had seen, more by token that it was the very day he had been mole-catching on Squire Cass's land, down by the old saw-pit. Some said Marner must have been in a "fit," a word which seemed to explain things otherwise incredible; but the argumentative Mr. Macey, clerk of the parish, shook his head, and asked if anybody was ever known to go off in a fit and not fall down. A fit was a stroke, was n't it? and it was in the nature of a stroke to partly take away the use of a man's limbs and throw him on the parish, if he 'd got no children to look to. No, no; it was no stroke that would let a man stand on his legs, like a horse between the shafts, and then walk off as soon as you can say " Gee!" But there might be such a thing as a man's soul being loose from his body, and going out and in, like a bird out of its nest and back; and that was how folks got over-wise, for they went to school in this shell-less state to those who could teach them more than their neighbors could learn with their five senses and the parson. And where did Master Marner get his knowledge of herbs from — and charms too, if he liked to give them away? Jem Rodney's story was no more than what might have been expected by anybody who had seen how Marner had cured Sally Oates, and made her sleep like a baby, when her heart had been beating enough to burst her body, for two months and more, while she had been under the doctor's care. He might cure more folks if he would; but he was worth speaking fair, if it was only to keep him from doing you a mischief.

It was partly to this vague fear that Marner was indebted for protecting him from the persecution that his singularities might have drawn upon him, but still more to the fact that, the old linen-weaver in the neighboring parish of Tarley being dead, his handicraft made him a highly welcome settler to the richer housewives of the district, and even to the more provident cottagers, who had their little stock of yarn at the year's

end. Their sense of his usefulness would have counteracted
any repugnance or suspicion which was not confirmed by a
deficiency in the quality or the tale of the cloth he wove for
them. And the years had rolled on without producing any
change in the impressions of the neighbors concerning Marner,
except the change from novelty to habit. At the end of fifteen
years the Raveloe men said just the same things about Silas
Marner as at the beginning : they did not say them quite so
often, but they believed them much more strongly when they
did say them. There was only one important addition which
the years had brought : it was, that Master Marner had laid
by a fine sight of money somewhere, and that he could buy up
"bigger men" than himself.

But while opinion concerning him had remained nearly sta-
tionary, and his daily habits had presented scarcely any visible
change, Marner's inward life had been a history and a meta-
morphosis, as that of every fervid nature must be when it has
fled, or been condemned to solitude. His life, before he came
to Raveloe, had been filled with the movement, the mental
activity, and the close fellowship, which, in that day as in
this, marked the life of an artisan early incorporated in a
narrow religious sect, where the poorest layman has the chance
of distinguishing himself by gifts of speech, and has, at the
very least, the weight of a silent voter in the government of
his community. Marner was highly thought of in that little
hidden world, known to itself as the church assembling in
Lantern Yard ; he was believed to be a young man of exem-
plary life and ardent faith ; and a peculiar interest had been
centred in him ever since he had fallen, at a prayer-meeting,
into a mysterious rigidity and suspension of consciousness,
which, lasting for an hour or more, had been mistaken for
death. To have sought a medical explanation for this phe-
nomenon would have been held by Silas himself, as well as by
his minister and fellow-members, a wilful self-exclusion from
the spiritual significance that might lie therein. Silas was
evidently a brother selected for a peculiar discipline ; and
though the effort to interpret this discipline was discouraged
by the absence, on his part, of any spiritual vision during his

outward trance, yet it was believed by himself and others that
its effect was seen in an accession of light and fervor. A less
truthful man than he might have been tempted into the subsequent creation of a vision in the form of resurgent memory;
a less sane man might have believed in such a creation; but
Silas was both sane and honest, though, as with many honest
and fervent men, culture had not defined any channels for his
sense of mystery, and so it spread itself over the proper pathway of inquiry and knowledge. He had inherited from his
mother some acquaintance with medicinal herbs and their
preparation — a little store of wisdom which she had imparted
to him as a solemn bequest — but of late years he had had
doubts about the lawfulness of applying this knowledge, believing that herbs could have no efficacy without prayer, and
that prayer might suffice without herbs; so that his inherited
delight to wander through the fields in search of foxglove and
dandelion and coltsfoot, began to wear to him the character of
a temptation.

Among the members of his church there was one young man,
a little older than himself, with whom he had long lived in
such close friendship that it was the custom of their Lantern
Yard brethren to call them David and Jonathan. The real
name of the friend was William Dane, and he, too, was regarded as a shining instance of youthful piety, though somewhat given to over-severity towards weaker brethren, and to
be so dazzled by his own light as to hold himself wiser than
his teachers. But whatever blemishes others might discern in
William, to his friend's mind he was faultless; for Marner had
one of those impressible self-doubting natures which, at an in-
experienced age, admire imperativeness and lean on contradiction. The expression of trusting simplicity in Marner's face,
heightened by that absence of special observation, that defenceless, deer-like gaze which belongs to large prominent eyes,
was strongly contrasted by the self-complacent suppression of
inward triumph that lurked in the narrow slanting eyes and
compressed lips of William Dane. One of the most frequent
topics of conversation between the two friends was Assurance
of salvation: Silas confessed that he could never arrive at any-

thing higher than hope mingled with fear, and listened with
longing wonder when William declared that he had possessed
unshaken assurance ever since, in the period of his conversion,
he had dreamed that he saw the words "calling and election
sure" standing by themselves on a white page in the open
Bible. Such colloquies have occupied many a pair of pale-
faced weavers, whose unnurtured souls have been like young
winged things, fluttering forsaken in the twilight.

It had seemed to the unsuspecting Silas that the friendship
had suffered no chill even from his formation of another
attachment of a closer kind. For some months he had been
engaged to a young servant-woman, waiting only for a little
increase to their mutual savings in order to their marriage;
and it was a great delight to him that Sarah did not object to
William's occasional presence in their Sunday interviews. It
was at this point in their history that Silas's cataleptic fit
occurred during the prayer-meeting; and amidst the various
queries and expressions of interest addressed to him by his
fellow-members, William's suggestion alone jarred with the
general sympathy towards a brother thus singled out for
special dealings. He observed that, to him, this trance looked
more like a visitation of Satan than a proof of divine favor,
and exhorted his friend to see that he hid no accursed thing
within his soul. Silas, feeling bound to accept rebuke and
admonition as a brotherly office, felt no resentment, but only
pain, at his friend's doubts concerning him; and to this was
soon added some anxiety at the perception that Sarah's manner towards him began to exhibit a strange fluctuation between an effort at an increased manifestation of regard and
involuntary signs of shrinking and dislike. He asked her if
she wished to break off their engagement; but she denied
this: their engagement was known to the church, and had
been recognized in the prayer-meetings; it could not be broken
off without strict investigation, and Sarah could render no
reason that would be sanctioned by the feeling of the community. At this time the senior deacon was taken dangerously
ill, and, being a childless widower, he was tended night and
day by some of the younger brethren or sisters. Silas fre-

quently took his turn in the night-watching with William, the
one relieving the other at two in the morning. The old man,
contrary to expectation, seemed to be on the way to recovery,
when one night Silas, sitting up by his bedside, observed that
his usual audible breathing had ceased. The candle was burning low, and he had to lift it to see the patient's face distinctly. Examination convinced him that the deacon was
dead — had been dead some time, for the limbs were rigid.
Silas asked himself if he had been asleep, and looked at the
clock: it was already four in the morning. How was it that
William had not come? In much anxiety he went to seek
for help, and soon there were several friends assembled in the
house, the minister among them, while Silas went away to his
work, wishing he could have met William to know the reason
of his non-appearance. But at six o'clock, as he was thinking
of going to seek his friend, William came, and with him the
minister. They came to summon him to Lantern Yard, to
meet the church members there; and to his inquiry concerning the cause of the summons the only reply was, "You will
hear." Nothing further was said until Silas was seated in
the vestry, in front of the minister, with the eyes of those
who to him represented God's people fixed solemnly upon him.
Then the minister, taking out a pocket-knife, showed it to
Silas, and asked him if he knew where he had left that knife?
Silas said, he did not know that he had left it anywhere out
of his own pocket — but he was trembling at this strange
interrogation. He was then exhorted not to hide his sin, but
to confess and repent. The knife had been found in the
bureau by the departed deacon's bedside — found in the place
where the little bag of church money had lain, which the
minister himself had seen the day before. Some hand had
removed that bag; and whose hand could it be, if not that of
the man to whom the knife belonged? For some time Silas
was mute with astonishment: then he said, "God will clear
me: I know nothing about the knife being there, or the money
being gone. Search me and my dwelling; you will find nothing but three pound five of my own savings, which William
Dane knows I have had these six months." At this William

groaned, but the minister said, "The proof is heavy against
you, brother Marner. The money was taken in the night last
past, and no man was with our departed brother but you, for
William Dane declares to us that he was hindered by sudden
sickness from going to take his place as usual, and you yourself said that he had not come ; and, moreover, you neglected
the dead body."

"I must have slept," said Silas. Then after a pause, he
added, "Or I must have had another visitation like that which
you have all seen me under, so that the thief must have come
and gone while I was not in the body, but out of the body.
But, I say again, search me and my dwelling, for I have been
nowhere else."

The search was made, and it ended — in William Dane's
finding the well-known bag, empty, tucked behind the chest
of drawers in Silas's chamber ! On this William exhorted his
friend to confess, and not to hide his sin any longer. Silas
turned a look of keen reproach on him, and said, " William,
for nine years that we have gone in and out together, have
you ever known me tell a lie ? But God will clear me."

" Brother," said William, " how do I know what you may
have done in the secret chambers of your heart, to give Satan
an advantage over you ? "

Silas was still looking at his friend. Suddenly a deep flush
came over his face, and he was about to speak impetuously,
when he seemed checked again by some inward shock, that
sent the flush back and made him tremble. But at last he
spoke feebly, looking at William.

" I remember now — the knife was n't in my pocket."

William said, " I know nothing of what you mean." The
other persons present, however, began to inquire where Silas
meant to say that the knife was, but he would give no further
explanation : he only said, " I am sore stricken ; I can say
nothing. God will clear me."

On their return to the vestry there was further deliberation.
Any resort to legal measures for ascertaining the culprit was
contrary to the principles of the church in Lantern Yard,
according to which prosecution was forbidden to Christians,

even had the case held less scandal to the community. But
the members were bound to take other measures for finding
out the truth, and they resolved on praying and drawing lots.
This resolution can be a ground of surprise only to those who
are unacquainted with that obscure religious life which has
gone on in the alleys of our towns. Silas knelt with his
brethren, relying on his own innocence being certified by
immediate divine interference, but feeling that there was
sorrow and mourning behind for him even then — that his
trust in man had been cruelly bruised. *The lots declared that
Silas Marner was guilty.* He was solemnly suspended from
church-membership, and called upon to render up the stolen
money : only on confession, as the sign of repentance, could
he be received once more within the folds of the church.
Marner listened in silence. At last, when every one rose to
depart, he went towards William Dane and said, in a voice
shaken by agitation —

"The last time I remember using my knife, was when I took
it out to cut a strap for you. I don't remember putting it in
my pocket again. *You* stole the money, and you have woven
a plot to lay the sin at my door. But you may prosper, for
all that : there is no just God that governs the earth right-
eously, but a God of lies, that bears witness against the
innocent."

There was a general shudder at this blasphemy.

William said meekly, "I leave our brethren to judge whether
this is the voice of Satan or not. I can do nothing but pray
for you, Silas."

Poor Marner went out with that despair in his soul — that
shaken trust in God and man, which is little short of madness
to a loving nature. In the bitterness of his wounded spirit,
he said to himself, " *She* will cast me off too." And he reflected that, if she did not believe the testimony against him,
her whole faith must be upset as his was. To people accustomed to reason about the forms in which their religious feeling has incorporated itself, it is difficult to enter into that
simple, untaught state of mind in which the form and the
feeling have never been severed by an act of reflection. We

are apt to think it inevitable that a man in Marner's position should have begun to question the validity of an appeal to the divine judgment by drawing lots; but to him this would have been an effort of independent thought such as he had never known; and he must have made the effort at a moment when all his energies were turned into the anguish of disappointed faith. If there is an angel who records the sorrows of men as well as their sins, he knows how many and deep are the sorrows that spring from false ideas for which no man is culpable.

Marner went home, and for a whole day sat alone, stunned by despair, without any impulse to go to Sarah and attempt to win her belief in his innocence. The second day he took refuge from benumbing unbelief, by getting into his loom and working away as usual; and before many hours were past, the minister and one of the deacons came to him with the message from Sarah, that she held her engagement to him at an end. Silas received the message mutely, and then turned away from the messengers to work at his loom again. In little more than a month from that time, Sarah was married to William Dane; and not long afterwards it was known to the brethren in Lantern Yard that Silas Marner had departed from the town.

CHAPTER II.

EVEN people whose lives have been made various by learning, sometimes find it hard to keep a fast hold on their habitual views of life, on their faith in the Invisible, nay, on the sense that their past joys and sorrows are a real experience, when they are suddenly transported to a new land, where the beings around them know nothing of their history, and share none of their ideas — where their mother earth shows another lap, and human life has other forms than those on which their souls have been nourished. Minds that have been unhinged from their old faith and love, have perhaps sought this Lethean influence of exile, in which the past becomes dreamy because its symbols have all vanished, and the present too is dreamy because it is linked with no memories. But even *their* experience may hardly enable them thoroughly to imagine what was the effect on a simple weaver like Silas Marner, when he left his own country and people and came to settle in Raveloe. Nothing could be more unlike his native town, set within sight of the widespread hillsides, than this low, wooded region, where he felt hidden even from the heavens by the screening trees and hedgerows. There was nothing here, when he rose in the deep morning quiet and looked out on the dewy brambles and rank tufted grass, that seemed to have any relation with that life centring in Lantern Yard, which had once been to him the altar-place of high dispensations. The whitewashed walls; the little pews where well-known figures entered with a subdued rustling, and where first one well-known voice and then another, pitched in a peculiar key of petition, uttered phrases at once occult and familiar, like the amulet worn on the heart; the pulpit where the minister delivered unquestioned doctrine, and swayed to and fro, and handled the book in a long-accustomed manner; the very pauses between the couplets of the hymn, as it was given out, and the recurrent swell of voices in song: these things had been the channel of divine influences to Marner — they were the fostering home of his religious emotions — they were Christianity and God's kingdom upon earth. A weaver who finds hard words in his hymn-book knows nothing of abstractions; as the little child knows nothing of parental love, but only knows one face and one lap towards which it stretches its arms for refuge and nurture.

And what could be more unlike that Lantern Yard world than the world in Raveloe? — orchards looking lazy with neglected plenty; the large church in the wide churchyard, which men gazed at lounging at their own doors in service-time; the purple-faced farmers jogging along the lanes or turning in at the Rainbow; homesteads, where men supped heavily and slept in the light of the evening hearth, and where women seemed to be laying up a stock of linen for the life to come. There were no lips in Raveloe from which a word could fall that would stir Silas Marner's benumbed faith to a sense of pain. In the early ages of the world, we know, it was believed that each territory was inhabited and ruled by its own divinities, so that a man could cross the bordering heights and be out of the reach of his native gods, whose presence was confined to the streams and the groves and the hills among which he had lived from his birth. And poor Silas was vaguely conscious of something not unlike the feeling of primitive men, when they fled thus, in fear or in sullenness, from the face of an unpropitious deity. It seemed to him that the Power he had vainly trusted in among the streets and at the prayer-meetings, was very far away from this land in which he had taken refuge, where men lived in careless abundance, knowing and needing nothing of that trust, which, for him, had been turned to bitterness. The little light he possessed spread its beams so narrowly, that frustrated belief was a curtain broad enough to create for him the blackness of night.

His first movement after the shock had been to work in his loom; and he went on with this unremittingly, never asking himself why, now he was come to Raveloe, he worked far on into the night to finish the tale of Mrs. Osgood's table-linen sooner than she expected — without contemplating beforehand the money she would put into his hand for the work. He seemed to weave, like the spider, from pure impulse, without reflection. Every man's work, pursued steadily, tends in this way to become an end in itself, and so to bridge over the loveless chasms of his life. Silas's hand satisfied itself with throwing the shuttle, and his eye with seeing the little squares in the cloth complete themselves under his effort. Then there were the calls of hunger; and Silas, in his solitude, had to provide his own breakfast, dinner, and supper, to fetch his own water from the well, and put his own kettle on the fire; and all these immediate promptings helped, along with the weaving, to reduce his life to the unquestioning activity of a spinning insect. He hated the thought of the past; there was nothing that called out his love and fellowship towards the strangers he had come among; and the future was all dark, for there was no Unseen Love that cared for him. Thought was arrested by utter bewilderment, now its old narrow pathway was closed, and affection seemed to have died under the bruise that had fallen on its keenest nerves.

But at last Mrs. Osgood's table-linen was finished, and Silas was paid in gold. His earnings in his native town, where he worked for a wholesale dealer, had been after a lower rate; he had been paid weekly, and of his weekly earnings a large proportion had gone to objects of piety and charity. Now, for the first time in his life, he had five bright guineas put into his hand; no man expected a share of them, and he loved no man that he should offer him a share. But what were the guineas to him who saw no vista beyond countless days of weaving? It was needless for him to ask that, for it was pleasant to him to feel them in his palm, and look at their bright faces, which were all his own: it was another element of life, like the weaving and the satisfaction of hunger, subsisting quite aloof from the life of belief and love from which he had been cut off. The weaver's hand had known the touch of hard-won money even before the palm had grown to its full breadth; for twenty years, mysterious money had stood to him as the symbol of earthly good, and the immediate object of toil. He had seemed to love it little in the years when every penny had its purpose for him; for he loved the *purpose* then. But now, when all purpose was gone, that habit of looking towards the money and grasping it with a sense of fulfilled effort made a loam that was deep enough for the seeds of desire; and as Silas walked homeward across the fields in the twilight, he drew out the money and thought it was brighter in the gathering gloom.

About this time an incident happened which seemed to open a possibility of some fellowship with his neighbors. One day, taking a pair of shoes to be mended, he saw the cobbler's wife seated by the fire, suffering from the terrible symptoms of heart-disease and dropsy, which he had witnessed as the precursors of his mother's death. He felt a rush of pity at the mingled sight and remembrance, and, recalling the relief his mother had found from a simple preparation of foxglove, he promised Sally Oates to bring her something that would ease her, since the doctor did her no good. In this office of charity, Silas felt, for the first time since he had come to Raveloe, a sense of unity between his past and present life, which might have been the beginning of his rescue from the insect-like existence into which his nature had shrunk. But Sally Oates's disease had raised her into a personage of much interest and importance among the neighbors, and the fact of her having found relief from drinking Silas Marner's "stuff" became a matter of general discourse. When Doctor Kimble gave physic, it was natural that it should have an effect ; but when a weaver, who came from nobody knew where, worked wonders with a bottle of brown waters, the occult character of the process was evident. Such a sort of thing had not been known since the Wise Woman at Tarley died ; and she had charms as well as "stuff :" everybody went to her when their children had fits. Silas Marner must be a person of the same sort, for how did he know what would bring back Sally Oates's breath, if he did n't know a fine sight more than that ? The Wise Woman had words that she muttered to herself, so that you could n't hear what they were, and if she tied a bit of red thread round the child's toe the while, it would keep off the water in the head. There were women in Raveloe, at that present time, who had worn one of the Wise Woman's little bags round their necks, and, in consequence, had never had an idiot child, as Ann Coulter had. Silas Marner could very likely do as much, and more ; and now it was all clear how he should have come from unknown parts, and be so "comical-looking." But Sally Oates must mind and not tell the doctor, for he would be sure to set his face against Marner : he was always angry about the Wise Woman, and used to threaten those who went to her that they should have none of his help any more.

Silas now found himself and his cottage suddenly beset by mothers who wanted him to charm away the whooping-cough, or bring back the milk, and by men who wanted stuff against the rheumatics or the knots in the hands ; and, to secure themselves against a refusal, the applicants brought silver in their palms. Silas might have driven a profitable trade in charms as well as in his small list of drugs; but money on this condition was no temptation to him: he had never known an impulse towards falsity, and he drove one after another away with growing irritation, for the news of him as a wise man had spread even to Tarley, and it was long before people ceased to take long walks for the sake of asking his aid. But the hope in his wisdom was at length changed into dread, for no one believed him when he said he knew no charms and could work no cures, and every man and woman who had an accident or a new attack after applying to him, set the misfortune down to Master Marner's ill-will and irritated glances. Thus it came to pass that his movement of pity towards Sally Oates, which had given him a transient sense of brotherhood, heightened the repulsion between him and his neighbors, and made his isolation more complete.

Gradually the guineas, the crowns, and the half-crowns, grew to a heap, and Marner drew less and less for his own wants, trying to solve the problem of keeping himself strong enough to work sixteen hours a day on as small an outlay as possible. Have not men, shut up in solitary imprisonment, found an interest in marking the moments by straight strokes of a certain length on the wall, until the growth of the sum of straight strokes, arranged in triangles, has become a mastering purpose? Do we not wile away moments of inanity or fatigued waiting by repeating some trivial movement or sound, until the repetition has bred a want, which is incipient habit? That will help us to understand how the love of accumulating money grows an absorbing passion in men whose imaginations, even in the very beginning of their hoard, showed them no purpose beyond it. Marner wanted the heaps of ten to grow into a square, and then into a larger square; and every added guinea, while it was itself a satisfaction, bred a new desire. In this strange world, made a hopeless riddle to him, he might, if he had had a less intense nature, have sat weaving, weaving — looking towards the end of his pattern, or towards the end of his web, till he forgot the riddle, and everything else but his immediate sensations; but the money had come to mark off his weaving into periods, and the money not only grew, but it remained with him. He began to think it was conscious of him, as his loom was, and he would on no account have exchanged those coins, which had become his familiars, for other coins with unknown faces. He handled them, he counted them, till their form and color were like the satisfaction of a thirst to him; but it was only in the night, when his work was done, that he drew them out to enjoy their companionship. He had taken up some bricks in his floor underneath his loom, and here he had made a hole in which he set the iron pot that contained his guineas and silver coins, covering the bricks with sand whenever he replaced them. Not that the idea of being robbed presented itself often or strongly to his mind: hoarding was common in country districts in those days; there were old laborers in the parish of Raveloe who were known to have their savings by them, probably inside their flock-beds; but their rustic neighbors, though not all of them as honest as their ancestors in the days of King Alfred, had not imaginations bold enough to lay a plan of burglary. How could they have spent the money in their own village without betraying themselves? They would be obliged to "run away" — a course as dark and dubious as a balloon journey.

So, year after year, Silas Marner had lived in this solitude, his guineas rising in the iron pot, and his life narrowing and hardening itself more and more into a mere pulsation of desire and satisfaction that had no relation to any other being. His life had reduced itself to the functions of weaving and hoarding, without any contemplation of an end towards which the functions tended. The same sort of process has perhaps been undergone by wiser men, when they have been cut off from faith and love — only, instead of a loom and a heap of guineas, they have had some erudite research, some ingenious project, or some well-knit theory. Strangely Marner's face and figure shrank and bent themselves into a constant mechanical relation to the objects of his life, so that he produced the same sort of impression as a handle or a crooked tube, which has no meaning standing apart. The prominent eyes that used to look trusting and dreamy, now looked as if they had been made to see only one kind of thing that was very small, like tiny grain, for which they hunted everywhere : and he was so withered and yellow, that, though he was not yet forty, the children always called him "Old Master Marner."

Yet even in this stage of withering a little incident happened, which showed that the sap of affection was not all gone. It was one of his daily tasks to fetch his water from a well a couple of fields off, and for this purpose, ever since he came to Raveloe, he had had a brown earthenware pot, which he held as his most precious utensil among the very few conveniences he had granted himself. It had been his companion for twelve years, always standing on the same spot, always lending its handle to him in the early morning, so that its form had an expression for him of willing helpfulness, and the impress of its handle on his palm gave a satisfaction mingled with that of having the fresh clear water. One day as he was returning from the well, he stumbled against the step of the stile, and his brown pot, falling with force against the stones that overarched the ditch below him, was broken in three pieces. Silas picked up the pieces and carried them home with grief in his heart. The brown pot could never be of use to him any more, but he stuck the bits together and propped the ruin in its old place for a memorial.

This is the history of Silas Marner, until the fifteenth year after he came to Raveloe. The livelong day he sat in his loom, his ear filled with its monotony, his eyes bent close down on the slow growth of sameness in the brownish web, his muscles moving with such even repetition that their pause seemed almost as much a constraint as the holding of his breath. But at night came his revelry : at night he closed his shutters, and made fast his doors, and drew forth his gold. Long ago the heap of coins had become too large for the iron pot to hold them, and he had made for them two thick leather bags, which wasted no room in their resting-place, but lent themselves flexibly to every corner. How the guineas shone as they came pouring out of the dark leather mouths! The silver bore no large proportion in amount to the gold, because the long pieces of linen which formed his chief work were always partly paid for in gold, and out of the silver he supplied his own bodily wants, choosing always the shillings and sixpences to spend in this way. He loved the guineas best, but he would not change the silver — the crowns and half-crowns that were his own earnings, begotten by his labor; he loved them all. He spread them out in heaps and bathed his hands in them; then he counted them and set them up in regular piles, and felt their rounded outline between his thumb and fingers, and thought fondly of the guineas that were only half earned by the work in his loom, as if they had been unborn children — thought of the guineas that were coming slowly through the coming years, through all his life, which spread far away before him, the end quite hidden by countless days of weaving. No wonder his thoughts were still with his loom and his money when he made his journeys through the fields and the lanes to fetch and carry home his work, so that his steps never wandered to the hedge-banks and the lane-side in search of the once familiar herbs: these too belonged to the past, from which his life had shrunk away, like a rivulet that has sunk far down from the grassy fringe of its old breadth into a little shivering thread, that cuts a groove for itself in the barren sand.

But about the Christmas of that fifteenth year, a second great change came over Marner's life, and his history became blent in a singular manner with the life of his neighbors.

CHAPTER III.

THE greatest man in Raveloe was Squire Cass, who lived in the large red house with the handsome flight of stone steps in front and the high stables behind it, nearly opposite the church. He was only one among several landed parishioners, but he alone was honored with the title of Squire; for though

Mr. Osgood's family was also understood to be of timeless origin — the Raveloe imagination having never ventured back to that fearful blank when there were no Osgoods — still, he merely owned the farm he occupied; whereas Squire Cass had a tenant or two, who complained of the game to him quite as if he had been a lord.

It was still that glorious war-time which was felt to be a peculiar favor of Providence towards the landed interest, and the fall of prices had not yet come to carry the race of small squires and yeomen down that road to ruin for which extravagant habits and bad husbandry were plentifully anointing their wheels. I am speaking now in relation to Raveloe and the parishes that resembled it; for our old-fashioned country life had many different aspects, as all life must have when it is spread over a various surface, and breathed on variously by multitudinous currents, from the winds of heaven to the thoughts of men, which are forever moving and crossing each other with incalculable results. Raveloe lay low among the bushy trees and the rutted lanes, aloof from the currents of industrial energy and Puritan earnestness: the rich ate and drank freely, accepting gout and apoplexy as things that ran mysteriously in respectable families, and the poor thought that the rich were entirely in the right of it to lead a jolly life; besides, their feasting caused a multiplication of orts, which were the heirlooms of the poor. Betty Jay scented the boiling of Squire Cass's hams, but her longing was arrested by the unctuous liquor in which they were boiled; and when the seasons brought round the great merry-makings, they were regarded on all hands as a fine thing for the poor. For the Raveloe feasts were like the rounds of beef and the barrels of ale — they were on a large scale, and lasted a good while, especially in the winter-time. After ladies had packed up their best gowns and top-knots in bandboxes, and had incurred the risk of fording streams on pillions with the precious burden in rainy or snowy weather, when there was no knowing how high the water would rise, it was not to be supposed that they looked forward to a brief pleasure. On this ground it was always contrived in the dark seasons, when there was little work to be done, and the hours were long, that several neighbors should keep open house in succession. So soon as Squire Cass's standing dishes diminished in plenty and freshness, his guests had nothing to do but to walk a little higher up the village to Mr. Osgood's, at the Orchards, and they found hams and chines uncut, pork-pies with the scent of the fire in them, spun butter in all its freshness — everything, in fact, that appetites at leisure could desire, in perhaps greater perfection, though not in greater abundance, than at Squire Cass's.

For the Squire's wife had died long ago, and the Red House was without that presence of the wife and mother which is the fountain of wholesome love and fear in parlor and kitchen; and this helped to account not only for there being more profusion than finished excellence in the holiday provisions, but also for the frequency with which the proud Squire condescended to preside in the parlor of the Rainbow rather than under the shadow of his own dark wainscot; perhaps, also, for the fact that his sons had turned out rather ill. Raveloe was not a place where moral censure was severe, but it was thought a weakness in the Squire that he had kept all his sons at home in idleness; and though some license was to be allowed to young men whose fathers could afford it, people shook their heads at the courses of the second son, Dunstan, commonly called Dunsey Cass, whose taste for swopping and betting might turn out to be a sowing of something worse than wild oats. To be sure, the neighbors said, it was no matter what became of Dunsey — a spiteful jeering fellow, who seemed to enjoy his drink the more when other people went dry — always provided that his doings did not bring trouble on a family like Squire Cass's, with a monument in the church, and tankards older than King George. But it would be a thousand pities if Mr. Godfrey, the eldest, a fine open-faced good-natured young man who was to come into the land some day, should take to going along the same road with his brother, as he had seemed to do of late. If he went on in that way, he would lose Miss Nancy Lammeter; for it was well known that she had looked very shyly on him ever since

last Whitsuntide twelvemonth, when there was so much talk
about his being away from home days and days together.
There was something wrong, more than common — that was
quite clear; for Mr. Godfrey did n't look half so fresh-colored
and open as he used to do. At one time everybody was saying, What a handsome couple he and Miss Nancy Lammeter
would make! and if she could come to be mistress at the Red
House, there would be a fine change, for the Lammeters had
been brought up in that way, that they never suffered a pinch
of salt to be wasted, and yet everybody in their household had
of the best, according to his place. Such a daughter-in-law
would be a saving to the old Squire, if she never brought a
penny to her fortune; for it was to be feared that, notwithstanding his incomings, there were more holes in his pocket
than the one where he put his own hand in. But if Mr. Godfrey did n't turn over a new leaf, he might say "Good-by" to
Miss Nancy Lammeter.

It was the once hopeful Godfrey who was standing, with
his hands in his side-pockets and his back to the fire, in the
dark wainscoted parlor, one late November afternoon in that
fifteenth year of Silas Marner's life at Raveloe. The fading
gray light fell dimly on the walls decorated with guns, whips,
and foxes' brushes, on coats and hats flung on the chairs, on
tankards sending forth a scent of flat ale, and on a half-choked
fire, with pipes propped up in the chimney-corners: signs of
a domestic life destitute of any hallowing charm, with which
the look of gloomy vexation on Godfrey's blond face was in
sad accordance. He seemed to be waiting and listening for
some one's approach, and presently the sound of a heavy step,
with an accompanying whistle, was heard across the large
empty entrance-hall.

The door opened, and a thick-set, heavy-looking young man
entered, with the flushed face and the gratuitously elated
bearing which mark the first stage of intoxication. It was
Dunsey, and at the sight of him Godfrey's face parted with
some of its gloom to take on the more active expression of
hatred. The handsome brown spaniel that lay on the hearth
retreated under the chair in the chimney-corner.

"Well, Master Godfrey, what do you want with me?" said Dunsey, in a mocking tone. "You're my elders and betters, you know; I was obliged to come when you sent for me."

"Why, this is what I want — and just shake yourself sober and listen, will you?" said Godfrey, savagely. He had himself been drinking more than was good for him, trying to turn his gloom into uncalculating anger. "I want to tell you, I must hand over that rent of Fowler's to the Squire, or else tell him I gave it you; for he's threatening to distrain for it, and it'll all be out soon, whether I tell him or not. He said, just now, before he went out, he should send word to Cox to distrain, if Fowler did n't come and pay up his arrears this week. The Squire's short o' cash, and in no humor to stand any nonsense; and you know what he threatened, if ever he found you making away with his money again. So, see and get the money, and pretty quickly, will you?"

"Oh!" said Dunsey, sneeringly, coming nearer to his brother and looking in his face. "Suppose, now, you get the money yourself, and save me the trouble, eh? Since you was so kind as to hand it over to me, you'll not refuse me the kindness to pay it back for me: it was your brotherly love made you do it, you know."

Godfrey bit his lips and clenched his fist. "Don't come near me with that look, else I'll knock you down."

"Oh no, you won't," said Dunsey, turning away on his heel, however. "Because I'm such a good-natured brother, you know. I might get you turned out of house and home, and cut off with a shilling any day. I might tell the Squire how his handsome son was married to that nice young woman, Molly Farren, and was very unhappy because he could n't live with his drunken wife, and I should slip into your place as comfortable as could be. But you see, I don't do it — I'm so easy and good-natured. You'll take any trouble for me. You'll get the hundred pounds for me — I know you will."

"How can I get the money?" said Godfrey, quivering. "I have n't a shilling to bless myself with. And it's a lie that you'd slip into my place: you'd get yourself turned out too, that's all. For if you begin telling tales, I'll follow. Bob's my father's favorite — you know that very well. He 'd only think himself well rid of you."

"Never mind," said Dunsey, nodding his head sideways as he looked out of the window. "It 'ud be very pleasant to me to go in your company — you 're such a handsome brother, and we 've always been so fond of quarrelling with one another, I should n't know what to do without you. But you 'd like better for us both to stay at home together; I know you would. So you 'll manage to get that little sum o' money, and I 'll bid you good-by, though I 'm sorry to part."

Dunstan was moving off, but Godfrey rushed after him and seized him by the arm, saying, with an oath —

"I tell you, I have no money: I can get no money."

"Borrow of old Kimble."

"I tell you, he won't lend me any more, and I shan't ask him."

"Well, then, sell Wildfire."

"Yes, that 's easy talking. I must have the money directly."

"Well, you 've only got to ride him to the hunt to-morrow. There 'll be Bryce and Keating there, for sure. You 'll get more bids than one."

"I daresay, and get back home at eight o'clock, splashed up to the chin. I 'm going to Mrs. Osgood's birthday dance."

"Oho!" said Dunsey, turning his head on one side, and trying to speak in a small mincing treble. "And there 's sweet Miss Nancy coming; and we shall dance with her, and promise never to be naughty again, and be taken into favor, and — "

"Hold your tongue about Miss Nancy, you fool," said Godfrey, turning red, "else I 'll throttle you."

"What for?" said Dunsey, still in an artificial tone, but taking a whip from the table and beating the butt-end of it on his palm. "You 've a very good chance. I 'd advise you to creep up her sleeve again: it 'ud be saving time, if Molly should happen to take a drop too much laudanum some day, and make a widower of you. Miss Nancy would n't mind being a second, if she did n't know it. And you 've got a good-natured brother, who 'll keep your secret well, because you 'll be so very obliging to him."

"I'll tell you what it is," said Godfrey, quivering, and pale again, "my patience is pretty near at an end. If you'd a little more sharpness in you, you might know that you may urge a man a bit too far, and make one leap as easy as another. I don't know but what it is so now: I may as well tell the Squire everything myself — I should get you off my back, if I got nothing else. And, after all, he'll know some time. She's been threatening to come herself and tell him. So, don't flatter yourself that your secrecy's worth any price you choose to ask. You drain me of money till I have got nothing to pacify *her* with, and she'll do as she threatens some day. It's all one. I'll tell my father everything myself, and you may go to the devil."

Dunsey perceived that he had overshot his mark, and that there was a point at which even the hesitating Godfrey might be driven into decision. But he said, with an air of unconcern —

"As you please; but I'll have a draught of ale first." And ringing the bell, he threw himself across two chairs, and began to rap the window-seat with the handle of his whip.

Godfrey stood, still with his back to the fire, uneasily moving his fingers among the contents of his side-pockets, and looking at the floor. That big muscular frame of his held plenty of animal courage, but helped him to no decision when the dangers to be braved were such as could neither be knocked down nor throttled. His natural irresolution and moral cow-ardice were exaggerated by a position in which dreaded conse-quences seemed to press equally on all sides, and his irritation had no sooner provoked him to defy Dunstan and anticipate all possible betrayals, than the miseries he must bring on him-self by such a step seemed more unendurable to him than the present evil. The results of confession were not contingent, they were certain; whereas betrayal was not certain. From the near vision of that certainty he fell back on suspense and vacillation with a sense of repose. The disinherited son of a small squire, equally disinclined to dig and to beg, was almost as helpless as an uprooted tree, which, by the favor of earth and sky, has grown to a handsome bulk on the spot where it first shot upward. Perhaps it would have been possible to think of digging with some cheerfulness if Nancy Lammeter were to be won on those terms; but, since he must irrevocably lose *her* as well as the inheritance, and must break every tie but the one that degraded him and left him without motive for trying to recover his better self, he could imagine no future for himself on the other side of confession but that of "'listing for a soldier" — the most desperate step, short of suicide, in the eyes of respectable families. No! he would rather trust to casualties than to his own resolve — rather go on sitting at the feast, and sipping the wine he loved, though with the sword hanging over him and terror in his heart, than rush away into the cold darkness where there was no pleasure left. The utmost concession to Dunstan about the horse began to seem easy, compared with the fulfilment of his own threat. But his pride would not let him recommence the conversation otherwise than by continuing the quarrel. Dunstan was waiting for this, and took his ale in shorter draughts than usual.

"It's just like you," Godfrey burst out, in a bitter tone, "to talk about my selling Wildfire in that cool way — the last thing I've got to call my own, and the best bit of horse-flesh I ever had in my life. And if you'd got a spark of pride in you, you'd be ashamed to see the stables emptied, and everybody sneering about it. But it's my belief you'd sell yourself, if it was only for the pleasure of making somebody feel he'd got a bad bargain."

"Ay, ay," said Dunstan, very placably, "you do me justice, I see. You know I'm a jewel for 'ticing people into bargains. For which reason I advise you to let *me* sell Wildfire. I'd ride him to the hunt to-morrow for you, with pleasure. I should n't look so handsome as you in the saddle, but it's the horse they'll bid for, and not the rider."

"Yes, I daresay — trust my horse to you!"

"As you please," said Dunstan, rapping the window-seat again with an air of great unconcern. "It's *you* have got to pay Fowler's money; it's none of my business. You received the money from him when you went to Bramcote, and *you* told the Squire it was n't paid. I 'd nothing to do with that; you chose to be so obliging as to give it me, that was all. If you don't want to pay the money, let it alone; it 's all one to me. But I was willing to accommodate you by undertaking to sell the horse, seeing it 's not convenient to you to go so far to-morrow."

Godfrey was silent for some moments. He would have liked to spring on Dunstan, wrench the whip from his hand, and flog him to within an inch of his life; and no bodily fear could have deterred him; but he was mastered by another sort of fear, which was fed by feelings stronger even than his resentment. When he spoke again it was in a half-conciliatory tone.

" Well, you mean no nonsense about the horse, eh? You 'll sell him all fair, and hand over the money? If you don't, you know, everything 'ull go to smash, for I 've got nothing else to trust to. And you 'll have less pleasure in pulling the house over my head, when your own skull 's to be broken too."

" Ay, ay," said Dunstan, rising; "all right. I thought you 'd come round. I 'm the fellow to bring old Bryce up to the scratch. I 'll get you a hundred and twenty for him, if I get you a penny."

" But it 'll perhaps rain cats and dogs to-morrow, as it did yesterday, and then you can't go," said Godfrey, hardly knowing whether he wished for that obstacle or not.

" Not *it*," said Dunstan. " I 'm always lucky in my weather. It might rain if you wanted to go yourself. You never hold trumps, you know — I always do. You 've got the beauty, you see, and I 've got the luck, so you must keep me by you for your crooked sixpence; you 'll *ne*-ver get along without me."

" Confound you, hold your tongue!" said Godfrey, impetu-ously. " And take care to keep sober to-morrow, else you 'll get pitched on your head coming home, and Wildfire might be the worse for it."

" Make your tender heart easy," said Dunstan, opening the door. " You never knew me see double when I 'd got a bar-gain to make; it 'ud spoil the fun. Besides, whenever I fall, I 'm warranted to fall on my legs."

With that, Dunstan slammed the door behind him, and left Godfrey to that bitter rumination on his personal circumstances which was now unbroken from day to day save by the excitement of sporting, drinking, card-playing, or the rarer and less oblivious pleasure of seeing Miss Nancy Lammeter. The subtle and varied pains springing from the higher sensibility that accompanies higher culture, are perhaps less pitiable than that dreary absence of impersonal enjoyment and consolation which leaves ruder minds to the perpetual urgent companionship of their own griefs and discontents. The lives of those rural forefathers, whom we are apt to think very prosaic figures — men whose only work was to ride round their land, getting heavier and heavier in their saddles, and who passed the rest of their days in the half-listless gratification of senses dulled by monotony — had a certain pathos in them nevertheless. Calamities came to *them* too, and their early errors carried hard consequences: perhaps the love of some sweet maiden, the image of purity, order, and calm, had opened their eyes to the vision of a life in which the days would not seem too long, even without rioting; but the maiden was lost, and the vision passed away, and then what was left to them, especially when they had become too heavy for the hunt, or for carrying a gun over the furrows, but to drink and get merry, or to drink and get angry, so that they might be independent of variety, and say over again with eager emphasis the things they had said already any time that twelvemonth? Assuredly, among these flushed and dull-eyed men there were some whom — thanks to their native human-kindness — even riot could never drive into brutality; men who, when their cheeks were fresh, had felt the keen point of sorrow or remorse, had been pierced by the reeds they leaned on, or had lightly put their limbs in fetters from which no struggle could loose them; and under these sad circumstances, common to us all, their thoughts could find no resting-place outside the ever-trodden round of their own petty history.

That, at least, was the condition of Godfrey Cass in this six-and-twentieth year of his life. A movement of compunction, helped by those small indefinable influences which every

personal relation exerts on a pliant nature, had urged him into
a secret marriage, which was a blight on his life. It was an
ugly story of low passion, delusion, and waking from delusion,
which needs not to be dragged from the privacy of Godfrey's
bitter memory. He had long known that the delusion was
partly due to a trap laid for him by Dunstan, who saw in his
brother's degrading marriage the means of gratifying at once
his jealous hate and his cupidity. And if Godfrey could have
felt himself simply a victim, the iron bit that destiny had put
into his mouth would have chafed him less intolerably. If
the curses he muttered half aloud when he was alone had had
no other object than Dunstan's diabolical cunning, he might
have shrunk less from the consequences of avowal. But he
had something else to curse — his own vicious folly, which now
seemed as mad and unaccountable to him as almost all our
follies and vices do when their promptings have long passed
away. For four years he had thought of Nancy Lammeter,
and wooed her with tacit patient worship, as the woman who
made him think of the future with joy: she would be his wife,
and would make home lovely to him, as his father's home had
never been; and it would be easy, when she was always near,
to shake off those foolish habits that were no pleasures, but
only a feverish way of annulling vacancy. Godfrey's was
an essentially domestic nature, bred up in a home where the
hearth had no smiles, and where the daily habits were not
chastised by the presence of household order. His easy disposition made him fall in unresistingly with the family courses,
but the need of some tender permanent affection, the longing
for some influence that would make the good he preferred
easy to pursue, caused the neatness, purity, and liberal order-
liness of the Lammeter household, sunned by the smile of
Nancy, to seem like those fresh bright hours of the morning
when temptations go to sleep and leave the ear open to the
voice of the good angel, inviting to industry, sobriety, and
peace. And yet the hope of this paradise had not been
enough to save him from a course which shut him out of it
forever. Instead of keeping fast hold of the strong silken
rope by which Nancy would have drawn him safe to the green

banks where it was easy to step firmly, he had let himself be
dragged back into mud and slime, in which it was useless to
struggle. He had made ties for himself which robbed him of
all wholesome motive and were a constant exasperation.

Still, there was one position worse than the present: it was
the position he would be in when the ugly secret was disclosed; and the desire that continually triumphed over every
other was that of warding off the evil day, when he would
have to bear the consequences of his father's violent resentment for the wound inflicted on his family pride — would
have, perhaps, to turn his back on that hereditary ease and
dignity which, after all, was a sort of reason for living, and
would carry with him the certainty that he was banished forever from the sight and esteem of Nancy Lammeter. The
longer the interval, the more chance there was of deliverance
from some, at least, of the hateful consequences to which he
had sold himself; the more opportunities remained for him to
snatch the strange gratification of seeing Nancy, and gathering
some faint indications of her lingering regard. Towards this
gratification he was impelled, fitfully, every now and then,
after having passed weeks in which he had avoided her as the
far-off bright-winged prize that only made him spring forward
and find his chain all the more galling. One of those fits of
yearning was on him now, and it would have been strong
enough to have persuaded him to trust Wildfire to Dunstan
rather than disappoint the yearning, even if he had not had
another reason for his disinclination towards the morrow's
hunt. That other reason was the fact that the morning's
meet was near Batherley, the market-town where the unhappy
woman lived, whose image became more odious to him every
day; and to his thought the whole vicinage was haunted by
her. The yoke a man creates for himself by wrong-doing will
breed hate in the kindliest nature; and the good-humored,
affectionate-hearted Godfrey Cass was fast becoming a bitter
man, visited by cruel wishes, that seemed to enter, and depart,
and enter again, like demons who had found in him a ready-
garnished home.

What was he to do this evening to pass the time? He

might as well go to the Rainbow, and hear the talk about the
cock-fighting: everybody was there, and what else was there
to be done? Though, for his own part, he did not care a
button for cock-fighting. Snuff, the brown spaniel, who had
placed herself in front of him, and had been watching him for
some time, now jumped up in impatience for the expected
caress. But Godfrey thrust her away without looking at her,
and left the room, followed humbly by the unresenting Snuff
— perhaps because she saw no other career open to her.

CHAPTER IV.

DUNSTAN CASS, setting off in the raw morning. at the judi-
ciously quiet pace of a man who is obliged to ride to cover on
his hunter, had to take his way along the lane which, at its
farther extremity, passed by the piece of unenclosed ground
called the Stone-pit, where stood the cottage, once a stone-
cutter's shed, now for fifteen years inhabited by Silas Marner.
The spot looked very dreary at this season, with the moist
trodden clay about it, and the red, muddy water high up in
the deserted quarry. That was Dunstan's first thought as he
approached it; the second was, that the old fool of a weaver,
whose loom he heard rattling already, had a great deal of
money hidden somewhere. How was it that he, Dunstan
Cass, who had often heard talk of Marner's miserliness, had
never thought of suggesting to Godfrey that he should frighten
or persuade the old fellow into lending the money on the
excellent security of the young Squire's prospects? The
resource occurred to him now as so easy and agreeable, especially as Marner's hoard was likely to be large enough to leave
Godfrey a handsome surplus beyond his immediate needs, and
enable him to accommodate his faithful brother, that he had .
almost turned the horse's head towards home again. Godfrey
would be ready enough to accept the suggestion: he would

snatch eagerly at a plan that might save him from parting
with Wildfire. But when Dunstan's meditation reached this
point, the inclination to go on grew strong and prevailed. He
did n't want to give Godfrey that pleasure : he preferred that
Master Godfrey should be vexed. Moreover, Dunstan enjoyed the self-important consciousness of having a horse to
sell, and the opportunity of driving a bargain, swaggering,
and possibly taking somebody in. He might have all the
satisfaction attendant on selling his brother's horse, and not
the less have the further satisfaction of setting Godfrey to
borrow Marner's money. So he rode on to cover.

Bryce and Keating were there, as Dunstan was quite sure
they would be — he was such a lucky fellow.

"Heyday!" said Bryce, who had long had his eye on Wildfire, "you 're on your brother's horse to-day : how 's that ?"

"Oh, I 've swopped with him," said Dunstan, whose delight
in lying, grandly independent of utility, was not to be diminished by the likelihood that his hearer would not believe him
— "Wildfire's mine now."

"What! has he swopped with you for that big-boned hack
of yours ?" said Bryce, quite aware that he should get another
lie in answer.

"Oh, there was a little account between us," said Dunsey,
carelessly, "and Wildfire made it even. I accommodated him
by taking the horse, though it was against my will, for I 'd
got an itch for a mare o' Jortin's — as rare a bit o' blood as
ever you threw your leg across. But I shall keep Wildfire,
now I 've got him, though I 'd a bid of a hundred and fifty for
him the other day, from a man over at Flitton — he 's buying
for Lord Cromleck — a fellow with a cast in his eye, and a
green waistcoat. But I mean to stick to Wildfire : I shan't
get a better at a fence in a hurry. The mare 's got more blood,
but she 's a bit too weak in the hind-quarters."

Bryce of course divined that Dunstan wanted to sell the
horse, and Dunstan knew that he divined it (horse-dealing is
only one of many human transactions carried on in this ingenious manner) ; and they both considered that the bargain
was in its first stage, when Bryce replied, ironically —

"I wonder at that now; I wonder you mean to keep him; for I never heard of a man who did n't want to sell his horse getting a bid of half as much again as the horse was worth. You'll be lucky if you get a hundred."

Keating rode up now, and the transaction became more complicated. It ended in the purchase of the horse by Bryce for a hundred and twenty, to be paid on the delivery of Wildfire, safe and sound, at the Batherley stables. It did occur to Dunsey that it might be wise for him to give up the day's hunting, proceed at once to Batherley, and, having waited for Bryce's return, hire a horse to carry him home with the money in his pocket. But the inclination for a run, encouraged by confidence in his luck, and by a draught of brandy from his pocket-pistol at the conclusion of the bargain, was not easy to overcome, especially with a horse under him that would take the fences to the admiration of the field. Dunstan, however, took one fence too many, and got his horse pierced with a hedge-stake. His own ill-favored person, which was quite unmarketable, escaped without injury; but poor Wildfire, unconscious of his price, turned on his flank and painfully panted his last. It happened that Dunstan, a short time before, having had to get down to arrange his stirrup, had muttered a good many curses at this interruption, which had thrown him in the rear of the hunt near the moment of glory, and under this exasperation had taken the fences more blindly. He would soon have been up with the hounds again, when the fatal accident happened; and hence he was between eager riders in advance, not troubling themselves about what happened behind them, and far-off stragglers, who were as likely as not to pass quite aloof from the line of road in which Wildfire had fallen. Dunstan, whose nature it was to care more for immediate annoyances than for remote consequences, no sooner recovered his legs, and saw that it was all over with Wildfire, than he felt a satisfaction at the absence of witnesses to a position which no swaggering could make enviable. Reinforcing himself, after his shake, with a little brandy and much swearing, he walked as fast as he could to a coppice on his right hand, through which it occurred to him that he could make his way

to Batherley without danger of encountering any member of
the hunt. His first intention was to hire a horse there and
ride home forthwith, for to walk many miles without a gun in
his hand and along an ordinary road, was as much out of the
question to him as to other spirited young men of his kind.
He did not much mind about taking the bad news to Godfrey,
for he had to offer him at the same time the resource of Marner's money; and if Godfrey kicked, as he always did, at the
notion of making a fresh debt from which he himself got the
smallest share of advantage, why, he wouldn't kick long:
Dunstan felt sure he could worry Godfrey into anything.
The idea of Marner's money kept growing in vividness, now
the want of it had become immediate; the prospect of having
to make his appearance with the muddy boots of a pedestrian
at Batherley, and to encounter the grinning queries of stable-
men, stood unpleasantly in the way of his impatience to be
back at Raveloe and carry out his felicitous plan; and a
casual visitation of his waistcoat-pocket, as he was ruminating,
awakened his memory to the fact that the two or three small
coins his fore-finger encountered there, were of too pale a color
to cover that small debt, without payment of which the stable-
keeper had declared he would never do any more business with
Dunsey Cass. After all, according to the direction in which
the run had brought him, he was not so very much farther
from home than he was from Batherley; but Dunsey, not
being remarkable for clearness of head, was only led to this
conclusion by the gradual perception that there were other
reasons for choosing the unprecedented course of walking
home. It was now nearly four o'clock, and a mist was gathering: the sooner he got into the road the better. He remembered having crossed the road and seen the finger-post only a
little while before Wildfire broke down; so, buttoning his coat,
twisting the lash of his hunting-whip compactly round the
handle, and rapping the tops of his boots with a self-possessed
air, as if to assure himself that he was not at all taken by surprise, he set off with the sense that he was undertaking a
remarkable feat of bodily exertion, which somehow and at
some time he should be able to dress up and magnify to the

admiration of a select circle at the Rainbow. When a young gentleman like Dunsey is reduced to so exceptional a mode of locomotion as walking, a whip in his hand is a desirable corrective to a too bewildering dreamy sense of unwontedness in his position; and Dunstan, as he went along through the gathering mist, was always rapping his whip somewhere. It was Godfrey's whip, which he had chosen to take without leave because it had a gold handle; of course no one could see, when Dunstan held it, that the name *Godfrey Cass* was cut in deep letters on that gold handle — they could only see that it was a very handsome whip. Dunsey was not without fear that he might meet some acquaintance in whose eyes he would cut a pitiable figure, for mist is no screen when people get close to each other; but when he at last found himself in the well-known Raveloe lanes without having met a soul, he silently remarked that that was part of his usual good-luck. But now the mist, helped by the evening darkness, was more of a screen than he desired, for it hid the ruts into which his feet were liable to slip — hid everything, so that he had to guide his steps by dragging his whip along the low bushes in advance of the hedgerow. He must soon, he thought, be getting near the opening at the Stone-pits: he should find it out by the break in the hedgerow. He found it out, however, by another circumstance which he had not expected — namely, by certain gleams of light, which he presently guessed to proceed from Silas Marner's cottage. That cottage and the money hidden within it had been in his mind continually during his walk, and he had been imagining ways of cajoling and tempting the weaver to part with the immediate possession of his money for the sake of receiving interest. Dunstan felt as if there must be a little frightening added to the cajolery, for his own arithmetical convictions were not clear enough to afford him any forcible demonstration as to the advantages of interest; and as for security, he regarded it vaguely as a means of cheating a man by making him believe that he would be paid. Altogether, the operation on the miser's mind was a task that Godfrey would be sure to hand over to his more daring and cunning brother: Dunstan had made up his mind to that; and

by the time he saw the light gleaming through the chinks of
Marner's shutters, the idea of a dialogue with the weaver had
become so familiar to him, that it occurred to him as quite a
natural thing to make the acquaintance forthwith. There
might be several conveniences attending this course: the
weaver had possibly got a lantern, and Dunstan was tired of
feeling his way. He was still nearly three-quarters of a mile
from home, and the lane was becoming unpleasantly slippery,
for the mist was passing into rain. He turned up the bank,
not without some fear lest he might miss the right way, since
he was not certain whether the light were in front or on the
side of the cottage. But he felt the ground before him cau-
tiously with his whip-handle, and at last arrived safely at the
door. He knocked loudly, rather enjoying the idea that the
old fellow would be frightened at the sudden noise. He heard
no movement in reply: all was silence in the cottage. Was
the weaver gone to bed, then? If so, why had he left a light?
That was a strange forgetfulness in a miser. Dunstan knocked
still more loudly, and, without pausing for a reply, pushed his
fingers through the latch-hole, intending to shake the door and
pull the latch-string up and down, not doubting that the door
was fastened. But, to his surprise, at this double motion the
door opened, and he found himself in front of a bright fire
which lit up every corner of the cottage — the bed, the loom,
the three chairs, and the table — and showed him that Marner
was not there.

Nothing at that moment could be much more inviting to
Dunsey than the bright fire on the brick hearth: he walked
in and seated himself by it at once. There was something in
front of the fire, too, that would have been inviting to a
hungry man, if it had been in a different stage of cooking. It
was a small bit of pork suspended from the kettle-hanger by
a string passed through a large door-key, in a way known to
primitive house-keepers unpossessed of jacks. But the pork
had been hung at the farthest extremity of the hanger, apparently to prevent the roasting from proceeding too rapidly during the owner's absence. The old staring simpleton had hot
meat for his supper, then? thought Dunstan. People had

always said he lived on mouldy bread, on purpose to check
his appetite. But where could he be at this time, and on such
an evening, leaving his supper in this stage of preparation,
and his door unfastened? Dunstan's own recent difficulty in
making his way suggested to him that the weaver had perhaps
gone outside his cottage to fetch in fuel, or for some such
brief purpose, and had slipped into the Stone-pit. That was
an interesting idea to Dunstan, carrying consequences of entire novelty. If the weaver was dead, who had a right to his
money? Who would know where his money was hidden?
Who would know that anybody had come to take it away? He
went no farther into the subtleties of evidence: the pressing
question, "Where *is* the money?" now took such entire possession of him as to make him quite forget that the weaver's
death was not a certainty. A dull mind, once arriving at an
inference that flatters a desire, is rarely able to retain the
impression that the notion from which the inference started
was purely problematic. And Dunstan's mind was as dull as
the mind of a possible felon usually is. There were only
three hiding-places where he had ever heard of cottagers'
hoards being found: the thatch, the bed, and a hole in the
floor. Marner's cottage had no thatch; and Dunstan's first
act, after a train of thought made rapid by the stimulus of
cupidity, was to go up to the bed; but while he did so, his
eyes travelled eagerly over the floor, where the bricks, distinct
in the fire-light, were discernible under the sprinkling of sand.
But not everywhere; for there was one spot, and one only,
which was quite covered with sand, and sand showing the
marks of fingers, which had apparently been careful to spread
it over a given space. It was near the treadles of the loom.
In an instant Dunstan darted to that spot, swept away the
sand with his whip, and, inserting the thin end of the hook
between the bricks, found that they were loose. In haste he
lifted up two bricks, and saw what he had no doubt was the
object of his search; for what could there be but money in
those two leathern bags? And, from their weight, they must
be filled with guineas. Dunstan felt round the hole, to be
certain that it held no more; then hastily replaced the bricks,

and spread the sand over them. Hardly more than five minutes had passed since he entered the cottage, but it seemed to Dunstan like a long while; and though he was without any distinct recognition of the possibility that Marner might be alive, and might re-enter the cottage at any moment, he felt an undefinable dread laying hold on him, as he rose to his feet with the bags in his hand. He would hasten out into the darkness, and then consider what he should do with the bags. He closed the door behind him immediately, that he might shut in the stream of light: a few steps would be enough to carry him beyond betrayal by the gleams from the shutter-chinks and the latch-hole. The rain and darkness had got thicker, and he was glad of it; though it was awkward walking with both hands filled, so that it was as much as he could do to grasp his whip along with one of the bags. But when he had gone a yard or two, he might take his time. So he stepped forward into the darkness.

CHAPTER V.

When Dunstan Cass turned his back on the cottage, Silas Marner was not more than a hundred yards away from it, plodding along from the village with a sack thrown round his shoulders as an over-coat, and with a horn lantern in his hand. His legs were weary, but his mind was at ease, free from the presentiment of change. The sense of security more frequently springs from habit than from conviction, and for this reason it often subsists after such a change in the conditions as might have been expected to suggest alarm. The lapse of time during which a given event has not happened, is, in this logic of habit, constantly alleged as a reason why the event should never happen, even when the lapse of time is precisely the added condition which makes the event imminent. A man will tell you that he has worked in a mine for forty years unhurt by an accident as a reason why he should apprehend no danger, though the roof is beginning to sink; and it is often observable, that the older a man gets, the more difficult it is to him to retain a believing conception of his own death. This influence of habit was necessarily strong in a man whose life was so monotonous as Marner's — who saw no new people and heard of no new events to keep alive in him the idea of the unexpected and the changeful; and it explains simply enough, why his mind could be at ease, though he had left his house and his treasure more defenceless than usual. Silas was thinking with double complacency of his supper: first, because it would be hot and savory; and secondly, because it would cost him nothing. For the little bit of pork was a present from that excellent housewife, Miss Priscilla Lammeter, to whom he had this day carried home a handsome piece of linen; and it was only on occasion of a present like this, that Silas indulged himself with roast meat. Supper was his favorite meal, because it came at his time of revelry, when his heart warmed over his gold; whenever he had roast meat, he always chose to have it for supper. But this evening, he had no sooner ingeniously knotted his string fast round his bit of pork, twisted the string according to rule over his door-key, passed it through the handle, and made it fast on the hanger, than he remembered that a piece of very fine twine was indispensable to his " setting up " a new piece of work in his loom early in the morning. It had slipped his memory, because, in coming from Mr. Lammeter's, he had not had to pass through the village; but to lose time by going on errands in the morning was out of the question. It was a nasty fog to turn out into, but there were things Silas loved better than his own comfort; so, drawing his pork to the extremity of the hanger, and arming himself with his lantern and his old sack, he set out on what, in ordinary weather, would have been a twenty minutes' errand. He could not have locked his door without undoing his well-knotted string and retarding his supper; it was not worth his while to make that sacrifice. What thief would find his way to the Stone-pits on such a night as this? and why should he come on this particular night, when he had never come through all the fifteen years before ? These questions were not distinctly present in Silas's mind; they merely serve to represent the vaguely-felt foundation of his freedom from anxiety.

He reached his door in much satisfaction that his errand was done : he opened it, and to his short-sighted eyes everything remained as he had left it, except that the fire sent out a welcome increase of heat. He trod about the floor while putting by his lantern and throwing aside his hat and sack, so as to merge the marks of Dunstan's feet on the sand in the marks of his own nailed boots. Then he moved his pork nearer to the fire, and sat down to the agreeable business of tending the meat and warming himself at the same time.

Any one who had looked at him as the red light shone upon his pale face, strange straining eyes, and meagre form, would perhaps have understood the mixture of contemptuous pity, dread, and suspicion with which he was regarded by his neighbors in Raveloe. Yet few men could be more harmless than poor Marner. In his truthful simple soul, not even the growing greed and worship of gold could beget any vice directly injurious to others. The light of his faith quite put out, and his affections made desolate, he had clung with all the force of his nature to his work and his money ; and like all objects to which a man devotes himself, they had fashioned him into correspondence with themselves. His loom, as he wrought in it without ceasing, had in its turn wrought on him, and confirmed more and more the monotonous craving for its monotonous response. His gold, as he hung over it and saw it grow, gathered his power of loving together into a hard isolation like its own.

As soon as he was warm he began to think it would be a long while to wait till after supper before he drew out his guineas, and it would be pleasant to see them on the table before him as he ate his unwonted feast. For joy is the best of wine, and Silas's guineas were a golden wine of that sort.

He rose and placed his candle unsuspectingly on the floor near his loom, swept away the sand without noticing any

change, and removed the bricks. The sight of the empty hole
made his heart leap violently, but the belief that his gold was
gone could not come at once — only terror, and the eager effort
to put an end to the terror. He passed his trembling hand all
about the hole, trying to think it possible that his eyes had
deceived him; then he held the candle in the hole and exam-
ined it curiously, trembling more and more. At last he shook
so violently that he let fall the candle, and lifted his hands to
his head, trying to steady himself, that he might think. Had
he put his gold somewhere else, by a sudden resolution last
night, and then forgotten it? A man falling into dark waters
seeks a momentary footing even on sliding stones; and Silas,
by acting as if he believed in false hopes, warded off the moment of despair. He searched in every corner, he turned his
bed over, and shook it, and kneaded it; he looked in his brick
oven where he laid his sticks. When there was no other place
to be searched, he kneeled down again and felt once more all
round the hole. There was no untried refuge left for a
moment's shelter from the terrible truth.

Yes, there was a sort of refuge which always comes with the
prostration of thought under an overpowering passion: it was
that expectation of impossibilities, that belief in contradictory
images, which is still distinct from madness, because it is
capable of being dissipated by the external fact. Silas got up
from his knees trembling, and looked round at the table:
did n't the gold lie there after all? The table was bare.
Then he turned and looked behind him — looked all round his
dwelling, seeming to strain his brown eyes after some possible
appearance of the bags where he had already sought them in
vain. He could see every object in his cottage — and his gold
was not there.

Again he put his trembling hands to his head, and gave a
wild ringing scream, the cry of desolation. For a few moments after, he stood motionless; but the cry had relieved
him from the first maddening pressure of the truth. He
turned, and tottered towards his loom, and got into the seat
where he worked, instinctively seeking this as the strongest
assurance of reality.

And now that all the false hopes had vanished, and the first shock of certainty was past, the idea of a thief began to present itself, and he entertained it eagerly, because a thief might be caught and made to restore the gold. The thought brought some new strength with it, and he started from his loom to the door. As he opened it the rain beat in upon him, for it was falling more and more heavily. There were no footsteps to be tracked on such a night — footsteps? When had the thief come? During Silas's absence in the daytime the door had been locked, and there had been no marks of any inroad on his return by daylight. And in the evening, too, he said to himself, everything was the same as when he had left it. The sand and bricks looked as if they had not been moved. *Was* it a thief who had taken the bags? or was it a cruel power that no hands could reach which had delighted in making him a second time desolate? He shrank from this vaguer dread, and fixed his mind with struggling effort on the robber with hands, who could be reached by hands. His thoughts glanced at all the neighbors who had made any remarks, or asked any questions which he might now regard as a ground of suspicion. There was Jem Rodney, a known poacher, and otherwise disreputable: he had often met Marner in his journeys across the fields, and had said something jestingly about the weaver's money; nay, he had once irritated Marner, by lingering at the fire when he called to light his pipe, instead of going about his business. Jem Rodney was the man — there was ease in the thought. Jem could be found and made to restore the money: Marner did not want to punish him, but only to get back his gold which had gone from him, and left his soul like a forlorn traveller on an unknown desert. The robber must be laid hold of. Marner's ideas of legal authority were confused, but he felt that he must go and proclaim his loss; and the great people in the village — the clergyman, the constable, and Squire Cass — would make Jem Rodney, or somebody else, deliver up the stolen money. He rushed out in the rain, under the stimulus of this hope, forgetting to cover his head, not caring to fasten his door; for he felt as if he had nothing left to lose. He ran swiftly, till want of breath compelled him to slacken his pace as he was entering the village at the turning close to the Rainbow.

The Rainbow, in Marner's view, was a place of luxurious resort for rich and stout husbands, whose wives had superfluous stores of linen ; it was the place where he was likely to find the powers and dignities of Raveloe, and where he could most speedily make his loss public. He lifted the latch, and turned into the bright bar or kitchen on the right hand, where the less lofty customers of the house were in the habit of assembling, the parlor on the left being reserved for the more select society in which Squire Cass frequently enjoyed the double pleasure of conviviality and condescension. But the parlor was dark to-night, the chief personages who ornamented its circle being all at Mrs. Osgood's birthday dance, as Godfrey Cass was. And in consequence of this, the party on the high-screened seats in the kitchen was more numerous than usual ; several personages, who would otherwise have been admitted into the parlor and enlarged the opportunity of hectoring and condescension for their betters, being content this evening to vary their enjoyment by taking their spirits-and-water where they could themselves hector and condescend in company that called for beer.

* * *

CHAPTER VI.

THE conversation, which was at a high pitch of animation when Silas approached the door of the Rainbow, had, as usual, been slow and intermittent when the company first assembled. The pipes began to be puffed in a silence which had an air of severity ; the more important customers, who drank spirits and sat nearest the fire, staring at each other as if a bet were depending on the first man who winked ; while the beer-drinkers, chiefly men in fustian jackets and smock-frocks, kept their eyelids down and rubbed their hands across their mouths, as if their draughts of beer were a funereal duty attended with embarrassing sadness. At last, Mr. Snell, the landlord, a man of a neutral disposition, accustomed to stand aloof from human differences as those of beings who were all alike in need of liquor, broke silence, by saying in a doubtful tone to his cousin the butcher —

"Some folks 'ud say that was a fine beast you druv in yesterday, Bob ?"

The butcher, a jolly, smiling, red-haired man, was not disposed to answer rashly. He gave a few puffs before he spat and replied, "And they would n't be fur wrong, John."

After this feeble delusive thaw, the silence set in as severely as before.

"Was it a red Durham ?" said the farrier, taking up the thread of discourse after the lapse of a few minutes.

The farrier looked at the landlord, and the landlord looked at the butcher, as the person who must take the responsibility of answering.

"Red it was," said the butcher, in his good-humored husky treble — "and a Durham it was."

"Then you need n't tell *me* who you bought it of," said the farrier, looking round with some triumph; "I know who it is has got the red Durhams o' this country-side. And she 'd a white star on her brow, I 'll bet a penny ?" The farrier leaned forward with his hands on his knees as he put this question, and his eyes twinkled knowingly.

"Well; yes — she might," said the butcher, slowly, considering that he was giving a decided affirmative. "I don't say contrairy."

"I knew that very well," said the farrier, throwing himself backward again, and speaking defiantly; "if *I* don't know Mr. Lammeter's cows, I should like to know who does — that 's all. And as for the cow you 've bought, bargain or no bargain, I 've been at the drenching of her — contradick me who will."

The farrier looked fierce, and the mild butcher's conversational spirit was roused a little.

"I 'm not for contradicking no man," he said; "I 'm for peace and quietness. Some are for cutting long ribs — I 'm for cutting 'em short myself; but I don't quarrel with 'em.

All I say is, it's a lovely carkiss — and anybody as was reasonable, it 'ud bring tears into their eyes to look at it."

"Well, it's the cow as I drenched, whatever it is," pursued the farrier, angrily; "and it was Mr. Lammeter's cow, else you told a lie when you said it was a red Durham."

"I tell no lies," said the butcher, with the same mild huskiness as before, "and I contradick none — not if a man was to swear himself black: he's no meat o' mine, nor none o' my bargains. All I say is, it's a lovely carkiss. And what I say I'll stick to; but I'll quarrel wi' no man."

"No," said the farrier, with bitter sarcasm, looking at the company generally; "and p'rhaps you ar n't pig-headed; and p'rhaps you did n't say the cow was a red Durham; and p'rhaps you did n't say she'd got a star on her brow — stick to that, now you're at it."

"Come, come," said the landlord; "let the cow alone. The truth lies atween you: you're both right and both wrong, as I allays say. And as for the cow's being Mr. Lammeter's, I say nothing to that; but this I say, as the Rainbow's the Rainbow. And for the matter o' that, if the talk is to be o' the Lammeters, *you* know the most upo' that head, eh, Mr. Macey? You remember when first Mr. Lammeter's father come into these parts, and took the Warrens?"

Mr. Macey, tailor and parish-clerk, the latter of which functions rheumatism had of late obliged him to share with a small-featured young man.who sat opposite him, held his white head on one side, and twirled his thumbs with an air of complacency, slightly seasoned with criticism. He smiled pityingly, in answer to the landlord's appeal, and said —

"Ay, ay; I know, I know; but I let other folks talk. I've laid by now, and gev up to the young uns. Ask them as have been to school at Tarley: they've learnt pernouncing; that's come up since my day."

"If you're pointing at me, Mr. Macey," said the deputy-clerk, with an air of anxious propriety, "I'm nowise a man to speak out of my place. As the psalm says —

'I know what's right, nor only so,
But also practise what I know.'"

" Well, then, I wish you 'd keep hold o' the tune, when it's set for you; if you 're for prac*ti*sing, I wish you 'd prac*ti*se that," said a large jocose-looking man, an excellent wheel-wright in his week-day capacity, but on Sundays leader of the choir. He winked, as he spoke, at two of the company, who were known officially as the "bassoon" and the "key-bugle," in the confidence that he was expressing the sense of the musical profession in Raveloe.

Mr. Tookey, the deputy-clerk, who shared the unpopularity common to deputies, turned very red, but replied, with careful moderation — "Mr. Winthrop, if you 'll bring me any proof as I 'm in the wrong, I 'm not the man to say I won't alter. But there 's people set up their own ears for a standard, and expect the whole choir to follow 'em. There may be two opinions, I hope."

" Ay, ay," said Mr. Macey, who felt very well satisfied with this attack on youthful presumption; "you 're right there, Tookey : there 's allays two 'pinions; there 's the 'pinion a man has of himsen, and there 's the 'pinion other folks have on him. There 'd be two 'pinions about a cracked bell, if the bell could hear itself."

" Well, Mr. Macey," said poor Tookey, serious amidst the general laughter, "I undertook to partially fill up the office of parish-clerk by Mr. Crackenthorp's desire, whenever your infirmities should make you unfitting; and it 's one of the rights thereof to sing in the choir — else why have you done the same yourself ? "

" Ah ! but the old gentleman and you are two folks," said Ben Winthrop. " The old gentleman 's got a gift. Why, the Squire used to invite him to take a glass, only to hear him sing the 'Red Rovier'; did n't he, Mr. Macey ? It 's a nat'ral gift. There 's my little lad Aaron, he 's got a gift — he can sing a tune off straight, like a throstle. But as for you, Master Tookey, you 'd better stick to your 'Amens': your voice is well enough when you keep it up in your nose. It 's your inside as is n't right made for music: it 's no better nor a hollow stalk."

This kind of unflinching frankness was the most piquant form of joke to the company at the Rainbow, and Ben Win-

throp's insult was felt by everybody to have capped Mr.
Macey's epigram.

"I see what it is plain enough," said Mr. Tookey, unable
to keep cool any longer. "There's a consperacy to turn me
out o' the choir, as I should n't share the Christmas money —
that's where it is. But I shall speak to Mr. Crackenthorp;
I 'll not be put upon by no man."

"Nay, nay, Tookey," said Ben Winthrop. "We 'll pay
you your share to keep out of it — that's what we 'll do.
There's things folks 'ud pay to be rid on, besides varmin."

"Come, come," said the landlord, who felt that paying
people for their absence was a principle dangerous to society;
"a joke's a joke. We 're all good friends here, I hope. We
must give and take. You 're both right and you 're both
wrong, as I say. I agree wi' Mr. Macey here, as there's two
opinions; and if mine was asked, I should say they 're both
right. Tookey's right and Winthrop's right, and they 've only
got to split the difference and make themselves even."

The farrier was puffing his pipe rather fiercely, in some
contempt at this trivial discussion. He had no ear for music
himself, and never went to church, as being of the medical
profession, and likely to be in requisition for delicate cows.
But the butcher, having music in his soul, had listened with
a divided desire for Tookey's defeat and for the preservation
of the peace.

"To be sure," he said, following up the landlord's conciliatory view, "we 're fond of our old clerk; it 's nat'ral and him
used to be such a singer, and got a brother as is known for the
first fiddler in this country-side. Eh, it 's a pity but what
Solomon lived in our village, and could give us a tune when
we liked; eh, Mr. Macey? I 'd keep him in liver and lights
for nothing — that I would."

"Ay, ay," said Mr. Macey, in the height of complacency;
"our family's been known for musicianers as far back as
anybody can tell. But them things are dying out, as I tell
Solomon every time he comes round; there's no voices like
what there used to be, and there's nobody remembers what
we remember, if it is n't the old crows."

"Ay, you remember when first Mr. Lammeter's father come into these parts, don't you, Mr. Macey?" said the landlord.

"I should think I did," said the old man, who had now gone through that complimentary process necessary to bring him up to the point of narration; "and a fine old gentleman he was — as fine, and finer nor the Mr. Lammeter as now is. He came from a bit north'ard, so far as I could ever make out. But there's nobody rightly knows about those parts: only it could n't be far north'ard, nor much different from this country, for he brought a fine breed o' sheep with him, so there must be pastures there, and everything reasonable. We heared tell as he'd sold his own land to come and take the Warrens, and that seemed odd for a man as had land of his own, to come and rent a farm in a strange place. But they said it was along of his wife's dying; though there's reasons in things as nobody knows on — that's pretty much what I've made out; yet some folks are so wise, they'll find you fifty reasons straight off, and all the while the real reason's winking at 'em in the corner, and they niver see 't. Howsomever, it was soon seen as we'd got a new parish'ner as know'd the rights and customs o' things, and kep a good house, and was well looked on by everybody. And the young man — that's the Mr. Lammeter as now is, for he'd niver a sister — soon begun to court Miss Osgood, that's the sister o' the Mr. Osgood as now is, and a fine handsome lass she was — eh, you can't think — they pretend this young lass is like her, but that's the way wi' people as don't know what come before 'em. *I* should know, for I helped the old rector, Mr. Drumlow as was, I helped him marry 'em."

Here Mr. Macey paused; he always gave his narrative in instalments, expecting to be questioned according to precedent.

"Ay, and a partic'lar thing happened, did n't it, Mr. Macey, so as you were likely to remember that marriage?" said the landlord, in a congratulatory tone.

"I should think there did — a *very* partic'lar thing," said Mr. Macey, nodding sideways. "For Mr. Drumlow — poor old gentleman, I was fond on him, though he'd got a bit confused in his head, what wi' age and wi' taking a drop o' summat warm when the service come of a cold morning. And young Mr. Lammeter he'd have no way but he must be married in Janiwary, which, to be sure, 's a unreasonable time to be married in, for it is n't like a christening or a burying, as you can't help; and so Mr. Drumlow — poor old gentleman, I was fond on him — but when he come to put the questions, he put 'em by the rule o' contrary, like, and he says, 'Wilt thou have this man to thy wedded wife?' says he, and then he says, 'Wilt thou have this woman to thy wedded husband?' says he. But the partic'larest thing of all is, as nobody took any notice on it but me, and they answered straight off 'yes,' like as if it had been me saying 'Amen' i' the right place, without listening to what went before."

"But *you* knew what was going on well enough, did n't you, Mr. Macey? You were live enough, eh?" said the butcher.

"Lor bless you!" said Mr. Macey, pausing, and smiling in pity at the impotence of his hearer's imagination — "why, I was all of a tremble: it was as if I'd been a coat pulled by the two tails, like; for I could n't stop the parson, I could n't take upon me to do that; and yet I said to myself, I says, 'Suppose they should n't be fast married, 'cause the words are contrary?' and my head went working like a mill, for I was allays un-common for turning things over and seeing all round 'em; and I says to myself, 'Is 't the meanin' or the words as makes folks fast i' wedlock?' For the parson meant right, and the bride and bridegroom meant right. But then, when I come to think on it, meanin' goes but a little way i' most things, for you may mean to stick things together and your glue may be bad, and then where are you? And so I says to mysen, 'It is n't the meanin', it 's the glue.' And I was worreted as if I'd got three bells to pull at once, when we went into the vestry, and they begun to sign their names. But where 's the use o' talking? — you can't think what goes on in a 'cute man's inside."

"But you held in for all that, did n't you, Mr. Macey?" said the landlord.

"Ay, I held in tight till I was by mysen wi' Mr. Drumlow, and then I out wi' everything, but respectful, as I allays did.

And he made light on it, and he says, 'Pooh, pooh, Macey, make yourself easy,' he says; 'it's neither the meaning nor the words — it's the re*ge*ster does it — that's the glue.' So you see he settled it easy; for parsons and doctors know everything by heart, like, so as they are n't worreted wi' thinking what's the rights and wrongs o' things, as I 'n been many and many's the time. And sure enough the wedding turned out all right, on'y poor Mrs. Lammeter — that's Miss Osgood as was — died afore the lasses was growed up; but for prosperity and everything respectable, there's no family more looked on."

Every one of Mr. Macey's audience had heard this story many times, but it was listened to as if it had been a favorite tune, and at certain points the puffing of the pipes was momentarily suspended, that the listeners might give their whole minds to the expected words. But there was more to come; and Mr. Snell, the landlord, duly put the leading question.

"Why, old Mr. Lammeter had a pretty fortin, did n't they say, when he come into these parts?"

"Well, yes," said Mr. Macey; "but I dare say it's as much as this Mr. Lammeter's done to keep it whole. For there was allays a talk as nobody could get rich on the Warrens: though he holds it cheap, for it's what they call Charity Land."

"Ay, and there's few folks know so well as you how it come to be Charity Land, eh, Mr. Macey?" said the butcher.

"How should they?" said the old clerk, with some contempt. "Why, my grandfather made the grooms' livery for that Mr. Cliff as came and built the big stables at the Warrens. Why, they're stables four times as big as Squire Cass's, for he thought o' nothing but hosses and hunting, Cliff did n't — a Lunnon tailor, some folks said, as had gone mad wi' cheating. For he could n't ride; lor bless you! they said he'd got no more grip o' the hoss than if his legs had been cross-sticks: my grandfather heared old Squire Cass say so many and many a time. But ride he would as if Old Harry had been a-driving him; and he'd a son, a lad o' sixteen; and nothing would his father have him do, but he must ride and ride — though the lad was frighted, they said. And it was a common saying as

the father wanted to ride the tailor out o' the lad, and make a
gentleman on him — not but what I 'm a tailor myself, but in
respect as God made me such, I 'm proud on it, for 'Macey,
tailor,' 's been wrote up over our door since afore the Queen's
heads went out on the shillings.   But Cliff, he was ashamed o'
being called a tailor, and he was sore vexed as his riding was
laughed at, and nobody o' the gentlefolks hereabout could abide
him.   Howsomever, the poor lad got sickly and died, and the
father did n't live long after him, for he got queerer nor ever,
and they said he used to go out i' the dead o' the night, wi' a
lantern in his hand, to the stables, and set a lot o' lights burning, for he got as he could n't sleep; and there he 'd stand,
cracking his whip and looking at his hosses; and they said it
was a mercy as the stables did n't get burned down wi' the
poor dumb creaturs in 'em.   But at last he died raving, and
they found as he 'd left all his property, Warrens and all, to
a Lunnon Charity, and that 's how the Warrens come to be
Charity Land; though, as for the stables, Mr. Lammeter never
uses 'em — they 're out o' all charicter — lor bless you! if you
was to set the doors a-banging in 'em, it 'ud sound like thunder
half o'er the parish."

   "Ay, but there 's more going on in the stables than what
folks see by daylight, eh, Mr. Macey?" said the landlord.

   "Ay, ay; go that way of a dark night, that 's all," said Mr.
Macey, winking mysteriously, "and then make believe, if you
like, as you did n't see lights i' the stables, nor hear the stamping o' the hosses, nor the cracking o' the whips, and howling,
too, if it 's tow'rt daybreak. 'Cliff's Holiday' has been the
name of it ever sin' I were a boy; that 's to say, some said as
it was the holiday Old Harry gev him from roasting, like.
That 's what my father told me, and he was a reasonable man,
though there 's folks nowadays know what happened afore
they were born better nor they know their own business."

   "What do you say to that, eh, Dowlas?" said the landlord,
turning to the farrier, who was swelling with impatience for
his cue.   "There 's a nut for _you_ to crack."

   Mr. Dowlas was the negative spirit in the company, and was
proud of his position.

"Say? I say what a man *should* say as does n't shut his eyes to look at a finger-post. I say, as I 'm ready to wager any man ten pound, if he 'll stand out wi' me any dry night in the pasture before the Warren stables, as we shall neither see lights nor hear noises, if it is n't the blowing of our own noses. That 's what I say, and I 've said it many a time ; but there 's nobody 'ull ventur a ten-pun' note on their ghos'es as they make so sure of."

" Why, Dowlas, that 's easy betting, that is," said Ben Winthrop. "You might as well bet a man as he would n't catch the rheumatise if he stood up to 's neck in the pool of a frosty night. It 'ud be fine fun for a man to win his bet as he 'd catch the rheumatise. Folks as believe in Cliff's Holiday are n't a-going to ventur near it for a matter o' ten pound."

"If Master Dowlas wants to know the truth on it," said Mr. Macey, with a sarcastic smile, tapping his thumbs together, " he 's no call to lay any bet — let him go and stan' by himself — there 's nobody 'ull hinder him ; and then he can let the parish'ners know if they 're wrong."

"Thank you ! I 'm obliged to you," said the farrier, with a snort of scorn. "If folks are fools, it 's no business o' mine. *I* don't want to make out the truth about ghos'es : I know it a'ready. But I 'm not against a bet — everything fair and open. Let any man bet me ten pound as I shall see Cliff's Holiday, and I 'll go and stand by myself. I want no company. I 'd as lief do it as I 'd fill this pipe."

"Ah, but who 's to watch you, Dowlas, and see you do it ? That 's no fair bet," said the butcher.

"No fair bet ? " replied Mr. Dowlas, angrily. "I should like to hear any man stand up and say I want to bet unfair. Come now, Master Lundy, I should like to hear you say it."

"Very like you would," said the butcher. "But it 's no business o' mine. You 're none o' my bargains, and I are n't a-going to try and 'bate your price. If anybody 'll bid for you at your own vallying, let him. I 'm for peace and quietness, I am."

"Yes, that 's what every yapping cur is, when you hold a stick up at him," said the farrier. "But I 'm afraid o' neither man nor ghost, and I'm ready to lay a fair bet. *I* are n't a turn-tail cur."

"Ay, but there's this in it, Dowlas," said the landlord, speaking in a tone of much candor and tolerance. "There's folks, i' my opinion, they can't see ghos'es, not if they stood as plain as a pike-staff before 'em. And there's reason i' that. For there's my wife, now, can't smell, not if she'd the strongest o' cheese under her nose. I never see'd a ghost myself; but then I says to myself, 'Very like I have n't got the smell for 'em.' I mean, putting a ghost for a smell, or else contrairiways. And so, I'm for holding with both sides; for, as I say, the truth lies between 'em. And if Dowlas was to go and stand, and say he'd never seen a wink o' Cliff's Holiday all the night through, I'd back him; and if anybody said as Cliff's Holiday was certain sure for all that, I'd back *him* too. For the smell's what I go by."

The landlord's analogical argument was not well received by the farrier — a man intensely opposed to compromise.

"Tut, tut," he said, setting down his glass with refreshed irritation; "what's the smell got to do with it? Did ever a ghost give a man a black eye? That's what I should like to know. If ghos'es want me to believe in 'em, let 'em leave off skulking i' the dark and i' lone places — let 'em come where there's company and candles."

"As if ghos'es 'ud want to be believed in by anybody so ignirant!" said Mr. Macey, in deep disgust at the farrier's crass incompetence to apprehend the conditions of ghostly phenomena.

CHAPTER VII.

YET the next moment there seemed to be some evidence that ghosts had a more condescending disposition than Mr. Macey attributed to them; for the pale thin figure of Silas Marner was suddenly seen standing in the warm light, uttering no word, but looking round at the company with his strange unearthly eyes. The long pipes gave a simultaneous movement, like the antennæ of startled insects, and every man present, not excepting even the sceptical farrier, had an impression that he saw, not Silas Marner in the flesh, but an apparition; for the door by which Silas had entered was hidden by the high-screened seats, and no one had noticed his approach. Mr. Macey, sitting a long way off the ghost, might be supposed to have felt an argumentative triumph, which would tend to neutralize his share of the general alarm. Had he not always said that when Silas Marner was in that strange trance of his, his soul went loose from his body? Here was the demonstration: nevertheless, on the whole, he would have been as well contented without it. For a few moments there was a dead silence, Marner's want of breath and agitation not allowing him to speak. The landlord, under the habitual sense that he was bound to keep his house open to all company, and confident in the protection of his unbroken neutrality, at last took on himself the task of adjuring the ghost.

"Master Marner," he said, in a conciliatory tone, "what's lacking to you? What's your business here?"

"Robbed!" said Silas, gaspingly. "I've been robbed! I want the constable — and the Justice — and Squire Cass — and Mr. Crackenthorp."

"Lay hold on him, Jem Rodney," said the landlord, the idea of a ghost subsiding; "he's off his head, I doubt. He's wet through."

Jem Rodney was the outermost man, and sat conveniently near Marner's standing-place; but he declined to give his services.

"Come and lay hold on him yourself, Mr. Snell, if you've a mind," said Jem, rather sullenly. "He's been robbed, and murdered too, for what I know," he added, in a muttering tone.

"Jem Rodney!" said Silas, turning and fixing his strange eyes on the suspected man.

"Ay, Master Marner, what do ye want wi' me?" said Jem, trembling a little, and seizing his drinking-can as a defensive weapon.

"If it was you stole my money," said Silas, clasping his

hands entreatingly, and raising his voice to a cry, " give it me back, — and I won't meddle with you. I won't set the constable on you. Give it me back, and I 'll let you — I 'll let you have a guinea."

" Me stole your money ! " said Jem, angrily. " I 'll pitch this can at your eye if you talk o' *my* stealing your money."

" Come, come, Master Marner," said the landlord, now rising resolutely, and seizing Marner by the shoulder, "if you 've got any information to lay, speak it out sensible, and show as you 're in your right mind, if you expect anybody to listen to you. You 're as wet as a drownded rat. Sit down and dry yourself, and speak straight forrard."

" Ah, to be sure, man," said the farrier, who began to feel that he had not been quite on a par with himself and the occasion. " Let 's have no more staring and screaming, else we 'll have you strapped for a madman. That was why I did n't speak at the first — thinks I, the man 's run mad."

" Ay, ay, make him sit down," said several voices at once, well pleased that the reality of ghosts remained still an open question.

The landlord forced Marner to take off his coat, and then to sit down on a chair aloof from every one else, in the centre of the circle and in the direct rays of the fire. The weaver, too feeble to have any distinct purpose beyond that of getting help to recover his money, submitted unresistingly. The transient fears of the company were now forgotten in their strong curiosity, and all faces were turned towards Silas, when the landlord, having seated himself again, said —

" Now then, Master Marner, what 's this you 've got to say — as you 've been robbed ? Speak out."

" He 'd better not say again as it was me robbed him," cried Jem Rodney, hastily. " What could I ha' done with his money ? I could as easy steal the parson's surplice, and wear it."

" Hold your tongue, Jem, and let 's hear what he 's got to say," said the landlord. "Now then, Master Marner."

Silas now told his story, under frequent questioning as the mysterious character of the robbery became evident.

This strangely novel situation of opening his trouble to his

Raveloe neighbors, of sitting in the warmth of a hearth not his own, and feeling the presence of faces and voices which were his nearest promise of help, had doubtless its influence on Marner, in spite of his passionate preoccupation with his loss. Our consciousness rarely registers the beginning of a growth within us any more than without us : there have been many circulations of the sap before we detect the smallest sign of the bud.

The slight suspicion with which his hearers at first listened to him, gradually melted away before the convincing simplicity of his distress: it was impossible for the neighbors to doubt that Marner was telling the truth, not because they were capable of arguing at once from the nature of his statements to the absence of any motive for making them falsely, but because, as Mr. Macey observed, " Folks as had the devil to back 'em were not likely to be so mushed " as poor Silas was. Rather, from the strange fact that the robber had left no traces, and had happened to know the nick of time, utterly incalculable by mortal agents, when Silas would go away from home without locking his door, the more probable conclusion seemed to be, that his disreputable intimacy in that quarter, if it ever existed, had been broken up, and that, in consequence, this ill turn had been done to Marner by somebody it was quite in vain to set the constable after. Why this preternatural felon should be obliged to wait till the door was left unlocked, was a question which did not present itself.

"It isn't Jem Rodney as has done this work, Master Marner," said the landlord. "You mustn't be a-casting your eye at poor Jem. There may be a bit of a reckoning against Jem for the matter of a hare or so, if anybody was bound to keep their eyes staring open, and niver to wink; but Jem's been a-sitting here drinking his can, like the decentest man i' the parish, since before you left your house, Master Marner, by your own account."

"Ay, ay," said Mr. Macey; "let's have no accusing o' the innicent. That isn't the law. There must be folks to swear again' a man before he can be ta'en up. Let's have no accusing o' the innicent, Master Marner."

Memory was not so utterly torpid in Silas that it could not be wakened by these words. With a movement of compunction as new and strange to him as everything else within the last hour, he started from his chair and went close up to Jem, looking at him as if he wanted to assure himself of the expression in his face.

"I was wrong," he said — "yes, yes — I ought to have thought. There's nothing to witness against you, Jem. Only you'd been into my house oftener than anybody else, and so you came into my head. I don't accuse you — I won't accuse anybody — only," he added, lifting up his hands to his head, and turning away with bewildered misery, "I try — I try to think where my guineas can be."

"Ay, ay, they're gone where it's hot enough to melt 'em, I doubt," said Mr. Macey.

"Tchuh!" said the farrier. And then he asked, with a cross-examining air, "How much money might there be in the bags, Master Marner?"

"Two hundred and seventy-two pounds, twelve and six-pence, last night when I counted it," said Silas, seating himself again, with a groan.

"Pooh! why, they'd be none so heavy to carry. Some tramp's been in, that's all; and as for the no footmarks, and the bricks and the sand being all right — why, your eyes are pretty much like a insect's, Master Marner; they're obliged to look so close, you can't see much at a time. It's my opinion as, if I'd been you, or you'd been me — for it comes to the same thing — you wouldn't have thought you'd found everything as you left it. But what I vote is, as two of the sensiblest o' the company should go with you to Master Kench, the constable's — he's ill i' bed, I know that much — and get him to appoint one of us his deppity; for that's the law, and I don't think anybody 'ull take upon him to contradick me there. It isn't much of a walk to Kench's; and then, if it's me as is deppity, I'll go back with you, Master Marner, and examine your premises; and if anybody's got any fault to find with that, I'll thank him to stand up and say it out like a man."

By this pregnant speech the farrier had re-established his self-complacency, and waited with confidence to hear himself named as one of the superlatively sensible men.

"Let us see how the night is, though," said the landlord, who also considered himself personally concerned in this proposition. "Why, it rains heavy still," he said, returning from the door.

"Well, I 'm not the man to be afraid o' the rain," said the farrier. "For it 'll look bad when Justice Malam hears as respectable men like us had a information laid before 'em and took no steps."

The landlord agreed with this view, and after taking the sense of the company, and duly rehearsing a small ceremony known in high ecclesiastical life as the *nolo episcopari*, he consented to take on himself the chill dignity of going to Kench's. But to the farrier's strong disgust, Mr. Macey now started an objection to his proposing himself as a deputy-constable; for that oracular old gentleman, claiming to know the law, stated, as a fact delivered to him by his father, that no doctor could be a constable.

"And you 're a doctor, I reckon, though you 're only a cow-doctor — for a fly 's a fly, though it may be a hoss-fly," concluded Mr. Macey, wondering a little at his own "'cuteness."

There was a hot debate upon this, the farrier being of course indisposed to renounce the quality of doctor, but contending that a doctor could be a constable if he liked — the law meant, he need n't be one if he did n't like. Mr. Macey thought this was nonsense, since the law was not likely to be fonder of doctors than of other folks. Moreover, if it was in the nature of doctors more than of other men not to like being constables, how came Mr. Dowlas to be so eager to act in that capacity?

"*I* don't want to act the constable," said the farrier, driven into a corner by this merciless reasoning; "and there 's no man can say it of me, if he 'd tell the truth. But if there 's to be any jealousy and envying about going to Kench's in the rain, let them go as like it — you won't get me to go, I can tell you."

By the landlord's intervention, however, the dispute was accommodated. Mr. Dowlas consented to go as a second person disinclined to act officially; and so poor Silas, furnished with some old coverings, turned out with his two companions into the rain again, thinking of the long night-hours before him, not as those do who long to rest, but as those who expect to "watch for the morning."

------------♦------------

CHAPTER VIII.

WHEN Godfrey Cass returned from Mrs. Osgood's party at midnight, he was not much surprised to learn that Dunsey had not come home. Perhaps he had not sold Wildfire, and was waiting for another chance — perhaps, on that foggy afternoon, he had preferred housing himself at the Red Lion at Batherley for the night, if the run had kept him in that neighborhood; for he was not likely to feel much concern about leaving his brother in suspense. Godfrey's mind was too full of Nancy Lammeter's looks and behavior, too full of the exasperation against himself and his lot, which the sight of her always produced in him, for him to give much thought to Wildfire, or to the probabilities of Dunstan's conduct.

The next morning the whole village was excited by the story of the robbery, and Godfrey, like every one else, was occupied in gathering and discussing news about it, and in visiting the Stone-pits. The rain had washed away all possibility of distinguishing foot-marks, but a close investigation of the spot had disclosed, in the direction opposite to the village, a tinder-box, with a flint and steel, half sunk in the mud. It was not Silas's tinder-box, for the only one he had ever had was still standing on his shelf; and the inference generally accepted was, that the tinder-box in the ditch was somehow connected with the robbery. A small minority shook their heads, and intimated their opinion that it was not a robbery to have much light thrown on it by tinder-boxes, that Master Marner's tale had a queer look with it, and that such things had been known as a man's doing himself a mischief, and then setting the justice to look for the doer. But when questioned closely as to their grounds for this opinion, and what Master Marner had to gain by such false pretences, they only shook their heads as before, and observed that there was no knowing what some folks counted gain; moreover, that everybody had a right to their own opinions, grounds or no grounds, and that the weaver, as everybody knew, was partly crazy. Mr. Macey, though he joined in the defence of Marner against all suspicions of deceit, also pooh-poohed the tinder-box; indeed, repudiated it as a rather impious suggestion, tending to imply that everything must be done by human hands, and that there was no power which could make away with the guineas without moving the bricks. Nevertheless, he turned round rather sharply on Mr. Tookey, when the zealous deputy, feeling that this was a view of the case peculiarly suited to a parish-clerk, carried it still further, and doubted whether it was right to inquire into a robbery at all when the circumstances were so mysterious.

"As if," concluded Mr. Tookey — "as if there was nothing but what could be made out by justices and constables."

"Now, don't you be for overshooting the mark, Tookey," said Mr. Macey, nodding his head aside admonishingly. "That's what you're allays at; if I throw a stone and hit, you think there's summat better than hitting, and you try to throw a stone beyond. What I said was against the tinder-box: I said nothing against justices and constables, for they're o' King George's making, and it 'ud be ill-becoming a man in a parish office to fly out again' King George."

While these discussions were going on among the group outside the Rainbow, a higher consultation was being carried on within, under the presidency of Mr. Crackenthorp, the Rector, assisted by Squire Cass and other substantial parishioners. It had just occurred to Mr. Snell, the landlord — he being, as he observed, a man accustomed to put two and two together — to connect with the tinder-box, which, as deputy-

constable, he himself had had the honorable distinction of
finding, certain recollections of a pedler who had called to
drink at the house about a month before, and had actually
stated that he carried a tinder-box about with him to light his
pipe. Here, surely, was a clew to be followed out. And as
memory, when duly impregnated with ascertained facts, is
sometimes surprisingly fertile, Mr. Snell gradually recovered
a vivid impression of the effect produced on him by the pedler's countenance and conversation. He had a "look with
his eye" which fell unpleasantly on Mr. Snell's sensitive
organism. To be sure, he did n't say anything particular —
no, except that about the tinder-box — but it is n't what a man
says, it 's the way he says it. Moreover, he had a swarthy
foreignness of complexion which boded little honesty.

"Did he wear ear-rings?" Mr. Crackenthorp wished to
know, having some acquaintance with foreign customs.

"Well — stay — let me see," said Mr. Snell, like a docile
clairvoyant, who would really not make a mistake if she
could help it. After stretching the corners of his mouth and
contracting his eyes, as if he were trying to see the ear-rings,
he appeared to give up the effort, and said, "Well, he 'd got
ear-rings in his box to sell, so it 's nat'ral to suppose he might
wear 'em. But he called at every house, a'most, in the village; there 's somebody else, mayhap, saw 'em in his ears,
though I can't take upon me rightly to say."

Mr. Snell was correct in his surmise, that somebody else
would remember the pedler's ear-rings. For on the spread
of inquiry among the villagers it was stated with gathering
emphasis, that the parson had wanted to know whether the
pedler wore ear-rings in his ears, and an impression was
created that a great deal depended on the eliciting of this
fact. Of course, every one who heard the question, not having any distinct image of the pedler as *without* ear-rings,
immediately had an image of him *with* ear-rings, larger or
smaller, as the case might be; and the image was presently
taken for a vivid recollection, so that the glazier's wife, a
well-intentioned woman, not given to lying, and whose house
was among the cleanest in the village, was ready to declare,

as sure as ever she meant to take the sacrament the very next
Christmas that was ever coming, that she had seen big ear-
rings, in the shape of the young moon, in the pedler's two
ears; while Jinny Oates, the cobbler's daughter, being a more
imaginative person, stated not only that she had seen them
too, but that they had made her blood creep, as it did at that
very moment while there she stood.

Also, by way of throwing further light on this clew of the
tinder-box, a collection was made of all the articles purchased
from the pedler at various houses, and carried to the Rainbow
to be exhibited there. In fact, there was a general feeling in
the village, that for the clearing-up of this robbery there must
be a great deal done at the Rainbow, and that no man need
offer his wife an excuse for going there while it was the scene
of severe public duties.

Some disappointment was felt, and perhaps a little indignation also, when it became known that Silas Marner, on being
questioned by the Squire and the parson, had retained no other
recollection of the pedler than that he had called at his door,
but had not entered his house, having turned away at once
when Silas, holding the door ajar, had said that he wanted
nothing. This had been Silas's testimony, though he clutched
strongly at the idea of the pedler's being the culprit, if only
because it gave him a definite image of a whereabout for his
gold after it had been taken away from its hiding-place: he
could see it now in the pedler's box. But it was observed
with some irritation in the village, that anybody but a "blind
creatur" like Marner would have seen the man prowling about,
for how came he to leave his tinder-box in the ditch close by,
if he had n't been lingering there? Doubtless, he had made
his observations when he saw Marner at the door. Anybody
might know — and only look at him — that the weaver was
a half-crazy miser. It was a wonder the pedler had n't murdered him; men of that sort, with rings in their ears, had
been known for murderers often and often; there had been
one tried at the 'sizes, not so long ago but what there were
people living who remembered it.

Godfrey Cass, indeed, entering the Rainbow during one of

Mr. Snell's frequently repeated recitals of his testimony, had treated it lightly, stating that he himself had bought a pen-knife of the pedler, and thought him a merry grinning fellow enough; it was all nonsense, he said, about the man's evil looks. But this was spoken of in the village as the random talk of youth, "as if it was only Mr. Snell who had seen something odd about the pedler!" On the contrary, there were at least half-a-dozen who were ready to go before Justice Malam, and give in much more striking testimony than any the land-lord could furnish. It was to be hoped Mr. Godfrey would not go to Tarley and throw cold water on what Mr. Snell said there, and so prevent the justice from drawing up a warrant. He was suspected of intending this, when, after mid-day, he was seen setting off on horseback in the direction of Tarley.

But by this time Godfrey's interest in the robbery had faded before his growing anxiety about Dunstan and Wildfire, and he was going, not to Tarley, but to Batherley, unable to rest in uncertainty about them any longer. The possibility that Dun-stan had played him the ugly trick of riding away with Wild-fire, to return at the end of a month, when he had gambled away or otherwise squandered the price of the horse, was a fear that urged itself upon him more, even, than the thought of an accidental injury; and now that the dance at Mrs. Os-good's was past, he was irritated with himself that he had trusted his horse to Dunstan. Instead of trying to still his fears he encouraged them, with that superstitious impression which clings to us all, that if we expect evil very strongly it is the less likely to come; and when he heard a horse ap-proaching at a trot, and saw a hat rising above a hedge beyond an angle of the lane, he felt as if his conjuration had succeeded. But no sooner did the horse come within sight, than his heart sank again. It was not Wildfire; and in a few moments more he discerned that the rider was not Dunstan, but Bryce, who pulled up to speak, with a face that implied something dis-agreeable.

"Well, Mr. Godfrey, that's a lucky brother of yours, that Master Dunsey, isn't he?"

"What do you mean?" said Godfrey, hastily.

" Why, has n't he been home yet ? " said Bryce.

" Home ? no. What has happened ? Be quick. What has he done with my horse ? "

" Ah, I thought it was yours, though he pretended you had parted with it to him."

" Has he thrown him down and broken his knees ? " said Godfrey, flushed with exasperation.

" Worse than that," said Bryce. " You see, I 'd made a bargain with him to buy the horse for a hundred and twenty — a swinging price, but I always liked the horse. And what does he do but go and stake him — fly at a hedge with stakes in it, atop of a bank with a ditch before it. The horse had been dead a pretty good while when he was found. So he has n't been home since, has he ? "

" Home ? no." said Godfrey, " and he 'd better keep away. Confound me for a fool ! I might have known this would be the end of it."

" Well, to tell you the truth," said Bryce, " after I 'd bargained for the horse, it did come into my head that he might be riding and selling the horse without your knowledge, for I did n't believe it was his own. I knew Master Dunsey was up to his tricks sometimes. But where can he be gone ? He 's never been seen at Batherley. He could n't have been hurt, for he must have walked off."

" Hurt ? " said Godfrey, bitterly. " He 'll never be hurt — he 's made to hurt other people."

" And so you *did* give him leave to sell the horse, eh ? " said Bryce.

" Yes ; I wanted to part with the horse — he was always a little too hard in the mouth for me," said Godfrey ; his pride making him wince under the idea that Bryce guessed the sale to be a matter of necessity. " I was going to see after him — I thought some mischief had happened. I 'll go back now," he added, turning the horse's head, and wishing he could get rid of Bryce ; for he felt that the long-dreaded crisis in his life was close upon him. " You 're coming on to Raveloe, are n't you ? "

" Well, no, not now," said Bryce. " I *was* coming round

there, for I had to go to Flitton, and I thought I might as well take you in my way, and just let you know all I knew myself about the horse. I suppose Master Dunsey did n't like to show himself till the ill news had blown over a bit. He's perhaps gone to pay a visit at the Three Crowns, by Whitbridge — I know he's fond of the house."

"Perhaps he is," said Godfrey, rather absently. Then rousing himself, he said, with an effort at carelessness, "We shall hear of him soon enough, I 'll be bound."

"Well, here's my turning," said Bryce, not surprised to perceive that Godfrey was rather "down;" "so I 'll bid you good-day, and wish I may bring you better news another time."

Godfrey rode along slowly, representing to himself the scene of confession to his father from which he felt that there was now no longer any escape. The revelation about the money must be made the very next morning; and if he withheld the rest, Dunstan would be sure to come back shortly, and, finding that he must bear the brunt of his father's anger, would tell the whole story out of spite, even though he had nothing to gain by it. There was one step, perhaps, by which he might still win Dunstan's silence and put off the evil day: he might tell his father that he had himself spent the money paid to him by Fowler; and as he had never been guilty of such an offence before, the affair would blow over after a little storming. But Godfrey could not bend himself to this. He felt that in letting Dunstan have the money, he had already been guilty of a breach of trust hardly less culpable than that of spending the money directly for his own behoof; and yet there was a distinction between the two acts which made him feel that the one was so much more blackening than the other as to be intolerable to him.

"I don't pretend to be a good fellow," he said to himself; "but I 'm not a scoundrel — at least, I 'll stop short somewhere. I 'll bear the consequences of what I *have* done sooner than make believe I 've done what I never would have done. I 'd never have spent the money for my own pleasure — I was tortured into it."

Through the remainder of this day Godfrey, with only occasional fluctuations, kept his will bent in the direction of a complete avowal to his father, and he withheld the story of Wildfire's loss till the next morning, that it might serve him as an introduction to heavier matter. The old Squire was accustomed to his son's frequent absence from home, and thought neither Dunstan's nor Wildfire's non-appearance a matter calling for remark. Godfrey said to himself again and again, that if he let slip this one opportunity of confession, he might never have another; the revelation might be made even in a more odious way than by Dunstan's malignity: *she* might come as she had threatened to do. And then he tried to make the scene easier to himself by rehearsal: he made up his mind how he would pass from the admission of his weakness in letting Dunstan have the money to the fact that Dunstan had a hold on him which he had been unable to shake off, and how he would work up his father to expect something very bad before he told him the fact. The old Squire was an implacable man: he made resolutions in violent anger, and he was not to be moved from them after his anger had subsided — as fiery volcanic matters cool and harden into rock. Like many violent and implacable men, he allowed evils to grow under favor of his own heedlessness, till they pressed upon him with exasperating force, and then he turned round with fierce severity and became unrelentingly hard. This was his system with his tenants: he allowed them to get into arrears, neglect their fences, reduce their stock, sell their straw, and otherwise go the wrong way, — and then, when he became short of money in consequence of this indulgence, he took the hardest measures and would listen to no appeal. Godfrey knew all this, and felt it with the greater force because he had constantly suffered annoyance from witnessing his father's sudden fits of unrelentingness, for which his own habitual irresolution deprived him of all sympathy. (He was not critical on the faulty indulgence which preceded these fits; *that* seemed to him natural enough.) Still there was just the chance, Godfrey thought, that his father's pride might see this marriage in a light that would induce him to hush it up, rather than turn his son out and make the family the talk of the country for ten miles round.

This was the view of the case that Godfrey managed to keep before him pretty closely till midnight, and he went to sleep thinking that he had done with inward debating. But when he awoke in the still morning darkness he found it impossible to reawaken his evening thoughts; it was as if they had been tired out and were not to be roused to further work. Instead of arguments for confession, he could now feel the presence of nothing but its evil consequences: the old dread of disgrace came back — the old shrinking from the thought of raising a hopeless barrier between himself and Nancy — the old disposition to rely on chances which might be favorable to him, and save him from betrayal. Why, after all, should he cut off the hope of them by his own act? He had seen the matter in a wrong light yesterday. He had been in a rage with Dunstan, and had thought of nothing but a thorough break-up of their mutual understanding; but what it would be really wisest for him to do, was to try and soften his father's anger against Dunsey, and keep things as nearly as possible in their old condition. If Dunsey did not come back for a few days (and Godfrey did not know but that the rascal had enough money in his pocket to enable him to keep away still longer), everything might blow over.

CHAPTER IX.

GODFREY rose and took his own breakfast earlier than usual, but lingered in the wainscoted parlor till his younger brothers had finished their meal and gone out; awaiting his father, who always took a walk with his managing-man before breakfast. Every one breakfasted at a different hour in the Red House, and the Squire was always the latest, giving a long chance to a rather feeble morning appetite before he tried it.

The table had been spread with substantial eatables nearly
two hours before he presented himself — a tall, stout man of
sixty, with a face in which the knit brow and rather hard
glance seemed contradicted by the slack and feeble mouth.
His person showed marks of habitual neglect, his dress was
slovenly; and yet there was something in the presence of the
old Squire distinguishable from that of the ordinary farmers
in the parish, who were perhaps every whit as refined as he,
but, having slouched their way through life with a consciousness of being in the vicinity of their "betters," wanted that
self-possession and authoritativeness of voice and carriage
which belonged to a man who thought of superiors as remote
existences with whom he had personally little more to do
than with America or the stars. The Squire had been used
to parish homage all his life, used to the presupposition that
his family, his tankards, and everything that was his, were
the oldest and best; and as he never associated with any
gentry higher than himself, his opinion was not disturbed by
comparison.

He glanced at his son as he entered the room, and said,
"What, sir! have n't *you* had your breakfast yet?" but there
was no pleasant morning greeting between them; not because
of any unfriendliness, but because the sweet flower of courtesy
is not a growth of such homes as the Red House.

"Yes, sir," said Godfrey, "I 've had my breakfast, but I was
waiting to speak to you."

"Ah! well," said the Squire, throwing himself indifferently
into his chair, and speaking in a ponderous coughing fashion,
which was felt in Raveloe to be a sort of privilege of his rank,
while he cut a piece of beef, and held it up before the deer-
hound that had come in with him. "Ring the bell for my
ale, will you? You youngsters' business is your own pleasure, mostly. There's no hurry about it for anybody but
yourselves."

The Squire's life was quite as idle as his sons', but it was a
fiction kept up by himself and his contemporaries in Raveloe
that youth was exclusively the period of folly, and that their
aged wisdom was constantly in a state of endurance mitigated

by sarcasm. Godfrey waited, before he spoke again, until the ale had been brought and the door closed — an interval during which Fleet, the deer-hound, had consumed enough bits of beef to make a poor man's holiday dinner.

"There's been a cursed piece of ill-luck with Wildfire," he began ; "happened the day before yesterday."

"What! broke his knees ?" said the Squire, after taking a draught of ale. "I thought you knew how to ride better than that, sir. I never threw a horse down in my life. If I had, I might ha' whistled for another, for *my* father was n't quite so ready to unstring as some other fathers I know of. But they must turn over a new leaf — *they* must. What with mortgages and arrears, I'm as short o' cash as a roadside pauper. And that fool Kimble says the newspaper's talking about peace. Why, the country would n't have a leg to stand on. Prices 'ud run down like a jack, and I should never get my arrears, not if I sold all the fellows up. And there's that damned Fowler, I won't put up with him any longer ; I've told Winthrop to go to Cox this very day. The lying scoundrel told me he'd be sure to pay me a hundred last month. He takes advantage because he's on that outlying farm, and thinks I shall forget him."

The Squire had delivered this speech in a coughing and interrupted manner, but with no pause long enough for Godfrey to make it a pretext for taking up the word again. He felt that his father meant to ward off any request for money on the ground of the misfortune with Wildfire, and that the emphasis he had thus been led to lay on his shortness of cash and his arrears was likely to produce an attitude of mind the utmost unfavorable for his own disclosure. But he must go on, now he had begun.

"It's worse than breaking the horse's knees — he's been staked and killed," he said, as soon as his father was silent, and had begun to cut his meat. "But I was n't thinking of asking you to buy me another horse ; I was only thinking I'd lost the means of paying you with the price of Wildfire, as I'd meant to do. Dunsey took him to the hunt to sell him for me the other day, and after he'd made a bargain for a hundred and twenty with Bryce, he went after the hounds, and took some fool's leap or other that did for the horse at once. If it had n't been for that, I should have paid you a hundred pounds this morning."

The Squire had laid down his knife and fork, and was staring at his son in amazement, not being sufficiently quick of brain to form a probable guess as to what could have caused so strange an inversion of the paternal and filial relations as this proposition of his son to pay him a hundred pounds.

"The truth is, sir — I'm very sorry — I was quite to blame," said Godfrey. "Fowler did pay that hundred pounds. He paid it to me, when I was over there one day last month. And Dunsey bothered me for the money, and I let him have it, because I hoped I should be able to pay it you before this."

The Squire was purple with anger before his son had done speaking, and found utterance difficult. "You let Dunsey have it, sir? And how long have you been so thick with Dunsey that you must *collogue* with him to embezzle my money? Are you turning out a scamp? I tell you I won't have it. I 'll turn the whole pack of you out of the house together, and marry again. I'd have you to remember, sir, my property 's got no entail on it ; — since my grandfather's time the Casses can do as they like with their land. Remember that, sir. Let Dunsey have the money! Why should you let Dunsey have the money ? There 's some lie at the bottom of it."

"There 's no lie, sir," said Godfrey. "I would n't have spent the money myself, but Dunsey bothered me, and I was a fool, and let him have it. But I meant to pay it, whether he did or not. That 's the whole story. I never meant to embezzle money, and I 'm not the man to do it. You never knew me do a dishonest trick, sir."

"Where 's Dunsey, then ? What do you stand talking there for ? Go and fetch Dunsey, as I tell you, and let him give account of what he wanted the money for, and what he 's done with it. He shall repent it. I 'll turn him out. I said I would, and I 'll do it. He sha'n't brave me. Go and fetch him."

"Dunsey is n't come back, sir."

"What! did he break his own neck, then ? " said the Squire, with some disgust at the idea that, in that case, he could not fulfil his threat.

"No, he was n't hurt, I believe, for the horse was found dead, and Dunsey must have walked off. I dare say we shall see him again by-and-by. I don't know where he is."

"And what must you be letting him have my money for ? Answer me that," said the Squire, attacking Godfrey again, since Dunsey was not within reach.

"Well, sir, I don't know," said Godfrey, hesitatingly. That was a feeble evasion, but Godfrey was not fond of lying, and, not being sufficiently aware that no sort of duplicity can long flourish without the help of vocal falsehoods, he was quite un-prepared with invented motives.

"You don't know ? I tell you what it is, sir. You 've been up to some trick, and you 've been bribing him not to tell," said the Squire, with a sudden acuteness which startled God-frey, who felt his heart beat violently at the nearness of his father's guess. The sudden alarm pushed him on to take the next step — a very slight impulse suffices for that on a down-ward road.

"Why, sir," he said, trying to speak with careless ease, "it was a little affair between me and Dunsey ; it 's no matter to anybody else. It 's hardly worth while to pry into young men's fooleries : it would n't have made any difference to you, sir, if I 'd not had the bad luck to lose Wildfire. I should have paid you the money."

"Fooleries ! Pshaw ! it 's time you 'd done with fooleries. And I 'd have you know, sir, you *must* ha' done with 'em," said the Squire, frowning and casting an angry glance at his son. "Your goings-on are not what I shall find money for any longer. There 's my grandfather had his stables full o' horses, and kept a good house, too, and in worse times, by what I can make out ; and so might I, if I had n't four good-for-nothing fellows to hang on me like horse-leeches. I 've been too good a father to you all — that 's what it is. But I shall pull up, sir."

Godfrey was silent. He was not likely to be very penetrating in his judgments, but he had always had a sense that his father's indulgence had not been kindness, and had had a vague longing for some discipline that would have checked his own errant weakness and helped his better will. The Squire ate his bread and meat hastily, took a deep draught of ale, then turned his chair from the table, and began to speak again.

"It'll be all the worse for you, you know — you'd need try and help me keep things together."

"Well, sir, I've often offered to take the management of things, but you know you've taken it ill always, and seemed to think I wanted to push you out of your place."

"I know nothing o' your offering or o' my taking it ill," said the Squire, whose memory consisted in certain strong impressions unmodified by detail; "but I know one while you seemed to be thinking o' marrying, and I didn't offer to put any obstacles in your way, as some fathers would. I'd as lieve you married Lammeter's daughter as anybody. I suppose, if I'd said you nay, you'd ha' kept on with it; but, for want o' contradiction, you've changed your mind. You're a shilly-shally fellow: you take after your poor mother. She never had a will of her own; a woman has no call for one, if she's got a proper man for her husband. But *your* wife had need have one, for you hardly know your own mind enough to make both your legs walk one way. The lass hasn't said downright she won't have you, has she?"

"No," said Godfrey, feeling very hot and uncomfortable; "but I don't think she will."

"Think! why haven't you the courage to ask her? Do you stick to it, you want to have *her* — that's the thing?"

"There's no other woman I want to marry," said Godfrey, evasively.

"Well, then, let me make the offer for you, that's all, if you haven't the pluck to do it yourself. Lammeter isn't likely to be loath for his daughter to marry into *my* family, I should think. And as for the pretty lass, she wouldn't have her cousin — and there's nobody else, as I see, could ha' stood in your way."

"I'd rather let it be, please sir, at present," said Godfrey, in alarm. "I think she's a little offended with me just now, and I should like to speak for myself. A man must manage these things for himself."

"Well, speak, then, and manage it, and see if you can't turn over a new leaf. That's what a man must do when he thinks o' marrying."

"I don't see how I can think of it at present, sir. You would n't like to settle me on one of the farms, I suppose, and I don't think she'd come to live in this house with all my brothers. It's a different sort of life to what she's been used to."

"Not come to live in this house? Don't tell me. You ask her, that's all," said the Squire, with a short, scornful laugh.

"I'd rather let the thing be, at present, sir," said Godfrey. "I hope you won't try to hurry it on by saying anything."

"I shall do what I choose," said the Squire, "and I shall let you know I'm master; else you may turn out, and find an estate to drop into somewhere else. Go out and tell Winthrop not to go to Cox's, but wait for me. And tell 'em to get my horse saddled. And stop: look out and get that hack o' Dunsey's sold, and hand me the money, will you? He'll keep no more hacks at my expense. And if you know where he's sneaking — I dare say you do — you may tell him to spare himself the journey o' coming back home. Let him turn ostler, and keep himself. He sha'n't hang on me any more."

"I don't know where he is; and if I did, it is n't my place to tell him to keep away," said Godfrey, moving towards the door.

"Confound it, sir, don't stay arguing, but go and order my horse," said the Squire, taking up a pipe.

Godfrey left the room, hardly knowing whether he were more relieved by the sense that the interview was ended without having made any change in his position, or more uneasy that he had entangled himself still further in prevarication and deceit. What had passed about his proposing to Nancy had raised a new alarm, lest by some after-dinner words of his father's to Mr. Lammeter he should be thrown into the em-

barrassment of being obliged absolutely to decline her when
she seemed to be within his reach. He fled to his usual refuge, that of hoping for some unforeseen turn of fortune, some
favorable chance which would save him from unpleasant consequences — perhaps even justify his insincerity by manifest-
ing its prudence.

In this point of trusting to some throw of fortune's dice,
Godfrey can hardly be called old-fashioned. Favorable Chance
is the god of all men who follow their own devices instead of
obeying a law they believe in. Let even a polished man of
these days get into a position he is ashamed to avow, and his
mind will be bent on all the possible issues that may deliver
him from the calculable results of that position. Let him live
outside his income, or shirk the resolute honest work that
brings wages, and he will presently find himself dreaming of
a possible benefactor, a possible simpleton who may be cajoled
into using his interest, a possible state of mind in some possible person not yet forthcoming. Let him neglect the re-
sponsibilities of his office, and he will inevitably anchor himself on the chance, that the thing left undone may turn out
not to be of the supposed importance. Let him betray his
friend's confidence, and he will adore that same cunning complexity called Chance, which gives him the hope that his
friend will never know. Let him forsake a decent craft that
he may pursue the gentilities of a profession to which nature
never called him, and his religion will infallibly be the worship of blessed Chance, which he will believe in as the mighty
creator of success. The evil principle deprecated in that religion, is the orderly sequence by which the seed brings forth
a crop after its kind.

CHAPTER X.

JUSTICE MALAM was naturally regarded in Tarley and Raveloe as a man of capacious mind, seeing that he could draw
much wider conclusions without evidence than could be expected of his neighbors who were not on the Commission of
the Peace. Such a man was not likely to neglect the clew of
the tinder-box, and an inquiry was set on foot concerning a
pedler, name unknown, with curly black hair and a foreign complexion, carrying a box of cutlery and jewelry, and wearing
large rings in his ears. But either because inquiry was too
slow-footed to overtake him, or because the description applied
to so many pedlers that inquiry did not know how to choose
among them, weeks passed away, and there was no other
result concerning the robbery than a gradual cessation of the
excitement it had caused in Raveloe. Dunstan Cass's absence
was hardly a subject of remark : he had once before had a
quarrel with his father, and had gone off, nobody knew
whither, to return at the end of six weeks, take up his old
quarters unforbidden and swagger as usual. His own family,
who equally expected this issue, with the sole difference that
the Squire was determined this time to forbid him the old
quarters, never mentioned his absence; and when his uncle
Kimble or Mr. Osgood noticed it, the story of his having killed
Wildfire and committed some offence against his father was
enough to prevent surprise. To connect the fact of Dunsey's
disappearance with that of the robbery occurring on the same
day, lay quite away from the track of every one's thought —
even Godfrey's, who had better reason than any one else to
know what his brother was capable of. He remembered no
mention of the weaver between them since the time, twelve
years ago, when it was their boyish sport to deride him ; and,
besides, his imagination constantly created an *alibi* for Dunstan : he saw him continually in some congenial haunt, to

which he had walked off on leaving Wildfire — saw him sponging on chance acquaintances, and meditating a return home to the old amusement of tormenting his elder brother. Even if any brain in Raveloe had put the said two facts together, I doubt whether a combination so injurious to the prescriptive respectability of a family with a mural monument and venerable tankards, would not have been suppressed as of unsound tendency. But Christmas puddings, brawn, and abundance of spirituous liquors, throwing the mental originality into the channel of nightmare, are great preservatives against a dangerous spontaneity of waking thought.

When the robbery was talked of at the Rainbow and elsewhere, in good company, the balance continued to waver between the rational explanation founded on the tinder-box, and the theory of an impenetrable mystery that mocked investigation. The advocates of the tinder-box-and-pedler view considered the other side a muddle-headed and credulous set, who, because they themselves were wall-eyed, supposed everybody else to have the same blank outlook; and the adherents of the inexplicable more than hinted that their antagonists were animals inclined to crow before they had found any corn — mere skimming-dishes in point of depth — whose clear-sightedness consisted in supposing there was nothing behind a barn-door because they could n't see through it; so that, though their controversy did not serve to elicit the fact concerning the robbery, it elicited some true opinions of collateral importance.

But while poor Silas's loss served thus to brush the slow current of Raveloe conversation, Silas himself was feeling the withering desolation of that bereavement about which his neighbors were arguing at their ease. To any one who had observed him before he lost his gold, it might have seemed that so withered and shrunken a life as his could hardly be susceptible of a bruise, could hardly endure any subtraction but such as would put an end to it altogether. But in reality it had been an eager life, filled with immediate purpose which fenced him in from the wide, cheerless unknown. It had been a clinging life; and though the object round which its fibres had clung was a dead disrupted thing, it satisfied the need for

clinging. But now the fence was broken down — the support
was snatched away. Marner's thoughts could no longer move
in their old round, and were baffled by a blank like that which
meets a plodding ant when the earth has broken away on its
homeward path. The loom was there, and the weaving, and
the growing pattern in the cloth ; but the bright treasure in
the hole under his feet was gone; the prospect of handling
and counting it was gone : the evening had no phantasm of
delight to still the poor soul's craving. The thought of the
money he would get by his actual work could bring no joy, for
its meagre image was only a fresh reminder of his loss ; and
hope was too heavily crushed by the sudden blow, for his
imagination to dwell on the growth of a new hoard from that
small beginning.

He filled up the blank with grief. As he sat weaving, he
every now and then moaned low, like one in pain : it was the
sign that his thoughts had come round again to the sudden
chasm — to the empty evening time. And all the evening, as
he sat in his loneliness by his dull fire, he leaned his elbows
on his knees, and clasped his head with his hands, and moaned
very low — not as one who seeks to be heard.

And yet he was not utterly forsaken in his trouble. The
repulsion Marner had always created in his neighbors was
partly dissipated by the new light in which this misfortune
had shown him. Instead of a man who had more cunning
than honest folks could come by, and, what was worse, had
not the inclination to use that cunning in a neighborly way, it
was now apparent that Silas had not cunning enough to keep
his own. He was generally spoken of as a "poor mushed
creatur ; " and that avoidance of his neighbors, which had
before been referred to his ill-will and to a probable addiction
to worse company, was now considered mere craziness.

This change to a kindlier feeling was shown in various ways.
The odor of Christmas cooking being on the wind, it was the
season when superfluous pork and black puddings are suggestive of charity in well-to-do families ; and Silas's misfortune
had brought him uppermost in the memory of housekeepers
like Mrs. Osgood. Mr. Crackenthorp, too, while he admon-

ished Silas that his money had probably been taken from him because he thought too much of it and never came to church, enforced the doctrine by a present of pigs' pettitoes, well calculated to dissipate unfounded prejudices against the clerical character. Neighbors who had nothing but verbal consolation to give showed a disposition not only to greet Silas and discuss his misfortune at some length when they encountered him in the village, but also to take the trouble of calling at his cottage and getting him to repeat all the details on the very spot; and then they would try to cheer him by saying. "Well, Master Marner, you're no worse off nor other poor folks, after all; and if you was to be crippled, the parish 'ud give you a 'lowance."

I suppose one reason why we are seldom able to comfort our neighbors with our words is that our goodwill gets adulterated, in spite of ourselves, before it can pass our lips. We can send black puddings and pettitoes without giving them a flavor of our own egoism; but language is a stream that is almost sure to smack of a mingled soil. There was a fair proportion of kindness in Raveloe; but it was often of a beery and bungling sort, and took the shape least allied to the complimentary and hypocritical.

Mr. Macey, for example, coming one evening expressly to let Silas know that recent events had given him the advantage of standing more favorably in the opinion of a man whose judgment was not formed lightly, opened the conversation by saying, as soon as he had seated himself and adjusted his thumbs —

"Come, Master Marner, why, you've no call to sit a-moaning. You're a deal better off to ha' lost your money, nor to ha' kep it by foul means. I used to think, when you first come into these parts, as you were no better nor you should be; you were younger a deal than what you are now; but you were allays a staring, white-faced creatur, partly like a bald-faced calf, as I may say. But there's no knowing: it isn't every queer-looksed thing as Old Harry's had the making of — I mean, speaking o' toads and such; for they're often harmless, and useful against varmin. And it's pretty much the same

wi' you, as fur as I can see. Though as to the yarbs and stuff
to cure the breathing, if you brought that sort o' knowledge
from distant parts, you might ha' been a bit freer of it. And
if the knowledge was n't well come by, why, you might ha'
made up for it by coming to church reg'lar; for as for the
children as the Wise Woman charmed, I 've been at the
christening of 'em again and again, and they took the water
just as well. And that 's reasonable; for if Old Harry 's a
mind to do a bit o' kindness for a holiday, like, who 's got
anything against it? That 's my thinking; and I 've been
clerk o' this parish forty year, and I know, when the parson
and me does the cussing of a Ash Wednesday, there 's no cussing o' folks as have a mind to be cured without a doctor, let
Kimble say what he will. And so, Master Marner, as I was
saying — for there 's windings i' things as they may carry you
to the fur end o' the prayer-book afore you get back to 'em —
my advice is, as you keep up your sperrits; for as for thinking
you 're a deep un, and ha' got more inside you nor 'ull bear
daylight, I 'm not o' that opinion at all, and so I tell the neighbors. For, says I, you talk o' Master Marner making out a tale
— why, it 's nonsense, that is : it 'ud take a 'cute man to make
a tale like that ; and, says I, he looked as scared as a rabbit."

During this discursive address Silas had continued motionless in his previous attitude, leaning his elbows on his knees,
and pressing his hands against his head. Mr. Macey, not
doubting that he had been listened to, paused, in the expectation of some appreciatory reply, but Marner remained silent.
He had a sense that the old man meant to be good-natured
and neighborly; but the kindness fell on him as sunshine falls
on the wretched — he had no heart to taste it, and felt that it
was very far off him.

"Come, Master Marner, have you got nothing to say to
that ? " said Mr. Macey at last, with a slight accent of
impatience.

"Oh," said Marner, slowly, shaking his head between his
hands, "I thank you — thank you — kindly."

"Ay, ay, to be sure : I thought you would," said Mr. Macey;
"and my advice is — have you got a Sunday suit ? "

"No," said Marner.

"I doubted it was so," said Mr. Macey. "Now, let me advise you to get a Sunday suit: there's Tookey, he's a poor creatur, but he's got my tailoring business, and some o' my money in it, and he shall make a suit at a low price, and give you trust, and then you can come to church, and be a bit neighborly. Why, you've never heared me say 'Amen' since you come into these parts, and I recommend you to lose no time, for it'll be poor work when Tookey has it all to himself, for I may n't be equil to stand i' the desk at all, come another winter." Here Mr. Macey paused, perhaps expecting some sign of emotion in his hearer; but not observing any, he went on. "And as for the money for the suit o' clothes, why, you get a matter of a pound a-week at your weaving, Master Marner, and you're a young man, eh, for all you look so mushed. Why, you couldn't ha' been five-and-twenty when you come into these parts, eh?"

Silas started a little at the change to a questioning tone, and answered mildly, "I don't know; I can't rightly say — it's a long while since."

After receiving such an answer as this, it is not surprising that Mr. Macey observed, later on in the evening at the Rainbow, that Marner's head was "all of a muddle," and that it was to be doubted if he ever knew when Sunday came round, which showed him a worse heathen than many a dog.

Another of Silas's comforters, besides Mr. Macey, came to him with a mind highly charged on the same topic. This was Mrs. Winthrop, the wheelwright's wife. The inhabitants of Raveloe were not severely regular in their church-going, and perhaps there was hardly a person in the parish who would not have held that to go to church every Sunday in the calendar would have shown a greedy desire to stand well with Heaven, and get an undue advantage over their neighbors — a wish to be better than the "common run," that would have implied a reflection on those who had had godfathers and godmothers as well as themselves, and had an equal right to the burying-service. At the same time, it was understood to be requisite for all who were not household servants, or young

men, to take the sacrament at one of the great festivals:
Squire Cass himself took it on Christmas-day; while those
who were held to be "good livers" went to church with
greater, though still with moderate, frequency.

Mrs. Winthrop was one of these: she was in all respects a
woman of scrupulous conscience, so eager for duties that life
seemed to offer them too scantily unless she rose at half-past
four, though this threw a scarcity of work over the more
advanced hours of the morning, which it was a constant problem with her to remove. Yet she had not the vixenish temper
which is sometimes supposed to be a necessary condition of
such habits: she was a very mild, patient woman, whose
nature it was to seek out all the sadder and more serious
elements of life, and pasture her mind upon them. She was
the person always first thought of in Raveloe when there
was illness or death in a family, when leeches were to be
applied, or there was a sudden disappointment in a monthly
nurse. She was a "comfortable woman" — good-looking,
fresh-complexioned, having her lips always slightly screwed,
as if she felt herself in a sick-room with the doctor or the
clergyman present. But she was never whimpering; no one
had seen her shed tears; she was simply grave and inclined
to shake her head and sigh, almost imperceptibly, like a
funereal mourner who is not a relation. It seemed surprising
that Ben Winthrop, who loved his quart-pot and his joke, got
along so well with Dolly; but she took her husband's jokes
and joviality as patiently as everything else, considering that
"men would be so," and viewing the stronger sex in the light
of animals whom it had pleased Heaven to make naturally
troublesome, like bulls and turkey-cocks.

This good wholesome woman could hardly fail to have her
mind drawn strongly towards Silas Marner, now that he appeared in the light of a sufferer; and one Sunday afternoon
she took her little boy Aaron with her, and went to call on
Silas, carrying in her hand some small lard-cakes, flat paste-
like articles much esteemed in Raveloe. Aaron, an apple-
cheeked youngster of seven, with a clean starched frill which
looked like a plate for the apples, needed all his adventurous

curiosity to embolden him against the possibility that the big-eyed weaver might do him some bodily injury; and his dubiety was much increased when, on arriving at the Stone-pits, they heard the mysterious sound of the loom.

"Ah, it is as I thought," said Mrs. Winthrop, sadly.

They had to knock loudly before Silas heard them; but when he did come to the door he showed no impatience, as he would once have done, at a visit that had been unasked for and unexpected. Formerly, his heart had been as a locked casket with its treasure inside; but now the casket was empty, and the lock was broken. Left groping in darkness, with his prop utterly gone, Silas had inevitably a sense, though a dull and half-despairing one, that if any help came to him it must come from without; and there was a slight stirring of expectation at the sight of his fellow-men, a faint consciousness of dependence on their good-will. He opened the door wide to admit Dolly, but without otherwise returning her greeting than by moving the arm-chair a few inches as a sign that she was to sit down in it. Dolly, as soon as she was seated, removed the white cloth that covered her lard-cakes, and said in her gravest way —

"I'd a baking yesterday, Master Marner, and the lard-cakes turned out better nor common, and I'd ha' asked you to accept some, if you'd thought well. I don't eat such things myself, for a bit o' bread's what I like from one year's end to the other; but men's stomichs are made so comical, they want a change — they do, I know, God help 'em."

Dolly sighed gently as she held out the cakes to Silas, who thanked her kindly and looked very close at them, absently, being accustomed to look so at everything he took into his hand — eyed all the while by the wondering bright orbs of the small Aaron, who had made an outwork of his mother's chair, and was peeping round from behind it.

"There's letters pricked on 'em," said Dolly. "I can't read 'em myself, and there's nobody, not Mr. Macey himself, rightly knows what they mean; but they've a good meaning, for they're the same as is on the pulpit-cloth at church. What are they, Aaron, my dear?"

Aaron retreated completely behind his outwork.

"Oh go, that's naughty," said his mother, mildly. "Well, whativer the letters are, they've a good meaning; and it's a stamp as has been in our house, Ben says, ever since he was a little un, and his mother used to put it on the cakes, and I've allays put it on too; for if there's any good, we've need of it i' this world."

"It's I. H. S.," said Silas, at which proof of learning Aaron peeped round the chair again.

"Well, to be sure, you can read 'em off," said Dolly. "Ben's read 'em to me many and many a time, but they slip out o' my mind again; the more's the pity, for they're good letters, else they would n't be in the church; and so I prick 'em on all the loaves and all the cakes, though sometimes they won't hold, because o' the rising — for, as I said, if there's any good to be got we've need of it i' this world — that we have; and I hope they'll bring good to you, Master Marner, for it's wi' that will I brought you the cakes; and you see the letters have held better nor common."

Silas was as unable to interpret the letters as Dolly, but there was no possibility of misunderstanding the desire to give comfort that made itself heard in her quiet tones. He said, with more feeling than before — "Thank you — thank you kindly." But he laid down the cakes and seated himself absently — drearily unconscious of any distinct benefit towards which the cakes and the letters, or even Dolly's kindness, could tend for him.

"Ah, if there's good anywhere, we've need of it," repeated Dolly, who did not lightly forsake a serviceable phrase. She looked at Silas pityingly as she went on. "But you did n't hear the church-bells this morning, Master Marner? I doubt you did n't know it was Sunday. Living so lone here, you lose your count, I dare say; and then, when your loom makes a noise, you can't hear the bells, more partic'lar now the frost kills the sound."

"Yes, I did; I heard 'em," said Silas, to whom Sunday bells were a mere accident of the day, and not part of its sacredness. There had been no bells in Lantern Yard.

"Dear heart!" said Dolly, pausing before she spoke again. "But what a pity it is you should work of a Sunday, and not clean yourself — if you *did n't* go to church; for if you'd a roasting bit, it might be as you could n't leave it, being a lone man. But there's the bakehus, if you could make up your mind to spend a twopence on the oven now and then, — not every week, in course — I should n't like to do that myself, — you might carry your bit o' dinner there, for it's nothing but right to have a bit o' summat hot of a Sunday, and not to make it as you can't know your dinner from Saturday. But now, upo' Christmas-day, this blessed Christmas as is ever coming, if you was to take your dinner to the bakehus, and go to church, and see the holly and the yew, and hear the anthim, and then take the sacramen', you'd be a deal the better, and you'd know which end you stood on, and you could put your trust i' Them as knows better nor we do, seein' you'd ha' done what it lies on us all to do."

Dolly's exhortation, which was an unusually long effort of speech for her, was uttered in the soothing persuasive tone with which she would have tried to prevail on a sick man to take his medicine, or a basin of gruel for which he had no appetite. Silas had never before been closely urged on the point of his absence from church, which had only been thought of as a part of his general queerness; and he was too direct and simple to evade Dolly's appeal.

"Nay, nay," he said, "I know nothing o' church. I've never been to church."

"No!" said Dolly, in a low tone of wonderment. Then bethinking herself of Silas's advent from an unknown country, she said, "Could it ha' been as they'd no church where you was born?"

"Oh yes," said Silas, meditatively, sitting in his usual posture of leaning on his knees, and supporting his head. "There was churches — a many — it was a big town. But I knew nothing of 'em — I went to chapel."

Dolly was much puzzled at this new word, but she was rather afraid of inquiring further, lest "chapel" might mean some haunt of wickedness. After a little thought, she said —

"Well, Master Marner, it's niver too late to turn over a new leaf, and if you've niver had no church, there's no telling the good it'll do you. For I feel so set up and comfortable as niver was, when I've been and heard the prayers, and the singing to the praise and glory o' God, as Mr. Macey gives out — and Mr. Crackenthorp saying good words, and more partic'lar on Sacramen' Day; and if a bit o' trouble comes, I feel as I can put up wi' it, for I've looked for help i' the right quarter, and gev myself up to Them as we must all give ourselves up to at the last; and if we 'n done our part, it is n't to be believed as Them as are above us 'ull be worse nor we are, and come short o' Their 'n."

Poor Dolly's exposition of her simple Raveloe theology fell rather unmeaningly on Silas's ears, for there was no word in it that could rouse a memory of what he had known as religion, and his comprehension was quite baffled by the plural pronoun, which was no heresy of Dolly's, but only her way of avoiding a presumptuous familiarity. He remained silent, not feeling inclined to assent to the part of Dolly's speech which he fully understood — her recommendation that he should go to church. Indeed, Silas was so unaccustomed to talk beyond the brief questions and answers necessary for the transaction of his simple business, that words did not easily come to him without the urgency of a distinct purpose.

But now, little Aaron, having become used to the weaver's awful presence, had advanced to his mother's side, and Silas, seeming to notice him for the first time, tried to return Dolly's signs of goodwill by offering the lad a bit of lard-cake. Aaron shrank back a little, and rubbed his head against his mother's shoulder, but still thought the piece of cake worth the risk of putting his hand out for it.

"Oh, for shame, Aaron," said his mother, taking him on her lap, however; "why, you don't want cake again yet awhile. He's wonderful hearty," she went on, with a little sigh — "that he is, God knows. He's my youngest, and we spoil him sadly, for either me or the father must allays hev him in our sight — that we must."

She stroked Aaron's brown head, and thought it must do

Master Marner good to see such a "pictur of a child." But
Marner, on the other side of the hearth, saw the neat-featured
rosy face as a mere dim round, with two dark spots in it.

"And he's got a voice like a bird — you would n't think,"
Dolly went on; "he can sing a Christmas carril as his father's
taught him; and I take it for a token as he'll come to good,
as he can learn the good tunes so quick. Come, Aaron, stan'
up and sing the carril to Master Marner, come."

Aaron replied by rubbing his forehead against his mother's
shoulder.

"Oh, that's naughty," said Dolly, gently. "Stan' up, when
mother tells you, and let me hold the cake till you've done."

Aaron was not indisposed to display his talents, even to an
ogre, under protecting circumstances; and after a few more
signs of coyness, consisting chiefly in rubbing the backs of his
hands over his eyes, and then peeping between them at Master
Marner, to see if he looked anxious for the "carril," he at
length allowed his head to be duly adjusted, and standing
behind the table, which let him appear above it only as far as
his broad frill, so that he looked like a cherubic head untroubled with a body, he began with a clear chirp, and in a
melody that had the rhythm of an industrious hammer —

> " God rest you, merry gentlemen,
> Let nothing you dismay,
> For Jesus Christ our Saviour
> Was born on Christmas-day."

Dolly listened with a devout look, glancing at Marner in
some confidence that this strain would help to allure him to
church.

"That's Christmas music," she said, when Aaron had ended,
and had secured his piece of cake again. "There's no other
music equil to the Christmas music — 'Hark the erol angils
sing.' And you may judge what it is at church, Master
Marner, with the bassoon and the voices, as you can't help
thinking you've got to a better place a'ready — for I would n't
speak ill o' this world, seeing as Them put us in it as knows
best — but what wi' the drink, and the quarrelling, and the

bad illnesses, and the hard dying, as I've seen times and times, one's thankful to hear of a better. The boy sings pretty, don't he, Master Marner?"

"Yes," said Silas, absently, "very pretty."

The Christmas carol, with its hammer-like rhythm, had fallen on his ears as strange music, quite unlike a hymn, and could have none of the effect Dolly contemplated. But he wanted to show her that he was grateful, and the only mode that occurred to him was to offer Aaron a bit more cake.

"Oh no, thank you, Master Marner," said Dolly, holding down Aaron's willing hands. "We must be going home now. And so I wish you good-by, Master Marner; and if you ever feel anyways bad in your inside, as you can't fend for yourself, I'll come and clean up for you, and get you a bit o' victual, and willing. But I beg and pray of you to leave off weaving of a Sunday, for it's bad for soul and body — and the money as comes i' that way 'ull be a bad bed to lie down on at the last, if it doesn't fly away, nobody knows where, like the white frost. And you'll excuse me being that free with you, Master Marner, for I wish you well — I do. Make your bow, Aaron."

Silas said "Good-by, and thank you kindly," as he opened the door for Dolly, but he couldn't help feeling relieved when she was gone — relieved that he might weave again and moan at his ease. Her simple view of life and its comforts, by which she had tried to cheer him, was only like a report of unknown objects, which his imagination could not fashion. The fountains of human love and of faith in a divine love had not yet been unlocked, and his soul was still the shrunken rivulet, with only this difference, that its little groove of sand was blocked up, and it wandered confusedly against dark obstruction.

And so, notwithstanding the honest persuasions of Mr. Macey and Dolly Winthrop, Silas spent his Christmas-day in loneliness, eating his meat in sadness of heart, though the meat had come to him as a neighborly present. In the morning he looked out on the black frost that seemed to press cruelly on every blade of grass, while the half-icy red pool shivered under the bitter wind; but towards evening the snow began to fall, and curtained from him even that dreary outlook, shutting him close up with his narrow grief. And he sat in his robbed home through the livelong evening, not caring to close his shutters or lock his door, pressing his head between his hands and moaning, till the cold grasped him and told him that his fire was gray.

Nobody in this world but himself knew that he was the same Silas Marner who had once loved his fellow with tender love, and trusted in an unseen goodness. Even to himself that past experience had become dim.

But in Raveloe village the bells rang merrily, and the church was fuller than all through the rest of the year, with red faces among the abundant dark-green boughs — faces prepared for a longer service than usual by an odorous breakfast of toast and ale. Those green boughs, the hymn and anthem never heard but at Christmas — even the Athanasian Creed, which was discriminated from the others only as being longer and of exceptional virtue, since it was only read on rare occasions — brought a vague exulting sense, for which the grown men could as little have found words as the children, that something great and mysterious had been done for them in heaven above and in earth below, which they were appropriating by their presence. And then the red faces made their way through the black biting frost to their own homes, feeling themselves free for the rest of the day to eat, drink, and be merry, and using that Christian freedom without diffidence.

At Squire Cass's family party that day nobody mentioned Dunstan — nobody was sorry for his absence, or feared it would be too long. The doctor and his wife, uncle and aunt Kimble, were there, and the annual Christmas talk was carried through without any omissions, rising to the climax of Mr. Kimble's experience when he walked the London hospitals thirty years back, together with striking professional anecdotes then gathered. Whereupon cards followed, with aunt Kimble's annual failure to follow suit, and uncle Kimble's irascibility concerning the odd trick which was rarely explicable to him, when it was not on his side, without a general visitation of tricks to see that they were formed on sound principles : the whole being accompanied by a strong steaming odor of spirits-and-water.

But the party on Christmas-day, being a strictly family party, was not the pre-eminently brilliant celebration of the season at the Red House. It was the great dance on New Year's Eve that made the glory of Squire Cass's hospitality, as of his forefathers', time out of mind. This was the occasion when all the society of Raveloe and Tarley, whether old acquaintances separated by long rutty distances, or cooled acquaintances separated by misunderstandings concerning run-away calves, or acquaintances founded on intermittent con-descension, counted on meeting and on comporting themselves with mutual appropriateness. This was the occasion on which fair dames who came on pillions sent their bandboxes before them, supplied with more than their evening costume ; for the feast was not to end with a single evening, like a paltry town entertainment, where the whole supply of eatables is put on the table at once, and bedding is scanty. The Red House was provisioned as if for a siege ; and as for the spare feather-beds ready to be laid on floors, they were as plentiful as might nat-urally be expected in a family that had killed its own geese for many generations.

Godfrey Cass was looking forward to this New Year's Eve with a foolish reckless longing, that made him half deaf to his importunate companion, Anxiety.

"Dunsey will be coming home soon : there will be a great blow-up, and how will you bribe his spite to silence ? " said Anxiety.

" Oh, he won't come home before New Year's Eve, perhaps," said Godfrey ; " and I shall sit by Nancy then, and dance with her, and get a kind look from her in spite of herself."

"But money is wanted in another quarter," said Anxiety, in a louder voice, "and how will you get it without selling your mother's diamond pin ? And if you don't get it . . . ? "

" Well, but something may happen to make things easier. At any rate, there's one pleasure for me close at hand : Nancy is coming."

"Yes, and suppose your father should bring matters to a pass that will oblige you to decline marrying her — and to give your reasons?"

"Hold your tongue, and don't worry me. I can see Nancy's eyes, just as they will look at me, and feel her hand in mine already."

But Anxiety went on, though in noisy Christmas company; refusing to be utterly quieted even by much drinking.

CHAPTER XI.

SOME women, I grant, would not appear to advantage seated on a pillion, and attired in a drab joseph and a drab beaver-bonnet, with a crown resembling a small stew-pan; for a garment suggesting a coachman's greatcoat, cut out under an exiguity of cloth that would only allow of miniature capes, is not well adapted to conceal deficiencies of contour, nor is drab a color that will throw sallow cheeks into lively contrast. It was all the greater triumph to Miss Nancy Lammeter's beauty that she looked thoroughly bewitching in that costume, as, seated on the pillion behind her tall, erect father, she held one arm round him, and looked down, with open-eyed anxiety, at the treacherous snow-covered pools and puddles, which sent up formidable splashings of mud under the stamp of Dobbin's foot. A painter would, perhaps, have preferred her in those moments when she was free from self-consciousness; but certainly the bloom on her cheeks was at its highest point of contrast with the surrounding drab when she arrived at the door of the Red House, and saw Mr. Godfrey Cass ready to lift her from the pillion. She wished her sister Priscilla had come up at the same time behind the servant, for then she would have contrived that Mr. Godfrey should have lifted off Priscilla first, and, in the meantime, she would have persuaded her father to go round to the horse-block instead of alighting at the door-steps. It was very painful, when you had made it quite clear to a young man that you were determined not to marry him, however much he might wish it, that he would still continue to pay you marked attentions; besides, why did n't he always show the same attentions, if he meant them sincerely, instead of being so strange as Mr. Godfrey Cass was, sometimes behaving as if he did n't want to speak to her, and taking no notice of her for weeks and weeks, and then, all on a sudden, almost making love again? Moreover, it was quite plain he had no real love for her, else he would not let people have *that* to say of him which they did say. Did he suppose that Miss Nancy Lammeter was to be won by any man, squire or no squire, who led a bad life? That was not what she had been used to see in her own father, who was the soberest and best man in that country-side, only a little hot and hasty now and then, if things were not done to the minute.

All these thoughts rushed through Miss Nancy's mind, in their habitual succession, in the moments between her first sight of Mr. Godfrey Cass standing at the door and her own arrival there. Happily, the Squire came out too and gave a loud greeting to her father, so that, somehow, under cover of this noise she seemed to find concealment for her confusion and neglect of any suitably formal behavior, while she was being lifted from the pillion by strong arms which seemed to find her ridiculously small and light. And there was the best reason for hastening into the house at once, since the snow was beginning to fall again, threatening an unpleasant journey for such guests as were still on the road. These were a small minority; for already the afternoon was beginning to decline, and there would not be too much time for the ladies who came from a distance to attire themselves in readiness for the early tea which was to inspirit them for the dance.

There was a buzz of voices through the house, as Miss Nancy entered, mingled with the scrape of a fiddle preluding in the kitchen; but the Lammeters were guests whose arrival had evidently been thought of so much that it had been watched for from the windows, for Mrs. Kimble, who did the honors at the Red House on these great occasions, came forward to meet Miss Nancy in the hall, and conduct her up-stairs. Mrs. Kimble was the Squire's sister, as well as the doctor's wife — a double dignity, with which her diameter was in direct proportion; so that, a journey up-stairs being rather fatiguing to her, she did not oppose Miss Nancy's request to be allowed to find her way alone to the Blue Room, where the Miss Lammeters' bandboxes had been deposited on their arrival in the morning.

There was hardly a bedroom in the house where feminine compliments were not passing and feminine toilettes going forward, in various stages, in space made scanty by extra beds spread upon the floor; and Miss Nancy, as she entered the Blue Room, had to make her little formal curtsy to a group of six. On the one hand, there were ladies no less important than the two Miss Gunns, the wine merchant's daughters from Lytherly, dressed in the height of fashion, with the tightest skirts and the shortest waists, and gazed at by Miss Ladbrook (of the Old Pastures) with a shyness not unsustained by inward criticism. Partly, Miss Ladbrook felt that her own skirt must be regarded as unduly lax by the Miss Gunns, and partly, that it was a pity the Miss Gunns did not show that judgment which she herself would show if she were in their place, by stopping a little on this side of the fashion. On the other hand, Mrs. Ladbrook was standing in skull-cap and front, with her turban in her hand, curtsying and smiling blandly and saying, "After you, ma'am," to another lady in similar circumstances, who had politely offered the precedence at the looking-glass.

But Miss Nancy had no sooner made her curtsy than an elderly lady came forward, whose full white muslin kerchief, and mob-cap round her curls of smooth gray hair, were in daring contrast with the puffed yellow satins and top-knotted caps of her neighbors. She approached Miss Nancy with much primness, and said, with a slow, treble suavity —

"Niece, I hope I see you well in health." Miss Nancy kissed her aunt's cheek dutifully, and answered, with the same sort of amiable primness, "Quite well, I thank you, aunt; and I hope I see you the same."

"Thank you, niece; I keep my health for the present. And how is my brother-in-law ? "

These dutiful questions and answers were continued until it was ascertained in detail that the Lammeters were all as well as usual, and the Osgoods likewise, also that niece Priscilla must certainly arrive shortly, and that travelling on pillions in snowy weather was unpleasant, though a joseph was a great protection. Then Nancy was formally introduced to her aunt's visitors, the Miss Gunns, as being the daughters of a mother known to *their* mother, though now for the first time induced to make a journey into these parts; and these ladies were so taken by surprise at finding such a lovely face and figure in an out-of-the-way country place, that they began to feel some curiosity about the dress she would put on when she took off her joseph. Miss Nancy, whose thoughts were always conducted with the propriety and moderation conspicuous in her manners, remarked to herself that the Miss Gunns were rather hard-featured than otherwise, and that such very low dresses as they wore might have been attributed to vanity if their shoulders had been pretty, but that, being as they were, it was not reasonable to suppose that they showed their necks from a love of display, but rather from some obligation not inconsistent with sense and modesty. She felt convinced, as she opened her box, that this must be her aunt Osgood's opinion, for Miss Nancy's mind resembled her aunt's to a degree that everybody said was surprising, considering the kinship was on Mr. Osgood's side ; and though you might not have supposed it from the formality of their greeting, there was a devoted attachment and mutual admiration between aunt and niece. Even Miss Nancy's refusal of her cousin Gilbert Osgood (on the ground solely that he was her cousin), though it had grieved her aunt greatly, had not in the least cooled the preference which had determined her to leave Nancy several of her hereditary ornaments, let Gilbert's future wife be whom she might.

Three of the ladies quickly retired, but the Miss Gunns were quite content that Mrs. Osgood's inclination to remain with her niece gave them also a reason for staying to see the rustic

beauty's toilette. And it was really a pleasure — from the
first opening of the bandbox, where everything smelt of lavender and rose-leaves, to the clasping of the small coral necklace
that fitted closely round her little white neck. Everything
belonging to Miss Nancy was of delicate purity and nattiness:
not a crease was where it had no business to be, not a bit of
her linen professed whiteness without fulfilling its profession;
the very pins on her pincushion were stuck in after a pattern
from which she was careful to allow no aberration; and as for
her own person, it gave the same idea of perfect unvarying
neatness as the body of a little bird. It is true that her light-
brown hair was cropped behind like a boy's, and was dressed
in front in a number of flat rings, that lay quite away from
her face; but there was no sort of coiffure that could make
Miss Nancy's cheek and neck look otherwise than pretty; and
when at last she stood complete in her silvery twilled silk, her
lace tucker, her coral necklace, and coral ear-drops, the Miss
Gunns could see nothing to criticise except her hands, which
bore the traces of butter-making, cheese-crushing, and even
still coarser work. But Miss Nancy was not ashamed of that,
for while she was dressing she narrated to her aunt how she
and Priscilla had packed their boxes yesterday, because this
morning was baking morning, and since they were leaving
home, it was desirable to make a good supply of meat-pies for
the kitchen; and as she concluded this judicious remark, she
turned to the Miss Gunns that she might not commit the rude-
ness of not including them in the conversation. The Miss
Gunns smiled stiffly, and thought what a pity it was that these
rich country people, who could afford to buy such good clothes
(really Miss Nancy's lace and silk were very costly), should
be brought up in utter ignorance and vulgarity. She actually
said " mate " for " meat," " 'appen " for " perhaps," and " oss "
for " horse," which, to young ladies living in good Lytherly
society, who habitually said 'orse, even in domestic privacy,
and only said 'appen on the right occasions, was necessarily
shocking. Miss Nancy, indeed, had never been to any school
higher than Dame Tedman's: her acquaintance with profane
literature hardly went beyond the rhymes she had worked in

her large sampler under the lamb and the shepherdess; and in order to balance an account, she was obliged to effect her subtraction by removing visible metallic shillings and sixpences from a visible metallic total. There is hardly a servant-maid in these days who is not better informed than Miss Nancy; yet she had the essential attributes of a lady — high veracity, delicate honor in her dealings, deference to others, and refined personal habits, — and lest these should not suffice to convince grammatical fair ones that her feelings can at all resemble theirs, I will add that she was slightly proud and exacting, and as constant in her affection towards a baseless opinion as towards an erring lover.

The anxiety about sister Priscilla, which had grown rather active by the time the coral necklace was clasped, was happily ended by the entrance of that cheerful-looking lady herself, with a face made blowsy by cold and damp. After the first questions and greetings, she turned to Nancy, and surveyed her from head to foot — then wheeled her round, to ascertain that the back view was equally faultless.

"What do you think o' *these* gowns, aunt Osgood?" said Priscilla, while Nancy helped her to unrobe.

"Very handsome indeed, niece," said Mrs. Osgood, with a slight increase of formality. She always thought niece Priscilla too rough.

"I'm obliged to have the same as Nancy, you know, for all I'm five years older, and it makes me look yellow; for she never *will* have anything without I have mine just like it, because she wants us to look like sisters. And I tell her, folks 'ull think it's my weakness makes me fancy as I shall look pretty in what she looks pretty in. For I *am* ugly — there's no denying that: I feature my father's family. But, law! I don't mind, do you?" Priscilla here turned to the Miss Gunns, rattling on in too much preoccupation with the delight of talking, to notice that her candor was not appreciated. "The pretty uns do for fly-catchers — they keep the men off us. I've no opinion o' the men, Miss Gunn — I don't know what *you* have. And as for fretting and stewing about what *they*'ll think of you from morning till night, and making

your life uneasy about what they're doing when they're out
o' your sight — as I tell Nancy, it's a folly no woman need
be guilty of, if she's got a good father and a good home: let
her leave it to them as have got no fortin, and can't help
themselves. As I say, Mr. Have-your-own-way is the best
husband, and the only one I'd ever promise to obey. I know
it isn't pleasant, when you've been used to living in a big
way, and managing hogsheads and all that, to go and put
your nose in by somebody else's fireside, or to sit down by
yourself to a scrag or a knuckle; but, thank God! my father's
a sober man and likely to live; and if you've got a man by
the chimney-corner, it doesn't matter if he's childish — the
business needn't be broke up."

The delicate process of getting her narrow gown over her
head without injury to her smooth curls, obliged Miss Priscilla to pause in this rapid survey of life, and Mrs. Osgood
seized the opportunity of rising and saying —

"Well, niece, you'll follow us. The Miss Gunns will like
to go down."

"Sister," said Nancy, when they were alone, "you've offended the Miss Gunns, I'm sure."

"What have I done, child?" said Priscilla, in some alarm.

"Why, you asked them if they minded about being ugly —
you're so very blunt."

"Law, did I? Well, it popped out: it's a mercy I said no
more, for I'm a bad un to live with folks when they don't
like the truth. But as for being ugly, look at me, child, in
this silver-colored silk — I told you how it'ud be — I look as
yallow as a daffadil. Anybody 'ud say you wanted to make
a mawkin of me."

"No, Priscy, don't say so. I begged and prayed of you not
to let us have this silk if you'd like another better. I was
willing to have your choice, you know I was," said Nancy, in
anxious self-vindication.

"Nonsense, child! you know you'd set your heart on this;
and reason good, for you're the color o' cream. It 'ud be fine
doings for you to dress yourself to suit my skin. What I find
fault with, is that notion o' yours as I must dress myself just

like you. But you do as you like with me — you always did,
from when first you begun to walk. If you wanted to go the
field's length, the field's length you'd go; and there was no
whipping you, for you looked as prim and innicent as a daisy
all the while."

"Priscy," said Nancy, gently, as she fastened a coral necklace, exactly like her own, round Priscilla's neck, which was
very far from being like her own, "I'm sure I'm willing to
give way as far as is right, but who should n't dress alike if it
is n't sisters? Would you have us go about looking as if we
were no kin to one another — us that have got no mother and
not another sister in the world? I'd do what was right, if I
dressed in a gown dyed with cheese-coloring; and I'd rather
you'd choose, and let me wear what pleases you."

"There you go again! You'd come round to the same
thing if one talked to you from Saturday night till Saturday
morning. It'll be fine fun to see how you'll master your husband and never raise your voice above the singing o' the kettle
all the while. I like to see the men mastered!"

"Don't talk so, Priscy," said Nancy, blushing. "You know
I don't mean ever to be married."

"Oh, you never mean a fiddlestick's end!" said Priscilla,
as she arranged her discarded dress, and closed her bandbox.
"Who shall I have to work for when father's gone, if you are
to go and take notions in your head and be an old maid, because some folks are no better than they should be? I
have n't a bit o' patience with you — sitting on an addled egg
forever, as if there was never a fresh un in the world. One
old maid's enough out o' two sisters; and I shall do credit to
a single life, for God A'mighty meant me for it. Come, we
can go down now. I'm as ready as a mawkin can be —
there's nothing awanting to frighten the crows, now I've got
my ear-droppers in."

As the two Miss Lammeters walked into the large parlor
together, any one who did not know the character of both
might certainly have supposed that the reason why the square-
shouldered, clumsy, high-featured Priscilla wore a dress the
facsimile of her pretty sister's, was either the mistaken vanity

of the one, or the malicious contrivance of the other in order
to set off her own rare beauty. But the good-natured self-
forgetful cheeriness and common-sense of Priscilla would soon
have dissipated the one suspicion ; and the modest calm of
Nancy's speech and manners told clearly of a mind free from
all disavowed devices.

Places of honor had been kept for the Miss Lammeters near
the head of the principal tea-table in the wainscoted parlor,
now looking fresh and pleasant with handsome branches of
holly, yew, and laurel, from the abundant growths of the old
garden; and Nancy felt an inward flutter, that no firmness
of purpose could prevent, when she saw Mr. Godfrey Cass
advancing to lead her to a seat between himself and Mr.
Crackenthorp, while Priscilla was called to the opposite side
between her father and the Squire. It certainly did make
some difference to Nancy that the lover she had given up was
the young man of quite the highest consequence in the parish
— at home in a venerable and unique parlor, which was the
extremity of grandeur in her experience, a parlor where *she*
might one day have been mistress, with the consciousness that
she was spoken of as " Madam Cass," the Squire's wife.
These circumstances exalted her inward drama in her own
eyes, and deepened the emphasis with which she declared to
herself that not the most dazzling rank should induce her to
marry a man whose conduct showed him careless of his character, but that, "love once, love always," was the motto of a
true and pure woman, and no man should ever have any right
over her which would be a call on her to destroy the dried
flowers that she treasured, and always would treasure, for
Godfrey Cass's sake. And Nancy was capable of keeping
her word to herself under very trying conditions. Nothing
but a becoming blush betrayed the moving thoughts that
urged themselves upon her as she accepted the seat next to
Mr. Crackenthorp; for she was so instinctively neat and
adroit in all her actions, and her pretty lips met each other
with such quiet firmness, that it would have been difficult for
her to appear agitated.

It was not the Rector's practice to let a charming blush

pass without an appropriate compliment. He was not in the least lofty or aristocratic, but simply a merry-eyed, small-featured, gray-haired man, with his chin propped by an ample many-creased white neckcloth which seemed to predominate over every other point in his person, and somehow to impress its peculiar character on his remarks; so that to have considered his amenities apart from his cravat would have been a severe, and perhaps a dangerous, effort of abstraction.

"Ha, Miss Nancy," he said, turning his head within his cravat and smiling down pleasantly upon her, "when anybody pretends this has been a severe winter, I shall tell them I saw the roses blooming on New Year's Eve — eh, Godfrey, what do *you* say ?"

Godfrey made no reply, and avoided looking at Nancy very markedly; for though these complimentary personalities were held to be in excellent taste in old-fashioned Raveloe society, reverent love has a politeness of its own which it teaches to men otherwise of small schooling. But the Squire was rather impatient at Godfrey's showing himself a dull spark in this way. By this advanced hour of the day, the Squire was always in higher spirits than we have seen him in at the breakfast-table, and felt it quite pleasant to fulfil the hereditary duty of being noisily jovial and patronizing: the large silver snuff-box was in active service and was offered without fail to all neighbors from time to time, however often they might have declined the favor. At present, the Squire had only given an express welcome to the heads of families as they appeared; but always as the evening deepened, his hospitality rayed out more widely, till he had tapped the youngest guests on the back and shown a peculiar fondness for their presence, in the full belief that they must feel their lives made happy by their belonging to a parish where there was such a hearty man as Squire Cass to invite them and wish them well. Even in this early stage of the jovial mood, it was natural that he should wish to supply his son's deficiencies by looking and speaking for him.

"Ay, ay," he began, offering his snuff-box to Mr. Lammeter, who for the second time bowed his head and waved his hand

in stiff rejection of the offer, "us old fellows may wish ourselves young to-night, when we see the mistletoe-bough in the
White Parlor. It's true, most things are gone back'ard in
these last thirty years — the country's going down since the
old king fell ill. But when I look at Miss Nancy here, I begin
to think the lasses keep up their quality; — ding me if I remember a sample to match her, not when I was a fine young
fellow, and thought a deal about my pigtail. No offence to
you, madam," he added, bending to Mrs. Crackenthorp, who
sat by him, "I did n't know *you* when you were as young as
Miss Nancy here."

Mrs. Crackenthorp — a small blinking woman, who fidgeted
incessantly with her lace, ribbons, and gold chain, turning her
head about and making subdued noises, very much like a
guinea-pig that twitches its nose and soliloquizes in all company indiscriminately — now blinked and fidgeted towards the
Squire, and said, "Oh no — no offence."

This emphatic compliment of the Squire's to Nancy was
felt by others besides Godfrey to have a diplomatic significance; and her father gave a slight additional erectness to his
back, as he looked across the table at her with complacent
gravity. That grave and orderly senior was not going to bate
a jot of his dignity by seeming elated at the notion of a match
between his family and the Squire's : he was gratified by any
honor paid to his daughter ; but he must see an alteration in
several ways before his consent would be vouchsafed. His
spare but healthy person, and high-featured firm face, that
looked as if it had never been flushed by excess, was in strong
contrast, not only with the Squire's, but with the appearance
of the Raveloe farmers generally — in accordance with a
favorite saying of his own, that "breed was stronger than
pasture."

"Miss Nancy's wonderful like what her mother was, though ;
is n't she, Kimble ?" said the stout lady of that name, looking
round for her husband.

But Doctor Kimble (country apothecaries in old days enjoyed that title without authority of diploma), being a thin
and agile man, was flitting about the room with his hands in

his pockets, making himself agreeable to his feminine patients, with medical impartiality, and being welcomed everywhere as a doctor by hereditary right — not one of those miserable apothecaries who canvass for practice in strange neighborhoods, and spend all their income in starving their one horse, but a man of substance, able to keep an extravagant table like the best of his patients. Time out of mind the Raveloe doctor had been a Kimble; Kimble was inherently a doctor's name; and it was difficult to contemplate firmly the melancholy fact that the actual Kimble had no son, so that his practice might one day be handed over to a successor with the incongruous name of Taylor or Johnson. But in that case the wiser people in Raveloe would employ Dr. Blick of Flitton — as less unnatural.

"Did you speak to me, my dear?" said the authentic doctor, coming quickly to his wife's side; but, as if foreseeing that she would be too much out of breath to repeat her remark, he went on immediately — "Ha, Miss Priscilla, the sight of you revives the taste of that super-excellent pork-pie. I hope the batch is n't near an end."

"Yes, indeed, it is, doctor," said Priscilla; "but I 'll answer for it the next shall be as good. My pork-pies don't turn out well by chance."

"Not as your doctoring does, eh, Kimble? — because folks forget to take your physic, eh?" said the Squire, who regarded physic and doctors as many loyal churchmen regard the church and the clergy — tasting a joke against them when he was in health, but impatiently eager for their aid when anything was the matter with him. He tapped his box, and looked round with a triumphant laugh.

"Ah, she has a quick wit, my friend Priscilla has," said the doctor, choosing to attribute the epigram to a lady rather than allow a brother-in-law that advantage over him. "She saves a little pepper to sprinkle over her talk — that 's the reason why she never puts too much into her pies. There 's my wife, now, she never has an answer at her tongue's end; but if I offend her, she 's sure to scarify my throat with black pepper the next day, or else give me the colic with watery greens.

That's an awful tit-for-tat." Here the vivacious doctor made
a pathetic grimace.

" Did you ever hear the like ? " said Mrs. Kimble, laughing
above her double chin with much good-humor, aside to Mrs.
Crackenthorp, who blinked and nodded, and amiably intended
to smile, but the intention lost itself in small twitchings and
noises.

" I suppose that's the sort of tit-for-tat adopted in your profession, Kimble, if you've a grudge against a patient," said
the Rector.

" Never do have a grudge against our patients," said Mr.
Kimble, " except when they leave us ; and then, you see, we
have n't the chance of prescribing for 'em. Ha, Miss Nancy,"
he continued, suddenly skipping to Nancy's side, " you won't
forget your promise ? You're to save a dance for me, you
know."

" Come, come, Kimble, don't you be too for'ard," said the
Squire. " Give the young uns fair-play. There's my son
Godfrey 'll be wanting to have a round with you if you run
off with Miss Nancy. He's bespoke her for the first dance,
I 'll be bound. Eh, sir! what do you say ? " he continued,
throwing himself backward, and looking at Godfrey. " Have n't
you asked Miss Nancy to open the dance with you ? "

Godfrey, sorely uncomfortable under this significant insistence about Nancy, and afraid to think where it would end by the
time his father had set his usual hospitable example of drinking
before and after supper, saw no course open but to turn to
Nancy and say, with as little awkwardness as possible —

" No; I 've not asked her yet, but I hope she 'll consent —
if somebody else has n't been before me."

" No, I 've not engaged myself," said Nancy, quietly, though
blushingly. (If Mr. Godfrey founded any hopes on her con-
senting to dance with him, he would soon be undeceived ; but
there was no need for her to be uncivil.)

" Then I hope you 've no objections to dancing with me,"
said Godfrey, beginning to lose the sense that there was anything uncomfortable in this arrangement.

" No, no objections," said Nancy, in a cold tone.

"Ah, well, you 're a lucky fellow, Godfrey," said uncle Kimble; "but you 're my godson, so I won't stand in your way. Else I 'm not so very old, eh, my dear ? " he went on, skipping to his wife's side again. "You would n't mind my having a second after you were gone — not if I cried a good deal first ? "

" Come, come, take a cup o' tea and stop your tongue, do," said good-humored Mrs. Kimble, feeling some pride in a husband who must be regarded as so clever and amusing by the company generally. If he had only not been irritable at cards !

While safe, well-tested personalities were enlivening the tea in this way, the sound of the fiddle approaching within a distance at which it could be heard distinctly, made the young people look at each other with sympathetic impatience for the end of the meal.

" Why, there 's Solomon in the hall," said the Squire, " and playing my fav'rite tune, *I* believe — 'The flaxen-headed ploughboy ' — he 's for giving us a hint as we are n't enough in a hurry to hear him play. Bob," he called out to his third long-legged son, who was at the other end of the room, " open the door, and tell Solomon to come in. He shall give us a tune here."

Bob obeyed, and Solomon walked in, fiddling as he walked, for he would on no account break off in the middle of a tune.

" Here, Solomon," said the Squire, with loud patronage. " Round here, my man. Ah, I knew it was 'The flaxen-headed ploughboy : ' there 's no finer tune."

Solomon Macey, a small hale old man, with an abundant crop of long white hair reaching nearly to his shoulders, advanced to the indicated spot, bowing reverently while he fiddled, as much as to say that he respected the company though he respected the key-note more. As soon as he had repeated the tune and lowered his fiddle, he bowed again to the Squire and the Rector, and said, " I hope I see your honor and your reverence well, and wishing you health and long life and a happy New Year. And wishing the same to you, Mr. Lammeter, sir ; and to the other gentlemen, and the madams, and the young lasses."

As Solomon uttered the last words, he bowed in all directions solicitously, lest he should be wanting in due respect. But thereupon he immediately began to prelude, and fell into the tune which he knew would be taken as a special compliment by Mr. Lammeter.

"Thank ye, Solomon, thank ye," said Mr. Lammeter when the fiddle paused again. "That 's 'Over the hills and far away,' that is. My father used to say to me, whenever we heard that tune, 'Ah, lad, *I* come from over the hills and far away.' There 's a many tunes I don't make head or tail of; but that speaks to me like the blackbird's whistle. I suppose it 's the name: there 's a deal in the name of a tune."

But Solomon was already impatient to prelude again, and presently broke with much spirit into "Sir Roger de Coverley," at which there was a sound of chairs pushed back, and laughing voices.

"Ay, ay, Solomon, we know what that means," said the Squire, rising. "It 's time to begin the dance, eh ? Lead the way, then, and we 'll all follow you."

So Solomon, holding his white head on one side, and playing vigorously, marched forward at the head of the gay procession into the White Parlor, where the mistletoe-bough was hung, and multitudinous tallow candles made rather a brilliant effect, gleaming from among the berried holly-boughs, and reflected in the old-fashioned oval mirrors fastened in the panels of the white wainscot. A quaint procession! Old Solomon, in his seedy clothes and long white locks, seemed to be luring that decent company by the magic scream of his fiddle — luring discreet matrons in turban-shaped caps, nay, Mrs. Crackenthorp herself, the summit of whose perpendicular feather was on a level with the Squire's shoulder — luring fair lasses complacently conscious of very short waists and skirts blameless of front-folds — luring burly fathers in large variegated waistcoats, and ruddy sons, for the most part shy and sheepish, in short nether garments and very long coat-tails.

Already Mr. Macey and a few other privileged villagers, who were allowed to be spectators on these great occasions, were seated on benches placed for them near the door; and

great was the admiration and satisfaction in that quarter
when the couples had formed themselves for the dance, and
the Squire led off with Mrs. Crackenthorp, joining hands with
the Rector and Mrs. Osgood. That was as it should be —
that was what everybody had been used to — and the charter
of Raveloe seemed to be renewed by the ceremony. It was
not thought of as an unbecoming levity for the old and
middle-aged people to dance a little before sitting down to
cards, but rather as part of their social duties. For what
were these if not to be merry at appropriate times, interchang-
ing visits and poultry with due frequency, paying each other
old-established compliments in sound traditional phrases, passing well-tried personal jokes, urging your guests to eat and
drink too much out of hospitality, and eating and drinking
too much in your neighbor's house to show that you liked
your cheer? And the parson naturally set an example in
these social duties. For it would not have been possible for
the Raveloe mind, without a peculiar revelation, to know that
a clergyman should be a pale-faced memento of solemnities,
instead of a reasonably faulty man whose exclusive authority
to read prayers and preach, to christen, marry, and bury you,
necessarily co-existed with the right to sell you the ground
to be buried in and to take tithe in kind ; on which last point,
of course, there was a little grumbling, but not to the extent
of irreligion — not of deeper significance than the grumbling
at the rain, which was by no means accompanied with a spirit
of impious defiance, but with a desire that the prayer for fine
weather might be read forthwith.

There was no reason, then, why the Rector's dancing should
not be received as part of the fitness of things quite as much
as the Squire's, or why, on the other hand, Mr. Macey's official respect should restrain him from subjecting the parson's
performance to that criticism with which minds of extraordi-
nary acuteness must necessarily contemplate the doings of
their fallible fellow-men.

"The Squire's pretty springe, considering his weight," said
Mr. Macey, "and he stamps uncommon well. But Mr. Lammeter beats 'em all for shapes: you see he holds his head like

a sodger, and he is n't so cushiony as most o' the oldish gentlefolks — they run fat in general ; and he 's got a fine leg. The
parson 's nimble enough, but he has n't got much of a leg :
it 's a bit too thick down'ard, and his knees might be a bit
nearer wi'out damage ; but he might do worse, he might do
worse. Though he has n't that grand way o' waving his hand
as the Squire has."

"Talk o' nimbleness, look at Mrs. Osgood," said Ben Winthrop, who was holding his son Aaron between his knees.
"She trips along with her little steps, so as nobody can see
how she goes — it 's like as if she had little wheels to her feet.
She does n't look a day older nor last year : she 's the finest-
made woman as is, let the next be where she will."

"I don't heed how the women are made," said Mr. Macey,
with some contempt. "They wear nayther coat nor breeches :
you can't make much out o' their shapes."

"Fayder," said Aaron, whose feet were busy beating out
the tune, "how does that big cock's-feather stick in Mrs.
Crackenthorp's yead ? Is there a little hole for it, like in
my shuttle-cock ? "

"Hush, lad, hush ; that 's the way the ladies dress their-
selves, that is," said the father, adding, however, in an under-
tone to Mr. Macey, "It does make her look funny, though —
partly like a short-necked bottle wi' a long quill in it. Hey,
by jingo, there 's the young Squire leading off now, wi' Miss
Nancy for partners ! There 's a lass for you ! — like a pink-
and-white posy — there 's nobody 'ud think as anybody could
be so pritty. I should n't wonder if she 's Madam Cass some
day, arter all — and nobody more rightfuller, for they 'd make
a fine match. You can find nothing against Master Godfrey's
shapes, Macey, I'll bet a penny."

Mr. Macey screwed up his mouth, leaned his head further on
one side, and twirled his thumbs with a presto movement as
his eyes followed Godfrey up the dance. At last he summed
up his opinion.

"Pretty well down'ard, but a bit too round i' the shoulder-
blades. And as for them coats as he gets from the Flitton
tailor, they 're a poor cut to pay double money for."

"Ah, Mr. Macey, you and me are two folks," said Ben, slightly indignant at this carping. "When I've got a pot o' good ale, I like to swaller it, and do my inside good, i'stead o' smelling and staring at it to see if I can't find faut wi' the brewing. I should like you to pick me out a finer-limbed young fellow nor Master Godfrey — one as 'ud knock you down easier, or 's more pleasanter looksed when he's piert and merry."

"Tchuh!" said Mr. Macey, provoked to increased severity, "he is n't come to his right color yet: he's partly like a slack-baked pie. And I doubt he's got a soft place in his head, else why should he be turned round the finger by that offal Dunsey as nobody's seen o' late, and let him kill that fine hunting hoss as was the talk o' the country? And one while he was allays after Miss Nancy, and then it all went off again, like a smell o' hot porridge, as I may say. That was n't my way when *I* went a-coorting."

"Ah, but mayhap Miss Nancy hung off like, and your lass did n't," said Ben.

"I should say she did n't," said Mr. Macey, significantly. "Before I said 'sniff,' I took care to know as she'd say 'snaff,' and pretty quick too. I was n't a-going to open *my* mouth, like a dog at a fly, and snap it to again, wi' nothing to swaller."

"Well, I think Miss Nancy's a-coming round again," said Ben, "for Master Godfrey does n't look so down-hearted to-night. And I see he's for taking her away to sit down, now they 're at the end o' the dance: that looks like sweethearting, that does."

The reason why Godfrey and Nancy had left the dance was not so tender as Ben imagined. In the close press of couples a slight accident had happened to Nancy's dress, which, while it was short enough to show her neat ankle in front, was long enough behind to be caught under the stately stamp of the Squire's foot, so as to rend certain stitches at the waist, and cause much sisterly agitation in Priscilla's mind, as well as serious concern in Nancy's. One's thoughts may be much oc-cupied with love-struggles, but hardly so as to be insensible to a disorder in the general framework of things. Nancy had no sooner completed her duty in the figure they were dancing than she said to Godfrey, with a deep blush, that she must go and sit down till Priscilla could come to her; for the sisters had already exchanged a short whisper and an open-eyed glance full of meaning. No reason less urgent than this could have prevailed on Nancy to give Godfrey this opportunity of sitting apart with her. As for Godfrey, he was feeling so happy and oblivious under the long charm of the country-dance with Nancy, that he got rather bold on the strength of her confusion, and was capable of leading her straight away, without leave asked, into the adjoining small parlor, where the card-tables were set.

"Oh no, thank you," said Nancy, coldly, as soon as she perceived where he was going, "not in there. I'll wait here till Priscilla's ready to come to me. I'm sorry to bring you out of the dance and make myself troublesome."

"Why, you'll be more comfortable here by yourself," said the artful Godfrey: "I'll leave you here till your sister can come." He spoke in an indifferent tone.

That was an agreeable proposition, and just what Nancy desired; why, then, was she a little hurt that Mr. Godfrey should make it? They entered, and she seated herself on a chair against one of the card-tables, as the stiffest and most unapproachable position she could choose.

"Thank you, sir," she said immediately. "I need n't give you any more trouble. I'm sorry you've had such an unlucky partner."

"That's very ill-natured of you," said Godfrey, standing by her without any sign of intended departure, "to be sorry you've danced with me."

"Oh no, sir, I don't mean to say what's ill-natured at all," said Nancy, looking distractingly prim and pretty. "When gentlemen have so many pleasures, one dance can matter but very little."

"You know that is n't true. You know one dance with you matters more to me than all the other pleasures in the world."

It was a long, long while since Godfrey had said anything so direct as that, and Nancy was startled. But her instinctive dignity and repugnance to any show of emotion made her sit perfectly still, and only throw a little more decision into her voice, as she said —

"No, indeed, Mr. Godfrey, that's not known to me, and I have very good reasons for thinking different. But if it's true, I don't wish to hear it."

"Would you never forgive me, then, Nancy — never think well of me, let what would happen — would you never think the present made amends for the past? Not if I turned a good fellow, and gave up everything you did n't like?"

Godfrey was half conscious that this sudden opportunity of speaking to Nancy alone had driven him beside himself; but blind feeling had got the mastery of his tongue. Nancy really felt much agitated by the possibility Godfrey's words suggested, but this very pressure of emotion that she was in danger of finding too strong for her roused all her power of self-command.

"I should be glad to see a good change in anybody, Mr. Godfrey," she answered, with the slightest discernible difference of tone, "but it 'ud be better if no change was wanted."

"You're very hard-hearted, Nancy," said Godfrey, pettishly. "You might encourage me to be a better fellow. I 'm very miserable — but you 've no feeling."

"I think those have the least feeling that act wrong to begin with," said Nancy, sending out a flash in spite of herself. Godfrey was delighted with that little flash, and would have liked to go on and make her quarrel with him; Nancy was so exasperatingly quiet and firm. But she was not indifferent to him *yet*.

The entrance of Priscilla, bustling forward and saying, "Dear heart alive, child, let us look at this gown," cut off Godfrey's hopes of a quarrel.

"I suppose I must go now," he said to Priscilla.

"It 's no matter to me whether you go or stay," said that frank lady, searching for something in her pocket, with a preoccupied brow.

"Do *you* want me to go?" said Godfrey, looking at Nancy, who was now standing up by Priscilla's order.

"As you like," said Nancy, trying to recover all her former coldness, and looking down carefully at the hem of her gown.

"Then I like to stay," said Godfrey, with a reckless determination to get as much of this joy as he could to-night, and think nothing of the morrow.

CHAPTER XII.

WHILE Godfrey Cass was taking draughts of forgetfulness from the sweet presence of Nancy, willingly losing all sense of that hidden bond which at other moments galled and fretted him so as to mingle irritation with the very sunshine, Godfrey's wife was walking with slow uncertain steps through the snow-covered Raveloe lanes, carrying her child in her arms.

This journey on New Year's Eve was a premeditated act of vengeance which she had kept in her heart ever since Godfrey, in a fit of passion, had told her he would sooner die than acknowledge her as his wife. There would be a great party at the Red House on New Year's Eve, she knew: her husband would be smiling and smiled upon, hiding *her* existence in the darkest corner of his heart. But she would mar his pleasure: she would go in her dingy rags, with her faded face, once as handsome as the best, with her little child that had its father's hair and eyes, and disclose herself to the Squire as his eldest son's wife. It is seldom that the miserable can help regarding their misery as a wrong inflicted by those who are less miserable. Molly knew that the cause of her dingy rags was not her husband's neglect, but the demon Opium to whom she was enslaved, body and soul, except in the lingering mother's tenderness that refused to give him her hungry child. She knew this well; and yet, in the moments of wretched unbenumbed consciousness, the sense of her want and degradation transformed itself continually into bitterness towards Godfrey. *He* was well off; and if she had her rights she would be well off too. The belief that he repented his marriage, and suffered from it, only aggravated her vindictiveness. Just and self-reproving thoughts do not come to us too thickly, even in the purest air and with the best lessons of heaven and earth; how should those white-winged delicate messengers make their way to Molly's poisoned chamber, inhabited by no higher memories than those of a barmaid's paradise of pink ribbons and gentlemen's jokes?

She had set out at an early hour, but had lingered on the road, inclined by her indolence to believe that if she waited under a warm shed the snow would cease to fall. She had waited longer than she knew, and now that she found herself belated in the snow-hidden ruggedness of the long lanes, even the animation of a vindictive purpose could not keep her spirit from failing. It was seven o'clock, and by this time she was not very far from Raveloe, but she was not familiar enough with those monotonous lanes to know how near she was to her journey's end. She needed comfort, and she knew but one comforter — the familiar demon in her bosom; but she hesitated a moment, after drawing out the black remnant, before she raised it to her lips. In that moment the mother's love pleaded for painful consciousness rather than oblivion — pleaded to be left in aching weariness, rather than to have the encircling arms benumbed so that they could not feel the dear burden. In another moment Molly had flung something away, but it was not the black remnant — it was an empty phial. And she walked on again under the breaking cloud, from which there came now and then the light of a quickly veiled star, for a freezing wind had sprung up since the snowing had ceased. But she walked always more and more drowsily, and clutched more and more automatically the sleeping child at her bosom.

Slowly the demon was working his will, and cold and weariness were his helpers. Soon she felt nothing but a supreme immediate longing that curtained off all futurity — the longing to lie down and sleep. She had arrived at a spot where her footsteps were no longer checked by a hedgerow, and she had wandered vaguely, unable to distinguish any objects, notwithstanding the wide whiteness around her, and the growing starlight. She sank down against a straggling furze bush, an easy pillow enough; and the bed of snow, too, was soft. She did not feel that the bed was cold, and did not heed whether the child would wake and cry for her. But her arms had not yet relaxed their instinctive clutch; and the little one slumbered on as gently as if it had been rocked in a lace-trimmed cradle.

But the complete torpor came at last: the fingers lost their tension, the arms unbent; then the little head fell away from the bosom, and the blue eyes opened wide on the cold starlight. At first there was a little peevish cry of "mammy," and an effort to regain the pillowing arm and bosom; but mammy's ear was deaf, and the pillow seemed to be slipping away backward. Suddenly, as the child rolled downward on its mother's knees, all wet with snow, its eyes were caught by a bright glancing light on the white ground, and, with the ready transition of infancy, it was immediately absorbed in watching the bright living thing running towards it, yet never arriving. That bright living thing must be caught; and in an instant the child had slipped on all fours, and held out one little hand to catch the gleam. But the gleam would not be caught in that way, and now the head was held up to see where the cunning gleam came from. It came from a very bright place; and the little one, rising on its legs, toddled through the snow, the old grimy shawl in which it was wrapped trailing behind it, and the queer little bonnet dangling at its back—toddled on to the open door of Silas Marner's cottage, and right up to the warm hearth, where there was a bright fire of logs and sticks, which had thoroughly warmed the old sack (Silas's greatcoat) spread out on the bricks to dry. The little one, accustomed to be left to itself for long hours without notice from its mother, squatted down on the sack, and spread its tiny hands towards the blaze, in perfect contentment, gurgling and making many inarticulate communications to the cheerful fire, like a new-hatched gosling beginning to find itself comfortable. But presently the warmth had a lulling effect, and the little golden head sank down on the old sack, and the blue eyes were veiled by their delicate half-transparent lids.

But where was Silas Marner while this strange visitor had come to his hearth? He was in the cottage, but he did not see the child. During the last few weeks, since he had lost his money, he had contracted the habit of opening his door and looking out from time to time, as if he thought that his money might be somehow coming back to him, or that some trace, some news of it, might be mysteriously on the road, and be caught by the listening ear or the straining eye. It was chiefly at night, when he was not occupied in his loom, that he fell into this repetition of an act for which he could have assigned no definite purpose, and which can hardly be understood except by those who have undergone a bewildering separation from a supremely loved object. In the evening twilight, and later whenever the night was not dark, Silas looked out on that narrow prospect round the Stone-pits, listening and gazing, not with hope, but with mere yearning and unrest.

This morning he had been told by some of his neighbors that it was New Year's Eve, and that he must sit up and hear the old year rung out and the new rung in, because that was good luck, and might bring his money back again. This was only a friendly Raveloe-way of jesting with the half-crazy oddities of a miser, but it had perhaps helped to throw Silas into a more than usually excited state. Since the on-coming of twilight he had opened his door again and again, though only to shut it immediately at seeing all distance veiled by the falling snow. But the last time he opened it the snow had ceased, and the clouds were parting here and there. He stood and listened, and gazed for a long while — there was really something on the road coming towards him then, but he caught no sign of it; and the stillness and the wide trackless snow seemed to narrow his solitude, and touched his yearning with the chill of despair. He went in again, and put his right hand on the latch of the door to close it — but he did not close it: he was arrested, as he had been already since his loss, by the invisible wand of catalepsy, and stood like a graven image, with wide but sightless eyes, holding open his door. powerless to resist either the good or evil that might enter there.

When Marner's sensibility returned, he continued the action which had been arrested, and closed his door, unaware of the chasm in his consciousness, unaware of any intermediate change, except that the light had grown dim, and that he was chilled and faint. He thought he had been too long standing at the door and looking out. Turning towards the hearth, where the two logs had fallen apart, and sent forth only a red uncertain glimmer, he seated himself on his fireside chair, and was stooping to push his logs together, when, to his blurred vision, it seemed as if there were gold on the floor in front of the hearth. Gold! — his own gold — brought back to him as mysteriously as it had been taken away! He felt his heart begin to beat violently, and for a few moments he was unable to stretch out his hand and grasp the restored treasure. The heap of gold seemed to glow and get larger beneath his agitated gaze. He leaned forward at last, and stretched forth his hand; but instead of the hard coin with the familiar resisting outline, his fingers encountered soft warm curls. In utter amazement, Silas fell on his knees and bent his head low to examine the marvel: it was a sleeping child — a round, fair thing, with soft yellow rings all over its head. Could this be his little sister come back to him in a dream — his little sister whom he had carried about in his arms for a year before she died, when he was a small boy without shoes or stockings? That was the first thought that darted across Silas's blank wonderment. *Was* it a dream? He rose to his feet again, pushed his logs together, and, throwing on some dried leaves and sticks, raised a flame; but the flame did not disperse the vision — it only lit up more distinctly the little round form of the child, and its shabby clothing. It was very much like his little sister. Silas sank into his chair powerless, under the double presence of an inexplicable surprise and a hurrying influx of memories. How and when had the child come in

without his knowledge ? He had never been beyond the door.
But along with that question, and almost thrusting it away,
there was a vision of the old home and the old streets leading
to Lantern Yard — and within that vision another, of the
thoughts which had been present with him in those far-off
scenes. The thoughts were strange to him now, like old
friendships impossible to revive; and yet he had a dreamy
feeling that this child was somehow a message come to him
from that far-off life : it stirred fibres that had never been
moved in Raveloe — old quiverings of tenderness — old impressions of awe at the presentiment of some Power presiding
over his life; for his imagination had not yet extricated itself
from the sense of mystery in the child's sudden presence, and
had formed no conjectures of ordinary natural means by which
the event could have been brought about.

But there was a cry on the hearth : the child had awaked,
and Marner stooped to lift it on his knee. It clung round his
neck, and burst louder and louder into that mingling of inarticulate cries with "mammy" by which little children express
the bewilderment of waking. Silas pressed it to him, and
almost unconsciously uttered sounds of hushing tenderness,
while he bethought himself that some of his porridge, which
had got cool by the dying fire, would do to feed the child with
if it were only warmed up a little.

He had plenty to do through the next hour. The porridge,
sweetened with some dry brown sugar from an old store which
he had refrained from using for himself, stopped the cries of
the little one, and made her lift her blue eyes with a wide
quiet gaze at Silas, as he put the spoon into her mouth. Presently she slipped from his knee and began to toddle about,
but with a pretty stagger that made Silas jump up and follow
her lest she should fall against anything that would hurt her.
But she only fell in a sitting posture on the ground, and began
to pull at her boots, looking up at him with a crying face as
if the boots hurt her. He took her on his knee again, but it
was some time before it occurred to Silas's dull bachelor mind
that the wet boots were the grievance, pressing on her warm
ankles. He got them off with difficulty, and baby was at once

happily occupied with the primary mystery of her own toes, inviting Silas, with much chuckling, to consider the mystery too. But the wet boots had at last suggested to Silas that the child had been walking on the snow, and this roused him from his entire oblivion of any ordinary means by which it could have entered or been brought into his house. Under the prompting of this new idea, and without waiting to form conjectures, he raised the child in his arms, and went to the door. As soon as he had opened it, there was the cry of "mammy" again, which Silas had not heard since the child's first hungry waking. Bending forward, he could just discern the marks made by the little feet on the virgin snow, and he followed their track to the furze bushes. "Mammy!" the little one cried again and again, stretching itself forward so as almost to escape from Silas's arms, before he himself was aware that there was something more than the bush before him — that there was a human body, with the head sunk low in the furze, and half-covered with the shaken snow.

CHAPTER XIII.

It was after the early supper-time at the Red House, and the entertainment was in that stage when bashfulness itself had passed into easy jollity, when gentlemen, conscious of unusual accomplishments, could at length be prevailed on to dance a hornpipe, and when the Squire preferred talking loudly, scattering snuff, and patting his visitors' backs, to sitting longer at the whist-table — a choice exasperating to uncle Kimble, who, being always volatile in sober business hours, became intense and bitter over cards and brandy, shuffled before his adversary's deal with a glare of suspicion, and turned up a mean trump-card with an air of inexpressible disgust, as if in a world where such things could happen one might as well enter on a course of reckless profligacy. When

the evening had advanced to this pitch of freedom and enjoyment, it was usual for the servants, the heavy duties of supper
being well over, to get their share of amusement by coming
to look on at the dancing; so that the back regions of the
house were left in solitude.

There were two doors by which the White Parlor was entered from the hall, and they were both standing open for the
sake of air; but the lower one was crowded with the servants
and villagers, and only the upper doorway was left free. Bob
Cass was figuring in a hornpipe, and his father, very proud
of this lithe son, whom he repeatedly declared to be just like
himself in his young days in a tone that implied this to be
the very highest stamp of juvenile merit, was the centre of a
group who had placed themselves opposite the performer, not
far from the upper door. Godfrey was standing a little way
off, not to admire his brother's dancing, but to keep sight of
Nancy, who was seated in the group, near her father. He
stood aloof, because he wished to avoid suggesting himself as
a subject for the Squire's fatherly jokes in connection with
matrimony and Miss Nancy Lammeter's beauty, which were
likely to become more and more explicit. But he had the
prospect of dancing with her again when the hornpipe was
concluded, and in the meanwhile it was very pleasant to get
long glances at her quite unobserved.

But when Godfrey was lifting his eyes from one of those
long glances, they encountered an object as startling to him
at that moment as if it had been an apparition from the dead.
It *was* an apparition from that hidden life which lies, like a
dark by-street, behind the goodly ornamented façade that
meets the sunlight and the gaze of respectable admirers. It
was his own child carried in Silas Marner's arms. That was
his instantaneous impression, unaccompanied by doubt, though
he had not seen the child for months past; and when the
hope was rising that he might possibly be mistaken, Mr.
Crackenthorp and Mr. Lammeter had already advanced to
Silas, in astonishment at this strange advent. Godfrey joined
them immediately, unable to rest without hearing every word
— trying to control himself, but conscious that if any one

noticed him, they must see that he was white-lipped and trembling.

But now all eyes at that end of the room were bent on Silas Marner; the Squire himself had risen, and asked angrily, "How's this? — what's this? — what do you do coming in here in this way?"

"I'm come for the doctor — I want the doctor," Silas had said, in the first moment, to Mr. Crackenthorp.

"Why, what's the matter, Marner?" said the Rector. "The doctor's here; but say quietly what you want him for."

"It's a woman," said Silas, speaking low, and half-breathlessly, just as Godfrey came up. "She's dead, I think — dead in the snow at the Stone-pits — not far from my door."

Godfrey felt a great throb: there was one terror in his mind at that moment: it was, that the woman might *not* be dead. That was an evil terror — an ugly inmate to have found a nestling-place in Godfrey's kindly disposition; but no disposition is a security from evil wishes to a man whose happiness hangs on duplicity.

"Hush, hush!" said Mr. Crackenthorp. "Go out into the hall there. I'll fetch the doctor to you. Found a woman in the snow — and thinks she's dead," he added, speaking low, to the Squire. "Better say as little about it as possible: it will shock the ladies. Just tell them a poor woman is ill from cold and hunger. I'll go and fetch Kimble."

By this time, however, the ladies had pressed forward, curious to know what could have brought the solitary linen-weaver there under such strange circumstances, and interested in the pretty child, who, half alarmed and half attracted by the brightness and the numerous company, now frowned and hid her face, now lifted up her head again and looked round placably, until a touch or a coaxing word brought back the frown, and made her bury her face with new determination.

"What child is it?" said several ladies at once, and, among the rest, Nancy Lammeter, addressing Godfrey.

"I don't know — some poor woman's who has been found in the snow, I believe," was the answer Godfrey wrung from himself with a terrible effort. ("After all, *am* I certain?" he hastened to add, in anticipation of his own conscience.)

"Why, you'd better leave the child here, then, Master Marner," said good-natured Mrs. Kimble, hesitating, however, to take those dingy clothes into contact with her own ornamented satin bodice. "I'll tell one o' the girls to fetch it."

"No — no — I can't part with it, I can't let it go," said Silas, abruptly. "It's come to me — I've a right to keep it."

The proposition to take the child from him had come to Silas quite unexpectedly, and his speech, uttered under a strong sudden impulse, was almost like a revelation to himself: a minute before, he had no distinct intention about the child.

"Did you ever hear the like?" said Mrs. Kimble, in mild surprise, to her neighbor.

"Now, ladies, I must trouble you to stand aside," said Mr. Kimble, coming from the card-room, in some bitterness at the interruption, but drilled by the long habit of his profession into obedience to unpleasant calls, even when he was hardly sober.

"It's a nasty business turning out now, eh, Kimble?" said the Squire. "He might ha' gone for your young fellow — the 'prentice, there — what's his name?"

"Might? ay — what's the use of talking about might?" growled uncle Kimble, hastening out with Marner, and followed by Mr. Crackenthorp and Godfrey. "Get me a pair of thick boots, Godfrey, will you? And stay, let somebody run to Winthrop's and fetch Dolly — she's the best woman to get. Ben was here himself before supper; is he gone?"

"Yes, sir, I met him," said Marner; "but I couldn't stop to tell him anything, only I said I was going for the doctor, and he said the doctor was at the Squire's. And I made haste and ran, and there was nobody to be seen at the back o' the house, and so I went in to where the company was."

The child, no longer distracted by the bright light and the smiling women's faces, began to cry and call for "mammy," though always clinging to Marner, who had apparently won her thorough confidence. Godfrey had come back with the boots, and felt the cry as if some fibre were drawn tight within him.

"I'll go," he said, hastily, eager for some movement; "I'll go and fetch the woman — Mrs. Winthrop."

"Oh, pooh — send somebody else," said uncle Kimble, hurrying away with Marner.

"You'll let me know if I can be of any use, Kimble," said Mr. Crackenthorp. But the doctor was out of hearing.

Godfrey, too, had disappeared: he was gone to snatch his hat and coat, having just reflection enough to remember that he must not look like a madman; but he rushed out of the house into the snow without heeding his thin shoes.

In a few minutes he was on his rapid way to the Stone-pits by the side of Dolly, who, though feeling that she was entirely in her place in encountering cold and snow on an errand of mercy, was much concerned at a young gentleman's getting his feet wet under a like impulse.

"You'd a deal better go back, sir," said Dolly, with respectful compassion. "You've no call to catch cold; and I'd ask you if you'd be so good as tell my husband to come, on your way back — he's at the Rainbow, I doubt — if you found him anyway sober enough to be o' use. Or else, there's Mrs. Snell 'ud happen send the boy up to fetch and carry, for there may be things wanted from the doctor's."

"No, I'll stay, now I'm once out — I'll stay outside here," said Godfrey, when they came opposite Marner's cottage. "You can come and tell me if I can do anything."

"Well, sir, you're very good: you've a tender heart," said Dolly, going to the door.

Godfrey was too painfully preoccupied to feel a twinge of self-reproach at this undeserved praise. He walked up and down, unconscious that he was plunging ankle-deep in snow, unconscious of everything but trembling suspense about what was going on in the cottage, and the effect of each alternative on his future lot. No, not quite unconscious of everything else. Deeper down, and half-smothered by passionate desire and dread, there was the sense that he ought not to be waiting on these alternatives; that he ought to accept the consequences of his deeds, own the miserable wife, and fulfil the claims of the helpless child. But he had not moral courage enough to contemplate that active renunciation of Nancy as possible for him: he had only conscience and heart enough to make him forever uneasy under the weakness that forbade the renunciation. And at this moment his mind leaped away from all restraint towards the sudden prospect of deliverance from his long bondage.

"Is she dead?" said the voice that predominated over every other within him. "If she is, I may marry Nancy; and then I shall be a good fellow in future, and have no secrets, and the child — shall be taken care of somehow." But across that vision came the other possibility — "She may live, and then it's all up with me."

Godfrey never knew how long it was before the door of the cottage opened and Mr. Kimble came out. He went forward to meet his uncle, prepared to suppress the agitation he must feel, whatever news he was to hear.

"I waited for you, as I'd come so far," he said, speaking first.

"Pooh, it was nonsense for you to come out: why did n't you send one of the men? There's nothing to be done. She's dead — has been dead for hours, I should say."

"What sort of woman is she?" said Godfrey, feeling the blood rush to his face.

"A young woman, but emaciated, with long black hair. Some vagrant — quite in rags. She's got a wedding-ring on, however. They must fetch her away to the workhouse to-morrow. Come, come along."

"I want to look at her," said Godfrey. "I think I saw such a woman yesterday. I'll overtake you in a minute or two."

Mr. Kimble went on, and Godfrey turned back to the cottage. He cast only one glance at the dead face on the pillow, which Dolly had smoothed with decent care; but he remembered that last look at his unhappy hated wife so well, that at the end of sixteen years every line in the worn face was present to him when he told the full story of this night.

He turned immediately towards the hearth, where Silas
Marner sat lulling the child. She was perfectly quiet now,
but not asleep — only soothed by sweet porridge and warmth
into that wide-gazing calm which makes us older human beings,
with our inward turmoil, feel a certain awe in the presence of
a little child, such as we feel before some quiet majesty or
beauty in the earth or sky — before a steady glowing planet,
or a full-flowered eglantine, or the bending trees over a silent
pathway. The wide-open blue eyes looked up at Godfrey's
without any uneasiness or sign of recognition : the child could
make no visible audible claim on its father ; and the father
felt a strange mixture of feelings, a conflict of regret and joy,
that the pulse of that little heart had no response for the half-
jealous yearning in his own, when the blue eyes turned away
from him slowly, and fixed themselves on the weaver's queer
face, which was bent low down to look at them, while the
small hand began to pull Marner's withered cheek with loving
disfiguration.

"You'll take the child to the parish to-morrow ?" asked
Godfrey, speaking as indifferently as he could.

"Who says so ?" said Marner, sharply. "Will they make
me take her ?"

"Why, you wouldn't like to keep her, should you — an old
bachelor like you ?"

"Till anybody shows they've a right to take her away
from me," said Marner. "The mother's dead, and I reckon
it's got no father : it's a lone thing — and I'm a lone thing.
My money's gone, I don't know where — and this is come
from I don't know where. I know nothing — I'm partly
mazed."

"Poor little thing !" said Godfrey. "Let me give something
towards finding it clothes."

He had put his hand in his pocket and found half-a-guinea,
and, thrusting it into Silas's hand, he hurried out of the cottage
to overtake Mr. Kimble.

"Ah, I see it's not the same woman I saw," he said, as he
came up. "It's a pretty little child : the old fellow seems to
want to keep it ; that's strange for a miser like him. But I

gave him a trifle to help him out: the parish is n't likely to quarrel with him for the right to keep the child."

"No; but I 've seen the time when I might have quarrelled with him for it myself. It 's too late now, though. If the child ran into the fire, your aunt 's too fat to overtake it: she could only sit and grunt like an alarmed sow. But what a fool you are, Godfrey, to come out in your dancing shoes and stockings in this way — and you one of the beaux of the evening, and at your own house! What do you mean by such freaks, young fellow? Has Miss Nancy been cruel, and do you want to spite her by spoiling your pumps?"

"Oh, everything has been disagreeable to-night. I was tired to death of jigging and gallanting, and that bother about the hornpipes. And I 'd got to dance with the other Miss Gunn," said Godfrey, glad of the subterfuge his uncle had suggested to him.

The prevarication and white lies which a mind that keeps itself ambitiously pure is as uneasy under as a great artist under the false touches that no eye detects but his own, are worn as lightly as mere trimmings when once the actions have become a lie.

Godfrey reappeared in the White Parlor with dry feet, and, since the truth must be told, with a sense of relief and gladness that was too strong for painful thoughts to struggle with. For could he not venture now, whenever opportunity offered, to say the tenderest things to Nancy Lammeter — to promise her and himself that he would always be just what she would desire to see him? There was no danger that his dead wife would be recognized: those were not days of active inquiry and wide report; and as for the registry of their marriage, that was a long way off, buried in unturned pages, away from every one's interest but his own. Dunsey might betray him if he came back; but Dunsey might be won to silence.

And when events turn out so much better for a man than he has had reason to dread, is it not a proof that his conduct has been less foolish and blameworthy than it might otherwise have appeared? When we are treated well, we naturally begin to think that we are not altogether unmeritorious, and that it is only just we should treat ourselves well, and not mar our own good fortune. Where, after all, would be the use of his confessing the past to Nancy Lammeter, and throwing away his happiness? — nay, hers? for he felt some confidence that she loved him. As for the child, he would see that it was cared for: he would never forsake it; he would do everything but own it. Perhaps it would be just as happy in life without being owned by its father, seeing that nobody could tell how things would turn out, and that — is there any other reason wanted? — well, then, that the father would be much happier without owning the child.

CHAPTER XIV.

THERE was a pauper's burial that week in Raveloe, and up Kench Yard at Batherley it was known that the dark-haired woman with the fair child, who had lately come to lodge there, was gone away again. That was all the express note taken that Molly had disappeared from the eyes of men. But the unwept death which, to the general lot, seemed as trivial as the summer-shed leaf, was charged with the force of destiny to certain human lives that we know of, shaping their joys and sorrows even to the end.

Silas Marner's determination to keep the "tramp's child" was matter of hardly less surprise and iterated talk in the village than the robbery of his money. That softening of feeling towards him which dated from his misfortune, that merging of suspicion and dislike in a rather contemptuous pity for him as lone and crazy, was now accompanied with a more active sympathy, especially among the women. Notable mothers, who knew what it was to keep children "whole and sweet;" lazy mothers, who knew what it was to be interrupted in folding their arms and scratching their elbows by the mischievous propensities of children just firm on their legs, were

equally interested in conjecturing how a lone man would manage with a two-year-old child on his hands, and were equally
ready with their suggestions: the notable chiefly telling him
what he had better do, and the lazy ones being emphatic in
telling him what he would never be able to do.

Among the notable mothers, Dolly Winthrop was the one
whose neighborly offices were the most acceptable to Marner,
for they were rendered without any show of bustling instruction. Silas had shown her the half-guinea given to him by
Godfrey, and had asked her what he should do about getting
some clothes for the child.

"Eh, Master Marner," said Dolly, "there's no call to buy,
no more nor a pair o' shoes; for I've got the little petticoats
as Aaron wore five years ago, and it's ill spending the money
on them baby-clothes, for the child 'ull grow like grass i' May,
bless it — that it will."

And the same day Dolly brought her bundle, and displayed
to Marner, one by one, the tiny garments in their due order of
succession, most of them patched and darned, but clean and
neat as fresh-sprung herbs. This was the introduction to a
great ceremony with soap and water, from which Baby came
out in new beauty, and sat on Dolly's knee, handling her toes
and chuckling and patting her palms together with an air of
having made several discoveries about herself, which she
communicated by alternate sounds of "gug-gug-gug," and
"mammy." The "mammy" was not a cry of need or uneasiness: Baby had been used to utter it without expecting either
tender sound or touch to follow.

"Anybody 'ud think the angils in heaven could n't be prettier," said Dolly, rubbing the golden curls and kissing them.
"And to think of its being covered wi' them dirty rags — and
the poor mother froze to death; but there's Them as took care
of it, and brought it to your door, Master Marner. The door
was open, and it walked in over the snow, like as if it had been
a little starved robin. Did n't you say the door was open?"

"Yes," said Silas, meditatively. "Yes — the door was
open. The money's gone I don't know where, and this is
come from I don't know where."

He had not mentioned to any one his unconsciousness of the child's entrance, shrinking from questions which might lead to the fact he himself suspected — namely, that he had been in one of his trances.

"Ah," said Dolly, with soothing gravity, "it's like the night and the morning, and the sleeping and the waking, and the rain and the harvest — one goes and the other comes, and we know nothing how nor where. We may strive and scrat and fend, but it's little we can do arter all — the big things come and go wi' no striving o' our'n — they do, that they do; and I think you're in the right on it to keep the little un, Master Marner, seeing as it's been sent to you, though there's folks as thinks different. You'll happen be a bit moithered with it while it's so little; but I'll come, and welcome, and see to it for you: I've a bit o' time to spare most days, for when one gets up betimes i' the morning, the clock seems to stan' still tow'rt ten, afore it's time to go about the victual. So, as I say, I'll come and see to the child for you, and welcome."

"Thank you—kindly," said Silas, hesitating a little. "I'll be glad if you'll tell me things. But," he added uneasily, leaning forward to look at Baby with some jealousy, as she was resting her head backward against Dolly's arm, and eying him contentedly from a distance — "but I want to do things for it myself, else it may get fond o' somebody else, and not fond o' me. I've been used to fending for myself in the house —I can learn, I can learn."

"Eh, to be sure," said Dolly, gently. "I've seen men as are wonderful handy wi' children. The men are awk'ard and contrairy mostly, God help 'em — but when the drink's out of 'em, they aren't unsensible, though they're bad for leeching and bandaging — so fiery and unpatient. You see this goes first, next the skin," proceeded Dolly, taking up the little shirt, and putting it on.

"Yes," said Marner, docilely, bringing his eyes very close, that they might be initiated in the mysteries; whereupon Baby seized his head with both her small arms, and put her lips against his face with purring noises.

"See there," said Dolly, with a woman's tender tact, "she's fondest o' you. She wants to go o' your lap, I'll be bound. Go, then: take her, Master Marner; you can put the things on, and then you can say as you've done for her from the first of her coming to you."

Marner took her on his lap, trembling with an emotion mysterious to himself, at something unknown dawning on his life. Thought and feeling were so confused within him, that if he had tried to give them utterance, he could only have said that the child was come instead of the gold — that the gold had turned into the child. He took the garments from Dolly, and put them on under her teaching; interrupted, of course, by Baby's gymnastics.

"There, then! why, you take to it quite easy, Master Marner," said Dolly; "but what shall you do when you're forced to sit in your loom? For she'll get busier and mischievouser every day — she will, bless her. It's lucky as you've got that high hearth i'stead of a grate, for that keeps the fire more out of her reach: but if you've got anything as can be spilt or broke, or as is fit to cut her fingers off, she'll be at it — and it is but right you should know."

Silas meditated a little while in some perplexity. "I'll tie her to the leg o' the loom," he said at last —"tie her with a good long strip o' something."

"Well, mayhap that'll do, as it's a little gell, for they're easier persuaded to sit i' one place nor the lads. I know what the lads are; for I've had four — four I've had, God knows — and if you was to take and tie 'em up, they'd make a fighting and a crying as if you was ringing the pigs. But I'll bring you my little chair, and some bits o' red rag and things for her to play wi'; an' she'll sit and chatter to 'em as if they was alive. Eh, if it was n't a sin to the lads to wish 'em made different, bless 'em, I should ha' been glad for one of 'em to be a little gell; and to think as I could ha' taught her to scour, and mend, and the knitting, and everything. But I can teach 'em this little un, Master Marner, when she gets old enough."

"But she'll be *my* little un," said Marner, rather hastily. "She'll be nobody else's."

"No, to be sure; you'll have a right to her, if you're a father to her, and bring her up according. But," added Dolly, coming to a point which she had determined beforehand to touch upon, "you must bring her up like christened folks's children, and take her to church, and let her learn her catechise, as my little Aaron can say off — the 'I believe,' and everything, and 'hurt nobody by word or deed,' — as well as if he was the clerk. That's what you must do, Master Marner, if you'd do the right thing by the orphin child."

Marner's pale face flushed suddenly under a new anxiety. His mind was too busy trying to give some definite bearing to Dolly's words for him to think of answering her.

"And it's my belief," she went on, "as the poor little creature has never been christened, and it's nothing but right as the parson should be spoke to; and if you was noways unwilling, I'd talk to Mr. Macey about it this very day. For if the child ever went anyways wrong, and you hadn't done your part by it, Master Marner — 'noculation, and everything to save it from harm — it 'ud be a thorn i' your bed forever o' this side the grave; and I can't think as it 'ud be easy lying down for anybody when they'd got to another world, if they hadn't done their part by the helpless children as come wi'out their own asking."

Dolly herself was disposed to be silent for some time now, for she had spoken from the depths of her own simple belief, and was much concerned to know whether her words would produce the desired effect on Silas. He was puzzled and anxious, for Dolly's word "christened" conveyed no distinct meaning to him. He had only heard of baptism, and had only seen the baptism of grown-up men and women.

"What is it as you mean by 'christened'?" he said at last, timidly. "Won't folks be good to her without it?"

"Dear, dear! Master Marner," said Dolly, with gentle distress and compassion. "Had you never no father nor mother as taught you to say your prayers, and as there's good words and good things to keep us from harm?"

"Yes," said Silas, in a low voice; "I know a deal about that — used to, used to. But your ways are different: my country was a good way off." He paused a few moments, and then added, more decidedly, "But I want to do everything as can be done for the child. And whatever's right for it i' this country, and you think 'ull do it good, I'll act according, if you'll tell me."

"Well, then, Master Marner," said Dolly, inwardly rejoiced, "I'll ask Mr. Macey to speak to the parson about it; and you must fix on a name for it, because it must have a name giv' it when it's christened."

"My mother's name was Hephzibah," said Silas, "and my little sister was named after her."

"Eh, that's a hard name," said Dolly. "I partly think it is n't a christened name."

"It's a Bible name," said Silas, old ideas recurring.

"Then I've no call to speak again' it," said Dolly, rather startled by Silas's knowledge on this head; "but you see I'm no scholard, and I'm slow at catching the words. My husband says I'm allays like as if I was putting the haft for the handle — that's what he says — for he's very sharp, God help him. But it was awk'ard calling your little sister by such a hard name, when you'd got nothing big to say, like — was n't it, Master Marner?"

"We called her Eppie," said Silas.

"Well, if it was noways wrong to shorten the name, it 'ud be a deal handier. And so I'll go now, Master Marner, and I'll speak about the christening afore dark; and I wish you the best o' luck, and it's my belief as it'll come to you, if you do what's right by the orphin child; — and there's the 'noculation to be seen to; and as to washing its bits o' things, you need look to nobody but me, for I can do 'em wi' one hand when I've got my suds about. Eh, the blessed angil! You'll let me bring my Aaron one o' these days, and he'll show her his little cart as his father's made for him, and the black-and-white pup as he's got a-rearing."

Baby *was* christened, the Rector deciding that a double baptism was the lesser risk to incur; and on this occasion Silas, making himself as clean and tidy as he could, appeared for the first time within the church, and shared in the observances held sacred by his neighbors. He was quite unable, by means of anything he heard or saw, to identify the Raveloe religion with his old faith; if he could at any time in his previous life have done so, it must have been by the aid of a strong feeling ready to vibrate with sympathy, rather than by a comparison of phrases and ideas : and now for long years that feeling had been dormant. He had no distinct idea about the baptism and the church-going, except that Dolly had said it was for the good of the child ; and in this way, as the weeks grew to months, the child created fresh and fresh links between his life and the lives from which he had hitherto shrunk continually into narrower isolation. Unlike the gold which needed nothing, and must be worshipped in close-locked solitude — which was hidden away from the daylight, was deaf to the song of birds, and started to no human tones — Eppie was a creature of endless claims and ever-growing desires, seeking and loving sunshine, and living sounds, and living movements ; making trial of everything, with trust in new joy, and stirring the human kindness in all eyes that looked on her. The gold had kept his thoughts in an ever-repeated circle, leading to nothing beyond itself ; but Eppie was an object compacted of changes and hopes that forced his thoughts onward, and carried them far away from their old eager pacing towards the same blank limit — carried them away to the new things that would come with the coming years, when Eppie would have learned to understand how her father Silas cared for her ; and made him look for images of that time in the ties and charities that bound together the families of his neighbors. The gold had asked that he should sit weaving longer and longer, deafened and blinded more and more to all things except the monotony of his loom and the repetition of his web; but Eppie called him away from his weaving, and make him think all its pauses a holiday, re-awakening his senses with her fresh life, even to the old winter-flies that came crawling forth in the early spring sunshine, and warming him into joy because *she* had joy.

And when the sunshine grew strong and lasting, so that the buttercups were thick in the meadows, Silas might be seen in the sunny mid-day, or in the late afternoon when the shadows were lengthening under the hedgerows, strolling out with uncovered head to carry Eppie beyond the Stone-pits to where the flowers grew, till they reached some favorite bank where he could sit down, while Eppie toddled to pluck the flowers, and make remarks to the winged things that murmured happily above the bright petals, calling "Dad-dad's" attention continually by bringing him the flowers. Then she would turn her ear to some sudden bird-note, and Silas learned to please her by making signs of hushed stillness, that they might listen for the note to come again : so that when it came, she set up her small back and laughed with gurgling triumph. Sitting on the banks in this way, Silas began to look for the once familiar herbs again ; and as the leaves, with their unchanged outline and markings, lay on his palm, there was a sense of crowding remembrances from which he turned away timidly, taking refuge in Eppie's little world, that lay lightly on his enfeebled spirit.

As the child's mind was growing into knowledge, his mind was growing into memory : as her life unfolded, his soul, long stupefied in a cold narrow prison, was unfolding too, and trembling gradually into full consciousness.

It was an influence which must gather force with every new year : the tones that stirred Silas's heart grew articulate, and called for more distinct answers ; shapes and sounds grew clearer for Eppie's eyes and ears, and there was more that "Dad-dad" was imperatively required to notice and account for. Also, by the time Eppie was three years old, she developed a fine capacity for mischief, and for devising ingenious ways of being troublesome, which found much exercise, not only for Silas's patience, but for his watchfulness and penetration. Sorely was poor Silas puzzled on such occasions by the incompatible demands of love. Dolly Winthrop told him that punishment was good for Eppie, and that, as for rearing a child without making it tingle a little in soft and safe places now and then, it was not to be done.

"To be sure, there's another thing you might do, Master Marner," added Dolly, meditatively : "you might shut her up once i' the coal-hole. That was what I did wi' Aaron; for I was that silly wi' the youngest lad, as I could never bear to smack him. Not as I could find i' my heart to let him stay i' the coal-hole more nor a minute, but it was enough to colly him all over, so as he must be new washed and dressed, and it was as good as a rod to him — that was. But I put it upo' your conscience, Master Marner, as there's one of 'em you must choose — ayther smacking or the coal-hole — else she'll get so masterful, there'll be no holding her."

Silas was impressed with the melancholy truth of this last remark; but his force of mind failed before the only two penal methods open to him, not only because it was painful to him to hurt Eppie, but because he trembled at a moment's contention with her, lest she should love him the less for it. Let even an affectionate Goliath get himself tied to a small tender thing, dreading to hurt it by pulling, and dreading still more to snap the cord, and which of the two, pray, will be master? It was clear that Eppie, with her short toddling steps, must lead father Silas a pretty dance on any fine morning when circumstances favored mischief.

For example. He had wisely chosen a broad strip of linen as a means of fastening her to his loom when he was busy: it made a broad belt round her waist, and was long enough to allow of her reaching the truckle-bed and sitting down on it, but not long enough for her to attempt any dangerous climbing. One bright summer's morning Silas had been more engrossed than usual in "setting up" a new piece of work, an occasion on which his scissors were in requisition. These scissors, owing to an especial warning of Dolly's, had been kept carefully out of Eppie's reach; but the click of them had had a peculiar attraction for her ear, and watching the results of that click, she had derived the philosophic lesson that the same cause would produce the same effect. Silas had seated himself in his loom, and the noise of weaving had begun; but he had left his scissors on a ledge which Eppie's arm was long enough to reach; and now, like a small mouse, watching her opportunity, she stole quietly from her corner, secured the scissors, and toddled to the bed again, setting up her back as a mode of concealing the fact. She had a distinct intention as to the use of the scissors; and having cut the linen strip in a jagged but effectual manner, in two moments she had run out at the open door where the sunshine was inviting her, while poor Silas believed her to be a better child than usual. It was not until he happened to need his scissors that the terrible fact burst upon him: Eppie had run out by herself — had perhaps fallen into the Stone-pit. Silas, shaken by the worst fear that could have befallen him, rushed out, calling "Eppie!" and ran eagerly about the unenclosed space, exploring the dry cavities into which she might have fallen, and then gazing with questioning dread at the smooth red surface of the water. The cold drops stood on his brow. How long had she been out? There was one hope — that she had crept through the stile and got into the fields, where he habitually took her to stroll. But the grass was high in the meadow, and there was no descrying her, if she were there, except by a close search that would be a trespass on Mr. Osgood's crop. Still, that misdemeanor must be committed; and poor Silas, after peering all round the hedgerows, traversed the grass, beginning with perturbed vision to see Eppie behind every group of red sorrel, and to see her moving always farther off as he approached. The meadow was searched in vain; and he got over the stile into the next field, looking with dying hope towards a small pond which was now reduced to its summer shallowness, so as to leave a wide margin of good adhesive mud. Here, however, sat Eppie, discoursing cheerfully to her own small boot, which she was using as a bucket to convey the water into a deep hoof-mark, while her little naked foot was planted comfortably on a cushion of olive-green mud. A red-headed calf was observing her with alarmed doubt through the opposite hedge.

Here was clearly a case of aberration in a christened child which demanded severe treatment; but Silas, overcome with convulsive joy at finding his treasure again, could do nothing but snatch her up, and cover her with half-sobbing kisses. It was not until he had carried her home, and had begun to think of the necessary washing, that he recollected the need that he should punish Eppie, and "make her remember." The idea that she might run away again and come to harm, gave him unusual resolution, and for the first time he determined to try the coal-hole — a small closet near the hearth.

"Naughty, naughty Eppie," he suddenly began, holding her on his knee, and pointing to her muddy feet and clothes — "naughty to cut with the scissors and run away. Eppie must go into the coal-hole for being naughty. Daddy must put her in the coal-hole."

He half-expected that this would be shock enough, and that Eppie would begin to cry. But instead of that, she began to shake herself on his knee, as if the proposition opened a pleasing novelty. Seeing that he must proceed to extremities, he put her into the coal-hole, and held the door closed, with a trembling sense that he was using a strong measure. For a moment there was silence, but then came a little cry, "Opy, opy!" and Silas let her out again, saying, "Now Eppie 'ull never be naughty again, else she must go in the coal-hole — a black naughty place."

The weaving must stand still a long while this morning, for now Eppie must be washed, and have clean clothes on; but it was to be hoped that this punishment would have a lasting effect, and save time in future — though, perhaps, it would have been better if Eppie had cried more.

In half an hour she was clean again, and Silas having turned his back to see what he could do with the linen band, threw it down again, with the reflection that Eppie would be good without fastening for the rest of the morning. He turned round again, and was going to place her in her little chair near the loom, when she peeped out at him with black face and hands again, and said, "Eppie in de toal-hole!"

This total failure of the coal-hole discipline shook Silas's belief in the efficacy of punishment. "She'd take it all for fun," he observed to Dolly, "if I didn't hurt her, and that I can't do, Mrs. Winthrop. If she makes me a bit o' trouble, I can bear it. And she's got no tricks but what she'll grow out of."

"Well, that's partly true, Master Marner," said Dolly, sym-
pathetically; "and if you can't bring your mind to frighten
her off touching things, you must do what you can to keep
'em out of her way. That's what I do wi' the pups as the
lads are allays a-rearing. They *will* worry and gnaw — worry
and gnaw they will, if it was one's Sunday cap as hung anywhere so as they could drag it. They know no difference,
God help 'em: it's the pushing o' the teeth as sets 'em on,
that's what it is."

So Eppie was reared without punishment, the burden of her
misdeeds being borne vicariously by father Silas. The stone
hut was made a soft nest for her, lined with downy patience:
and also in the world that lay beyond the stone hut she knew
nothing of frowns and denials.

Notwithstanding the difficulty of carrying her and his yarn
or linen at the same time, Silas took her with him in most of
his journeys to the farm-houses, unwilling to leave her behind
at Dolly Winthrop's, who was always ready to take care of
her; and little curly-headed Eppie, the weaver's child, became
an object of interest at several outlying homesteads, as well as
in the village. Hitherto he had been treated very much as if
he had been a useful gnome or brownie — a queer and unaccountable creature, who must necessarily be looked at with
wondering curiosity and repulsion, and with whom one would
be glad to make all greetings and bargains as brief as possible,
but who must be dealt with in a propitiatory way, and occasionally have a present of pork or garden stuff to carry home
with him, seeing that without him there was no getting the
yarn woven. But now Silas met with open smiling faces and
cheerful questioning, as a person whose satisfactions and difficulties could be understood. Everywhere he must sit a little
and talk about the child, and words of interest were always
ready for him: "Ah, Master Marner, you'll be lucky if she
takes the measles soon and easy!" — or, "Why, there isn't
many lone men 'ud ha' been wishing to take up with a little
un like that: but I reckon the weaving makes you handier
than men as do out-door work — you're partly as handy as a
woman, for weaving comes next to spinning." Elderly mas-

ters and mistresses, seated observantly in large kitchen arm-chairs, shook their heads over the difficulties attendant on rearing children, felt Eppie's round arms and legs, and pro-nounced them remarkably firm, and told Silas, that, if she turned out well (which, however, there was no telling), it would be a fine thing for him to have a steady lass to do for him when he got helpless. Servant maidens were fond of carrying her out to look at the hens and chickens, or to see if any cherries could be shaken down in the orchard; and the small boys and girls approached her slowly, with cautious movement and steady gaze, like little dogs face to face with one of their own kind, till attraction had reached the point at which the soft lips were put out for a kiss. No child was afraid of approaching Silas when Eppie was near him : there was no repulsion around him now, either for young or old; for the little child had come to link him once more with the whole world. There was love between him and the child that blent them into one, and there was love between the child and the world — from men and women with parental looks and tones, to the red lady-birds and the round pebbles.

Silas began now to think of Raveloe life entirely in relation to Eppie : she must have everything that was a good in Rave-loe; and he listened docilely, that he might come to under-stand better what this life was, from which, for fifteen years, he had stood aloof as from a strange thing, wherewith he could have no communion : as some man who has a precious plant to which he would give a nurturing home in a new soil, thinks of the rain, and the sunshine, and all influences, in relation to his nursling, and asks industriously for all knowledge that will help him to satisfy the wants of the searching roots, or to guard leaf and bud from invading harm. The disposition to hoard had been utterly crushed at the very first by the loss of his long-stored gold : the coins he earned afterwards seemed as irrelevant as stones brought to complete a house suddenly buried by an earthquake; the sense of bereavement was too heavy upon him for the old thrill of satisfaction to arise again at the touch of the newly-earned coin. And now something had come to replace his hoard which gave a growing purpose to the earnings, drawing his hope and joy continually onward beyond the money.

In old days there were angels who came and took men by the hand and led them away from the city of destruction. We see no white-winged angels now. But yet men are led away from threatening destruction : a hand is put into theirs, which leads them forth gently towards a calm and bright land, so that they look no more backward ; and the hand may be a little child's.

CHAPTER XV.

There was one person, as you will believe, who watched with keener though more hidden interest than any other, the prosperous growth of Eppie under the weaver's care. He dared not do anything that would imply a stronger interest in a poor man's adopted child than could be expected from the kindliness of the young Squire, when a chance meeting suggested a little present to a simple old fellow whom others noticed with goodwill ; but he told himself that the time would come when he might do something towards furthering the welfare of his daughter without incurring suspicion. Was he very uneasy in the meantime at his inability to give his daughter her birthright ? I cannot say that he was. The child was being taken care of, and would very likely be happy, as people in humble stations often were — happier, perhaps, than those brought up in luxury.

That famous ring that pricked its owner when he forgot duty and followed desire — I wonder if it pricked very hard when he set out on the chase, or whether it pricked but lightly then, and only pierced to the quick when the chase had long been ended, and hope, folding her wings, looked backward and became regret ?

Godfrey Cass's cheek and eye were brighter than ever now. He was so undivided in his aims, that he seemed like a man of firmness. No Dunsey had come back: people had made up their minds that he was gone for a soldier, or gone "out of the country," and no one cared to be specific in their inquiries on a subject delicate to a respectable family. Godfrey had ceased to see the shadow of Dunsey across his path; and the path now lay straight forward to the accomplishment of his best, longest-cherished wishes. Everybody said Mr. Godfrey had taken the right turn; and it was pretty clear what would be the end of things, for there were not many days in the week that he was not seen riding to the Warrens. Godfrey himself, when he was asked jocosely if the day had been fixed, smiled with the pleasant consciousness of a lover who could say "yes," if he liked. He felt a reformed man, delivered from temptation; and the vision of his future life seemed to him as a promised land for which he had no cause to fight. He saw himself with all his happiness centred on his own hearth, while Nancy would smile on him as he played with the children.

And that other child, not on the hearth — he would not forget it; he would see that it was well provided for. That was a father's duty.

PART II.

CHAPTER XVI.

It was a bright autumn Sunday, sixteen years after Silas Marner had found his new treasure on the hearth. The bells of the old Raveloe church were ringing the cheerful peal which told that the morning service was ended; and out of the arched doorway in the tower came slowly, retarded by friendly greetings and questions, the richer parishioners who had chosen this bright Sunday morning as eligible for church-going. It was the rural fashion of that time for the more important members of the congregation to depart first, while their humbler neighbors waited and looked on, stroking their bent heads or dropping their curtsies to any large ratepayer who turned to notice them.

Foremost among these advancing groups of well-clad people, there are some whom we shall recognize, in spite of Time, who has laid his hand on them all. The tall blond man of forty is not much changed in feature from the Godfrey Cass of six-and-twenty: he is only fuller in flesh, and has only lost the indefinable look of youth — a loss which is marked even when the eye is undulled and the wrinkles are not yet come. Perhaps the pretty woman, not much younger than he, who is leaning on his arm, is more changed than her husband: the lovely bloom that used to be always on her cheek now comes but fitfully, with the fresh morning air or with some strong surprise; yet to all who love human faces best for what they tell of human experience, Nancy's beauty has a heightened interest. Often the soul is ripened into fuller goodness while age has spread an ugly film, so that mere glances can never

divine the preciousness of the fruit. But the years have not
been so cruel to Nancy. The firm yet placid mouth, the clear
veracious glance of the brown eyes, speak now of a nature
that has been tested and has kept its highest qualities; and
even the costume, with its dainty neatness and purity, has
more significance now the coquetries of youth can have
nothing to do with it.

Mr. and Mrs. Godfrey Cass (any higher title has died away
from Raveloe lips since the old Squire was gathered to his
fathers and his inheritance was divided) have turned round
to look for the tall aged man and the plainly dressed woman
who are a little behind — Nancy having observed that they
must wait for "father and Priscilla" — and now they all turn
into a narrower path leading across the churchyard to a small
gate opposite the Red House. We will not follow them now;
for may there not be some others in this departing congregation
whom we should like to see again — some of those who are not
likely to be handsomely clad, and whom we may not recognize
so easily as the master and mistress of the Red House?

But it is impossible to mistake Silas Marner. His large
brown eyes seem to have gathered a longer vision, as is the
way with eyes that have been short-sighted in early life, and
they have a less vague, a more answering gaze; but in everything else one sees signs of a frame much enfeebled by the
lapse of the sixteen years. The weaver's bent shoulders and
white hair give him almost the look of advanced age, though
he is not more than five-and-fifty; but there is the freshest
blossom of youth close by his side — a blond dimpled girl of
eighteen, who has vainly tried to chastise her curly auburn
hair into smoothness under her brown bonnet: the hair ripples
as obstinately as a brooklet under the March breeze, and the
little ringlets burst away from the restraining comb behind
and show themselves below the bonnet-crown. Eppie cannot
help being rather vexed about her hair, for there is no other
girl in Raveloe who has hair at all like it, and she thinks hair
ought to be smooth. She does not like to be blameworthy
even in small things: you see how neatly her prayer-book is
folded in her spotted handkerchief.

That good-looking young fellow, in a new fustian suit, who
walks behind her, is not quite sure upon the question of hair
in the abstract, when Eppie puts it to him, and thinks that
perhaps straight hair is the best in general, but he does n't
want Eppie's hair to be different. She surely divines that
there is some one behind her who is thinking about her very
particularly, and mustering courage to come to her side as
soon as they are out in the lane, else why should she look
rather shy, and take care not to turn away her head from her
father Silas, to whom she keeps murmuring little sentences
as to who was at church, and who was not at church, and how
pretty the red mountain-ash is over the Rectory wall!

"I wish *we* had a little garden, father, with double daisies
in, like Mrs. Winthrop's," said Eppie, when they were out in
the lane; "only they say it 'ud take a deal of digging and
bringing fresh soil — and you could n't do that, could you,
father? Anyhow, I should n't like you to do it, for it 'ud be
too hard work for you."

"Yes, I could do it, child, if you want a bit o' garden: these
long evenings, I could work at taking in a little bit o' the
waste, just enough for a root or two o' flowers for you; and
again, i' the morning, I could have a turn wi' the spade before
I sat down to the loom. Why did n't you tell me before as
you wanted a bit o' garden?"

"*I* can dig it for you, Master Marner," said the young man
in fustian, who was now by Eppie's side, entering into the
conversation without the trouble of formalities. "It 'll be
play to me after I 've done my day's work, or any odd bits o'
time when the work 's slack. And I 'll bring you some soil
from Mr. Cass's garden — he 'll let me, and willing."

"Eh, Aaron, my lad, are you there?" said Silas; "I was n't
aware of you; for when Eppie 's talking o' things, I see nothing but what she 's a-saying. Well, if you could help me with
the digging, we might get her a bit o' garden all the sooner."

"Then, if you think well and good," said Aaron, "I 'll come
to the Stone-pits this afternoon, and we 'll settle what land 's
to be taken in, and I 'll get up an hour earlier i' the morning,
and begin on it."

" But not if you don't promise me not to work at the hard digging, father," said Eppie. " For I should n't ha' said anything about it," she added, half-bashfully half-roguishly, " only Mrs. Winthrop said as Aaron 'ud be so good. and — "

" And you might ha' known it without mother telling you," said Aaron. " And Master Marner knows too, I hope, as I 'm able and willing to do a turn o' work for him, and he won't do me the unkindness to anyways take it out o' my hands."

" There, now, father, you won't work in it till it 's all easy," said Eppie, " and you and me can mark out the beds, and make holes and plant the roots. It 'll be a deal livelier at the Stone-pits when we 've got some flowers, for I always think the flowers can see us and know what we 're talking about. And I 'll have a bit o' rosemary, and bergamot, and thyme, because they 're so sweet-smelling; but there 's no lavender only in the gentlefolks' gardens, I think."

" That 's no reason why you should n't have some," said Aaron, " for I can bring you slips of anything; I 'm forced to cut no end of 'em when I 'm gardening, and throw 'em away mostly. There 's a big bed o' lavender at the Red House : the missis is very fond of it."

" Well," said Silas, gravely, " so as you don't make free for us, or ask for anything as is worth much at the Red House : for Mr. Cass's been so good to us, and built us up the new end o' the cottage, and given us beds and things, as I could n't abide to be imposin' for garden-stuff or anything else."

" No, no, there 's no imposin'," said Aaron; " there 's never a garden in all the parish but what there 's endless waste in it for want o' somebody as could use everything up. It 's what I think to myself sometimes, as there need nobody run short o' victuals if the land was made the most on. and there was never a morsel but what could find its way to a mouth. It sets one thinking o' that — gardening does. But I must go back now, else mother 'ull be in trouble as I are n't there."

" Bring her with you this afternoon, Aaron," said Eppie; " I should n't like to fix about the garden, and her not know everything from the first — should you, father ? "

" Ay, bring her if you can, Aaron," said Silas ; " she 's sure

to have a word to say as 'll help us to set things on their right
end."

Aaron turned back up the village, while Silas and Eppie
went on up the lonely sheltered lane.

"Oh daddy!" she began, when they were in privacy, clasping and squeezing Silas's arm, and skipping round to give him
an energetic kiss. "My little old daddy! I'm so glad. I
don't think I shall want anything else when we've got a little
garden; and I knew Aaron would dig it for us," she went on
with roguish triumph — "I knew that very well."

"You're a deep little puss, you are," said Silas, with the
mild passive happiness of love-crowned age in his face; "but
you'll make yourself fine and beholden to Aaron."

"Oh no, I sha'n't," said Eppie, laughing and frisking; "he
likes it."

"Come, come, let me carry your prayer-book, else you'll be
dropping it, jumping i' that way."

Eppie was now aware that her behavior was under observation, but it was only the observation of a friendly donkey,
browsing with a log fastened to his foot — a meek donkey,
not scornfully critical of human trivialities, but thankful to
share in them, if possible, by getting his nose scratched; and
Eppie did not fail to gratify him with her usual notice, though
it was attended with the inconvenience of his following them,
painfully, up to the very door of their home.

But the sound of a sharp bark inside, as Eppie put the key
in the door, modified the donkey's views, and he limped away
again without bidding. The sharp bark was the sign of an
excited welcome that was awaiting them from a knowing
brown terrier, who, after dancing at their legs in a hysterical
manner, rushed with a worrying noise at a tortoise-shell kitten
under the loom, and then rushed back with a sharp bark again,
as much as to say, "I have done my duty by this feeble creature, you perceive;" while the lady-mother of the kitten sat
sunning her white bosom in the window, and looked round
with a sleepy air of expecting caresses, though she was not
going to take any trouble for them.

The presence of this happy animal life was not the only

change which had come over the interior of the stone cottage. There was no bed now in the living-room, and the small space was well filled with decent furniture, all bright and clean enough to satisfy Dolly Winthrop's eye. The oaken table and three-cornered oaken chair were hardly what was likely to be seen in so poor a cottage: they had come, with the beds and other things, from the Red House; for Mr. Godfrey Cass, as every one said in the village, did very kindly by the weaver; and it was nothing but right a man should be looked on and helped by those who could afford it, when he had brought up an orphan child, and been father and mother to her — and had lost his money too, so as he had nothing but what he worked for week by week, and when the weaving was going down too — for there was less and less flax spun — and Master Marner was none so young. Nobody was jealous of the weaver, for he was regarded as an exceptional person, whose claims on neighborly help were not to be matched in Raveloe. Any superstition that remained concerning him had taken an entirely new color; and Mr. Macey, now a very feeble old man of fourscore and six, never seen except in his chimney-corner or sitting in the sunshine at his door-sill, was of opinion that when a man had done what Silas had done by an orphan child, it was a sign that his money would come to light again, or leastwise that the robber would be made to answer for it — for, as Mr. Macey observed of himself, his faculties were as strong as ever.

Silas sat down now and watched Eppie with a satisfied gaze as she spread the clean cloth, and set on it the potato-pie, warmed up slowly in a safe Sunday fashion, by being put into a dry pot over a slowly-dying fire, as the best substitute for an oven. For Silas would not consent to have a grate and oven added to his conveniences: he loved the old brick hearth as he had loved his brown pot — and was it not there when he had found Eppie? The gods of the hearth exist for us still; and let all new faith be tolerant of that fetichism, lest it bruise its own roots.

Silas ate his dinner more silently than usual, soon laying down his knife and fork, and watching half-abstractedly

Eppie's play with Snap and the cat, by which her own dining was made rather a lengthy business. Yet it was a sight that might well arrest wandering thoughts: Eppie, with the rippling radiance of her hair and the whiteness of her rounded chin and throat set off by the dark-blue cotton gown, laughing merrily as the kitten held on with her four claws to one shoulder, like a design for a jug-handle, while Snap on the right hand and Puss on the other put up their paws towards a morsel which she held out of the reach of both — Snap occasionally desisting in order to remonstrate with the cat by a cogent worrying growl on the greediness and futility of her conduct; till Eppie relented, caressed them both, and divided the morsel between them.

But at last Eppie, glancing at the clock, checked the play, and said, "Oh daddy, you're wanting to go into the sunshine to smoke your pipe. But I must clear away first, so as the house may be tidy when godmother comes. I'll make haste — I won't be long."

Silas had taken to smoking a pipe daily during the last two years, having been strongly urged to it by the sages of Raveloe, as a practice "good for the fits;" and this advice was sanctioned by Dr. Kimble, on the ground that it was as well to try what could do no harm — a principle which was made to answer for a great deal of work in that gentleman's medical practice. Silas did not highly enjoy smoking, and often wondered how his neighbors could be so fond of it; but a humble sort of acquiescence in what was held to be good, had become a strong habit of that new self which had been developed in him since he had found Eppie on his hearth: it had been the only clew his bewildered mind could hold by in cherishing this young life that had been sent to him out of the darkness into which his gold had departed. By seeking what was needful for Eppie, by sharing the effect that everything produced on her, he had himself come to appropriate the forms of custom and belief which were the mould of Raveloe life; and as, with reawakening sensibilities, memory also reawakened, he had begun to ponder over the elements of his old faith, and blend them with his new impressions, till he recovered a consciousness of unity between his past and present. The sense of presiding goodness and the human trust which come with all pure peace and joy, had given him a dim impression that there had been some error, some mistake, which had thrown that dark shadow over the days of his best years; and as it grew more and more easy to him to open his mind to Dolly Winthrop, he gradually communicated to her all he could describe of his early life. The communication was necessarily a slow and difficult process, for Silas's meagre power of explanation was not aided by any readiness of interpretation in Dolly, whose narrow outward experience gave her no key to strange customs, and made every novelty a source of wonder that arrested them at every step of the narrative. It was only by fragments, and at intervals which left Dolly time to revolve what she had heard till it acquired some familiarity for her, that Silas at last arrived at the climax of the sad story — the drawing of lots, and its false testimony concerning him; and this had to be repeated in several interviews, under new questions on her part as to the nature of this plan for detecting the guilty and clearing the innocent.

"And yourn's the same Bible, you're sure o' that, Master Marner — the Bible as you brought wi' you from that country — it's the same as what they've got at church, and what Eppie's a-learning to read in?"

"Yes," said Silas, "every bit the same; and there's drawing o' lots in the Bible, mind you," he added in a lower tone.

"Oh dear, dear," said Dolly in a grieved voice, as if she were hearing an unfavorable report of a sick man's case. She was silent for some minutes; at last she said —

"There's wise folks, happen, as know how it all is; the parson knows, I'll be bound; but it takes big words to tell them things, and such as poor folks can't make much out on. I can never rightly know the meaning o' what I hear at church, only a bit here and there, but I know it's good words — I do. But what lies upo' your mind — it's this, Master Marner: as, if Them above had done the right thing by you, They'd never ha' let you be turned out for a wicked thief when you was innicent."

"Ah!" said Silas, who had now come to understand Dolly's phraseology, "that was what fell on me like as if it had been red-hot iron; because, you see, there was nobody as cared for me or clave to me above nor below. And him as I'd gone out and in wi' for ten year and more, since when we was lads and went halves — mine own familiar friend in whom I trusted, had lifted up his heel again' me, and worked to ruin me."

"Eh, but he was a bad un — I can't think as there's another such," said Dolly. "But I'm o'ercome, Master Marner; I'm like as if I'd waked and did n't know whether it was night or morning. I feel somehow as sure as I do when I've laid something up though I can't justly put my hand on it, as there was a rights in what happened to you, if one could but make it out; and you'd no call to lose heart as you did. But we'll talk on it again; for sometimes things come into my head when I'm leeching or poulticing, or such, as I could never think on when I was sitting still."

Dolly was too useful a woman not to have many opportunities of illumination of the kind she alluded to, and she was not long before she recurred to the subject.

"Master Marner," she said, one day that she came to bring home Eppie's washing, "I've been sore puzzled for a good bit wi' that trouble o' yourn and the drawing o' lots; and it got twisted back'ards and for'ards, as I did n't know which end to lay hold on. But it come to me all clear like, that night when I was sitting up wi' poor Bessy Fawkes, as is dead and left her children behind, God help 'em — it come to me as clear as daylight; but whether I've got hold on it now, or can anyways bring it to my tongue's end, that I don't know. For I've often a deal inside me as 'll never come out; and for what you talk o' your folks in your old country niver saying prayers by heart nor saying 'em out of a book, they must be wonderful cliver; for if I did n't know 'Our Father,' and little bits o' good words as I can carry out o' church wi' me, I might down o' my knees every night, but nothing could I say."

"But you can mostly say something as I can make sense on, Mrs. Winthrop," said Silas.

"Well, then, Master Marner, it come to me summat like

this: I can make nothing o' the drawing o' lots and the answer coming wrong; it 'ud mayhap take the parson to tell that, and he could only tell us i' big words. But what come to me as clear as the daylight, it was when I was troubling over poor Bessy Fawkes, and it allays comes into my head when I 'm sorry for folks, and feel as I can't do a power to help 'em, not if I was to get up i' the middle o' the night — it comes into my head as Them above has got a deal tenderer heart nor what I 've got — for I can't be anyways better nor Them as made me; and if anything looks hard to me, it 's because there 's things I don't know on; and for the matter o' that, there may be plenty o' things I don't know on, for it 's little as I know — that it is. And so, while I was thinking o' that, you come into my mind, Master Marner, and it all come pouring in: — if *I* felt i' my inside what was the right and just thing by you, and them as prayed and drawed the lots, all but that wicked un, if *they* 'd ha' done the right thing by you if they could, is n't there Them as was at the making on us, and knows better and has a better will? And that 's all as ever I can be sure on, and everything else is a big puzzle to me when I think on it. For there was the fever come and took off them as were full-growed, and left the helpless children; and there 's the breaking o' limbs; and them as 'ud do right and be sober have to suffer by them as are contrairy — eh, there 's trouble i' this world, and there 's things as we can niver make out the rights on. And all as we 've got to do is to trusten, Master Marner — to do the right thing as fur as we know, and to trusten. For if us as knows so little can see a bit o' good and rights, we may be sure as there 's a good and a rights bigger nor what we can know — I feel it i' my own inside as it must be so. And if you could but ha' gone on trustening, Master Marner, you would n't ha' run away from your fellow-creaturs and been so lone."

"Ah, but that 'ud ha' been hard," said Silas, in an undertone; "it 'ud ha' been hard to trusten then."

"And so it would," said Dolly, almost with compunction; "them things are easier said nor done; and I 'm partly ashamed o' talking."

"Nay, nay," said Silas, "you 're i' the right, Mrs. Winthrop — you 're i' the right. There 's good i' this world — I 've a feeling o' that now ; and it makes a man feel as there 's a good more nor he can see, i' spite o' the trouble and the wickedness. That drawing o' the lots is dark ; but the child was sent to me : there 's dealings with us — there 's dealings."

This dialogue took place in Eppie's earlier years, when Silas had to part with her for two hours every day, that she might learn to read at the dame school, after he had vainly tried himself to guide her in that first step to learning. Now that she was grown up, Silas had often been led, in those moments of quiet outpouring which come to people who live together in perfect love, to talk with *her* too of the past, and how and why he had lived a lonely man until she had been sent to him. For it would have been impossible for him to hide from Eppie that she was not his own child : even if the most delicate reticence on the point could have been expected from Raveloe gossips in her presence, her own questions about her mother could not have been parried, as she grew up, without that complete shrouding of the past which would have made a painful barrier between their minds. So Eppie had long known how her mother had died on the snowy ground, and how she herself had been found on the hearth by father Silas, who had taken her golden curls for his lost guineas brought back to him. The tender and peculiar love with which Silas had reared her in almost inseparable companionship with himself, aided by the seclusion of their dwelling, had preserved her from the lowering influences of the village talk and habits, and had kept her mind in that freshness which is sometimes falsely supposed to be an invariable attribute of rusticity. Perfect love has a breath of poetry which can exalt the relations of the least-instructed human beings ; and this breath of poetry had surrounded Eppie from the time when she had followed the bright gleam that beckoned her to Silas's hearth; so that it is not surprising if, in other things besides her delicate prettiness, she was not quite a common village maiden, but had a touch of refinement and fervor which came from no

other teaching than that of tenderly-nurtured unvitiated feeling. She was too childish and simple for her imagination to
rove into questions about her unknown father; for a long
while it did not even occur to her that she must have had a
father; and the first time that the idea of her mother having
had a husband presented itself to her, was when Silas showed
her the wedding-ring which had been taken from the wasted
finger, and had been carefully preserved by him in a little
lacquered box shaped like a shoe. He delivered this box into
Eppie's charge when she had grown up, and she often opened
it to look at the ring: but still she thought hardly at all about
the father of whom it was the symbol. Had she not a father
very close to her, who loved her better than any real fathers
in the village seemed to love their daughters? On the contrary, who her mother was, and how she came to die in that
forlornness, were questions that often pressed on Eppie's mind.
Her knowledge of Mrs. Winthrop, who was her nearest friend
next to Silas, made her feel that a mother must be very
precious; and she had again and again asked Silas to tell her
how her mother looked, whom she was like, and how he had
found her against the furze bush, led towards it by the little
footsteps and the outstretched arms. The furze bush was
there still; and this afternoon, when Eppie came out with
Silas into the sunshine, it was the first object that arrested her
eyes and thoughts.

"Father," she said, in a tone of gentle gravity, which sometimes came like a sadder, slower cadence across her playful-
ness, "we shall take the furze bush into the garden; it'll
come into the corner, and just against it I'll put snowdrops
and crocuses, 'cause Aaron says they won't die out, but'll always get more and more."

"Ah, child," said Silas, always ready to talk when he had
his pipe in his hand, apparently enjoying the pauses more than
the puffs, "it wouldn't do to leave out the furze bush; and
there's nothing prettier to my thinking, when it's yellow
with flowers. But it's just come into my head what we're to
do for a fence — mayhap Aaron can help us to a thought; but
a fence we must have, else the donkeys and things 'ull come

and trample everything down. And fencing's hard to be got at, by what I can make out."

"Oh, I 'll tell you, daddy," said Eppie, clasping her hands suddenly, after a minute's thought. "There's lots o' loose stones about, some of 'em not big, and we might lay 'em atop of one another, and make a wall. You and me could carry the smallest, and Aaron 'ud carry the rest — I know he would."

"Eh, my precious un," said Silas, "there is n't enough stones to go all round; and as for you carrying, why, wi' your little arms you could n't carry a stone no bigger than a turnip. You 're dillicate made, my dear," he added, with a tender intonation — "that's what Mrs. Winthrop says."

"Oh, I 'm stronger than you think, daddy," said Eppie; "and if there was n't stones enough to go all round, why they 'll go part o' the way, and then it 'll be easier to get sticks and things for the rest. See here, round the big pit, what a many stones!"

She skipped forward to the pit, meaning to lift one of the stones and exhibit her strength, but she started back in surprise.

"Oh, father, just come and look here," she exclaimed — "come and see how the water's gone down since yesterday. Why, yesterday the pit was ever so full!"

"Well, to be sure," said Silas, coming to her side. "Why, that's the draining they 've begun on, since harvest, i' Mr. Osgood's fields, I reckon. The foreman said to me the other day, when I passed by 'em, 'Master Marner,' he said, 'I should n't wonder if we lay your bit o' waste as dry as a bone.' It was Mr. Godfrey Cass, he said, had gone into the draining: he 'd been taking these fields o' Mr. Osgood."

"How odd it 'll seem to have the old pit dried up!" said Eppie, turning away, and stooping to lift rather a large stone. "See, daddy, I can carry this quite well," she said, going along with much energy for a few steps, but presently letting it fall.

"Ah, you 're fine and strong, ar n't you?" said Silas, while Eppie shook her aching arms and laughed. "Come, come, let us go and sit down on the bank against the stile there, and have no more lifting. You might hurt yourself, child. You'd need have somebody to work for you — and my arm is n't over strong."

Silas uttered the last sentence slowly, as if it implied more than met the ear; and Eppie, when they sat down on the bank, nestled close to his side, and, taking hold caressingly of the arm that was not over strong, held it on her lap, while Silas puffed again dutifully at the pipe, which occupied his other arm. An ash in the hedgerow behind made a fretted screen from the sun, and threw happy playful shadows all about them.

"Father," said Eppie, very gently, after they had been sitting in silence a little while, "if I was to be married, ought I to be married with my mother's ring ? "

Silas gave an almost imperceptible start, though the question fell in with the under-current of thought in his own mind, and then said, in a subdued tone, "Why, Eppie, have you been a-thinking on it ? "

"Only this last week, father," said Eppie, ingenuously, "since Aaron talked to me about it."

"And what did he say ? " said Silas, still in the same subdued way, as if he were anxious lest he should fall into the slightest tone that was not for Eppie's good.

"He said he should like to be married, because he was a-going in four-and-twenty, and had got a deal of gardening work, now Mr. Mott's given up; and he goes twice a-week regular to Mr. Cass's, and once to Mr. Osgood's, and they're going to take him on at the Rectory."

"And who is it as he's wanting to marry ? " said Silas, with rather a sad smile.

"Why, me, to be sure, daddy," said Eppie, with dimpling laughter, kissing her father's cheek; "as if he'd want to marry anybody else ! "

"And you mean to have him, do you ? " said Silas.

"Yes, some time," said Eppie, "I don't know when. Everybody's married some time, Aaron says. But I told him that was n't true: for, I said, look at father — he's never been married."

"No, child," said Silas, "your father was a lone man till you was sent to him."

"But you'll never be lone again, father," said Eppie, tenderly. "That was what Aaron said — 'I could never think o' taking you away from Master Marner, Eppie.' And I said, 'It'ud be no use if you did, Aaron.' And he wants us all to live together, so as you need n't work a bit, father, only what's for your own pleasure; and he'd be as good as a son to you — that was what he said."

"And should you like that, Eppie?" said Silas, looking at her.

"I should n't mind it, father," said Eppie, quite simply. "And I should like things to be so as you need n't work much. But if it was n't for that, I'd sooner things did n't change. I'm very happy: I like Aaron to be fond of me, and come and see us often, and behave pretty to you — he always *does* behave pretty to you, does n't he, father?"

"Yes, child, nobody could behave better," said Silas, emphatically. "He's his mother's lad."

"But I don't want any change," said Eppie. "I should like to go on a long, long while, just as we are. Only Aaron does want a change; and he made me cry a bit — only a bit — because he said I did n't care for him, for if I cared for him I should want us to be married, as he did."

"Eh, my blessed child," said Silas, laying down his pipe as if it were useless to pretend to smoke any longer, "you're o'er young to be married. We'll ask Mrs. Winthrop — we'll ask Aaron's mother what *she* thinks: if there's a right thing to do, she'll come at it. But there's this to be thought on, Eppie: things *will* change, whether we like it or no; things won't go on for a long while just as they are and no difference. I shall get older and helplesser, and be a burden on you, belike, if I don't go away from you altogether. Not as I mean you'd think me a burden — I know you would n't — but it'ud be hard upon you; and when I look for'ard to that, I like to think as you'd have somebody else besides me — somebody young and strong, as'll outlast your own life, and take care on you to the end." Silas paused, and, resting his wrists on his knees, lifted his hands up and down meditatively as he looked on the ground.

"Then, would you like me to be married, father?" said Eppie, with a little trembling in her voice.

"I'll not be the man to say no, Eppie," said Silas, emphatically; "but we'll ask your godmother. She'll wish the right thing by you and her son too."

"There they come then," said Eppie. "Let us go and meet 'em. Oh the pipe! won't you have it lit again, father?" said Eppie, lifting that medicinal appliance from the ground.

"Nay, child," said Silas, "I've done enough for to-day. I think, mayhap, a little of it does me more good than so much at once."

———•———

CHAPTER XVII.

WHILE Silas and Eppie were seated on the bank discoursing in the fleckered shade of the ash-tree, Miss Priscilla Lammeter was resisting her sister's arguments, that it would be better to take tea at the Red House, and let her father have a long nap, than drive home to the Warrens so soon after dinner. The family party (of four only) were seated round the table in the dark wainscoted parlor, with the Sunday dessert before them, of fresh filberts, apples, and pears, duly ornamented with leaves by Nancy's own hand before the bells had rung for church.

A great change has come over the dark wainscoted parlor since we saw it in Godfrey's bachelor days, and under the wifeless reign of the old Squire. Now all is polish, on which no yesterday's dust is ever allowed to rest, from the yard's width of oaken boards round the carpet, to the old Squire's gun and whips and walking-sticks, ranged on the stag's antlers above the mantelpiece. All other signs of sporting and out-door occupation Nancy has removed to another room; but she has brought into the Red House the habit of filial reverence, and preserves sacredly in a place of honor these relics of her husband's departed father. The tankards are on the side-table still, but the bossed silver is undimmed by handling, and there are no dregs to send forth unpleasant suggestions : the only prevailing scent is of the lavender and rose-leaves that fill the vases of Derbyshire spar. All is purity and order in this once dreary room, for, fifteen years ago, it was entered by a new presiding spirit.

"Now, father," said Nancy, "*is* there any call for you to go home to tea? May n't you just as well stay with us? — such a beautiful evening as it 's likely to be."

The old gentleman had been talking with Godfrey about the increasing poor-rate and the ruinous times, and had not heard the dialogue between his daughters.

"My dear, you must ask Priscilla," he said, in the once firm voice, now become rather broken. "She manages me and the farm too."

"And reason good as I should manage you, father," said Priscilla, "else you 'd be giving yourself your death with rheumatism. And as for the farm, if anything turns out wrong, as it can't but do in these times, there 's nothing kills a man so soon as having nobody to find fault with but him-self. It 's a deal the best way o' being master, to let some-body else do the ordering, and keep the blaming in your own hands. It 'ud save many a man a stroke, *I* believe."

"Well, well, my dear," said her father, with a quiet laugh, "I did n't say you don't manage for everybody's good."

"Then manage so as you may stay tea, Priscilla," said Nancy, putting her hand on her sister's arm affectionately. "Come now; and we 'll go round the garden while father has his nap."

"My dear child, he 'll have a beautiful nap in the gig, for I shall drive. And as for staying tea, I can't hear of it; for there 's this dairymaid, now she knows she 's to be married, turned Michaelmas, she 'd as lief pour the new milk into the pig-trough as into the pans. That 's the way with 'em all: it 's as if they thought the world 'ud be new-made because they 're to be married. So come and let me put my bonnet on, and there 'll be time for us to walk round the garden while the horse is being put in."

When the sisters were treading the neatly-swept garden-walks, between the bright turf that contrasted pleasantly with the dark cones and arches and wall-like hedges of yew, Priscilla said —

"I'm as glad as anything at your husband's making that exchange o' land with cousin Osgood, and beginning the dairying. It's a thousand pities you didn't do it before; for it'll give you something to fill your mind. There's nothing like a dairy if folks want a bit o' worrit to make the days pass. For as for rubbing furniture, when you can once see your face in a table there's nothing else to look for; but there's always something fresh with the dairy; for even in the depths o' winter there's some pleasure in conquering the butter, and making it come whether or no. My dear," added Priscilla, pressing her sister's hand affectionately as they walked side by side, "you'll never be low when you've got a dairy."

"Ah, Priscilla," said Nancy, returning the pressure with a grateful glance of her clear eyes, "but it won't make up to Godfrey: a dairy's not so much to a man. And it's only what he cares for that ever makes me low. I'm contented with the blessings we have, if he could be contented."

"It drives me past patience," said Priscilla, impetuously, "that way o' the men — always wanting and wanting, and never easy with what they've got: they can't sit comfortable in their chairs when they've neither ache nor pain, but either they must stick a pipe in their mouths, to make 'em better than well, or else they must be swallowing something strong, though they're forced to make haste before the next meal comes in. But joyful be it spoken, our father was never that sort o' man. And if it had pleased God to make you ugly, like me, so as the men wouldn't ha' run after you, we might have kept to our own family, and had nothing to do with folks as have got uneasy blood in their veins."

"Oh don't say so, Priscilla," said Nancy, repenting that she had called forth this outburst; "nobody has any occasion to find fault with Godfrey. It's natural he should be disappointed at not having any children: every man likes to have

somebody to work for and lay by for, and he always counted
so on making a fuss with 'em when they were little. There's
many another man 'ud hanker more than he does. He's the
best of husbands."

"Oh, I know," said Priscilla, smiling sarcastically, "I know
the way o' wives; they set one on to abuse their husbands,
and then they turn round on one and praise 'em as if they
wanted to sell 'em. But father 'll be waiting for me; we must
turn now."

The large gig with the steady old gray was at the front door,
and Mr. Lammeter was already on the stone steps, passing the
time in recalling to Godfrey what very fine points Speckle had
when his master used to ride him.

"I always *would* have a good horse, you know," said the old
gentleman, not liking that spirited time to be quite effaced
from the memory of his juniors.

"Mind you bring Nancy to the Warrens before the week's
out, Mr. Cass," was Priscilla's parting injunction, as she took
the reins, and shook them gently, by way of friendly incite-
ment to Speckle.

"I shall just take a turn to the fields against the Stone-pits,
Nancy, and look at the draining," said Godfrey.

"You'll be in again by tea-time, dear?"

"Oh yes, I shall be back in an hour."

It was Godfrey's custom on a Sunday afternoon to do a
little contemplative farming in a leisurely walk. Nancy seldom accompanied him; for the women of her generation —
unless, like Priscilla, they took to outdoor management — were
not given to much walking beyond their own house and garden, finding sufficient exercise in domestic duties. So, when
Priscilla was not with her, she usually sat with Mant's Bible
before her, and after following the text with her eyes for a
little while, she would gradually permit them to wander as
her thoughts had already insisted on wandering.

But Nancy's Sunday thoughts were rarely quite out of keeping with the devout and reverential intention implied by the
book spread open before her. She was not theologically in-
structed enough to discern very clearly the relation between the

sacred documents of the past which she opened without method, and her own obscure, simple life; but the spirit of rectitude, and the sense of responsibility for the effect of her conduct on others, which were strong elements in Nancy's character, had made it a habit with her to scrutinize her past feelings and actions with self-questioning solicitude. Her mind not being courted by a great variety of subjects, she filled the vacant moments by living inwardly, again and again, through all her remembered experience, especially through the fifteen years of her married time, in which her life and its significance had been doubled. She recalled the small details, the words, tones, and looks, in the critical scenes which had opened a new epoch for her by giving her a deeper insight into the relations and trials of life, or which had called on her for some little effort of forbearance, or of painful adherence to an imagined or real duty —asking herself continually whether she had been in any respect blamable. This excessive rumination and self-questioning is perhaps a morbid habit inevitable to a mind of much moral sensibility when shut out from its due share of outward activity and of practical claims on its affections — inevitable to a noble-hearted, childless woman, when her lot is narrow. "I can do so little — have I done it all well ? " is the perpetually recurring thought; and there are no voices calling her away from that soliloquy, no peremptory demands to divert energy from vain regret or superfluous scruple.

There was one main thread of painful experience in Nancy's married life, and on it hung certain deeply-felt scenes, which were the oftenest revived in retrospect. The short dialogue with Priscilla in the garden had determined the current of retrospect in that frequent direction this particular Sunday afternoon. The first wandering of her thought from the text, which she still attempted dutifully to follow with her eyes and silent lips, was into an imaginary enlargement of the defence she had set up for her husband against Priscilla's implied blame. The vindication of the loved object is the best balm affection can find for its wounds: — "A man must have so much on his mind," is the belief by which a wife often supports a cheerful face under rough answers and unfeeling words.

And Nancy's deepest wounds had all come from the perception that the absence of children from their hearth was dwelt on in her husband's mind as a privation to which he could not reconcile himself.

Yet sweet Nancy might have been expected to feel still more keenly the denial of a blessing to which she had looked forward with all the varied expectations and preparations, solemn and prettily trivial, which fill the mind of a loving woman when she expects to become a mother. Was there not a drawer filled with the neat work of her hands, all unworn and untouched, just as she had arranged it there fourteen years ago — just, but for one little dress, which had been made the burial-dress? But under this immediate personal trial Nancy was so firmly unmurmuring, that years ago she had suddenly renounced the habit of visiting this drawer, lest she should in this way be cherishing a longing for what was not given.

Perhaps it was this very severity towards any indulgence of what she held to be sinful regret in herself, that made her shrink from applying her own standard to her husband. "It is very different — it is much worse for a man to be disappointed in that way: a woman can always be satisfied with devoting herself to her husband, but a man wants something that will make him look forward more — and sitting by the fire is so much duller to him than to a woman." And always, when Nancy reached this point in her meditations — trying, with predetermined sympathy, to see everything as Godfrey saw it — there came a renewal of self-questioning. *Had* she done everything in her power to lighten Godfrey's privation? Had she really been right in the resistance which had cost her so much pain six years ago, and again four years ago — the resistance to her husband's wish that they should adopt a child? Adoption was more remote from the ideas and habits of that time than of our own; still Nancy had her opinion on it. It was as necessary to her mind to have an opinion on all topics, not exclusively masculine, that had come under her notice, as for her to have a precisely marked place for every article of her personal property: and her opinions were always principles to be unwaveringly acted on. They were firm, not because of their basis, but because she held them with a tenacity inseparable from her mental action. On all the duties and proprieties of life, from filial behavior to the arrangements of the evening toilet, pretty Nancy Lammeter, by the time she was three-and-twenty, had her unalterable little code, and had formed every one of her habits in strict accordance with that code. She carried these decided judgments within her in the most unobtrusive way: they rooted themselves in her mind, and grew there as quietly as grass. Years ago, we know, she insisted on dressing like Priscilla, because "it was right for sisters to dress alike," and because "she would do what was right if she wore a gown dyed with cheese-coloring." That was a trivial but typical instance of the mode in which Nancy's life was regulated.

It was one of those rigid principles, and no petty egoistic feeling, which had been the ground of Nancy's difficult resistance to her husband's wish. To adopt a child, because children of your own had been denied you, was to try and choose your lot in spite of Providence : the adopted child, she was convinced, would never turn out well, and would be a curse to those who had wilfully and rebelliously sought what it was clear that, for some high reason, they were better without. When you saw a thing was not meant to be, said Nancy, it was a bounden duty to leave off so much as wishing for it. And so far, perhaps, the wisest of men could scarcely make more than a verbal improvement in her principle. But the conditions under which she held it apparent that a thing was not meant to be, depended on a more peculiar mode of thinking. She would have given up making a purchase at a particular place if, on three successive times, rain, or some other cause of Heaven's sending, had formed an obstacle; and she would have anticipated a broken limb or other heavy misfortune to any one who persisted in spite of such indications.

"But why should you think the child would turn out ill?" said Godfrey, in his remonstrances. "She has thriven as well as child can do with the weaver; and *he* adopted her. There is n't such a pretty little girl anywhere else in the parish, or one fitter for the station we could give her. Where can be the likelihood of her being a curse to anybody?"

"Yes, my dear Godfrey," said Nancy, who was sitting with her hands tightly clasped together, and with yearning, regretful affection in her eyes. "The child may not turn out ill with the weaver. But, then, he did n't go to seek her, as we should be doing. It will be wrong: I feel sure it will. Don't you remember what that lady we met at the Royston Baths told us about the child her sister adopted? That was the only adopting I ever heard of: and the child was transported when it was twenty-three. Dear Godfrey, don't ask me to do what I know is wrong: I should never be happy again. I know it 's very hard for *you* — it 's easier for me — but it 's the will of Providence."

It might seem singular that Nancy — with her religious theory pieced together out of narrow social traditions, fragments of church doctrine imperfectly understood, and girlish reasonings on her small experience — should have arrived by herself at a way of thinking so nearly akin to that of many devout people whose beliefs are held in the shape of a system quite remote from her knowledge: singular, if we did not know that human beliefs, like all other natural growths, elude the barriers of system.

Godfrey had from the first specified Eppie, then about twelve years old, as a child suitable for them to adopt. It had never occurred to him that Silas would rather part with his life than with Eppie. Surely the weaver would wish the best to the child he had taken so much trouble with, and would be glad that such good fortune should happen to her: she would always be very grateful to him, and he would be well provided for to the end of his life — provided for as the excellent part he had done by the child deserved. Was it not an appropriate thing for people in a higher station to take a charge off the hands of a man in a lower? It seemed an eminently appropriate thing to Godfrey, for reasons that were known only to himself; and by a common fallacy, he imagined the measure would be easy because he had private motives for desiring it. This was rather a coarse mode of estimating

Silas's relation to Eppie; but we must remember that many of the impressions which Godfrey was likely to gather concerning the laboring people around him would favor the idea that deep affections can hardly go along with callous palms and scant means; and he had not had the opportunity, even if he had had the power, of entering intimately into all that was exceptional in the weaver's experience. It was only the want of adequate knowledge that could have made it possible for Godfrey deliberately to entertain an unfeeling project: his natural kindness had outlived that blighting time of cruel wishes, and Nancy's praise of him as a husband was not founded entirely on a wilful illusion.

"I was right," she said to herself, when she had recalled all their scenes of discussion — "I feel I was right to say him nay, though it hurt me more than anything; but how good Godfrey has been about it! Many men would have been very angry with me for standing out against their wishes; and they might have thrown out that they'd had ill-luck in marrying me; but Godfrey has never been the man to say me an unkind word. It's only what he can't hide: everything seems so blank to him, I know; and the land — what a difference it 'ud make to him, when he goes to see after things, if he'd children growing up that he was doing it all for! But I won't murmur; and perhaps if he'd married a woman who'd have had children, she'd have vexed him in other ways."

This possibility was Nancy's chief comfort; and to give it greater strength, she labored to make it impossible that any other wife should have had more perfect tenderness. She had been *forced* to vex him by that one denial. Godfrey was not insensible to her loving effort, and did Nancy no injustice as to the motives of her obstinacy. It was impossible to have lived with her fifteen years and not be aware that an unselfish clinging to the right, and a sincerity clear as the flower-born dew, were her main characteristics; indeed, Godfrey felt this so strongly, that his own more wavering nature, too averse to facing difficulty to be unvaryingly simple and truthful, was kept in a certain awe of this gentle wife who watched his looks with a yearning to obey them. It seemed to him impos-

sible that he should ever confess to her the truth about Eppie:
she would never recover from the repulsion the story of his
earlier marriage would create, told to her now, after that long
concealment. And the child, too, he thought, must become an
object of repulsion: the very sight of her would be painful.
The shock to Nancy's mingled pride and ignorance of the world's
evil might even be too much for her delicate frame. Since he
had married her with that secret on his heart, he must keep it
there to the last. Whatever else he did, he could not make an
irreparable breach between himself and this long-loved wife.

Meanwhile, why could he not make up his mind to the
absence of children from a hearth brightened by such a wife?
Why did his mind fly uneasily to that void, as if it were the
sole reason why life was not thoroughly joyous to him? I
suppose it is the way with all men and women who reach
middle age without the clear perception that life never *can* be
thoroughly joyous: under the vague dulness of the gray hours,
dissatisfaction seeks a definite object, and finds it in the privation of an untried good. Dissatisfaction seated musingly on
a childless hearth, thinks with envy of the father whose
return is greeted by young voices — seated at the meal where
the little heads rise one above another like nursery plants,
it sees a black care hovering behind every one of them, and
thinks the impulses by which men abandon freedom, and seek
for ties, are surely nothing but a brief madness. In Godfrey's
case there were further reasons why his thoughts should be
continually solicited by this one point in his lot: his conscience, never thoroughly easy about Eppie, now gave his
childless home the aspect of a retribution; and as the time
passed on, under Nancy's refusal to adopt her, any retrieval
of his error became more and more difficult.

On this Sunday afternoon it was already four years since
there had been any allusion to the subject between them, and
Nancy supposed that it was forever buried.

"I wonder if he'll mind it less or more as he gets older,"
she thought, "I'm afraid more. Aged people feel the miss
of children: what would father do without Priscilla? And
if I die, Godfrey will be very lonely — not holding together

with his brothers much. But I won't be over-anxious, and trying to make things out beforehand : I must do my best for the present."

With that last thought Nancy roused herself from her revery, and turned her eyes again towards the forsaken page. It had been forsaken longer than she imagined, for she was presently surprised by the appearance of the servant with the tea-things. It was, in fact, a little before the usual time for tea; but Jane had her reasons.

"Is your master come into the yard, Jane ?"

"No 'm, he is n't," said Jane, with a slight emphasis, of which, however, her mistress took no notice.

"I don't know whether you 've seen 'em, 'm," continued Jane, after a pause, "but there 's folks making haste all one way, afore the front window. I doubt something 's happened. There 's niver a man to be seen i' the yard, else I 'd send and see. I 've been up into the top attic, but there 's no seeing anything for trees. I hope nobody 's hurt, that 's all."

"Oh, no, I dare say there 's nothing much the matter," said Nancy. "It 's perhaps Mr. Snell's bull got out again, as he did before."

"I wish he may n't gore anybody then, that 's all," said Jane, not altogether despising a hypothesis which covered a few imaginary calamities.

"That girl is always terrifying me," thought Nancy ; "I wish Godfrey would come in."

She went to the front window and looked as far as she could see along the road, with an uneasiness which she felt to be childish, for there were now no such signs of excitement as Jane had spoken of, and Godfrey would not be likely to return by the village road, but by the fields. She continued to stand, however, looking at the placid churchyard with the long shadows of the gravestones across the bright green hillocks, and at the glowing autumn colors of the Rectory trees beyond. Before such calm external beauty the presence of a vague fear is more distinctly felt — like a raven flapping its slow wing across the sunny air. Nancy wished more and more that Godfrey would come in.

CHAPTER XVIII.

Some one opened the door at the other end of the room, and
Nancy felt that it was her husband. She turned from the
window with gladness in her eyes, for the wife's chief dread
was stilled.

"Dear, I'm so thankful you're come," she said, going
towards him. "I began to get — "

She paused abruptly, for Godfrey was laying down his hat
with trembling hands, and turned towards her with a pale face
and a strange unanswering glance, as if he saw her indeed, but
saw her as part of a scene invisible to herself. She laid her
hand on his arm, not daring to speak again; but he left the
touch unnoticed, and threw himself into his chair.

Jane was already at the door with the hissing urn.

"Tell her to keep away, will you?" said Godfrey; and
when the door was closed again he exerted himself to speak
more distinctly.

"Sit down, Nancy — there," he said, pointing to a chair opposite him. "I came back as soon as I could, to hinder anybody's telling you but me. I've had a great shock — but I
care most about the shock it'll be to you."

"It isn't father and Priscilla?" said Nancy, with quivering
lips, clasping her hands together tightly on her lap.

"No, it's nobody living," said Godfrey, unequal to the con-
siderate skill with which he would have wished to make his
revelation. "It's Dunstan — my brother Dunstan, that we
lost sight of sixteen years ago. We've found him — found
his body — his skeleton."

The deep dread Godfrey's look had created in Nancy made
her feel these words a relief. She sat in comparative calmness
to hear what else he had to tell. He went on:

"The Stone-pit has gone dry suddenly — from the draining,
I suppose; and there he lies — has lain for sixteen years,

wedged between two great stones. There's his watch and seals, and there's my gold-handled hunting-whip, with my name on: he took it away, without my knowing, the day he went hunting on Wildfire, the last time he was seen."

Godfrey paused: it was not so easy to say what came next.

"Do you think he drowned himself?" said Nancy, almost wondering that her husband should be so deeply shaken by what had happened all those years ago to an unloved brother, of whom worse things had been augured.

"No, he fell in," said Godfrey, in a low but distinct voice, as if he felt some deep meaning in the fact. Presently he added: "Dunstan was the man that robbed Silas Marner."

The blood rushed to Nancy's face and neck at this surprise and shame, for she had been bred up to regard even a distant kinship with crime as a dishonor.

"Oh, Godfrey!" she said, with compassion in her tone, for she had immediately reflected that the dishonor must be felt still more keenly by her husband.

"There was the money in the pit," he continued — "all the weaver's money. Everything's been gathered up, and they're taking the skeleton to the Rainbow. But I came back to tell you: there was no hindering it; you must know."

He was silent, looking on the ground for two long minutes. Nancy would have said some words of comfort under this disgrace, but she refrained, from an instinctive sense that there was something behind — that Godfrey had something else to tell her. Presently he lifted his eyes to her face, and kept them fixed on her, as he said —

"Everything comes to light, Nancy, sooner or later. When God Almighty wills it, our secrets are found out. I've lived with a secret on my mind, but I'll keep it from you no longer. I wouldn't have you know it by somebody else, and not by me — I wouldn't have you find it out after I'm dead. I'll tell you now. It's been 'I will' and 'I won't' with me all my life — I'll make sure of myself now."

Nancy's utmost dread had returned. The eyes of the husband and wife met with awe in them, as at a crisis which suspended affection.

"Nancy," said Godfrey, slowly, "when I married you, I hid
something from you — something I ought to have told you.
That woman Marner found dead in the snow — Eppie's mother
— that wretched woman — was my wife : Eppie is my child."

He paused, dreading the effect of his confession. But Nancy
sat quite still, only that her eyes dropped and ceased to meet
his. She was pale and quiet as a meditative statue, clasping
her hands on her lap.

"You'll never think the same of me again," said Godfrey,
after a little while, with some tremor in his voice.

She was silent.

"I ought n't to have left the child unowned : I ought n't to
have kept it from you. But I could n't bear to give you up,
Nancy. I was led away into marrying her — I suffered for it."

Still Nancy was silent, looking down; and he almost expected that she would presently get up and say she would go
to her father's. How could she have any mercy for faults
that must seem so black to her, with her simple severe
notions ?

But at last she lifted up her eyes to his again and spoke.
There was no indignation in her voice — only deep regret.

"Godfrey, if you had but told me this six years ago, we
could have done some of our duty by the child. Do you think
I'd have refused to take her in, if I'd known she was yours ?"

At that moment Godfrey felt all the bitterness of an error
that was not simply futile, but had defeated its own end. He
had not measured this wife with whom he had lived so long.
But she spoke again, with more agitation.

"And — oh, Godfrey — if we'd had her from the first, if
you'd taken to her as you ought, she'd have loved me for her
mother — and you'd have been happier with me : I could
better have bore my little baby dying, and our life might have
been more like what we used to think it 'ud be."

The tears fell, and Nancy ceased to speak.

"But you would n't have married me then, Nancy, if I'd
told you," said Godfrey, urged, in the bitterness of his self-
reproach, to prove to himself that his conduct had not been
utter folly. "You may think you would now, but you

would n't then. With your pride and your father's, you 'd have hated having anything to do with me after the talk there 'd have been."

"I can't say what I should have done about that, Godfrey. I should never have married anybody else. But I was n't worth doing wrong for — nothing is in this world. Nothing is so good as it seems beforehand — not even our marrying was n't, you see." There was a faint sad smile on Nancy's face as she said the last words.

"I 'm a worse man than you thought I was, Nancy," said Godfrey, rather tremulously. "Can you forgive me ever?"

"The wrong to me is but little, Godfrey: you 've made it up to me — you 've been good to me for fifteen years. It 's another you did the wrong to; and I doubt it can never be all made up for."

"But we can take Eppie now," said Godfrey. "I won't mind the world knowing at last. I 'll be plain and open for the rest o' my life."

"It 'll be different coming to us, now she 's grown up," said Nancy, shaking her head sadly. "But it 's your duty to acknowledge her and provide for her; and I 'll do my part by her, and pray to God Almighty to make her love me."

"Then we 'll go together to Silas Marner's this very night, as soon as everything 's quiet at the Stone-pits."

CHAPTER XIX.

BETWEEN eight and nine o'clock that evening, Eppie and Silas were seated alone in the cottage. After the great excitement the weaver had undergone from the events of the afternoon, he had felt a longing for this quietude, and had even begged Mrs. Winthrop and Aaron, who had naturally lingered behind every one else, to leave him alone with his child. The excitement had not passed away: it had only reached that

stage when the keenness of the susceptibility makes external
stimulus intolerable — when there is no sense of weariness,
but rather an intensity of inward life, under which sleep is
an impossibility. Any one who has watched such moments
in other men remembers the brightness of the eyes and the
strange definiteness that comes over coarse features from that
transient influence. It is as if a new fineness of ear for all
spiritual voices had sent wonder-working vibrations through
the heavy mortal frame — as if "beauty born of murmuring
sound" had passed into the face of the listener.

Silas's face showed that sort of transfiguration, as he sat in
his arm-chair and looked at Eppie. She had drawn her own
chair towards his knees, and leaned forward, holding both his
hands, while she looked up at him. On the table near them,
lit by a candle, lay the recovered gold — the old long-loved
gold, ranged in orderly heaps, as Silas used to range it in the
days when it was his only joy. He had been telling her how
he used to count it every night, and how his soul was utterly
desolate till she was sent to him.

"At first, I'd a sort o' feeling come across me now and
then," he was saying in a subdued tone, "as if you might be
changed into the gold again; for sometimes, turn my head
which way I would, I seemed to see the gold; and I thought
I should be glad if I could feel it, and find it was come back.
But that did n't last long. After a bit, I should have thought
it was a curse come again, if it had drove you from me, for
I'd got to feel the need o' your looks and your voice and the
touch o' your little fingers. You did n't know then, Eppie,
when you were such a little un — you did n't know what your
old father Silas felt for you."

"But I know now, father," said Eppie. "If it had n't been
for you, they'd have taken me to the workhouse, and there'd
have been nobody to love me."

"Eh, my precious child, the blessing was mine. If you
had n't been sent to save me, I should ha' gone to the grave
in my misery. The money was taken away from me in time;
and you see it's been kept — kept till it was wanted for you.
It's wonderful — our life is wonderful."

Silas sat in silence a few minutes, looking at the money. "It takes no hold of me now," he said, ponderingly — "the money does n't. I wonder if it ever could again — I doubt it might; if I lost you, Eppie. I might come to think I was forsaken again, and lose the feeling that God was good to me."

At that moment there was a knocking at the door; and Eppie was obliged to rise without answering Silas. Beautiful she looked, with the tenderness of gathering tears in her eyes and a slight flush on her cheeks, as she stepped to open the door. The flush deepened when she saw Mr. and Mrs. Godfrey Cass. She made her little rustic curtsy, and held the door wide for them to enter.

"We 're disturbing you very late, my dear," said Mrs. Cass, taking Eppie's hand, and looking in her face with an expression of anxious interest and admiration. Nancy herself was pale and tremulous.

Eppie, after placing chairs for Mr. and Mrs. Cass, went to stand against Silas, opposite to them.

"Well, Marner," said Godfrey, trying to speak with perfect firmness, "it 's a great comfort to me to see you with your money again, that you 've been deprived of so many years. It was one of my family did you the wrong — the more grief to me — and I feel bound to make up to you for it in every way. Whatever I can do for you will be nothing but paying a debt, even if I looked no further than the robbery. But there are other things I 'm beholden — shall be beholden to you for, Marner."

Godfrey checked himself. It had been agreed between him and his wife that the subject of his fatherhood should be approached very carefully, and that, if possible, the disclosure should be reserved for the future, so that it might be made to Eppie gradually. Nancy had urged this, because she felt strongly the painful light in which Eppie must inevitably see the relation between her father and mother.

Silas, always ill at ease when he was being spoken to by "betters," such as Mr. Cass — tall, powerful, florid men, seen chiefly on horseback — answered with some constraint —

"Sir, I've a deal to thank you for a'ready. As for the robbery, I count it no loss to me. And if I did, you couldn't help it: you aren't answerable for it."

"You may look at it in that way, Marner, but I never can; and I hope you'll let me act according to my own feeling of what's just. I know you're easily contented: you've been a hard-working man all your life."

"Yes, sir, yes," said Marner, meditatively. "I should ha' been bad off without my work: it was what I held by when everything else was gone from me."

"Ah," said Godfrey, applying Marner's words simply to his bodily wants, "it was a good trade for you in this country, because there's been a great deal of linen-weaving to be done. But you're getting rather past such close work, Marner: it's time you laid by and had some rest. You look a good deal pulled down, though you're not an old man, *are* you?"

"Fifty-five, as near as I can say, sir," said Silas.

"Oh, why, you may live thirty years longer — look at old Macey! And that money on the table, after all, is but little. It won't go far either way — whether it's put out to interest, or you were to live on it as long as it would last: it wouldn't go far if you'd nobody to keep but yourself, and you've had two to keep for a good many years now."

"Eh, sir," said Silas, unaffected by anything Godfrey was saying, "I'm in no fear o' want. We shall do very well — Eppie and me 'ull do well enough. There's few working-folks have got so much laid by as that. I don't know what it is to gentlefolks, but I look upon it as a deal — almost too much. And as for us, it's little we want."

"Only the garden, father," said Eppie, blushing up to the ears the moment after.

"You love a garden, do you, my dear?" said Nancy, thinking that this turn in the point of view might help her husband. "We should agree in that: I give a deal of time to the garden."

"Ah, there's plenty of gardening at the Red House," said Godfrey, surprised at the difficulty he found in approaching a proposition which had seemed so easy to him in the distance.

"You've done a good part by Eppie, Marner, for sixteen years. It'ud be a great comfort to you to see her well provided for, wouldn't it? She looks blooming and healthy, but not fit for any hardships: she doesn't look like a strapping girl come of working parents. You'd like to see her taken care of by those who can leave her well off, and make a lady of her; she's more fit for it than for a rough life, such as she might come to have in a few years' time."

A slight flush came over Marner's face, and disappeared, like a passing gleam. Eppie was simply wondering Mr. Cass should talk so about things that seemed to have nothing to do with reality, but Silas was hurt and uneasy.

"I don't take your meaning, sir," he answered, not having words at command to express the mingled feelings with which he had heard Mr. Cass's words.

"Well, my meaning is this, Marner," said Godfrey, determined to come to the point. "Mrs. Cass and I, you know, have no children — nobody to be the better for our good home and everything else we have — more than enough for ourselves. And we should like to have somebody in the place of a daughter to us — we should like to have Eppie, and treat her in every way as our own child. It'ud be a great comfort to you in your old age, I hope, to see her fortune made in that way, after you've been at the trouble of bringing her up so well. And it's right you should have every reward for that. And Eppie, I'm sure, will always love you and be grateful to you: she'd come and see you very often, and we should all be on the look-out to do everything we could towards making you comfortable."

A plain man like Godfrey Cass, speaking under some embarrassment, necessarily blunders on words that are coarser than his intentions, and that are likely to fall gratingly on susceptible feelings. While he had been speaking, Eppie had quietly passed her arm behind Silas's head, and let her hand rest against it caressingly: she felt him trembling violently. He was silent for some moments when Mr. Cass had ended — powerless under the conflict of emotions, all alike painful. Eppie's heart was swelling at the sense that her father was in distress; and she was just going to lean down and speak to him, when one struggling dread at last gained the mastery over every other in Silas, and he said, faintly —

"Eppie, my child, speak. I won't stand in your way. Thank Mr. and Mrs. Cass."

Eppie took her hand from her father's head, and came forward a step. Her cheeks were flushed, but not with shyness this time: the sense that her father was in doubt and suffering banished that sort of self-consciousness. She dropped a low curtsy, first to Mrs. Cass and then to Mr. Cass, and said —

"Thank you, ma'am — thank you, sir. But I can't leave my father, nor own anybody nearer than him. And I don't want to be a lady — thank you all the same" (here Eppie dropped another curtsy). "I couldn't give up the folks I've been used to."

Eppie's lip began to tremble a little at the last words. She retreated to her father's chair again, and held him round the neck: while Silas, with a subdued sob, put up his hand to grasp hers.

The tears were in Nancy's eyes, but her sympathy with Eppie was, naturally, divided with distress on her husband's account. She dared not speak, wondering what was going on in her husband's mind.

Godfrey felt an irritation inevitable to almost all of us when we encounter an unexpected obstacle. He had been full of his own penitence and resolution to retrieve his error as far as the time was left to him; he was possessed with all-important feelings, that were to lead to a predetermined course of action which he had fixed on as the right, and he was not prepared to enter with lively appreciation into other people's feelings counteracting his virtuous resolves. The agitation with which he spoke again was not quite unmixed with anger.

"But I've a claim on you, Eppie — the strongest of all claims. It's my duty, Marner, to own Eppie as my child, and provide for her. She's my own child: her mother was my wife. I've a natural claim on her that must stand before every other."

Eppie had given a violent start, and turned quite pale. Silas, on the contrary, who had been relieved, by Eppie's answer, from the dread lest his mind should be in opposition to hers, felt the spirit of resistance in him set free, not without a touch of parental fierceness. "Then, sir," he answered, with an accent of bitterness that had been silent in him since the memorable day when his youthful hope had perished — "then, sir, why did n't you say so sixteen year ago, and claim her before I 'd come to love her, i 'stead o' coming to take her from me now, when you might as well take the heart out o' my body? God gave her to me because you turned your back upon her, and He looks upon her as mine: you 've no right to her! When a man turns a blessing from his door, it falls to them as take it in."

"I know that, Marner. I was wrong. I 've repented of my conduct in that matter," said Godfrey, who could not help feeling the edge of Silas's words.

"I 'm glad to hear it, sir," said Marner, with gathering excitement; "but repentance does n't alter what 's been going on for sixteen year. Your coming now and saying 'I 'm her father,' does n't alter the feelings inside us. It 's me she 's been calling her father ever since she could say the word."

"But I think you might look at the thing more reasonably, Marner," said Godfrey, unexpectedly awed by the weaver's direct truth-speaking. "It is n't as if she was to be taken quite away from you, so that you 'd never see her again. She 'll be very near you, and come to see you very often. She 'll feel just the same towards you."

"Just the same?" said Marner, more bitterly than ever. "How 'll she feel just the same for me as she does now, when we eat o' the same bit, and drink o' the same cup, and think o' the same things from one day's end to another? Just the same? That 's idle talk. You 'd cut us i' two."

Godfrey, unqualified by experience to discern the pregnancy of Marner's simple words, felt rather angry again. It seemed to him that the weaver was very selfish (a judgment readily passed by those who have never tested their own power of sacrifice) to oppose what was undoubtedly for Eppie's welfare;

and he felt himself called upon, for her sake, to assert his authority.

"I should have thought, Marner," he said, severely — "I should have thought your affection for Eppie would make you rejoice in what was for her good, even if it did call upon you to give up something. You ought to remember your own life's uncertain, and she's at an age now when her lot may soon be fixed in a way very different from what it would be in her father's home: she may marry some low working-man, and then, whatever I might do for her, I could n't make her well-off. You're putting yourself in the way of her welfare; and though I'm sorry to hurt you after what you've done, and what I've left undone, I feel now it's my duty to insist on taking care of my own daughter. I want to do my duty."

It would be difficult to say whether it were Silas or Eppie that was more deeply stirred by this last speech of Godfrey's. Thought had been very busy in Eppie as she listened to the contest between her old long-loved father and this new unfamiliar father who had suddenly come to fill the place of that black featureless shadow which had held the ring and placed it on her mother's finger. Her imagination had darted backward in conjectures, and forward in previsions, of what this revealed fatherhood implied; and there were words in Godfrey's last speech which helped to make the previsions especially definite. Not that these thoughts, either of past or future, determined her resolution — *that* was determined by the feelings which vibrated to every word Silas had uttered; but they raised, even apart from these feelings, a repulsion towards the offered lot and the newly-revealed father.

Silas, on the other hand, was again stricken in conscience, and alarmed lest Godfrey's accusation should be true — lest he should be raising his own will as an obstacle to Eppie's good. For many moments he was mute, struggling for the self-conquest necessary to the uttering of the difficult words. They came out tremulously.

"I'll say no more. Let it be as you will. Speak to the child. I'll hinder nothing."

Even Nancy, with all the acute sensibility of her own affections, shared her husband's view, that Marner was not justifiable in his wish to retain Eppie, after her real father had avowed himself. She felt that it was a very hard trial for the poor weaver, but her code allowed no question that a father by blood must have a claim above that of any foster-father. Besides, Nancy, used all her life to plenteous circumstances and the privileges of "respectability," could not enter into the pleasures which early nurture and habit connect with all the little aims and efforts of the poor who are born poor: to her mind Eppie, in being restored to her birthright, was entering on a too long withheld but unquestionable good. Hence she heard Silas's last words with relief, and thought, as Godfrey did, that their wish was achieved.

"Eppie, my dear," said Godfrey, looking at his daughter, not without some embarrassment, under the sense that she was old enough to judge him, "it'll always be our wish that you should show your love and gratitude to one who's been a father to you so many years, and we shall want to help you to make him comfortable in every way. But we hope you'll come to love us as well; and though I haven't been what a father should ha' been to you all these years, I wish to do the utmost in my power for you for the rest of my life, and provide for you as my only child. And you'll have the best of mothers in my wife—that'll be a blessing you haven't known since you were old enough to know it."

"My dear, you'll be a treasure to me," said Nancy, in her gentle voice. "We shall want for nothing when we have our daughter."

Eppie did not come forward and curtsy, as she had done before. She held Silas's hand in hers, and grasped it firmly —it was a weaver's hand, with a palm and finger-tips that were sensitive to such pressure — while she spoke with colder decision than before.

"Thank you, ma'am — thank you, sir, for your offers — they're very great, and far above my wish. For I should have no delight i' life any more if I was forced to go away from my father, and knew he was sitting at home, a-thinking of me and feeling lone. We've been used to be happy together every day, and I can't think o' no happiness without him. And he says he'd nobody i' the world till I was sent to him, and he'd have nothing when I was gone. And he's took care of me and loved me from the first, and I'll cleave to him as long as he lives, and nobody shall ever come between him and me."

"But you must make sure, Eppie," said Silas, in a low voice — "you must make sure as you won't ever be sorry, because you've made your choice to stay among poor folks, and with poor clothes and things, when you might ha' had everything o' the best."

His sensitiveness on this point had increased as he listened to Eppie's words of faithful affection.

"I can never be sorry, father," said Eppie. "I shouldn't know what to think on or to wish for with fine things about me, as I haven't been used to. And it 'ud be poor work for me to put on things, and ride in a gig, and sit in a place at church, as 'ud make them as I'm fond of think me unfitting company for 'em. What could I care for then?"

Nancy looked at Godfrey with a pained questioning glance. But his eyes were fixed on the floor, where he was moving the end of his stick, as if he were pondering on something absently. She thought there was a word which might perhaps come better from her lips than from his.

"What you say is natural, my dear child — it's natural you should cling to those who've brought you up," she said, mildly; "but there's a duty you owe to your lawful father. There's perhaps something to be given up on more sides than one. When your father opens his home to you, I think it's right you shouldn't turn your back on it."

"I can't feel as I've got any father but one," said Eppie, impetuously, while the tears gathered. "I've always thought of a little home where he'd sit i' the corner, and I should fend and do everything for him: I can't think o' no other home. I wasn't brought up to be a lady, and I can't turn my mind to it. I like the working-folks, and their victuals, and their ways. And," she ended passionately, while the tears fell, "I'm promised to marry a working-man, as 'll live with father, and help me to take care of him."

Godfrey looked up at Nancy with a flushed face and smarting dilated eyes. This frustration of a purpose towards which he had set out under the exalted consciousness that he was about to compensate in some degree for the greatest demerit of his life, made him feel the air of the room stifling.

"Let us go," he said, in an under-tone.

"We won't talk of this any longer now," said Nancy, rising. "We're your well-wishers, my dear — and yours too, Marner. We shall come and see you again. It's getting late now."

In this way she covered her husband's abrupt departure, for Godfrey had gone straight to the door, unable to say more.

CHAPTER XX.

Nancy and Godfrey walked home under the starlight in silence. When they entered the oaken parlor, Godfrey threw himself into his chair, while Nancy laid down her bonnet and shawl, and stood on the hearth near her husband, unwilling to leave him even for a few minutes, and yet fearing to utter any word lest it might jar on his feeling. At last Godfrey turned his head towards her, and their eyes met, dwelling in that meeting without any movement on either side. That quiet mutual gaze of a trusting husband and wife is like the first moment of rest or refuge from a great weariness or a great danger — not to be interfered with by speech or action which would distract the sensations from the fresh enjoyment of repose.

But presently he put out his hand, and as Nancy placed hers within it, he drew her towards him, and said —

"That's ended!"

She bent to kiss him, and then said, as she stood by his side, "Yes, I'm afraid we must give up the hope of having her for a daughter. It would n't be right to want to force her to come to us against her will. We can't alter her bringing up and what 's come of it."

"No," said Godfrey, with a keen decisiveness of tone, in contrast with his usually careless and unemphatic speech — "there 's debts we can't pay like money debts, by paying extra for the years that have slipped by. While I 've been putting off and putting off, the trees have been growing — it 's too late now. Marner was in the right in what he said about a man's turning away a blessing from his door : it falls to somebody else. I wanted to pass for childless once, Nancy — I shall pass for childless now against my wish."

Nancy did not speak immediately, but after a little while she asked — "You won't make it known, then, about Eppie's being your daughter ? "

"No : where would be the good to anybody ? — only harm. I must do what I can for her in the state of life she chooses. I must see who it is she 's thinking of marrying."

"If it won't do any good to make the thing known," said Nancy, who thought she might now allow herself the relief of entertaining a feeling which she had tried to silence before, "I should be very thankful for father and Priscilla never to be troubled with knowing what was done in the past, more than about Dunsey : it can't be helped, their knowing that."

"I shall put it in my will — I think I shall put it in my will. I should n't like to leave anything to be found out, like this about Dunsey," said Godfrey, meditatively. "But I can't see anything but difficulties that 'ud come from telling it now. I must do what I can to make her happy in her own way. I 've a notion," he added, after a moment's pause, "it 's Aaron Winthrop she meant she was engaged to. I remember seeing him with her and Marner going away from church."

"Well, he 's very sober and industrious," said Nancy, trying to view the matter as cheerfully as possible.

Godfrey fell into thoughtfulness again. Presently he looked up at Nancy sorrowfully, and said —

"She 's a very pretty, nice girl, is n't she, Nancy ? "

" Yes, dear ; and with just your hair and eyes : I wondered it had never struck me before."

" I think she took a dislike to me at the thought of my being her father : I could see a change in her manner after that."

" She could n't bear to think of not looking on Marner as her father," said Nancy, not wishing to confirm her husband's painful impression.

" She thinks I did wrong by her mother as well as by her. She thinks me worse than I am. But she *must* think it : she can never know all. It 's part of my punishment, Nancy, for my daughter to dislike me. I should never have got into that trouble if I 'd been true to you — if I had n't been a fool. I 'd no right to expect anything but evil could come of that marriage — and when I shirked doing a father's part too."

Nancy was silent : her spirit of rectitude would not let her try to soften the edge of what she felt to be a just compunction. He spoke again after a little while, but the tone was rather changed : there was tenderness mingled with the previous self-reproach.

" And I got *you*, Nancy, in spite of all ; and yet I 've been grumbling and uneasy because I had n't something else — as if I deserved it."

" You 've never been wanting to me, Godfrey," said Nancy, with quiet sincerity. " My only trouble would be gone if you resigned yourself to the lot that 's been given us."

" Well, perhaps it is n't too late to mend a bit there. Though it *is* too late to mend some things, say what they will."

CHAPTER XXI.

THE next morning, when Silas and Eppie were seated at their breakfast, he said to her —

" Eppie, there 's a thing I 've had on my mind to do this two year, and now the money 's been brought back to us, we can do it. I've been turning it over and over in the night, and I think we'll set out to-morrow, while the fine days last. We'll leave the house and everything for your godmother to take care on, and we'll make a little bundle o' things and set out."

"Where to go, daddy?" said Eppie, in much surprise.

"To my old country — to the town where I was born — up Lantern Yard. I want to see Mr. Paston, the minister: something may ha' come out to make 'em know I was inni-cent o' the robbery. And Mr. Paston was a man with a deal o' light — I want to speak to him about the drawing o' the lots. And I should like to talk to him about the religion o' this country-side, for I partly think he does n't know on it."

Eppie was very joyful, for there was the prospect not only of wonder and delight at seeing a strange country, but also of coming back to tell Aaron all about it. Aaron was so much wiser than she was about most things — it would be rather pleasant to have this little advantage over him. Mrs. Win-throp, though possessed with a dim fear of dangers attendant on so long a journey, and requiring many assurances that it would not take them out of the region of carriers' carts and slow wagons, was nevertheless well pleased that Silas should revisit his own country, and find out if he had been cleared from that false accusation.

"You'd be easier in your mind for the rest o' your life, Master Marner," said Dolly — "that you would. And if there's any light to be got up the Yard as you talk on, we've need of it i' this world, and I'd be glad on it myself, if you could bring it back."

So on the fourth day from that time, Silas and Eppie, in their Sunday clothes, with a small bundle tied in a blue linen handkerchief, were making their way through the streets of a great manufacturing town. Silas, bewildered by the changes thirty years had brought over his native place, had stopped several persons in succession to ask them the name of this town, that he might be sure he was not under a mistake about it.

"Ask for Lantern Yard, father — ask this gentleman with the tassels on his shoulders a-standing at the shop door; he is n't in a hurry like the rest," said Eppie, in some distress at her father's bewilderment, and ill at ease, besides, amidst the noise, the movement, and the multitude of strange indifferent faces.

"Eh, my child, he won't know anything about it," said Silas; "gentlefolks did n't ever go up the Yard. But happen somebody can tell me which is the way to Prison Street, where the jail is. I know the way out o' that as if I'd seen it yesterday."

With some difficulty, after many turnings and new inquiries, they reached Prison Street; and the grim walls of the jail, the first object that answered to any image in Silas's memory, cheered him with the certitude, which no assurance of the town's name had hitherto given him, that he was in his native place.

"Ah," he said, drawing a long breath, "there's the jail, Eppie; that's just the same: I are n't afraid now. It's the third turning on the left hand from the jail doors — that's the way we must go."

"Oh, what a dark ugly place!" said Eppie. "How it hides the sky! It's worse than the workhouse. I'm glad you don't live in this town now, father. Is Lantern Yard like this street?"

"My precious child," said Silas, smiling, "it is n't a big street like this. I never was easy i' this street myself, but I was fond o' Lantern Yard. The shops here are all altered, I think — I can't make 'em out; but I shall know the turning, because it's the third."

"Here it is," he said, in a tone of satisfaction, as they came to a narrow alley. "And then we must go to the left again, and then straight for'ard for a bit, up Shoe Lane: and then we shall be at the entry next to the o'erhanging window, where there's the nick in the road for the water to run. Eh, I can see it all."

"Oh father, I'm like as if I was stifled," said Eppie. "I could n't ha' thought as any folks lived i' this way, so close

together.   How pretty the Stone-pits 'ull look when we get
back ! "

" It looks comical to *me*, child, now — and smells bad.   I
can't think as it usened to smell so."

Here and there a sallow, begrimed face looked out from a
gloomy doorway at the strangers, and increased Eppie's uneasiness, so that it was a longed-for relief when they issued
from the alleys into Shoe Lane, where there was a broader
strip of sky.

" Dear heart ! " said Silas, " why, there 's people coming out
o' the Yard as if they 'd been to chapel at this time o' day —
a weekday noon ! "

Suddenly he started and stood still with a look of distressed
amazement, that alarmed Eppie.   They were before an opening in front of a large factory, from which men and women
were streaming for their mid-day meal.

"Father," said Eppie, clasping his arm, " what 's the
matter ? "

But she had to speak again and again before Silas could
answer her.

" It 's gone, child," he said, at last, in strong agitation —
" Lantern Yard 's gone.   It must ha' been here, because here 's
the house with the o'erhanging window — I know that — it 's
just the same; but they 've made this new opening; and see
that big factory !   It 's all gone — chapel and all."

" Come into that little brush-shop and sit down, father —
they 'll let you sit down," said Eppie, always on the watch
lest one of her father's strange attacks should come on.
" Perhaps the people can tell you all about it."

But neither from the brush-maker, who had come to Shoe
Lane only ten years ago, when the factory was already built,
nor from any other source within his reach, could Silas learn
anything of the old Lantern Yard friends, or of Mr. Paston
the minister.

" The old place is all swep' away," Silas said to Dolly Winthrop on the night of his return — " the little graveyard and
everything.   The old home 's gone; I 've no home but this
now.   I shall never know whether they got at the truth o' the

robbery, nor whether Mr. Paston could ha' given me any light about the drawing o' the lots. It's dark to me, Mrs. Winthrop, that is; I doubt it'll be dark to the last."

"Well, yes, Master Marner," said Dolly, who sat with a placid listening face, now bordered by gray hairs; "I doubt it may. It's the will o' Them above as a many things should be dark to us; but there's some things as I've never felt i' the dark about, and they're mostly what comes i' the day's work. You were hard done by that once, Master Marner, and it seems as you'll never know the rights of it; but that doesn't hinder there *being* a rights, Master Marner, for all it's dark to you and me."

"No," said Silas, "no; that doesn't hinder. Since the time the child was sent to me and I've come to love her as myself, I've had light enough to trusten by; and now she says she'll never leave me, I think I shall trusten till I die."

CONCLUSION.

THERE was one time of the year which was held in Raveloe to be especially suitable for a wedding. It was when the great lilacs and laburnums in the old-fashioned gardens showed their golden and purple wealth above the lichen-tinted walls, and when there were calves still young enough to want bucketfuls of fragrant milk. People were not so busy then as they must become when the full cheese-making and the mowing had set in; and besides, it was a time when a light bridal dress could be worn with comfort and seen to advantage.

Happily the sunshine fell more warmly than usual on the lilac tufts the morning that Eppie was married, for her dress was a very light one. She had often thought, though with a feeling of renunciation, that the perfection of a wedding-dress would be a white cotton, with the tiniest pink sprig at wide intervals; so that when Mrs. Godfrey Cass begged to provide one, and asked Eppie to choose what it should be, previous meditation had enabled her to give a decided answer at once.

Seen at a little distance as she walked across the churchyard and down the village, she seemed to be attired in pure white, and her hair looked like the dash of gold on a lily. One hand was on her husband's arm, and with the other she clasped the hand of her father Silas.

"You won't be giving me away, father," she had said before they went to church; "you'll only be taking Aaron to be a son to you."

Dolly Winthrop walked behind with her husband; and there ended the little bridal procession.

There were many eyes to look at it, and Miss Priscilla Lammeter was glad that she and her father had happened to drive up to the door of the Red House just in time to see this pretty sight. They had come to keep Nancy company to-day, because Mr. Cass had had to go away to Lytherley, for special reasons. That seemed to be a pity, for otherwise he might have gone, as Mr. Crackenthorp and Mr. Osgood certainly would, to look on at the wedding-feast which he had ordered at the Rainbow, naturally feeling a great interest in the weaver who had been wronged by one of his own family.

"I could ha' wished Nancy had had the luck to find a child like that and bring her up," said Priscilla to her father, as they sat in the gig; "I should ha' had something young to think of then, besides the lambs and the calves."

"Yes, my dear, yes," said Mr. Lammeter; "one feels that as one gets older. Things look dim to old folks: they'd need have some young eyes about 'em, to let 'em know the world's the same as it used to be."

Nancy came out now to welcome her father and sister; and the wedding group had passed on beyond the Red House to the humbler part of the village.

Dolly Winthrop was the first to divine that old Mr. Macey, who had been set in his arm-chair outside his own door, would expect some special notice as they passed, since he was too old to be at the wedding-feast.

"Mr. Macey's looking for a word from us," said Dolly; "he'll be hurt if we pass him and say nothing — and him so racked with rheumatiz."

So they turned aside to shake hands with the old man. He had looked forward to the occasion, and had his premeditated speech.

"Well, Master Marner," he said, in a voice that quavered a good deal, "I've lived to see my words come true. I was the first to say there was no harm in you, though your looks might be again' you; and I was the first to say you'd get your money back. And it's nothing but rightful as you should. And I'd ha' said the 'Amens,' and willing, at the holy matrimony; but Tookey's done it a good while now, and I hope you'll have none the worse luck."

In the open yard before the Rainbow the party of guests were already assembled, though it was still nearly an hour before the appointed feast-time. But by this means they could not only enjoy the slow advent of their pleasure; they had also ample leisure to talk of Silas Marner's strange history, and arrive by due degrees at the conclusion that he had brought a blessing on himself by acting like a father to a lone motherless child. Even the farrier did not negative this sentiment: on the contrary, he took it up as peculiarly his own, and invited any hardy person present to contradict him. But he met with no contradiction; and all differences among the company were merged in a general agreement with Mr. Snell's sentiment, that when a man had deserved his good luck, it was the part of his neighbors to wish him joy.

As the bridal group approached, a hearty cheer was raised in the Rainbow yard; and Ben Winthrop, whose jokes had retained their acceptable flavor, found it agreeable to turn in there and receive congratulations; not requiring the proposed interval of quiet at the Stone-pits before joining the company.

Eppie had a larger garden than she had ever expected there now; and in other ways there had been alterations at the expense of Mr. Cass, the landlord, to suit Silas's larger family. For he and Eppie had declared that they would rather stay at the Stone-pits than go to any new home. The garden was fenced with stones on two sides, but in front there was an open fence, through which the flowers shone with answering gladness, as the four united people came within sight of them.

"Oh father," said Eppie, "what a pretty home ours is! I think nobody could be happier than we are."

THE END.

University Press, Cambridge: John Wilson & Son.